Remus Gabriel Anghel, Eva Gerharz,
Gilberto Rescher, Monika Salzbrunn (eds.)
The Making of World Society

Remus Gabriel Anghel, Eva Gerharz,
Gilberto Rescher, Monika Salzbrunn (eds.)
The Making of World Society
Perspectives from Transnational Research

[transcript]

This book was printed with the financial support of the

Westfälisch-Lippische Universitätsgesellschaft

and

DFG Graduate School 844 »World Society.
Making and Representing the Global«.

**Bibliographic information published
by the Deutsche Nationalbibliothek**
The Deutsche Nationalbibliothek lists this publication in the Deutsche Nationalbibliografie; detailed bibliographic data are available in the Internet at http://dnb.d-nb.de

© 2008 transcript Verlag, Bielefeld

All rights reserved. No part of this book may be reprinted or reproduced or utilized in any form or by any electronic, mechanical, or other means, now known or hereafter invented, including photocopying and recording, or in any information storage or retrieval system, without permission in writing from the publisher.

Cover layout: Kordula Röckenhaus, Bielefeld
Cover: location: Tijuana, Mexico, © María Guadalupe Rivera Garay, Bielefeld, 2008
Typeset by: Stiewe & Lieber GmbH
Printed and bound in Great Britain by
Marston Book Services Ltd, Oxfordshire
ISBN 978-3-89942-835-3

Contents

Preface — 9

Introduction: The Making of World Society — 11
REMUS ANGHEL, EVA GERHARZ, GILBERTO RESCHER, MONIKA SALZBRUNN

Transnationality: Theoretical and Methodological Challenges

**Transnationalisation in North and South:
Concepts, Methodology and Venues for Research** — 25
THOMAS FAIST

**Transnationalisation, Translocal Spaces, Gender and
Development – Methodological Challenges** — 51
GUDRUN LACHENMANN

**World Society, Transnationalism and *Champs Migratoires*:
Reflections on German, Anglo-Saxon and French Academic Debates** — 75
MONIKA SALZBRUNN

Transnationalism, Political Participation and New Forms of Belonging

Euro-Alevis: From *Gastarbeiter* to Transnational Community — 103
BESIM CAN ZIRH

**Identity Politics as an Expression of
European Citizenship Practice: Participation of
Transnational Migrants in Local Political Conflicts** 133

MICHAEL JANOSCHKA

**Mothering in Migration:
Transnational Strategies of Polish Women in Italy** 153

GERMANA D'OTTAVIO

Transnationalism and Development

**Opening to the World:
Translocal Post-War Reconstruction in Northern Sri Lanka** 173

EVA GERHARZ

**Transnationality, Translocal Citizenship and Gender Relations:
Transformation of Rural Community Organisation,
Local Politics and Development** 195

GILBERTO RESCHER

Networks, Hubs, Localities

**A Global City-State of Finance – the Staging of Singapore as
Financial Hub between Global and Local Rhetoric** 221

STEPHANIE HERING

The Transnational Management of Hazardous Chemicals 237

ALEXANDRA LINDENTHAL

IT Usage and Transnational Identity Formations

**'Do you really talk about emotions on the phone..?':
Content of Distance Communication as a Structuring Moment
of the Modern World Society**   253

Magdalena Nowicka

**Does It Matter Where You Are? – Transnational Migration,
Internet Usage and the Emergence of Global Togetherness**   275

Heike Mónika Greschke

The Indernet – A German Network in a Transnational Space   291

Urmila Goel

Afterword: Are We All Transnationalists Now?   311

Joanna Pfaff-Czarnecka

Contributors   325

Preface

REMUS GABRIEL ANGHEL, EVA GERHARZ, GILBERTO RESCHER, MONIKA SALZBRUNN

World Society: Perspectives from Transnational Research is the result of two years of theoretical work based on empirical studies carried out on four continents. A conference on this topic, organised by Remus Gabriel Anghel, Eva Gerharz, Heike Greschke and Sven Kleinekathöfer, took place at the University of Bielefeld in November 2005. This conference was held within the framework of the Graduate School 844 "World Concepts and Global Structural Patterns" funded by the German Research Council (DFG). The event brought together junior and senior scholars from ten countries. The fruitful exchange that came out of this conference was deepened through international working groups which met virtually and physically over two years.

    We would like to thank all of those who helped us along the way and made the publication of this volume possible. We greatly appreciate the support of the DFG Graduate School 844 "World Society. Making and Representing the Global" for financing the conference and contributing to the publication. Financial help was also provided by the Westfälisch-Lippische Universitätsgesellschaft in Bielefeld. Thomas Faist has generously supported us throughout the publication process. We owe particular thanks to Joanna Pfaff-Czarnecka. Without her generosity and encouragement we would not have been able to share the outcome of our working group through this publication.

    We are also deeply grateful to several scholars who participated in the conference but whose contribution could not be integrated in this volume, particulary R. Cheran and Petra Dannecker. We also express our gratitude to all those who assisted us in copy editing, especially Sandrine Gukelberger and Mary Kenney. Karin Werner, Roswitha Gost and our project manager Alexander Masch at Transcript believed in this project from the very beginning and guided us with great professionalism and friendship.

Introduction: The Making of World Society

REMUS ANGHEL, EVA GERHARZ, GILBERTO RESCHER, MONIKA SALZBRUNN

As a result of the emergence of global communicative connectivity the world has become more integrated than ever before. Movements of people, exchange of commodities, ideas and values have contributed to the increasing integration of the world as a whole and the fact that the world can not be thought of as a conglomerate of separate entities as it was before. Related to these observations, studying world society is a great challenge facing social scientists today, because the notion itself reinforces a perspective which understands the world as a single, comprehensive texture: World society encompasses the totality of social relationships linking the inhabitants of the Earth. Similar views of such a vision are suggested by notions such as *dependencia* (André Gunder Frank 1969), world system (Wallerstein 1974), global village (McLuhan 1968; McLuhan/Powers 1992), or world culture (Meyer 2005). Moreover, John Urry introduced the concept of global complexity, taking the "global" as a complex perspective for analysing social processes (Urry 2002). Ulrich Beck (2006) has developed the notion of cosmopolitanism in a context of growing worldwide accessible reference systems. A critical standpoint in regard to Urry's and Beck's approaches is expressed by Eleonore Kofman (2005), who has criticised these views on cosmopolitanism as too narrow in scope. According to her, they are directed towards politically and economically privileged groups, leaving aside considerations about others. She also criticises the optimistic view of cosmopolitans, arguing that independent cosmopolitan individuals or networks can also be perceived as a threat in the eyes of representatives of the nation-state. Finally, an approach to synchronic meanings of worldwide phenomena is offered by historians like Osterhammel and Petersson (2003), who have analysed the world society from a diachronic perspective.

This general shifting perspective brings a number of new challenges for social science research which necessitate rethinking the notion of society in more fundamental ways. In social sciences, but also in popular understanding, society usually refers to bounded, territorially localised entities, especially to those confined by nation-states. The emphasis on world society, in contrast seeks to overcome this narrow perspective which, in times of mobility and border-crossing, can not be regarded any longer as the dominant conceptual framework for analysing and understanding society. This does not mean that the boundaries of nation-states have lost their relevance entirely, but the meanings and significance of nation-states as societal entities and, of their boundaries, is changing . This, in turn, bears important implications for identities and modes of belonging, as well as for the perspectives we need to apply while understanding and analysing social formations and society. This is the case, for instance, when we investigate multiple border-crossing practices, forms of transnational or global togetherness and new forms of internet-mediated sociality between people living in different parts of the world.

One particular aspect of the discussion on new meanings of boundaries in the world society consists of investigating transnationalisation processes. We understand the crossing of territorial and symbolic boundaries, like those of nation-states, as an intrinsic aspect of today's characteristics of the global as such and thus, a constitutive element in the making of world society. In this introduction we wish to highlight a few aspects of the ongoing constitution of world society. Furthermore, we attempt to clarify some of our conceptual tools and relate them to other discourses and notions, such as globalisation. This leads us to a more clear-cut understanding of world society, less as an object of sociological theory, but rather as an analytical concept describing the "global situation" (Tsing 2000). Transnationalisation, as the second constitutive concept within the framework of this anthology, also requires some clarifications. The social sciences have produced a multitude of empirical works related to various phenomena of transnationalisation during the last two decades, and based on these a great deal of conceptual work has been made. We attempt to narrow our focus in this discussion on its relationship with the notion of world society and intend to show some linkages related in the following chapters.

World Society as a Framing Concept

World-system theory, which can perhaps be regarded as a predecessor of perspectives on world society, dealt with the expansion of the capitalist economic system and categorised the opposition between centre and periphery. Immanuel Wallerstein (1974) and earlier Fernand Braudel (1949) developed approaches that linked various ways of thinking from social history, economy and the sociological tradition. Marxism and development theory have proceeded, using the approach of a world system, with influence on area studies. The global expansion of capitalism across national borders continued to be a central question of world-system theory. This was further developed and deepened by the pioneering works of mainly Latin American social scientists in the 1950's and 1960's. These scholars developed the concept of *dependencia*, which later on was further elaborated and globally revealed by André Gunder Frank (1969) in his theory of *the development of underdevelopment*. This influential perspective is concerned with the phenomena of underdevelopment as a result of a greater degree of integration into global structures dominated by First World countries and thus studies the relationship between dependent accumulation and underdevelopment of the Third World.[1]

The notion of world society was first introduced into the sociological debates by the Bielefeld system-theoretician Niklas Luhmann (1971), who assumed that under the condition of so called modernity, the world should be thought of as a system which transcends nation-states, stretching as a separate coordinated system (Wobbe 2000: 6).[2] In other words, the world can be conceived only as one irreducible entity, or social system. As such, this serves as a macro-sociological explanatory framework. According to Luhmann, world society is constituted by communication comprising all kinds of human interaction. Thinking of world society as a single social system which is not reducible to smaller geographical units (states, regions, locales) and which is constituted by communication, causes a number of difficulties for empirical research and theory building. This is because it remains incompatible with attempts to develop middle range theory based on empirical grounds.[3] Moreover, world society, as conceptualised in Luhmann's theory, is constituted solely through communication between *equalised* partners who are related to each other through inclusion, while the rest remain excluded (Kößler 2001: 24). This means also, that this approach cannot adequately capture the inequalities and asymmetries inside world society, which are, nevertheless, apparent and empirically evident, for example in regional disparities. These are crucial issues in development sociology and approaches to global social inequality. Luhmann's successor, Rudolf Stichweh (2000), tried to adapt this theoretical framework, paying attention to the obvious regional disparities, by introducing the idea of asynchrony (*Ungleichzeitigkeit*). However, this partial solution ignores the various modes of interrelatedness between the world's regions[4] (Kößler 2001: 25) since the disparities are frequently a direct result of global connectedness and integration into worldwide relations.

From our point of view, the notion of world society helps to depict interconnections between geographical and social subjects. We attempt to figure out hierarchies and power relations between different actors situated in distinct positions

---

1 A good overview is provided by the volume "The Underdevelopment of Development" edited by Chew/Denemark (1996).
2 Almost simultaneously Peter Heintz (1973) referred to world society as well.
3 Herewith we refer to R.K. Merton's (1949) differentiation between theories of various range. The aim of empirically grounded research is not to develop an all-embracing theory of society, but to understand the various dimensions of society based on observable phenomena.
4 Hence, any analysis in terms of asynchrony falls back into the concept of backwardness.

at different scales. In their latest reflections on rescaling processes, Nina Glick Schiller and Ayse Çağlar (forthcoming) analyse the positioning of localities within broader fields of power that are shaping opportunity structures, cultural politics, and pathways of migrants' local and transnational incorporation. We favour an understanding of world society inspired by the insights of system-theory and other macro perspectives, but which emphasise interrelatedness and rescaling processes. Social spaces, emerging between actors situated in different world regions and the localities therein, are constituted by differences in positions in power relations, possession of resources, and other general inequalities. In doing this, we also suppose that empirical perspectives on such issues will not lead us to a view of world society divided into territorial entities, such as nation-states. We rather envisage the world as a single global connectivity with a multitude of overlapping social spaces being continuously constructed and reconstructed.

Much literature on globalisation focuses on describing phenomena of worldwide mechanisms of diffusion, integration and shifting of boundaries, paying less attention to the notion of society and its characteristics under conditions of globality. In contrast, an approach focusing on world society helps to describe society under globalised conditions. Thereby, we follow Glick Schiller's (2005) lead in understanding globalisation as a myriad of cultural, social, political and economic processes that integrate the world into a single system of relationships and values: world society.

Moreover, we emphasise that world society, as an encompassing system and as an emergent reality, is created by the social actors involved: Their concrete interactions, negotiations, agency, struggles, conflicts and coalitions establish social space, which we regard as a constitutive element ordering society. This provides an opportunity to move away from macroscopic perspectives on world society, as it has been understood in some conventional approaches. Allowing us to analyse social processes at different levels and scales, however, this approach helps us to overcome the supposed gap between the macro-perspective of world society and social actors with an interaction approach. This also prevents us from applying a top-down perspective to the constitution of world society but instead to develop theoretical assumptions based on empirical, often ethnographic research on global or translocal phenomena.

Transnationalisation Processes Constituting World Society

Transnationalisation is one particular dimension contributing to the making of world society. Research on trans-border social formations such as transnational fields (for example: Glick Schiller/Basch/Szanton Blanc 1999) or social spaces (Faist 1998; Pries 1999) has contributed greatly to a shift in the understanding of society. Instead of clinging to a static 'container' concept of society, confined within the borders of the nation states where social actors are located and bounded inside a national society, transnational perspectives pinpoint social relations crossing societies or cultures. Thereby they highlight the social phenomenon being located in at least two, or multiple localised social contexts, thus constituting pluri-local social formations. In contrast to older perspectives on migration which focused on migrants' incorporation and later assimilation in the destination countries (Park/Burgess 1921), transnational approaches analyse the situatedness of migrants inbetween different territorial states. Migrants' 'inbetween-ness', however, accentuates a condition in which social actors are involved simultaneously in more than a single place and highlights the ambivalence of many transnational social processes going on in the world. This ambivalence stands at the core of a process of redefining sociality in the sense of *Vergesellschaftung*. By having provided means of distance communication, through internet and cheap telephone calls (Vertovec 2004), new forms of virtual sociality emerge, as is shown in the articles of Heike Greschke and Urmila Goel in this book. This may raise intriguing questions about the role of present and virtual communication, and identity change. Transnational research, however, highlights migrants' delocalisation and the trans-border interaction, which can be conceptualised in terms of transnational social spaces or fields. Moreover, Glick Schiller/Basch/Szanton Blanc (1999: 76) argue that the tendency to use the adjective *transnational* has contributed to the emergence of a transnational anthropology, that analyses, among other things, transformations of the ways in which time and space is experienced and represented (cf. Harvey 1990). Central to this argument are not just shifting representations and contestations of the nation-state and of its boundaries, but the scrutiny of localities and other spatially constructed entities.

In contrast to systemic world society perspectives, transnational approaches are rather process-oriented and actor-centred. They are often based on multi-situated or global ethnography (Burawoy et al. 2000), sometimes even on long-term empirical research. One of the commonalities transnationalisation perspectives have with world society approaches is that it presupposes a view of society detached from specific locations, regions, or states. It forms an encouraging and productive starting point that enables the researcher to avoid the pitfalls of a "methodological nationalism" (Wimmer/Glick Schiller 2002) consisting of a narrow analytical focus on nation-states. Some of the authors prefer to speak of translocalisation processes (see, among many others, the contributions of Gudrun Lachenmann, Monika Salzbrunn, Eva Gerharz and Gilberto Rescher in this volume). Geographical entities, constitutive of social formation and belonging are not necessarily constructed as nation-states, occupying a clearly demarcated territory. Disputed territories in countries with ethnic conflict for example, can be a much more meaningful reference producing subjective and collective feelings of belongingness among their (virtual) neighbourhoods (Appadurai 1995) than the nation-state. Moreover even in relation to social processes and phenomena which cross borders, the attachment to a specific locality can frequently be found to prevail over that owed to a nation-state. It has been pointed out that locality also can be an important concept for representing society (Pfaff-Czarnecka 2005). Localities can, like nation-states, be meaningful geographical spaces with great symbolical value and they serve, in some cases, as the crucial locus of social identification. In contexts of migration and transnationalisation, it can be observed how localities are constructed as localised and virtual neighbourhoods. The local is thus something to be created, organised and reproduced in social and phenomenological terms (Appadurai 1995).

Accordingly, observing transnationalisation and translocalisation processes constitutes an important research avenue for understanding the dynamics constituting world society. In contrast to the obvious macro-determinacy, inherent in conventional world society approaches, the perspective oriented towards 'the making of world society', is more oriented to the empirically observable features of the 'global situation'. This perspective facilitates the taking into account of the processes of interaction which, in the end, constitute macroscopic phenomena.

Finally, one has to acknowledge that the growing global interconnectedness indeed implies homogenising tendencies or decreasing diversity, as was proposed by Ritzer (1992) with his metaphor 'McDonaldisation of the World'. But at the same time, it reinforces global interconnectedness and complexity, to look at the diversification of world views which drives us towards an attempt to research and understand empirically the emergence of the world society. A plurality of theoretical and research views on world society, we hope, contributes, and brings us closer to grasping the dynamics of its constitution. With this book, we attempt to bring together some major perspectives, hoping to instigate further discussion and open new venues for future research.

The papers included in this book deal with a variety of, mainly empirically grounded, perspectives on transnational processes that are constitutive of world society. Most papers were presented at a conference organised by four former members of the research training group "World Concepts and Global Structural Patterns" in the Department of Sociology, in Bielefeld in November 24-25, 2005. This conference aimed at gathering contributions on the relationship between concepts of world society and transnationalisation from a cross-disciplinary perspective. The chapters greatly vary in terms of their themes, approaches, methodologies and styles but we believe that the diversity of our book's topics provides a fruitful basis for the further research on how world society can be analysed from an empirical perspective, and conceptualised from such a perspective.

Structure of the Book

This book is structured into five sections: an introductory part and four major topics around which various empirically informed contributions are centred. The first section focuses on the discussion of general questions concerning theory and methodology in the papers of Thomas Faist, Gudrun Lachenmann and Monika Salzbrunn. Thomas Faist critically analyses the state of affairs in migration research in the English and German literature and raises several questions concerning transnationalism and development: First, how has academic and policy thinking on "development" cast the role of transnational social formations and non-state organisations? Secondly, in what ways are the activities of transnational cliques, groups and organisations, which embody some of the community principles, complementary or incompatible with those of other institutions functioning according to the logics of states and markets? Gudrun Lachenmann focuses on methodological challenges deriving from attempts to conceptualize the interrelatedness of global and local dimensions and exemplifies these by referring to recent research on gender and Islam. She draws the connection between globalisation and localisation, in the sense of empirically grounding globalisation theories, and elaborates new venues for doing transcultural research and conceptualising global flows and landscapes in a translocal way. Lachenmann highlights the centrality of agency, relationality and dynamics which need to be unravelled when analysing the constitution of social spaces, knowledge, structuring and networking. She is doing this analysis emphasising the role of gender. Finally, she argues that globalisation is constituted through new forms of organisation and epistemic communities with the development world as a global knowledge framework. Monika Salzbrunn discusses and compares theoretical concepts of world society, transnationalisation and migratory fields with a focus on German, Anglo-Saxon and French debates. Entangled as well as parallel and isolated tracks lead to similar conclusions in contemporary research on migration, transnationalism and urban rescaling processes. Festive events in a context of migration provide examples of how to overcome the initial intellectual divergences by means of a focus which links transnationalisation with urban rescaling processes.

The second part of the book presents the works of Besim Can Zirh, Michael Janoschka, and Germana D'Ottavio on transnationalisation and migration. The contributions focus on new forms of political participation and identity formation in transnational contexts. Zirh analyses the evolution of the ways in which Alevi political participation has evolved in Turkey and Germany. He argues that the Euro-Alevis can be comprehended as a nascent transnational community that has emerged as a result of diasporisation of Alevis in relation to global transformations and changes in Turkish and German socio-political contexts. Janoschka inquires into the democratic participation of Northern Europeans in Spain. His paper provides a conceptual analysis of how transnational political practices and identity politics can be evaluated as an expression of European citizenship. Germana D'Ottavio looks at transnational mobility of Polish migrant women working in Italy. While the first two contributions explicitly address issues of political involvement among migrants, this article deals with changing identities and concepts of self among migrant women. It shows how Polish migrants organize transnational motherhood and demonstrates that mobility strategies are interconnected in transnational spaces. Migrant women use their agency within these spaces to create particular arrangements that allow them to achieve their goals in emigration and immigration societies.

The third part includes papers concerned with the linkage between translocalisation and development. Eva Gerharz shows the multiple forms of translocalisation of the Tamil Diaspora in respect to the reconstruction process which was initiated in Northern Sri Lanka after the Ceasefire of 2002. Her paper investigates the evolution of translocal spaces which are constituted through intensifying interaction between different actors and which are becoming increasingly relevant for post-conflict reconstruction. She argues that development, as a local endeavour, is constituted through translocal interactions. Based on an empirically grounded analysis, Gerharz shows how translocalisation processes lead to the re-negotiation of Tamil identity and development. Parting from everyday forms of translocality in rural Mexico, Gilberto Rescher analyses the transformation of rural indigenous communities that have become transnationalised in a way that reflects the flexibility of the particular rules and customs governing life in their villages. This process is discussed with respect to the renegotiation of local citizenship into transnational citizenship and the transformation of gender relations inside the transnationalised communities. Applying a focus on the communities of origin and herein the important position of women in the construction and maintenance of transnational social spaces, Rescher shows how social change is continuously negotiated and how it relates to broader transformations in the field of politics and development. He stresses the ambivalent outcomes of this process which show that in contrast to certain visions transnationalisation can not be understood per se as exclusively fostering processes of democratisation, emancipation and development, but indicate that such processes have to be studied in their totality.

The fourth part deals with networks and hubs in world society. Stephanie Herings contribution analyses the construction of Singapore as a financial center of South-East Asia. Starting with the assumption that finance is the most abstract and disembedded branch in global economy, often regarded as the vanguard of globalisation, Hering argues for the image of globality as constituting and contributing to the making of financial sites. The references to the specific locality proves indispensable for the rhetoric of globalisation – contrary to a naive perception of globalisation as a worldwide levelling of local and regional differences. She highlights the strategic use of rhetorics of local specifics and cultural distinctiveness as a transnational practice. Further on, Alexandra Lindenthal deals with networks of organisations specialised in the management of hazardous chemicals. Lindenthal asks in how far do corporations, which are involved in global production processes, handle hazardous chemicals across national or supranational territories and thereby contribute to the protection of health and environment.

The last part deals with the ways in which Information Technology changes the ways in which identity is conceptualised in different migration contexts. Magdalena Nowicka analyses how proximity and distance play a crucial role in the ways in which highly qualified mobile workers communicate with their families and friends. She argues that in networks, distance is not always metric, and that the interplay of proximity and distance influences the patterns of social inclusion and exclusion. Heike Greschke looks at the significance of co-presence and internet communication in the case of Paraguayan migrants living in different parts of the world. She shows that national identity can be regarded as a functional pattern of social organisation and structuring within global public spheres. Urmila Goel looks at the ways in which the second-generation Indians in Germany construct their identity through the mediation of an internet portal. She shows in detail how, why and with what consequences the transnational space theinder.net is positioned in national categories and at the same time remains a transnational space.

In her afterword, Joanna Pfaff-Czarnecka draws a conclusion about the empirically based reflections about the making of world society through transnational practices. Moreover, she critically discusses the scope of the transnationalisation paradigm in the world society project.

References

Appadurai, Arjun (1995) "The Production of Locality." In: Fardon, Richard (ed.) *Counterworks. Managing the Diversity of Knowledge*, London: Routledge, pp. 204-225.
Beck, Ulrich (2004) "Cosmopolitical Realism. On the Distinction Between Cosmopolitism and Philosophy and the Social Sciences." Global Networks 4/2, pp. 131-156.
Beck. Ulrich (2006) *The Cosmopolitan Vision*, Cambridge: Polity Press.
Braudel, Fernand (1949) *Méditerranée et le Monde Méditerranéen à l'époque de Philippe II*, Paris: Flammarion.
Burawoy, Michael/Blum, Joseph/George, Sheba/Gille, Zsuzsa/Gowan, Teresa/Haney, Lynne/Klawitter, Maren/Lopez, Steven/Riain, Seán Ó./Thayer, Millie (eds.) (2000) *Global Ethnography. Forces, Connections and Imaginations in a Postmodern World*, Berkeley: University of California Press.
Chew, Sing C./Denmark, Robert A. (eds.) (1996) *The Underdevelopment of Development. Essays in Honor of Andre Gunder Frank*, Thousand Oaks et al.: Sage Publications.
Faist, Thomas (1998) "Transnational Social Spaces out of International Migration: Evolution, Significance and Future Prospects." Archives Européennes de Sociologie/European Journal of Sociology 39/2, pp. 213-247.

Faist, Thomas (2000) "Transnationalization in International Migration: Implications for the Study of Citizenship and Culture." Ethnic and Racial Studies 23/2, pp. 189-222.

Frank, André Gunder (1969) *Kapitalismus und Unterentwicklung in Lateinamerika*, Frankfurt a.M.: Europäische Verlagsanstalt.

Glick Schiller, Nina (2005) "Transnational Social Fields and Imperialism. Bringing a Theory of Power to Transnational Studies." Anthropological Theory 5/4, pp. 439-461.

Glick Schiller, Nina/Basch, Linda/Szanton Blanc, Christina (1999) "From Immigrant to Transmigrant: Theorizing Transnational Migration." In: Ludger Pries (ed.) *Migration and Transnational Social Spaces*, Aldershot: Ashgate Publishing, pp. 73-104.

Glick Schiller, Nina/Çağlar, Ayse (forthcoming) "Towards a Theory of Locality in Migration Studies: Migrant Incorporation and City Scale." In: Nina Glick Schiller/Ayse Çağlar (eds.) *Rescaling Cities* (working title), Ithaca: Cornell University Press.

Harvey, David (1990) *The Condition of Postmodernity: An Enquiry into the Origins of Cultural Change*, Malden/Oxford: Blackwell Publishers.

Heintz, Peter (1973) *The Future of Development*, Bern: Huber Verlag.

Kofman, Eleonore (2005) "Figures of the Cosmopolitan. Privileged Nationals and National Outsiders." Innovation 18/1, pp. 83-97.

Kößler, Reinhart (2001) "Grenzen der Weltgesellschaft: Zu den Problemen der Homogenität und der Exklusion." Peripherie 83, pp. 7-35.

Luhmann, Niklas (1971) *Soziologische Aufklärung. Ausgewählte Aufsätze zur Theorie der Gesellschaft*. Opladen: Westdeutscher Verlag.

McLuhan, Marshall (1968) *War and Peace in the Global Village*, New York: Bantam Books.

McLuhan, Marshall/Bruce P. Powers (1992) *The Global Village: Transformations in World Life and Media in the 21st Century*, New York: Communication and Society.

Merton, Robert K. (1949) *Social Theory and Social Structure*, New York: Free Press.

Meyer, John (2005) *Weltkultur. Wie die westlichen Prinzipien die Welt durchdringen*, Frankfurt a. M.: Suhrkamp Taschenbuch Verlag.

Osterhammel, Jürgen/Petersson, Niels (2003) *Geschichte der Globalisierung. Dimensionen, Prozesse, Epochen*, München: C.H.Beck.

Park, Robert Ezra/Burgess, Ernest (1921) *Introduction to the Science of Sociology*, Chicago: University of Chicago Press.

Pfaff-Czarnecka, Joanna (2005) "Das Lokale als Ressource im entgrenzten Wettbewerb: Das Verhandeln kollektiver Repräsentation in Nepal – Himalaya." Zeitschrift für Soziologie, Sonderheft "Weltgesellschaft", pp. 479-499.

Pries, Ludger (1999) *Migration and Transnational Social Spaces,* Aldershot: Ashgate.

Ritzer, George (1992) *The McDonaldization of Society: An Investigation into the Changing Character of Contemporary Social Life*, London: Pine Forge Press.
Stichweh, Rudolf (2000) *Die Weltgesellschaft*, Frankfurt a. M.: Surkamp Verlag.
Tsing, Anna (2000) "The Global Situation." Cultural Anthropology 15/3, pp. 327-360.
Urry, John (2002) *Global Ccomplexity*, Cambridge: Polity Press.
Vertovec, Steven (2004) "Cheap Calls. The Social Glue of Migrant Transnationalism." Global Networks 4/2, pp. 219-224.
Wallerstein, Immanuel (1974) *The Modern World-System, I: Capitalist Agriculture and the Origins of European World-Economy in the Sixteenth Century*, New York/London: Academic Press.
Wimmer, Andreas/Glick Schiller, Nina (2002) "Methodological Nationalism and Beyond: Nation-State Building, Migration, and the Social Sciences." Global Networks 2, pp. 301-334.
Wobbe, Theresa (2000) *Weltgesellschaft,* Bielefeld: transcript Verlag, pp. 66-73.

Transnationality: Theoretical and Methodological Challenges

Transnationalisation in North and South: Concepts, Methodology and Venues for Research

THOMAS FAIST

Discussions of globalisation have amply and aptly described the increase in the intensity, velocity and scope of cross-border exchanges. These include financial transactions, the exchange of goods and services, and various efforts to deal with these challenges, including the supranational advancement of global governance (see e.g. Lechner/Boli 2003). Much less attention has been devoted to conceptualizing cross-border social and symbolic ties and their concatenation, such as the life-worlds of persons and the organisational activities of associations who move around and maintain ties in a cross-borderised world. In order to capture the societal dimensions of cross-border social life, terms such as transnational social spaces, transnational social fields or transnational social formations usually refer to sustained ties of geographically mobile persons, networks and organisations across the borders of multiple nation-states (Basch et al. 1994; Faist 2000a; Faist 2000b; Portes et al. 1999). To list but a few examples, transnational families practise complex forms of livelihood which imply geographical distance and social proximity in earning a living and raising children (e.g. Murray 1981). Chinese entrepreneurs have long been known to rely on guanxi – friendship-communal – networks dating back to hometown ties in China in order to integrate economically in a great variety of countries all over the globe (Ong 1992). Kurdish political activists in various European countries have organised in various associations to address both governments of immigration states and rulers in Turkey in order to advance their cause of an autonomous 'Kurdistan'. And in the UK, Muslim organisations made up of migrants from South Asia, have sought to gain recognition as a religious association while forming part of a global umma. Such border-crossing social – political, economic and cultural – formations are not only found in the North and West but are probably equally widespread in the South and East. After all, cross-border migration is not only South-North and

North-South but also runs in directions such as South-South or East-East and North-North.[1]

It is rather obvious that, although transnational approaches have centred on cross-border interactions and social formations in the context of international migration, and have thus has pointed to sustained and dense cross-border transactions involving North and South, East and West, most research has focused on and been carried out in the West and North. But not only has research focused on these regions – not surprising in view of the fact that most scholars working in a transnational vein were socialised and work in these regions. What is noteworthy is that comparatively little attention has been given to a balanced description of North-South linkages, including not only sites in the North and South but also the linkages. If the South is included, they are mostly valuable studies on locales in the South (for example Haugen/Carling 2005; Leichtman 2005). What is needed is certainly a strengthening of research on the South and East, giving perspectives to scholars from the South. Short of such mid-term goals, a short-term and first step involves a more rigorous analysis of the interlinkages between North and South, East and West. One of the venues for this much-needed step in research on transnationalisation is the newly rediscovered migration-development nexus, that is, the two-way link between migration and development.

In particular, transnational migrant networks and migrant associations have lately been at the centre of the optimistic visions of national governments in the OECD world and international economic development policy establishments such as the World Bank (for an overview, see Maimba/Ratha 2005; on optimistic claims, see World Bank 2006). First, the surge in financial remittances over the past three decades transferred by transnational migrants has given rise to a kind of euphoria. Annual remittances from economically developed to developing and transformation countries more than doubled during the 1990s and have been approximately twenty percent higher than official development assistance (ODA) to these countries. Second, knowledge transferred through networks of scientists and experts from North to South is increasingly seen as "brain circulation" beneficial to all parties involved (cf. Lowell/Findlay/Stewart 2004). The transfer of ideas is seen as helping developing and transformation countries to participate in knowledge societies, which are the basis for innovation, productivity, and development. In a wide sense this knowledge transfer includes networks of scientists

---

[1] The United Nations (UN) defines migrants as persons living outside their country of birth or citizenship for over a year. The world total of migrants amounted to about 100 million in 1980. Of those were ca. 50 million in the North, compared with 52 million in the South. By 2006, out of a global total of some 190 million migrants, 61 million had moved South-South, 53 million North-North, 14 million North-South and 62 million South-North (UNDESA 2006). Obviously, categories such as North and South represent gross over-simplifications, since many countries cannot be readily classified as either North or South. For example, there are also quite a few transformation or transition countries in the former Eastern block, or emerging powers such as China.

and experts from the USA to China, or the diffusion of the practice of participation in the formal labour market by women migrants from Bangladesh who stayed in Malaysia and returned to their country of origin (Dannecker 2004). Thirdly, there are social remittances, which involve the transfer of ideas regarding the rule of law, good governance, democracy, gender equity and human rights. Politically, social remittances have achieved a growing prominence in the aftermath of interventions into armed conflicts and efforts at reconstructing countries ravaged by civil war – evidenced lately in Somalia, Afghanistan, and Iraq. Occasionally diasporas made up of exiles, refugees, and labour migrants are hailed as mediators in conflict resolution, for example in the cases of South Africa or Nigeria. However, all these mechanisms of transfer also have their dark sides. For example, refugee and exile communities that have fuelled conflicts in their countries of origin from abroad, such as Kosovo Albanians or Chechen freedom fighters.

The newest round of the migration-development nexus is the idea of what in French has been called *co-développement*. Co-development means that migrants are productive development agents. It very well describes the public policy approaches of immigration countries to the migration-development nexus, at least those propagated by several states such as France, the Netherlands, the UK and international organisations such as the World Bank. Co-development does not build upon the permanent return of migrants to their countries of origin but tries to tap into existing transnational ties of migrants who are seen to be transmission belts of development cooperation. The question comes up how this new enthusiasm (Faist 2007a) can be fruitfully analysed from a transnational perspective. What is puzzling from a transnational view is that the new optimism envisages one-way flows from North to South, occluding reverse flows.

The central puzzle then is: On the one hand we can observe that public and academic debates in the newest round of the migration-development nexus address mostly one-way flows, the transfer of resources from North to South – financial remittances, human capital, knowledge and even so-called social remittances, such as the export of democracy and human rights. The newest round of the migration-development debate, like the older ones in the 1960s and 1980s, is couched in terms of development and development cooperation. On the other hand, studies taking a transnational approach suggest that we do not see one-way traffic but two-way flows. Certainly, we can still observe brain drain, as evidence in research on "brain strain hotspots", such as the health care sector in much of Sub-Saharan Africa, where the nurses and doctors who migrated abroad cannot be replaced (cf. Lowell et al. 2004). Also, countries such as the USA and the UK have benefited tremendously from tuition fees from students hailing from the South and East. Moreover, we may think of findings which indicate "reverse remittances", for example, families of migrants in Accra, Ghana paying for their kinfolk in Amsterdam to "get their papers", that is, to legalize their status in the Netherlands. And taking a broader historical perspective, it seems odd that the migration-development debate would focus predominantly on North-South transfers, as it is well-established that only colonial and imperial domination of large regions of Africa and Asia set the conditions in which migration systems could develop (Wallerstein 1983).

The first part of the analysis delineates three levels of transnational analysis, located in the realms of lifeworlds, associations and systems respectively. While the focus of transnational approaches is on the associational level (meso-level; Faist 1997), the lifeworld or interaction level (micro-level) and the systems level (macro-level) are to be included. The second part shifts attention to various types of meso-level social formations, called transnational social spaces. Transnational spaces can be conceptualised as being inbetween a space of places and a space of flows (Faist 2000a: chapter 1). The third part deals with transnational methodology, arguing that research should strive to consider multi-sited research, and research dealing with meso-level formations – not only associations but also the "spaces inbetween associations" and organisations. In the fourth part the analysis then moves on to consider an application of transnational methodology, the recently rediscovered migration-development nexus.

Transnational Approaches: Life-worlds, Associations and Systems

The Oxford Dictionary of English dates the emergence of the term "transnational" to ca. 1920, documented with a quotation from an economic text that saw Europe after World War One as characterised by its "international or more correctly transnational economy" (ODE 2003: 1762). Indeed, the term re-emerged in the late 1960s to denote increasing economic and political interdependence between industrialised countries and the spread of trans- or multinational companies operating across the globe (Keohane/Nye 1977). The newest round of the term transnational, which started in the late 1980s and early 1990s, took a bottom-up perspective and asked about migrants as agents in constellations of increased cross-border flows, not only of goods, but also of people (Basch et al. 1994). It is within this latest context that transnational approaches have flourished. They have explored counter-trends to the dis-embedding of social systems in an increasingly globalised world. Transnational studies look at processes of re-embedding the social in cross-border societal formations.

Transnational social formations – fields, spaces – consist of combinations of social and symbolic ties and their contents, positions in networks and organisations, and networks of organisations that cut across the borders of at least two national states. In other words, the term refers to sustained and continuous pluri-local transactions crossing state borders. Most of these formations are located inbetween the life-world of personal interactions, on the one hand, and the functional systems of differentiated spheres, such as the economy, polity, law, science and religion. The smallest element of transnational social formations is transactions, that is, bounded communications between at least three persons. More aggregated levels encompass groups, households, organisations and firms.

There are various ways to conceptualize transnational social formations, which can be thought to be part of more general cross border societal configurations. Transnational approaches, as do globalisation theories, world society and world polity theories, look at the current waves of global connectivity not as a new material phenomenon. Cultural pluralisation is not anything new in world history but has been the rule for centuries. Colonialism, wars of conquest, mass migrations, the slave trade, world wars, and refugee movements have been processes with global dimensions for several centuries. Viewed in a world-system perspective, capitalist markets required migration across borders of states and empires (Wallerstein 1974). What is new is not so much cultural pluralisation as a result of increasing global connectivity – more a matter of degree than a new quality – but global awareness of it. This awareness can be described as one important dimension of globalisation (Robertson 1992). It is reflected in academic analyses and in mass media.

Nonetheless, transnational approaches differ from both world society and world polity theories, on the one hand, and more general globalisation studies, on the other hand. On an epistemological level, transnational views argue against a simplistic top down world society or world polity version of global or glocal conditions, which suffer from a neo-functionalist oversimplification in the first case and an exogenous rational actor model in the second. World society theories view societal processes from the vantage point of an already existing world society. The systems-theoretic notion of world society presupposes that global communicative connectivity already exists. According to theorists such as Niklas Luhmann, society is the most encompassing social system, defined as the sum total of all communication connected to communication. As communication is geared towards global connectivity, only one society exists: world society (Luhmann 1975: 57). World society theory places a high premium on functional differentiation. In a functionally differentiated society, each subsystem fulfils one specific function coded in a binary way. For example, the political system decides on power or not to have power, the science system on truth or not truth, the economic system on money or not to have money, and so forth. Such functional differentiation is a form of homogenisation. Social formations other than those which are functionally differentiated, such as segmented or stratified forms, play only a secondary role. World society is the inevitable result of functional differentiation (Luhmann 1997: 809). In the world polity theory of John W. Meyer and the Stanford School, the starting point is the existence of a world culture, which is culture exogenous to local contexts, worldwide, and based on the premises of modern rationalisation in Max Weber's sense (Meyer et al. 2000). This world culture is rationalistic in that it does not primarily consist of values and norms which are debated and towards which actors orient their behaviour, but on "cognitive models". Actors accept such standards, that is, cognitive models, even though they may not be ready to act according to the standards prescribed; for example, in taking over English language curricula without adapting them to local circumstances.

There are various problems with both world society and world polity theory. Firstly, these theories postulate a priori and without further systematic empirical consideration that a world society or world polity actually exists. We can certainly observe the emergence of global institutions, for example, in the realm of political governance, such as the United Nations and its sub-organisations or the World Trade Organisation (WTO). Other prominent examples are the national state as a universal principle of political organisation, the use of money as a medium of economic exchange, and global standards in travel, time and communication. Yet such global structures or globally diffused institutions only exist in selected policy domains. Even if we turn to the universal semantics of human rights, rule of law, democracy or gender equity – terms which fulfil the function of meta-norms of meta-cognitive models – we observe that they do not rule universally. Also, functionally differentiated structures exist only to a very narrowly confined extent in many parts of the world. Social protection and social insurance in many parts of the world are just one crucial example (Faist 2007c). While some policy fields such as trade have been regulated by a complex and evolving international regimes, which may amount to elements of global governance, cross-cutting issue areas such as geographical mobility are a long way from being regulated by such mechanisms. Even in the realm of the United Nations various UN agencies compete for competence in these fields.

Secondly, both world society and world polity approaches are top down approaches which define the properties of lower order elements. Moreover, according to such views, it is modern organisations and networks which rule the societal world, while social formations such as families, tribes, and communities play a negligible role, if at all. World polity theory maintains that cognitive models shape the actors although authors working in this mould have conceded that it is not only world polity and world culture that shapes actors but it is also actors who shape world polity. For example, the very fact that the World Bank has championed the diaspora model of development has very real consequences for conceiving development. Different agents – a term used to ascribe the effectiveness of actors in influencing the social world – hold different notions of development. These notions change as a result of new paradigms. As a consequence, it still has to be shown how world society or world polity models shape local or national patterns. We can name many local or national patterns which do not necessarily go back to global models. For example, states in the OECD countries have employed very different models of incorporating migrants at the national level, ranging from assimilationist to multicultural paradigms (Castles/Miller 2003). Moreover, states have viewed very differently the desirability of migrants' transnational ties. While former colonial powers with a long experience in penetrating developing countries have seised quickly upon the idea of co-development, that is, employing migrants as development agents, others, often characterised by less intense transnational and international ties, have only recently started to think about such models. Examples for the former category are national states such as France, the UK, Spain and the Netherlands, for the latter Germany, Austria and Sweden (cf. de Haas 2006).

Thirdly, neo-functionalist approaches neglect the crucial aspect of legitimation and thus the whole realm of normatively bounded agency (Peters 1993). And the world polity approach suggests that actors reap benefits from adapting to cognitive models such as the mainstreaming of tertiary education models, for example, the "Bologna Process" in the European Union. Political conflict over the very definition of such processes is merely semantic. However, to reduce the analysis of social and societal formations to instrumental concerns, and to occlude normative and ethical or expressive dimensions is to truncate the rich variety of the orientation of agency. Conflicts over whether social orders or systems are legitimate are a driving force of social change and transformation. For example, political agents active in pushing for gender equity criticize existing political arrangements and justify their strategies by reference to overall meta-norms such as human rights. In a similar way, those trying to establish a national state from abroad through secession may refer to norms such as national self-determination. In these two very different cases it is the legitimacy of existing orders which is at stake, both on the level of empirically observable acceptance of authority and power and on the level of normative criteria used to evaluate institutions.

Transnational approaches also need to be carefully distinguished from globalisation theories. Transnational views refer to overlapping ties and linkages of non-state agents between various national states. The hunch that political transnationalisation is a set of processes with a potentially global scope has implications for the functions of states, supra- and international organisations. In contrast, globalisation approaches focus on processes transcending state territories. Various aspects of society and governance on the local, national, regional and global levels can be thought of as nested within each other – always connected by potentially global communication. This characteristic also applies to global governance, namely the rapid emergence of multilateral cooperation and international organisations.

On a methodological level, transnational approaches – along with world society and world polity theories – aim to overcome "methodological territorialism" (Scholte 2000: 56), that is, conflating society, state and *territory*. Such methodological territorialism is evident in many analyses which prioritise state agency in the traditional Weberian trilogy of the congruence of territory, authority and people. Yet it is evident from empirical observation that processes such as migration challenge national institutions such as citizenship, and – in conjunction with processes such as gender equity and denizenship rights – favour dual citizenship (Faist 2007b). In addition, transnational approaches also strive to overcome "methodological nationalism", the conflation of society, state and *nation* (Wimmer/Glick Schiller 2003). Again, the increasing tolerance of dual citizenship suggests that affiliations to nations may not be exclusive and monogamous but overlapping and plural.

Transnational perspectives on cross-border societal formations relate to the concepts of fields and spaces. While the former connotes the systemic dimensions of societal formations, the latter refers to associations and life-worlds. The notion of fields refers to the inner logic of social action of functionally differentiated realms. Although Pierre Bourdieu's notion of fields points towards the internal logic of systems, such as the economy, polity, science or law, transnational approaches do not presume an evolutionary and linear logic in a trend towards a functionally differentiated world society. The notion of transnational social fields is much more concerned with issues of agency and diverse social formations. In contrast, the notion of space denotes the spatial dimension of social life (Faist/Özveren 2004; Pries 2001). Transnational social spaces are not synonymous with concepts such as "network society" which postulate a trend towards societal life as a "space of flows" (Castells 1996). Undoubtedly, the intensity and velocity of the transfer of goods, capital, and ideas across borders has increased. And so has, in less spectacular rates of increase, cross-border migration. However, the dynamics of migration cannot be understood without considering the life worlds of persons, and the social and symbolic ties they entertain across regions of origin, destination and onward mobility.

Social space in particular has been neglected for several decades in the social sciences (Faist 2004b). In globalist or cosmopolitan approaches time definitively trumps place. The now often-used description of the world as a "space of flows" are creative reformulations of Marx's and Engels' famous dictum on capitalism: "all that is solid melts into air". The latter statement is still the clearest expression of the claim that there is an annihilation of space by time (Marx/Engels 1972 [1918]). Systems theory argues that migration can be substituted by routines (cf. Stichweh 2005). The core argument is that functional differentiation leads to the disappearance of social space and to the diminishing relevance of face-to-face communication in social systems. In a way, it is the end of geography. The counter-argument is equally simple but based on empirical evidence: social geographers have firmly established that face-to-face contact is the main functional reason for the spatial clustering of knowledge and skills. This is exactly why nowadays there is great fanfare about clusters of excellence in academia, such as Oxbridge in the UK, or clusters of growth in industry, such as the Rhine Valley or Shanghai. Other examples are international financial centres in places like New York, London or Frankfurt (see, for example, Thrift 1996). We observe a spatial clustering of practical knowledge, tacit knowledge and scientific knowledge. This trend is tied to production processes, which require simultaneous inputs and feedbacks (Sassen 2006: 72). Social spaces expand and direct contacts grow as technological possibilities grow, and the short-term and even long-term mobility of persons certainly does not decline but has steadily increased. It is not only true in the world of business but also in the life-worlds of migrants, and new telecommunications that technology is a complement to, rather than a substitute for, face-to-face contact. It appears that information is still an "experience good" and that face-to-face contact still helps to build the trust needed to close deals (Rauch 2001), or to build reciprocity and solidarity in kinship groups. This example indicates that spaces of flows – not only those of persons but also of goods – are embedded in spaces of places. In other words, intensive and continuous cross-border flows of persons, ideas and goods do not necessarily result in a de-bordered world.

Flows are tied to the experience of place(s). The production of space can be considered a dialectical process. On the one hand, globalisation allows a de-placing from concrete territorial places – space of flows. On the other hand, global flows have to be anchored locally in specific places – space of places. Space is conceived as a relational process of structuring relative positions of social and symbolic ties between social actors, social resources and goods inherent in social ties, and the connection of these ties to places. On a meso- or associational level – the main focus of transnational approaches – the dialectics of flows and places goes hand in hand with the possibility for transfer of resources in space. Financial capital, for example, is distinctly more mobile than social capital. It is therefore often seen as the prototype of a global good. In contrast, social capital, such as networks of solidarity and trust, are place-bound, local assets, which can only be rendered mobile across space by the social ties in kinship groups, organisations, communities, which connect distinct places. Any conceptualisation of space across borders would therefore depend on the type of ties and (social) goods to be exchanged. At the interstices of the space of flows and space of places are processes of glocalisation. Glocalisation then means, first, that the local is produced – to a large extent – on the global or transnational level. Secondly, the local is also important in reconfiguring place. An empirical example of this approach is transnational social spaces. The concept of transnational social spaces probes into the question of by what principles geographical propinquity, which implies the embeddedness of ties in place, is supplemented or transformed by transnational flows.

Ultimately, these analyses have to be reconnected to macro-level analysis in the realm of systems or fields. On a macro-level, the reconfiguration of social space is visible, for example, in the political realm. In a process of "unbundling" territoriality (Ruggie 1993), various types of functional regimes have come to intersect territorially-defined nation-states. Such institutions include common markets, border-crossing political communities and inter- and supranational organisations. Non-territorial functional space-as-flows and territorial nation-states as space-of-places are the grids wherein international or global society is anchored. Such ruptures render the conventional distinction between internal and external increasingly problematic because there are various tiers for making collectively binding decisions. It also calls into question the concept of state sovereignty as an expression of a single fixed viewpoint and the research strategy of 'methodological nationalism', which takes for granted national states as container-like units, defined by the congruence of a fixed state territory, an intergenerational political community and a legitimate state authority. In its stead, multi-layered systems of rule, such as the European Union, demand a multi-perspective framework.

Types of Transnational Social Spaces

The reality of transnational social spaces made up of migrants indicates, first, that migration and re-migration may not be definite, irrevocable and irreversible decisions – transnational lives in themselves may become a strategy of survival and betterment. Also, transnational webs include relatively immobile persons and collectives. Secondly, even those migrants who have settled for a considerable time outside the original countries of origin, frequently maintain strong transnational links. Thirdly, these links can be of a more informal nature, such as intra-household or family ties, or they can be institutionalised, such as political parties maintaining branches in various countries of immigration and emigration.

Under propitious conditions transnational social spaces find a fertile breeding ground. Favourable conditions for the reproduction of transnational ties include (1) modern technologies such as satellite or cable TV, instant mass communication, personal communication bridging long distances via telephone and fax, mass affordable short-term long-distance travel, (2) liberal state policies, such as poly-ethnic rights and anti-discrimination policies, or the opposite (3) cultural discrimination and socio-economic exclusion of migrants in immigration states, and (4) changing emigration state policies which reach out to migrants living abroad for remittances, investment, and political support.

There are three stylised types of transnational social spaces: small groups, particularly kinship systems; issue networks; and transnational organisations or associations.

(1) Formalised transboundary relations within *small groups* like households and wider kinship systems, are representative of many migrants. Families may live apart because one or more members work abroad as contract workers (like the former 'guestworkers' in Germany) or as employees of multinational companies. Small household and family groups have a strong sense of belonging to a common home. A classic example of such relations are transnational families, who conceive of themselves as both an economic unit and a unit of solidarity and who keep, besides their main house, a kind of shadow household in another country. Economic assets are mostly transferred from abroad to those who con-

tinue to run the household 'back home'. It is estimated that a vast amount of financial remittances are transferred within such small groups of kinship systems.

(2) Transnational issue networks are sets of ties between persons and organisations in which information and services are exchanged for the purpose of achieving a common goal. Linkage patterns may concatenate into advocacy networks (Keck/Sikkink 1998), business networks, or scientists' networks. These issue-specific networks engage in areas such as human rights and environmental protection. While issue networks have a long tradition in the realm of human rights, and are making steady progress in ecology, they are also emerging among migrants who have moved from the so-called third countries to the European Union (EU). Among the immigrant and citizenship associations are, for example, the European Citizenship Action Service (ECAS), and the Migration Policy Group (MPG). The latter network includes the British NGO Justice, the Immigration Lawyers Practitioners' Association and the Dutch Standing Group of Experts on Immigration and Asylum. Some of these networks – usually headed by non-migrant EU citizens – have succeeded in bringing issues such as discrimination onto the agendas of Intergovernmental Conferences (IGC), and, ultimately, into the Treaty of Maastricht (1997).

(3) Transnational organisations: an early type of transnational organisation – interstate non-governmental organisations (INGOS) – developed out of issue networks like the Red Cross, Amnesty International and Greenpeace. At the other extreme there are organisations which are based in one specific country but whose sphere of influence extends abroad, as with the ethno-nationalist Tamil Tigers which seek an autonomous Tamil state on the territory of contemporary Sri Lanka. Transnational enterprises constitute a further type of cross-border organisation. These businesses are differentiated transboundary organisations with an extremely detailed internal division of labour.

Transnational social spaces have cultural, political and economic aspects. Syncretist cultural practices – for example, music styles, language diffusion and mixing – and hybrid identities – such as German-Turkish or French-Algerian – are phenomena that tend to accompany processes of transnational migration. Although such phenomena may range from evanescent and temporary to more enduring and stable patterns over time, their observable existence has implications for the self-conception of individuals and groups, and for the definition of these same actors by others. How intensive this trend really is remains a matter of dispute. In principle, the idea of transnational cultural diffusion and syncretism implies the cross-border movement of people, symbols, practices, texts – all of which help to establish a pattern of common cultural beliefs across borders and patterns of reciprocal transactions between separate places, whereby cultural ideas in one place influence those in another.

Transnational migrant culture cannot be seen as baggage or a template, not as something to be figuratively packed and unpacked, uprooted (assimilationists) and transplanted from one national context to another (cultural pluralists and multiculturalists). Transnational cultures are cross-border mixes, which not only involve novel elements but also "hardware" found in national or local cultures from regions of origin and destination. Syncretist identities and practices do not imply a diaspora consciousness. Nor do these mixing identities necessarily denote a successful stage in the transition from one collective identity to another, such as the prototypical development: Sicilian → Italian → Italian-American → US-American. Rather, it is an outcome of transnational ties and often segmented cultural communities that do refer to a successful synthesis in some cases – such as hip-hop musicians among the cultural elite. Also, there may be religious hybridity, mixing a Protestant attitude of an individualist relationship to God with Islam (Roy 2004). On an organisational level, it is sometimes religious communities called by some observers as Islamist, such as Milli Görüş – an organisation originating in Turkey with branches all over Europe – which have moved more than Islamic organisations supported by the Turkish state to a Christian-type model of religious activity. For example, they have given the Imam a more prominent role than in traditional "folk Islam", more akin to Christian pastors. Quite important, syncretism and migrant incorporation are not necessarily opposite processes. For example, while many Chinese migrants in Canada may be incorporated socio-economically, they may engage in syncretist cultural practices related to both Canada and their home region.

In the political realm, over the last few decades more than half of all sovereign states have come to tolerate dual or multiple citizenship for various reasons (Faist 2007b; Faist/Kivisto 2007). This is astonishing when one considers that a few decades ago citizenship and political loyalty to a state were still considered inseparable. Dual citizenship could be conceived of as the political foundation of the transnational experience, enabling transnational migrants and their children to lead multiple lives across borders. There has been a push towards tolerating dual nationality from both ends, from immigration and emigration countries, albeit for somewhat different reasons. In immigration countries it has been the spread of an equal rights perspective, advanced by considerations of gender equity and equal political freedom for all residents, which has provided the momentum towards increasing tolerance. Categories of persons to which tolerance has been shown have continued to grow, starting from stateless persons, those not allowed to renounce their nationality that is, not released from their original citizenship, and, finally, spouses and children in bi-national marriages. In emigration countries, the reasons for increasing tolerance often have been pronounced in more instrumental ways. For instance, representatives of political regimes have attempted to forge continuous links to expatriates living abroad.

While political transnationalisation is not a new phenomenon, the transnational activists of today, unlike those of the 19th and the first half of the 20th centuries, are not comprised solely of professionals. A major difference between today and the turn of the 20th century may be that today, in addition to nationalist activists or diasporists, ethnic business persons and their associates, there is probably a greater proportion of groups concerned with human rights and fundamental rights issues. Transnational activists are not merely internationally oriented cosmopolitans but rather need a firm grounding in local or national contexts. In order to inquire into the rootedness of transnational political actors, it is necessary to distinguish the organisational form their activities take: First, there are transnationally active non-government organisations (NGOs), such as cultural organisations; diasporic organisations; and organisations founded by political exiles and dissidents with the intention of overturning authoritarian regimes in their country of origin. Secondly, there are also genuinely transnational NGOs or international NGOs (INGOs), in which migrant activists operate, such as Greenpeace or Amnesty International (Tarrow 1998).

Methodology: "Spaces inbetween" Associations and National States

Most empirical studies on the process of forming and reproducing transnational social spaces – transnationalisation – focus on association and organisations (cf. Moja 2005). Such studies need to be complemented by those looking at the "spaces inbetween associations", that is transactions criss-crossing multiple associations, networks forming within associations, and non-organised engagement. For example, village cultural associations of Overseas Chinese in Southeast Asia nowadays also function as an arena for businesspersons planning to invest in China (Hong Liu 1998). In such cases, associations function as platforms for persons who are participating in other social groups as well, an instance of cross-cutting social circles (cf. Simmel 1955).

Methodologically, the exhortation of transnational approaches to "follow the flow of persons, money, ideas and so forth" has not really been taken very seriously, contrary to most announcements. A more systematic network approach, not only in the metaphorical sense is necessary. Taking multi-sited fieldwork seriously – that is, simultaneous research in locations – would mean to follow financial or other transactions in tracing lateral connectivities to other immigration and emigration regions. A case at hand is a five-year study meticulously tracing transactions involving persons, groups and organisations in the case of networks of Ghanaian migrants located in Amsterdam back to locations in Ghana and in other regions of the world (Mazzucato 2008). Such a methodological approach does not presume concepts of world society which presuppose too much unity and systemic differentiation. In sum, exploring transnational connectivities through multi-sited fieldwork enables us to look at the great variety of societal forms – associations, small groups, networks of associations (issue networks) and informal social networks. In particular, it allows us to trace the combination of a high degree of local clustering with a relatively low average path distance between nodes and hubs, which are located in different national states.

Networks in the "spaces inbetween" and within associations can be built around various categorical distinctions, such as ethnicity, race, gender, schooling, professional training, political affiliation, and sexual preference. Ethnicity constitutes a particularly vexing issue in transnational studies. On the one hand a transnational approach should be able to overcome the "ethnic" bias inherent in much migration scholarship. The fallacy is to label migrants immediately by means of "ethnic" or "national" categories. Often scholars presuppose prematurely that categories such as Turks, Brazilians and so forth matter a lot, since they do in public discourse. On the other hand, methods should be able to trace actually existing ethnic social formations, such as networks of reciprocity, which are of great importance, for example, in informal transfer systems of financial remittances. Yet ethnic networks may be complemented by networks in the financial sector which are not ethnically based at all. For example, informal remittance networks extending from Manchester, UK to Lahore in Pakistan rely on intermediaries or financial brokers in Dubai (Ballard 2005). In such cases we may speak of network of networks characterised by overlapping categories. In essence, a network approach means to turn the issue of the importance of ethnicity into an empirical question.

Transnational agents, such as groups, associations, organisations, and diasporas, cannot be treated as unitary actors if one wants to understand the tensions inherent in transnational social formations. Certainly, the opportunities for transnational agents have changed in the process of globalisation, not only for migrant-based collectives (cf. Evans 2000). Because of the apparent increase in interconnectedness through long-distance communication, facilitated face-to-face communication and interaction through travel and interaction, and the diffusion of ideas and knowledge, social life extending across the borders of states has become more dense and extensive. The spaces "inbetween" states have multiplied. Some of the cherished concepts of migration research need to be questioned because they may not be adequate to capture more fluid life-styles, modes of action, and collective behaviour. The lives of migrants are not necessarily characterised by one-time settlement and commitment to one society or associations and groups in one society. Therefore, dichotomous distinctions such as "origin" vs. "destination" and "emigration" vs. "immigration" no longer hold, if only because many traditional emigration countries have become both transit and immigration countries. Turkey is a typical example. Less obviously, other dichotomies such as "temporary vs. permanent" or "labour migrant vs. refugee" also no longer hold if the goal is to map trajectories of mobile populations. One first step has been a renewed interest in the notion of social space. This has implied, among other things, the need to conceptualize migration beyond its demographic construction as "flows" and "stocks" of people and to look at the "inbetween places." Nonetheless, overcoming unhelpful binary conceptual oppositions does not mean occluding political conflicts in policy fields such as migration and development.

Venues for Research – The Example of Transnationalisation and Development

Public debate and research on the relationship between migration & development has increased considerably over the past years. To be more precise, it has experienced yet another climax after two previous ones, in the 1960s and 1980s. From a simple cost-benefit point of view the basic idea has always been that the flow of emigrants and the loss of brains are partly or wholly compensated by a reverse flow of money, ideas and knowledge. Yet there is very little systematic thought given to what is recently "new". A transnational approach means looking at the emergence of a new transnational agent in development discourse – intermittently called "migrants", "diaspora", or "transnational community". In the eyes of some international organisations, states and development agencies they have turned into development agents. Increasingly, the cross-border ties of geographically mobile persons and collectives have been moved to the centre of attention. And national states, local governments, inter- and supranational organisations and development agencies seek to co-opt and establish ties to such agents, who are engaged in sustained and continuous cross-border relationships on a personal, collective and organisational level. Also, and this is crucial for any kind of scientific endeavour, the emergence of this new type of development agent can be tackled by means of a decidedly transnational methodology just sketched. Only then can we hope to look at what is usually called "development" in both North and South, and what the different agents involved understand by "development", hence one may use the plural "development(s)". Development is a decidedly normative term and may be of little value analytically. However, its main purpose for this discussion is that it concentrates academic and public debates on the conflicting and evolving notions of what different agents understand as leading a "good life".

Various agents have repositioned themselves locally in the global changes over the past decades. Both public policies and rhetoric have changed. A prominent example of the transformed political semantics is the discursive and institutional changes the People's Republic of China has implemented. Discursively, the slogan to "serve the country" (*wei guo fuwu*) has replaced the previous motto of "return to serve" (*huiguo fuwu*) (Cheng Xi in Nyíri 2001: 637). Such rhetoric has been complemented by various public policy changes. Examples are easy to spot, including adaptations through mechanisms such as dual citizenship for emigrants and immigrants, voting rights for absentees, tax incentives for citizens abroad, and cooptation of migrant organisations by local, regional and state governments for development cooperation. Instead of permanent return migration, temporary returns, visits and other forms of transactions have moved to the centre of attention. Thus, in recent years the notion of migrants' return as an asset of development has been complemented by the idea that even if there is no eventual return, the commitment of migrants living abroad could be tapped, not only, for example, through hometown associations but also through informal "diaspora knowledge networks" (Meyer 2006). These are networks of scientists and R&D personnel, business networks, and networks of professionals working for multinational companies (Kuznetsov 2006). States, development agencies and international organisations try to support the circulatory mobility of persons involved. The keyword is "temporary return": An example is the Migration and Development in Africa (MIDA) program of the International Organisation of Migration (IOM), which send migrants as experts back to their countries of origin for short periods of time (cf. Kapur/McHale 2005). And, of course, governments try to tap into the activities of hometown associations. A prominent example is the Mexican *tres-por-uno* (3x1) program, in which each "migradollar" sent by migrants from abroad is complemented by three dollars from various governmental levels. More recently, banks have joined the fray and announced 4x1 programs. The examples given suggest that states and organisations have started to build programs based on the obligations and commitments felt by migrants towards "home country" institutions.

Much of the semantics focuses on community. The two most fashionable terms are diaspora and transnational communities. There is an interesting difference: diaspora is used frequently in the development discourse, and refers to individuals dispersed all over the globe, while the term transnational community is found more often in the transnationalist literature. Both terminologies refer to "communities without propinquity" (Faist 2000b): Such communities are not primarily built upon geographical closeness but on a series of social and symbolic ties which connect ethnic, religious and professional diasporas. Yet the notions of diaspora and transnational community need to be unbundled and even rejected in order to get closer to a systematic analysis. Rogers Brubaker cogently observed that the "universalisation of the diaspora, paradoxically, means the disappearance of the diaspora" (Brubaker 2005: 3). In recent decades there has been a telling change of meaning. First, in the classical meaning diaspora referred to forced migration and violent dispersal, nowadays it denotes any kind of migration, hence the talk of labour diaspora, trade diaspora, business diaspora, and refugee diasporas. Secondly, in a classical sense diaspora implied a return to an imagined or real homeland. Nowadays, this simply means some sort of sustained ties back to the home country, and in post-modern usage even lateral ties – that is, ties not only from emigration to one immigration country but connectivity all over the globe. Thirdly, in the old meaning diaspora referred to various forms of diaspora segregation in the immigration country, but in the new meaning a sort of culturally pluralist boundary maintenance in the host country. While these are interesting shifts in meaning, the term diaspora – as well as transnational community – is too restrictive a term. It imagines a rather homogeneous cross-border social formation. It repeats the same mistake as much migration scholarship which assumes rather homogenous national, ethnic or religious groupings. In sum, in a transnational approach terms such as "community" and "diaspora" do play a role. Nonetheless, they should not be used in a conceptually inflationary manner because this leads to an essentialisation of these categories.

The newest wave of the migration-development nexus raises a couple of challenges to transnational approaches:

Incorporation and Development

So far, incorporation and development studies are disjointed, even in transnational studies. Studies either take the perspective of the country or region, in which immigrants live, and deal from a transnational angle with issues of incorporation into labour markets, housing, education and cultural pluralism, but also social security, state security, wage differentials, and so forth. Or studies deal with the effects of transnational ties on home countries, villages, formations from which migrants originate, such as demographic dynamics, remittance flows, and cultural impacts and often involve an analysis of transnational flows. The former studies, preoccupied with effects on immigration regions, have entered into a dialogue with assimilation and multiculturalism perspectives, and the latter, focusing on emigration regions, with development studies. Yet the two areas are still awkward dance partners. For example, studies have found in the case of immigrants from Mexico, the Dominican Republic and Colombia in the USA that transnational immigrant organisations' members are older, better-established, and possess above-average levels of education (Portes et al. 2007). This could be interpreted, depending on one's conceptual predisposition, as transnationalism and assimilation not being opposites, or as a strong transnational orientation indicating a specific path of incorporation.

However, if not carried onwards, such discussions miss the essence of a transnational approach. From such a perspective incorporation in national polities of immigration is one of several dimensions, the other being emigration countries and transnational social formations themselves. This is clearly visible in two-way flows. From an integrated South-North-South perspective one has to look not only at remittances as North-South transfers but also at potential "reverse remittances." There are indeed empirical findings of "reverse remittances" or two way flows: They can be important especially at the beginning stages of migration of persons or groups, for example to help undocumented migrants to get papers and thus to legalize their stay. In this particular case reverse remittances may be indicative of an immigrant incorporation policy which externalises the costs of integration. Yet such support structures only function if there are cross border formations, consisting of various elements, such as kinship groups or brokers.

It is questionable whether terms such as immigrant integration or incorporation are able to capture how two-way flows shape the associational life connecting emigration and immigration regions. They are valid perspectives, of course, centring on regions of destination and origin. Nonetheless, the in-between transactions constitute social facts *sui generis*. Yet we have not yet found an appropriate terminology to deal with these social facts. For example, migrant associations in immigration regions cannot be neatly categorised into those concerned with social integration and those interested in development cooperation. It is thus not surprising that local governments in some European countries have started to link incorporation, development and migration policies. This opens up new ways of thinking about the link between incorporation and development: Not only may those best incorporated be most active in migrant organisations dealing with development (a result which is not really surprising) but development cooperation can also be seen as incorporation – yet the sphere is not restricted then to immigration states but extends to regions of origin. In Spanish metropolitan areas such as Madrid and Barcelona, for example, there has been a marked shift by local governments to not just support co-development but to tie incorporation in Spain to development abroad. Co-operation between local authorities and migrants is then directed not only at development in the countries of origin but also seen as a means to foster incorporation in Spain. The questions which arise are: Is this an example of co-optation of migrant organisations by local state agencies, or do we see collaboration between migrant associations and state power? What are the functions of local cooperation for migration control or management? Why do we see the triangulation of development, migration control and incorporation in countries which have only recently emerged as major receiving countries, such as Spain? And, ultimately, given the pluri-locality of incorporation in multiple sites in Spain and abroad: incorporation into what? In addition, it stands to reason why the combination of development, migration control and incorporation now and the motives behind it? In the end, the issue of co-development on the local level and the plurality of agents involved suggest that we need to pay more attention to different layers of statehood to understand the triangulation. After all, it is the national state which is explicitly engaged in migration control, while at the local level issues of incorporation achieve a prime importance.

Public Policy, Politics and Inequality

Many studies look positively at remittances – financial, knowledge and social – because they may reduce poverty or even eradicate it and contribute to economic growth. However, there is almost no discussion of the mechanisms of how this may work – it is almost as if an "invisible hand" transforms remittances into poverty reduction and economic growth. Needless to say, this is a very myopic view of the public policy relevance of remittances. If they tie transnational migration to global social inequality, then remittances must be examined in their relevance for social policy. Seen in this way, they do not constitute explicit social policies, of course, but they form a basis for fostering social solidarity among citizens.

There is, first, an interesting nexus between remittances, social policy and development with remittances constituting a sort of intervening variable because they are an expression of the diffuse solidarity and generalised reciprocity upon which any kind of social policy has to be built. Secondly, only by integrating transnational migrants and their associations into policy circuits on various governance levels can such potentials be realised. At the very least, we need to analyse the social policy potential inherent in transnational flows with respect to state agencies on various levels, non-governmental organisations and economic organisations such as firms.

Therefore, the crucial policy question is how to fit remittances into universal social policies. How can remittances be factored into what a recent publication by the United Nations Research Institute for Social Development (UNRISD) calls "developmental welfare"? Social policy and social rights are not something that might merely evolve after a certain level of development has been reached. Rather "social policy is a key instrument for economic and social development" (UNRISD 2007: 2). Since there is no simple remittance-development-nexus, we need to look at policies which can forge social solidarity and are thus based on social citizenship across the borders of national states (Faist 2007c). All the great theorists of societal membership – from Aristotle, Cicero, J.S. Mill, Hannah Arendt, T.H. Marshall – have agreed that in order to participate fully in public life, persons need to be in a certain socio-economic and political position – in Marshall's tradition we may call it social citizenship; more recently the term "capabilities" has been introduced by Amartya Sen to capture the same thought (Marshall 1950; Sen 1999).

However, for remittances to play a role in social policy, one has to consider the obvious difficulties involved in the exchange of financial flows (cf. Guarnizo 2003). For various reasons, macro-political agents such as governments and international organisations have tried to control such flows. States in the North, the USA in particular, have tried to redirect flows through the *hawala* and *hindi* systems to the formal banking system. Officially, this has been part of the effort of states to gain political control over resource flows after 9/11 in the "war against terrorism". From a state control point of view, remittances transferred through informal channels exemplify the transgressive behaviour of migrants, not only their entrepreneurial spirit; remittances do not go to countries as such but to particular households, villages and regions, and emigration states try to get control of the money. For international organisations, remittances are one of the instances in which the control over development finance is at stake. The World Bank and the regional development banks, such as the Asian Development Bank and the Inter-American Development Bank give loans to poor countries. The profit made comes from the small margin of interest rates imposed. However, in the aftermath of structural adjustment programs, and above all alternative sources for credit (e.g. China in Africa), more and more developing countries seem to be less and less interested in development finance issued with all the strings attached, such as the rule of law, democracy, respect for human rights, scaling down social subsidies. China imposes none of these stifling conditions. As a result, the World Bank issues fewer loans and thus the volume of transactions decreases. This state of affairs constitutes indeed a challenge to the mandate of the World Bank. A transnational perspective must take into account the frictions and sometimes even the political conflicts caused by the efforts to control financial remittances.

With respect to all forms of remittances, whether financial, human capital or social, the issue of their use for purposes such as social and economic welfare points towards a deeper question. They signal different and often divergent visions around the notion of development. If one uses the notion of development, the questions are: what kind of development, whose development and for whom? Is there a congruence of development visions of diaspora groups on the one hand and development agencies on the other hand? Do transfers imply transformations? The cooperation and sometimes cooptation of migrant associations by development agencies and local governments raises the issue of who sets the standards for the goals to be achieved. Listening to the voices of migrants and communities affected by migration may involve re-defining the goals and indicators of development to focus on human well-being rather than monetary wealth. Yet it would be naïve to ascribe an emphasis on community and equality to migrant agency, and more instrumental aims to development agencies, governments of national states and international organisations.

Transnationalisation through Coupling Migration Control and Development Aid

Paradoxically, restrictive migration policies may be conducive to financial remittances and the maintenance of transnational kinship groups. Contemporary international borders are much more akin to sieves than to medieval stone walls. Their principal function is to protect the integrity of the socio-economic, demographic and cultural integrity of the population which lies behind them. One important measure is to filter unacceptable or illegitimate migrants and welcome those who increase the competitiveness of the economy. The hewers of wood and the drawers of water are implicitly "wanted but not welcome" (Zolberg 1987). By contrast, those regarded as highly skilled migrants who transmit knowledge and foreign investments are not only wanted but also quite welcome. The migration-development link is usually mentioned in its function of reducing the propensities for migration to Europe. Coupled with such controls are policies making development aid to states in the European periphery conditional upon their willingness to control undocumented migration (Faist/Ette 2007). In other words, emigration countries need to show their willingness to control illegal migration to immigration countries in order to get development aid. A good example for such conditionality is Morocco, which partly depends on the EU for financial contributions.

Transnational Concepts and the Concept of the Transnational

Not all "national" concepts can or should be "transnationalised". It is very nebulous what terms such as "transnational citizenship" could mean. Sometimes the term is used to connote the membership of migrants to local communities (Fitzgerald 2004). However, it then does not have a legal referent. Citizenship usually connotes equal political freedom, equal rights of full members, and affiliation to a politically-bounded group (Faist 2007b). A very lose definition of citizenship as transnational does not help analytical work. On the level of national states it is therefore more precise to speak of dual or multiple citizenships. "And on the level of supra-state polities such as European Union citizenship, we find that several layers of citizenship are nested within each other – regional, national and European. In this case the term nested citizenship is appropriate" (Faist 2001). Therefore, we are better off speaking of transnational membership when discussing the involvement of geographically mobile persons in local communities in two or more countries. The situation may be different when talking about transnational civil society. Civil society and rule of law or even democratic statehood are mutually constitutive: Civil society is usually held to be a sphere distinct from "market" and "state", and as such can only be thought of in terms of basic human and civil rights guaranteed by state structures. Migrant organisations may be part of groups active in the civil sphere (Faist 2000b: chapter 9).

The difficulties involved in transnationalising concepts such as citizenship and civil society points towards a larger *problématique*. Too often the term "trans" means only overcoming unhelpful binary oppositions. And indeed, from a transnational angle oppositions such as emigrant and immigrant can partly be dissolved in the concept of a transnational migrant. Also, as mentioned above, there is no necessary opposition between transnational ties and the incorporation of geographically mobile persons in different and distinct local and national civil, economic and political spheres. However, it should not be forgotten that "trans" does not simply imply going beyond, namely beyond conflicts created by the very transnationality of ties and social structures. For example, there are numerous documented instances of conflicts between development visions of hometown associations on the one hand and those remaining in the locales of origin on the other hand. While the former may see stipends for bright students for study abroad as an appropriate tool of development, the latter may be interested in the improvement of local infrastructures (for examples, see Waldinger 2006).

Conclusion: Bringing Legitimation Back in

Transnational approaches offer a counter-balance to macro-oriented, top-down approaches of globalisation, world society and world polity theory. Although they are less integrated theoretically than these three broad groups of approaches, they offer much-needed heuristic tools to call into question the unrealistic notions of these other cross border theories in at least two respects. First, transnational approaches occupy the conceptual space inbetween "container" social sciences fraught by problems such as methodological territorialism and methodological nationalism on the one hand and world society and world polity theories on the other hand (on related but differing concepts such as "cosmopolitanism", see Beck/Sznaider 2006). Transnational approaches perform this function because they emphasise the tension between space as place and space as flows. Although the boundaries of many national institutions, including the national states themselves, are rapidly changing, binary oppositions are not going to dissolve. If one is interested in emergent structures of world society or world polity, one has to take very seriously the nexus between local and global models and look at how they shape each other. Doing so requires attention to cross border agency. This means allowing for both tendencies towards homogeneity and heterogeneity, incorporation and disintegration of societal formations across the globe. Second, globalisation and world society approaches usually do not pose the central question any political sociology has to put at its centre – the problem of legitimacy of social orders and social systems. Issues of legitimate social order, here shown in an exemplary way regarding the migration-development nexus, are at the root of social change and transformation in any kind of societal formation.

References

Ballard, Roger (2005) "Coalitions of Reciprocity and the Maintenance of Financial Integrity within Informal Value Transmission Systems: the Operational Dynamics of Contemporary Hawala Networks." Journal of Banking Regulations 6/4, pp. 319-352.

Basch, Linda/Glick Schiller, Nina/Szanton Blanc, Cristina (1994) *Nations Unbound: Transnational Projects, Postcolonial Predicaments, and Deterritorialized Nation-States*, Langhorne, PA: Gordon and Breach.

Beck, Ulrich/Sznaider, Nathan (2006) "Unpacking Cosmopolitanism for the Social Sciences: a Research Agenda." The British Journal of Sociology 57/1, pp. 1-23.

Brubaker, Rogers (2005) "The 'Diaspora' Diaspora." Ethnic and Racial Studies 28/1, pp. 1-19.

Castells, Manuel (1996) *The Rise of the Network Society. The Information Age: Economy, Society and Culture, Volume 1*, Oxford/Malden: Blackwell Publishing.

Castles, Stephen/Miller, Mark J. (2003) *The Age of Migration: International Population Movements in the Modern World*, Houndmills: Palgrave Macmillan.

Dannecker, Petra (2004) "Transnational Migration and the Transformation of

Gender Relations: The Case of Bangladeshi Labour Migrants." Current Sociology 53/4, pp. 655-674.

Evans, Peter (2000) "Fighting Marginalization with Transnational Networks: Counter-Hegemonic Globalization." Contemporary Sociology 29/1, pp. 230-241.

Faist, Thomas (1997) "The Crucial Meso-Level." In: Tomas Hammar/Grete Brochmann/Kristof Tamas/Thomas Faist (eds.) *International Migration, Immobility and Development: Multidisciplinary Perspective,* Oxford: Berg, pp. 187-217.

Faist, Thomas (2000a) *Transstaatliche Räume. Politik, Wirtschaft und Kultur in und zwischen Deutschland und der Türkei,* Bielefeld: transcript.

Faist, Thomas (2000b) *The Volume and Dynamics of International Migration and Transnational Social Spaces,* Oxford: Oxford University Press.

Faist, Thomas (2001) "Social Citizenship in the European Union, Nested Membership." Journal of Common Market Studies 39/1, pp. 39-60.

Faist, Thomas/Özveren, Eyüp (2004a) *Transnational Social Spaces: Agents, Networks and Institutions,* Aldershot: Ashgate.

Faist, Thomas (2004b) "Social Space." In: George Ritzer (ed.) *Encyclopedia of Social Theory,* Beverly Hills: Sage, pp. 760-773.

Faist, Thomas (2007a) *Transstate Social Spaces and Development: Exploring the Changing Balance between Communities, States and Markets,* International Institute for Labour Studies (IILS), Discussion paper DP/169/2007, Decent Work Research Programme, Geneva: ILO.

Faist, Thomas (ed.) (2007b) *Dual Citizenship in Europe: From Nationhood to Societal Integration,* Avebury: Ashgate.

Faist, Thomas (2007c) *The Transnational Social Question: Social Rights and Citizenship in Global Perspective,* Working Paper 14, Bielefeld: COMCAD – Center on Migration, Citizenship and Development, www.comcad-bielefeld.de.

Faist, Thomas/Ette, Andreas (eds.) (2007) *Between Autonomy and the European Union: The Europeanization of National Immigration Policies,* Houndmills: Palgrave Macmillan.

Faist, Thomas/Kivisto, Peter (2007) *Dual Citizenship in Global Perspective: From Unitary to Multiple Citizenship,* Houndmills: Palgrave Macmillan.

Fitzgerald, David (2004) "Beyond 'Transnationalism': Mexican Hometown Politics at an American Labour Union." Ethnic and Racial Studies 27/2, pp. 228-247.

Guarnizo, Luis Eduardo (2003) "The Economics of Transnational Living." International Migration Review 37/3, pp. 666-699.

Haas, Hein de (2006) *Engaging Diasporas: How Governments and Development Agencies Can Support Diaspora Involvement in the Development of Origin Countries,* A Study for Oxfam Novib, Oxford: University of Oxford, International Migration Institute.

Haugen, Heidi Østbø/Carling, Jørgen (2005) "On the Edge of the Chinese Diaspora: The Surge of Baihuo Business in an African City." Ethnic and Racial Studies 28/4, pp. 639-662.

Kapur, Devesh/McHale, John (2005) *Give Us Your Best and Brightest: The Global Hunt for Talent and Its Impact on the Developing World*, Cambridge, MA: Center for Global Development.

Keck, Margaret/Sikkink, Kathryn (eds.) (1998) *Activists Beyond Borders: Transnational Advocacy Networks in International Politics*, Ithaca: Cornell University Press.

Keohane, Robert O./Nye, Joseph S. (1977) *Power and Interdependence: World Politics in Transition*, Boston: Little, Brown.

Kuznetsov, Yevgeny (ed.) (2006) *Diaspora Networks and the International Migration of Skills: How Countries Can Draw on Their Talent Abroad*, Washington D.C.: The World Bank.

Lechner, Frank J./Boli, John (eds.) (2003) *The Globalization Reader*, Oxford: Blackwell.

Leichtman, Mara (2005) "The Legacy of Transnational Lives: Beyond the First Generation of Lebanese in Senegal." Ethnic and Racial Studies 28/4, pp. 663-686.

Lowell, Lindsay B./Findlay, Allan/Stewart, Emma (2004) *Brain Strain: Optimising Highly Skilled Migration from Developing Countries*, Asylum and Migration Working Paper 3, London: Institute for Public Policy Research.

Luhmann, Niklas (1975) "Die Weltgesellschaft." In: *Soziologische Aufklärung 2*, Opladen: Westdeutscher Verlag, pp. 51-71.

Luhmann, Niklas (1997) *Die Gesellschaft der Gesellschaft*, Frankfurt a. M.: Suhrkamp.

Maimba, Samuel Munzele/Ratha, Dilip (eds.) (2005) *Remittances. Development Impact and Future Prospects*, Washington D.C.: The World Bank.

Marshall, T.H. (1973 [1950]) *Citizenship and Social Class*, Cambridge: Cambridge University Press.

Marx, Karl/Engels, Friedrich (1972) "Manifest der kommunistischen Partei 1848." In: Karl Marx/Friedrich Engels (eds.) *Werke*, Vol. 4, Edited by the Institut für Marxismus-Leninismus beim Zentralkommitee der Sozialistischen Einheitspartei Deutschlands, Berlin: Dietz Verlag, pp. 461-474.

Meyer, Jean-Baptiste (2006) "Connaissance et développement: un lien à actualiser." In: Carton Michel/Jean-Baptiste Meyer (eds.) *La société des savoirs: trompe l'œil ou perspectives?*, Paris: L'Harmattan.

Meyer, John W./Boli, John/Thomas, George M./Ramirez, Francisco O. (2000) "World Society and the Nation State." American Journal of Sociology 103/1, pp. 144-181.

Moja, Jose C. (2005) "Immigrants and Associations: A Global and Historical Perspective." Journal of Ethnic and Migration Studies 31/5, pp. 833-864.

Münch, Richard (1998) *Globale Dynamik, lokale Lebenswelten: Der schwierige Weg in die Weltgesellschaft*, Frankfurt a. M.: Suhrkamp.

Murray, Colin (1981) *Families Divided: The Impact of Migrant Labour in Lesotho*, Cambridge: Cambridge University Press.

Mazzucato, Valentina (2008) "Simultaneity and networks in transnational migration: lessons learned from a simultaneous matched sample methodology." In: Josh DeWind/Jeanette Holdaway (eds.) *Migration and Development Within and Across Borders*, Geneva: International Organization for Migration (IOM).

Nyíri, Pál (2001) "Expatriating is Patriotic? The Discourse on "New Migrants" in the People's Republic of China and Identity Construction among Recent Migrants from the PRC." Journal of Ethnic and Migration Studies 27/4, pp. 635-654.

Ong, Aihwa (1992) "Limits to Cultural Accumulation: Chinese Capitalists on the American Pacific Rim." Annals of the New York Academy of Sciences 645, pp. 125-43.

Oxford Dictionary of English (ODE) (2003) 2nd edition, Edited by Catherine Soanes, Oxford: Oxford University Press.

Peters, Bernhard (1993) *Die Integration moderner Gesellschaften*, Frankfurt a.M.: Suhrkamp.

Portes, Alejandro/Guarnizo, Luis E./Landolt, Patricia (1999) "The Study of Transnationalism: Pitfalls and Promises of an Emergent Research Field." Ethnic and Racial Studies 22/2, pp. 217-237.

Portes, Alejandro/Escobar, Cristina/Radford, Alexandria Walton (2007) "Immigrant Transnational Organizations and Development: A Comparative Study." International Migration Review 41/1, pp. 242-281.

Pries, Ludger (2001) "The Approach of Transnational Social Spaces: Responding to New Configurations of the Social and the Spatial." In: Ludger Pries (ed.) *New Transnational Social Spaces: International Migration and Transnational Companies*, London: Routledge, pp. 3-33.

Rauch, James (2001) "Business and Social Networks in International Trade." Journal of Economic Literature 34, pp. 1177-1204.

Robertson, Ronald (1992) *Globalization: Social Theory and Global Culture*, London: Sage.

Roy, Olivier (2004) *L'islam mondialisé*, Paris: Seuil.

Ruggie, John Gerard (1993) "Territoriality and Beyond: Problematizing Modernity in International Relations." International Organization 47/2, pp. 139-174.

Sassen, Saskia (2006) *Territory, Authority, Rights: From Medieval to Global Assemblages*, Princeton: Princeton University Press.

Scholte, Jan Aart (2000) *Globalization: A Critical Introduction*, Basingstoke: Macmillan.

Sen, Amartya K. (1999) *Development as Freedom*, New York: Knopf.

Sieveking, Nadine/Fauser, Margit/Faist, Thomas (2007) *Die afrikanische Diaspora und Entwicklungskooperation*, Working Paper 18, Bielefeld: COMCAD – Center on Migration, Citizenship and Development, www.comcad-bielefeld.de.

Simmel, Georg (1955 [1922]) *Conflict & the Web of Group-Affiliations*, Translated by Kurt H. Wolff and Reinhard Bendix, New York: The Free Press.

Stichweh, Rudolf (2005) *Migration und Weltgesellschaft*, Working Paper 3/2005, Bielefeld: Institute for World Society Studies, June 20, 2007 (http://www.uni-bielefeld.de/soz/iw/pdf/stw.migration.PDF).

Tarrow, Sidney (1996) *Fishnets, Internets and Catnets: Globalization and Transnational Collective Action*, Working Paper 78, Madrid: Instituto Juan March de Estudios e Investigaciones.

Thrift, Nigel (1996) *Spatial Formations,* Thousand Oaks, CA: Sage.

United Nations Department of Economic and Social Affairs (UNDESA) (2006) *International Migration and Development: Analysis Prepared by UN Department of Economic and Social Affairs*, New York: UN Department of Public Information.

United Nations, Department of Economic and Social Affairs (2004) *World Economic and Social Survey. Part II: International Migration*, New York: UN.

United Nations Research Institute for Social Development (UNRISD) (2007) *Transformative Social Policy: Lessons from UNRISD Research*, Research and Policy Briefs 5, May 28, 2007 (http://www.unrisd.org /UNRISD /website/ document.nsf/ab82a6805797760f80256b4f005da1ab/c77a2891bc2fd07fc125 72130 020b2ac/ $FILE/RPB5e.pdf).

Waldinger, Roger (2006) *Conflict and Contestation in the Cross-Border Community: Hometown Associations Reassessed*, Los Angeles: University of California Digital Repositories Department of Sociology, UCLA, June 20, 2007 (http://repositories.cdlib.org/uclasoc/11).

Wallerstein, Immanuel (1974) *The Modern World System: Capitalist Agriculture and the Origins of the European World-Economy in the Sixteenth Century,* New York: Academic Press.

Wallerstein, Immanuel (1983) *Historical Capitalism,* London: Verso.

Wimmer, Andreas/Glick-Schiller, Nina (2003) "Methodological Nationalism, the Social Sciences, and the Study of Migration: An Essay in Historical Epistemology." International Migration Review 37, pp. 576-610.

World Bank (2006) *Global Economic Prospects: Economic Implications of Remittances and Migration*, Washington D.C.: The World Bank.

Zolberg, Aristide R. (1987) "'Wanted but Not Welcome': Alien Labor in Western Development." In: William Alonso (ed.) *Population in an Interacting World*, Cambridge, MA: Harvard University Press, pp. 36-73.

Transnationalisation, Translocal Spaces, Gender and Development – Methodological Challenges

GUDRUN LACHENMANN

Transcultural Research: Transnationalism and Development

In the approach presented in this article, we want to empirically ground globalisation theories and consider migration research as one very important methodological perspective. The other perspective important for our analysis is gender and agency.

This approach reflects the process of connecting development research (especially at the Department of Sociology in Bielefeld, see Schrader and Kaiser 2001) to a new concept of bridging migration and transnationalism. Migration is now seen as constituting a transnational space for negotiating development through translocal interactions which form an everyday life activity of 'transmigrants'. Their concepts of development, of societal well-being and of social transformation in general are probably quite different from the mainstream development ideas into which they are supposed to be integrated by 'developers'. These may be very modernistic, or traditionalistic in other concerns, not really democratic but with a high degree of ownership.

In order to investigate these processes, questions of methodology and design have to be asked in quite a different way than has been the case in development research, sociology and social anthropology up to now. Many are sceptical of regarding the adequacy of doing comparative research across different societies, first world and third world, between different cultures or civilisations, given the very heterogeneous and context specific developments. After the long tradition of regional studies, case studies in social anthropology and fear of transfer of Eurocentric concepts in development research, there is a necessity for a fundamental reconsidering of methodological approaches within a process of globalising social science. Concepts connected to specific cases and regions enter more and more into generalising debates, following a methodology of transcultural 'comparative global' social research.

Therefore, there is an increased interest in strengthening qualitative methodology and in empirically grounding certain theoretical fields such as the sociology of Islam, gender, social movements (Lachenmann 1993, 1998b) which can be made fruitful for migration and development studies and can be considered to be basic features of globalisation 'in the making'. There are three different approaches: qualitative analysis of concepts and phenomena considered to be constitutive of globalisation, such as social movements, networks, civil society within a framework of transcultural sociology, thereby avoiding dualisms of blocks, cultures etc.; globalisation studied through its constitutional element of interlinking, global flows, translocal social spaces, networks and movements; and globalisation looked at as it is generated from below, making use of knowledge accumulated by means of regional studies and looking at glocalisation and localisation. The paradigm of translocality refers to the interactive construction of social reality whereby boundaries of multiple social worlds, identities, and communities are renegotiated.

The article is mainly based on the research project "Negotiating Development in Translocal Gendered Spaces in Muslim Societies".[1] The women's movements which we studied in their own societies, referring to global concepts such as CEDAW, family law and with regard to translocality ascribed to their local and regional activities, were, together with migrants, among the early transnational actors of globalisation. In this article, I shall try to explain the theoretical concepts and methodology developed in this context to study the constitution of translocal spaces. We aim at bringing different recent venues together, such as engendering social fields and interface of knowledge systems on the one hand and approaches to new forms of field research on the other, linking up to internationally debated concepts of multi-sited respectively global ethnography. An important aspect of further developing the study of translocal spaces will be bringing together concepts of (translocal) agency, institutionalisation and structuration. It will be shown how these considerations can be applied to three case studies of Muslim societies. The theoretical outcome of empirically grounding globalisation theory will be based on contrasting concepts of 'othering' vs. glocalisation, transfer vs. interconnectedness and analysing the restructuring and overlapping of public spheres. Finally concrete methods of field research, as applied in the research project mentioned above will be explained.

In this project we argued that globalisation is being constituted through new social forms of organisation and epistemic communities, with the development of the world as a global knowledge framework. Within a framework of theory of agency, relationality and dynamics, we analyse the constitution of social spaces,

---

[1] Financed by the Volkswagen Foundation, see www.uni-bielefeld/trdc, and coordinated by the author and Dr. Petra Dannecker, together with Dr. Salma Nageeb, Dr. Nadine Sieveking and Anna Spiegel Dipl.Soz.

which are structured through gender, and look at othering and fundamentalisms as globalising forces negotiated locally at different interfaces. We want to contribute to deepening globalisation theory by looking at how spaces, knowledge, structuring through agency and networking of women in the development field are constituting flows and landscapes in a translocal way. We do this in the sense of empirically grounding approaches of Appadurai (1998, 2000), Robertson (1995) or Hannerz (2000) etc.. In our view the structuration of social fields is gendered, and the female negotiation of development and constitution of translocal and transnational spaces present very pertinent cases for consideration. Migration is a second important dimension of structuration and agency.

We can consider migration theory and transnationalism as one field of globalisation processes in which migrants are actors and carriers of ideas and concepts being localised and also globalised in the sense of feeding back to the North. Of course, the structuration of power of these translocal spaces, interfaces and interactions, is one of the main challenges to be analysed. Our approach intends to be transnational, overcoming methodological nationalism (although the interface between the state and i.a. its development policy can be focused upon as well) and methodological ethnicity (Glick-Schiller/Basch/Szanton Blanc 1992) by looking at diversity and intersectionality in the social and cultural construction of reality in a transcultural approach.

In general it is astonishing how little explicit debate and writing exists on how to do empirical research which captures translocality (Appadurai 1998; Freitag/von Oppen 2005) and transnationalism (Hannerz 2000; Faist 1998; Faist 2007; Pries 2001). It is clear that we cannot separate an interactive and translocal approach from a comparative approach when studying processes, relations, or flows. Comparison, respectively interface-analysis, does not imply one logic, but rather the construction of meaning from situatedness and contextualisation. Therefore, it seems very fruitful to make comparisons by deconstructing concepts regarding certain phenomena, such as citizenship and participation. The adequacy of the methods has to be discussed by looking at the newly observed processes and problems which are constitutive of globalisation. These include local/ national confrontations and questions of autonomy, political ethnicity, identity etc., the constitution of the public sphere and social spaces, knowledge production and transfer.

It is also very important to see that, although there is a global regime in development with very dominant conceptualisations, interactions and transfers, as in migration, are not mainly North – South any longer. However the South – South relations are often invisible. Such is the case with traders' networks[2] for example, which transform into transnational South – South firms, transnational

---

2   See Evers/Schrader (1994). They elaborated on the so called "traders' dilemma", showing that trade is mainly organised by non-locals who can avoid social obligations.

women's and other social movements and civil society, constituting new translocal public spheres.

Engendering Methodology, Researching Constitution of Translocal Spaces

We are aspiring to empirically ground globalisation theories in the sense of "grounded theory" (Strauss 1987; Strauss/Corbin 1998) and are doing transcultural comparison and research in the sense of "global ethnography" (Burawoy et al. 2000), and "multi-sited ethnography" (Marcus 1998). Therefore we study the social spaces constituted in different arenas, platforms for public debate, considering different flows and fields, such as development, through the agency and perspective of actors such as migrants and members of women organisations. The constitution of interactive social spaces through networks, especially through IT in a virtual space, is a very interesting concomitant feature of migration which transcends the division of everyday life and lifeworld, mid-level organisations and national boundaries (Harcourt 1999; Saloma-Akpedonu 2006).

From our point of view it is important to widen the epistemological and theoretical approach to embrace translocal social spaces in general by using the concept of overlapping knowledge systems and their interfaces (Long 1992). This implies broadening migration approaches and generalising development studies, but in very clear cut fields. This position should not be equated with the assumption that the nation state should or does lose certain functions. The difference in methodology lies in referring to certain dimensions of analysis such as interfaces with state authorities, politics, and institutions, instead of focusing on them as units of analysis.

We take recourse to phenomenological social theory and interpretative methodology and share the assumption that methodological deficits should be overcome by focusing on renegotiating and overcoming frontiers, constituting crosscutting and overlapping social spaces and institutions. This brings into focus the negotiation of meaning and constitution of social spaces. According to our view, this necessitates a methodological approach of structuration and hybridisation with a focus on negotiation of meaning of institutions in translocal/transnational spaces. This also implies to investigate new forms of social cohesion and collective agency of society including social movements and civil society organisations, and the constitution of crosscutting spaces for negotiating meaning. Another methodological requisite would be a systematic analyis of (encounters at) interfaces (of knowledge systems) and the interconnectedness or redrawing of boundaries between different sites and spaces.

We think that we can thereby overcome in our analysis the tendency to conceptualise institutions in very formalistic and modernistic ways, distinguishing between formal and informal institutions and sectors as well as social security, public and private, traditional and modern forms of governance, civil society and the state. This would imply drawing strict boundaries without taking into account interfaces, crosscutting knowledge and resource transfers and management, the social embeddedness of institutions, the permanent renegotiation of social identities, i.e. the enormous flexibility of structures and agency. However, we would look at processes of formalisation, organisation-building, development in translocal/transnational spaces, of participation, ownership and transformation of 'traditional' institutions.

Unfortunately, in mainstream transnationalism studies in general there is hardly any explicit engendering of analysis, although a gender perspective is very pertinent and fruitful. This is especially true regarding the structuration of social fields where gender clearly makes a difference and provides relevant insights into the construction of social reality.[3] However, there are some very thorough and rich empirical studies, mainly in the field of transnational identity formation (e.g. Thapan (ed.) 2005; Thapan 2005; Chaudhuri 2005). Often, only a conventional number-taking or comparison of men and women takes place. This looks at the very statically conceived 'role of women' in 'households', without taking into account research on translocal gender relations and their renegotiation, gendered modes of (circular) migration, construction of gender in institutions and organisations, including policies, and societal gender order.

When applying this gender perspective (Lachenmann 2004a; Lachenmann 2004b; Dannecker 2005), we realised that there are gendered (translocal) social spaces on the one hand, where the instrumentalisation of women in migration, identity and poverty reduction policies takes place. The construction of gender is often very essentialist, with gender constructs influencing, to a great extent, the orientalisation of migrants. This occurs through concepts such as vulnerable groups, forced marriage, oppression of women, thereby characterising the sending countries as underdeveloped and culturally inferior. On the other hand, far-fetched implications about what these 'suppressed' women should do are implied in policies. Also the gendered structure of transnational migration and the very big gender differences and interesting gendered networks are hardly taken into account.

Furthermore, it is very important to development and localisation, as Nina Glick Schiller has stressed, to study localities within the global 'new economy', overcoming the 'ethnic economy' approach. To do this she suggests a scaling approach to transnational migration research, including the positioning of nation-states and global cities within global fields of power affecting the "processes through which migrants move, settle, and maintain transnational connection" (Glick Schiller 2007: 6).

There is certainly a need for a global perspective, but at the same time we need to strengthen the methodological links between localities, localising pro-

---

3   Sarah J. Mahler and Patricia R. Pessar (2006) put it nicely: "Gender matters: ethnographers bring gender from the periphery toward the core of migration studies".

cesses, interfaces at different levels and crosscutting and overlapping social spaces. Of course we cannot consider migrants as 'actors of globalisation' (in the sense that political scientists often do) without unravelling underlying power structures. Agency and (power) structuration of translocal fields are constituting globalisation which is also 'made by migrants' in the sense of 'social worlds', establishing relations and institutions. We would refer to modes of structuration, dimensions, even think of strategies. A methodological consequence is to overcome dichotomies by showing that new cultural spaces are created – what could be called 'spaces of migration' (intersecting at many borders and internally structured) – in contrast to a concept of container culture (see e.g. Pries 2001).

The constitution of spaces can lead to formation of communities, but the more interesting approach of global ethnography would be to analyse negotiation within, e.g. between concepts of culture, development and obligations, gender relations etc. between migrants and people at home. Otherwise there is the danger of assuming a framework of 'global capitalism' without showing how combined power structures work on a local level. This is what can be conceived as a paradigm of 'translocality' (Appadurai 1998; Freitag/von Oppen 2005).

Development, in a framework of globalisation, must be conceived of as "social transformation" in a broad sense such as "multiple modernities". This concept implies looking at othering processes, different institutional solutions but also informalisation processes (e.g. of social services). These need to be defined in terms of knowledge production and use, as well as arenas of the negotiation of meaning in a scalar sense on different levels. In general, transnationalisation, including migration, should overcome tendencies to become closed epistemic communities. Following a translocal paradigm, our questions with regard to development and migrants as carriers of flows (in the sense of Appadurai 1998) would be: What concepts do they carry? Can they overcome the 'stranger'-'natives' divide which is used in development co-operation, addressed by social concepts such as local knowledge, participation, ownership etc. We are introducing methodological approaches in order to do analysis based on sociology of knowledge, including ideas of authority of knowledge, dominant knowledge etc. (e.g. article by Eva Gerharz in this volume).

The phenomenological approach of structuration, which is connected to the theory and methodological approach of social action – necessarily goes beyond an "actors" approach. This can not be done by concentrating on transnational organisations (Pries 2001). In our view, agency and the negotiation of meaning leading to structuration must be the basis for studying social spaces. Social space would be conceived of as the operationalisation of the life-world concept, which includes the dimension of "borders" or "boundaries". Instead of conceptualising fixed units of analysis, we suggest analysing dynamic interfaces of systems of knowledge in social spaces by showing how they are constituted. If globalisation and localisation are produced in a constructivist sense by migrants, or like in our project case study by women activists and researchers, everyday life and organisational life and linkages between these have to be brought together. We consider the micro-macro relation as best captured through the structuration and institutionalisation approach. Regarding the defining levels, we can indeed distinguish different complexities of societal organisation. However the linkages and interactions appear to be increasingly important. Very interesting indeed are the crossing of levels and the multiple entanglements.

Translocal Agency and Institutionalisation

Given the global and translocal phenomena of connectedness, methodological challenges are indeed to replace classical comparison because independent units of analysis cannot be distinguished any more. We analyse how social spaces are constituted through agency (e.g. Peleikis 2003 on Lebanon – Ivory Coast migrants) and we can formulate certain dimensions and perspectives in order to look at processes and dynamics in other cases. Such relational studies need to include systematic contextualisation thereby overcoming methodological nationalism by considering e.g. the interaction with the state when negotiating concepts in different spheres as only one of several dimensions.

Often organisations are considered as the relevant actors, whereas social movements are neglected. Social movements are typical actors in social spaces with blurred boundaries between formal and informal contexts. Relevant social spaces can be constituted by organisations, which, however, are not social spaces per se. Instead, we look at crosscutting spaces and multiple social worlds, not as concentric circles but as overlapping spheres, also regarding everyday life in and with the economy which is socially organised and transnationally embedded. Perspectives on both need to be combined in analysis. The methodological imperative of structuration has to be taken seriously. Pertinent here are some Bielefeld studies such as "The Traders' dilemma" (Evers/Schrader 1994), or "Doing IT in the Philippines" (Saloma-Akpedonu 2006), where the everyday life and organisational boundaries are blurred and where translocal interaction amongst actors within organisations or individually takes place. One example is the exchanging of IT knowledge and contracts with Philippine migrants to the United States. We assume that this blurring of the relations with organisations is one of the phenomena of globalisation which has to be understood. The way the global economy is structured for example by Bolivian migrants living and working in private sweat shops in Argentina ("cama dentro" lit. bed inside the sweatshop, Spiegel 2005), includes all forms of outsourcing, privatising and precarious working relations. Another relevant case would be cleaning staff and housemaids in global cities. Analysis can be based on concepts of modes of transformation, processes of institutionalisation and of organisation building.

With regard to the question of the institutionalisation of agency in social spaces, thereby contributing to the analysis of the migration/development nexus, we suggest studying interfaces between formal and informal institutions (such as social security or finance), crosscutting boundaries of formal institutions and formally employed persons including migrants overcoming distances. There are innovative forms of linking, conceiving and combating poverty by taking into account social networks, livelihoods, and cooperation between genders. These also take into account the exchange of resources and labour, boundary crossing between different logics of economic agency such as the reproductive and productive field, for example between women in informal business interacting with men in institutions and the other way round. It is important to analyse how boundaries are drawn and the interfaces between local governance and civil society organisations are take place. These can be analysed by looking at the social spaces for negotiating public issues or developing formal institutions. Examples are social forestry or informal institutions such as rehabilitation of irrigation schemes or male/female groups and organisations.

A phenomenological methodology clearly helps to overcome the 'society equals nation state' syndrome. We can render relational and interactive approaches more visible by using systematic dense methodology which includes the study of trajectories. Contextualisation can also be done systematically according to structures of relevance in the field. I am afraid the trap of territorial reference remains if cross-cutting worlds and boundaries are not examined; we have to study how these are permanently (re)produced and negotiated. This can be done by using concepts such as arena, platforms and public sphere(s) where power relations are generated and challenged and the meanings of policy issues are negotiated as well as the images of (gendered) migrants are constructed.

In our project we use the concept of 'translocal' social spaces in a broader sense, looking at processes of 'othering' and negotiating multiple feminisms, Islams, Islamic feminism, African feminism etc. (Lachenmann 2005). I consider "African" not as an ethnic but rather a political concept. In these debates 'migrants' from the respective countries play a decisive role. We talk about a 'cosmopolitan epistemic community' which brings together gender researchers, activists and experts on different levels of international organisations and links between their social movement/organisational base and regional regimes which influence and conceive global policy and rights concepts and debates, e.g. regarding UN women conferences.

M. Salzbrunn (see contribution in this volume) discusses different approaches to theorising locality in migration studies, "local-global embedding processes" and "globalisation from below" (a term used quite early in gender research). Following these approaches she very convincingly suggests studying certain "political and cultural events in a context of migration" in order to "recognise the rooting of transnational networks". Her epistemological focus considers them to be "platforms for the negotiation of inclusion/exclusion and transformation processes" (i.e. boundary drawing regarding power of definition). She avoids conceptualising "ethnic" essentialised communities by using the 'neutral' definition of "minorities", and looks at processes of communitarisation. In this process she sees the formation of "new identity" based on "experience of circulation".

I think these are very interesting directions in a 'localisation' approach, which can be connected to concepts of 'politics of the place' (Harcourt 2000; Gupta/Ferguson 1997) and 'translocality', in the sense of the constitution of social spaces where new hybrid social worlds, identities, interactions, modes of transformation and gender order are negotiated, showing how they are constructed in translocal social spaces.

The dimension of comparison applied in the sense mentioned above, when looking at agency in public spheres, is seen in the relationship and the location e.g. of Muslim minorities in a secular state, thereby applying a situational approach, elaborating on arrangements, modes of interaction etc., and doing systematic contextualisation. The instrument applied is event analysis. These new forms of comparison are concerned with dimensions such as "religious references in the public sphere" (Salzbrunn in this volume). This I consider to be a meso level of social organisation, as well as a middle range theorising approach, including the phenomena of sociality (*Vergesellschaftung*). Methodologically this implies institutionalisation processes and social change. The production of hybridity, a concept which is supposed to overcome old dichotomies between developed and underdeveloped countries (Nederveen Pieterse/Parekh eds. 1995), is shown in translocal spaces through interactions as well as economic, cultural and social structures and institutions.

In order to further study globalisation processes, and even if we regard them to be constitutive of a "world society", it is certainly fruitful to use hermeneutics to open up stocks of knowledge on non Western societies. The sociology of knowledge laid the necessary methodological foundations rather early through the works of Peter Berger and Thomas Luckmann (1966). These works are still very relevant for studying the social construction of reality through the situated negotiation of meaning. Following this approach ensures that cultural relativism is avoided .

We attempt to do systematic contextualisation, in transcultural global social research, elaborating on translocal social spaces, referring to these foundations in sociology of knowledge and trying to come up with different possible interpretations of meaning (such as implied in Geertz 1983; Knoblauch ed. 1996 etc.). When our methodology is based on "grounded theory", we come up with key categories and working (hypo)thesis, which demonstrate the explanatory power of various concepts. The idea of 'different meanings' has always been implied in constructivism along with logics of actions, interfaces of systems of knowledge and the multiplicity of social worlds .

The idea of "multi-sited ethnography" (Marcus 1998) has influenced social anthropology. In this approach I would claim that the "sociological" view should be highlighted more explicitly. We have used it in several forms, combining "thick and complex methods" such as trajectories, multi-level analysis (Berg-Schlosser 2000; Lang 2005), mobile research (Schlee 1985), and structured designs including triangulation. We have also developed new forms of comparison, where it is not the same researcher who has to do all the different studies, but rather works with collectively elaborated dimensions, and typologies as developed in interpretative sociology.

This debate has been highly enriched through the work of Michael Burawoy and his research group in California, and also by debates in social anthropology, which refer to global power structures and ask how new forms of power structuration can be taken into account in what they call "Global ethnography. Forces, connections, and imaginations in a postmodern world" (Burawoy et al. 2000). They want to overcome the restrictedness of the ethnographic site represented by the Chicago school in this new approach. "Within any field, whether it had global reach or was bounded by community or nation, our fieldwork had to assemble a picture of the whole by recognising diverse perspectives from the parts, from singular but connected sites", striving at a "historically grounded, theoretically driven, macro ethnography" (Burawoy 2000: 4). Inda and Rosaldo (2002) use the term "anthropology of globalisation", Long (2000: 184pp) talks about "exploring local/global transformations". This approach can be combined with systematising structuration, translocality and contextualisation, in the sense of empirically grounding globalisation theory.

Studying Translocality and Comparison Through Case Studies

In our research project we studied, through field studies as well as common workshops, how global development concepts are localised and negotiated in translocal social spaces in three different Muslim societies – Senegal, Sudan, and Malaysia. We study how women academics, activists and movements interact with civil society and the state, thereby restructuring the public sphere. We restricted the scope of our studies by looking very specifically at female activities and the gendered structure of development processes including concepts of vulnerability and rights. Nevertheless, we have been able to arrive at more generalised conclusions beyond merely comparing the three cases. Our research process is guided thus by the question of how comparative research can contribute in a fruitful way to theory building and at the same time to understanding our 'special cases'.

The diversity of concepts and constructs of gender, development and religious identity, that we came across in our research project, is not only pre-determined because of the highly contrasting case studies we did in countries and societies which have completely different constellations in regard to Islam. In these three countries, Islam varies in its importance for state and society, type of development and socio-economic issues, as well as the influence of religion on societal and international conflicts. The theoretical sampling of these countries was complemented by the results which emerged when theory was grounded in empirical findings. In Senegal – a secular state – Islam is hardly relevant at all for development efforts. However, it is omnipresent, in a localised Brotherhood structure, and in some newly Islamising forces which are starting to compete on a national level with state legitimacy (e.g. with regard to family code debates). In our empirical results the Senegal case shows how local development works and how women network, linking it to women rights in a very basic way – even in some discourses such as those against equality (when women want to uphold family obligations of men).

Sudan – as an Islamist state – stands for Islam as the permanent force as against which to negotiate room for manoeuvre by women and defining the meaning of global as against popular Islam. At the same time, development issues resulting from poverty are omnipresent in all women's groups. Their social spaces seem to have grown enormously in the context of the present day conflict and of the peace debates being supported by the international and donor community. These spaces constitute a very interesting arena of societal transformation. In our comparative design, Sudan therefore indicates that the interface between the state and the civil society is being strengthened and the public sphere restructured.

The case of Malaysia, on the other hand, has shown that the force of women's and feminist organisations and networks is struggling in a complex national context based on political ethnicity and national Islam. Its power of negotiation and conquered space seems not to refer to the development model per se: There are astonishingly conventional welfare or service oriented women's organisations reflecting the typical developmentalist constructs of 'vulnerable women'. At the same time, rather conventional left-wing 'progressive' organisations seem to have little power to change the miserable working and rights situations of mainly labourers belonging to ethnic minorities (plantation workers etc.). However, there are very important feminist organisations and networks which have entered an inner Islamic debate on situated interpretations of Islam relating to women's rights and which seriously challenge hegemonic religious authorities, Islamic practices and the state. This question, which we have conceptualised as "authority of knowledge", is an interesting feature of all three societies. However, in Malaysia it seems to be on a high scholarly level and is especially crucial at this point in time before the possible institutionalisation of *Sharia* law. At the same time women groups seem to get their main legitimacy from their important transnational presence and reputation in networking. Here, of course, the feminist Islamic exchange is one important field, but at least as important is the participation in regional and global debates about globally defined rights (see CEDAW) from which they draw their power for national activism.

It became clear that the relevant issues being discussed are very different in the three countries. For example, discussions of sexualised violence or illegitimate children, an issue raised in Malaysia, are still taboo in Sudan. There is no single uniform globalising force called Islamisation. We can, on the contrary, see more and more diversified processes of Islamisation going on in very different settings.

However, on the national/societal level we have worked out ideal types of power in civil society which could be applied to and compared with other societies. In Malaysia we see strongly gendered public spaces and networking in order to negotiate national forms of Islamisation by means of human rights discourses. This action is – nearly exclusively – legitimised to a very high degree by external networking, thereby influencing and contributing strongly to inter-Islamic gender discourses. In Sudan a strong Islamist State is fighting the diversity of Islam often including local, and popular Islam of women, and with strong pressure to open up to Western and global development donors. This is leading to development discourses on poverty, but is combined with peace keeping and conflict resolution processes and activities. In Senegal there is increasing neglect of the Muslim societal context in favour of very liberal, Western oriented development concepts. Also, the degree of influence on negotiating development concepts in the public sphere seems to be less with regard to gender issues. There are Islamisation processes going on within the global discourse with very clear implications for gender and development, and these are considered to be politically critical.

New Interactive Methodological Perspectives

Othering processes vs. glocalisation

We have been able to observe developments taking place within the international women's organisations and positioning in the international arena. We could witness that othering processes are not uniform and sometimes absent. In Malaysia activists claim not to be anti-Western but rather – as in global feminist discourse – anti neo-liberalism and denounce the impact of globalisation. Here, the present discourse goes in the direction of very generalised criticism, which often very simply claims that human and women rights discourses should be linked to or replace macro-economic debates.

Although there is a consensus on the diversity of feminisms in a global arena, this might indeed cause certain new boundaries to be drawn and othering processes and exclusions to be produced. Moreover, since the Malaysian women's movement claims global solidarity with women and sisterhood, this might be constituted in global female spaces where globalisation and relevant concepts seem indeed to be negotiated. In Senegal the othering works through different constructions of gender and, thereby, conceptions of (universal human) equality, which sometimes does not address the global feminist discourses on difference. This debate takes place between feeling labelled by the term 'Muslim' women and claiming universal exchange on the one hand, and working for the consideration of specific, nationally relevant, contexts of culture and tradition on the other. Development can mean neo-traditional reconstruction of community. When theorising about new global forms of diversity and difference, we can refer to these translocal relations, where it is clear that neither economy nor women's movements nor NGOs are bound to one place.

We have found references to different Islams, and claims of everyday Islam against global homogenisation and fundamentalisms, as well as different feminisms reflecting regional and political diversity. These phenomena can be interpreted as different modernities in relation to public space, secularism, economic institutions, cultural re-vitalisation, social movements and civil society.

Translocal Public Spheres

The constitution of public spheres where universal concepts are being negotiated, has been a very interesting aspect of comparison in our project. Forms of activism were discovered (such as those taking place at Women's days) to be very global culture oriented (consumerism, popular music etc. in shopping malls in Malaysia), as well as very conventional and state dominated (Senegal) or even ambivalent such like Sudan where womens' groups are part of the peace making process but enter very little into the constitutional debates. In Malaysia the importance of the women's movement in entering and restructuring the public sphere is shown in the remarkable "shadow report" elaborated for the (World Conference on Women in) Beijing plus 10 process. In Senegal the official national Strategy for Gender Equality and Equity (SNEEG) adopted in 2005 lacks professional quality regarding agency in society and a vision of any sort of gender movement. This is the case although it is supported and even contributed to by a large women's organisation. In Sudan, one can say that women groups have for quite some time been, in a less conspicuous way than Human Rights activists, upholding a public discourse by occupying spaces concerning women's issues, poverty, and now peace and democracy.

Sociology, including that of "world society", mostly neglects these new interactions and spheres. These relations are not addressed when studying the 'impacts' of globalisation or new global regimes of development and social policies. Mostly, relevant interactions become invisible as seen from a modernist view on the one hand and a paternalistic antipoverty and diffusionist perspective on the other. Transnational relations in migration, new forms of shadow economy in formerly socialist regimes, social embeddedness, interface between all so called informal forms of economy and politics have only recently been discovered (see e.g. Yurkowa 2004). The relational approach goes far beyond studying reactions to impacts, survival strategies etc. which are discovered in an exotised sense. These are structurations and institutionalisations which take place in very crosscutting ways.[4]

Transfer vs. Interconnectedness

Modernity implies pluralism and globalisation implies diversity yet in an interrelated system of interactions, constitution of spaces and negotiation of meanings as understood by the term of battlefields of knowledge (Long/Long 1992). There is clearly no doubt any more about the transfer of knowledge, patterns of modernity and so forth. Thus theorisation about globalisation has to be based especially on these glocalisation and localisation processes. At the same time, this does not mean that we should and can study 'the impact' of globalisation processes in general or of certain global governance policies, economic policies etc. in particular. This has been the case especially within the feminist global arena, i.a. generated within different UN-environments, and of global movements often criticising in a too general way and constructing 'neo-liberalism' as a global antiforce. Neither should we look at 'reactions' of societies or groups even if we envision active coping or survival strategies. This also means that we cannot just look at the transfer, diffusion or movement of concepts and institutional arrangements in different policy domains (such as gender policies, local governance, and social services) without analysing the contexts and problem solutions in the respective situations. This forces us to introduce completely different perspectives, crosscutting unquestioned analytical concepts such as formal and informal, market and subsistence, public and private.

Often it is not a question of diffusion or transfer of models and solutions. When exploring interconnectedness and localisation, the perspective changes and one no longer oversees phenomena of glocalisation within a given societal context. This is neither impact nor resistance, but it is also not some completely new alternative or independent idea.

---

4   The Internet, or information technology per se, could be considered to be a new form of translocal public space (Spiegel, Harig rapp. 2002). It is a matter of a (gendered) structure of knowledge, which means combining agency and knowledge, and added to the new debates on knowledge management in development agencies (Worldbank 1999, 2000). Feminist economists (Lachenmann 1998a; Marchand/Parpart eds. 1995,) are what could be called a strategic global group of women activists and researchers – an epistemic community which has partly become virtual, with many members who are cosmopolitan migrants (Hannerz 2000). They argue very strongly that the socio-economic consequences of globalisation are especially harmful because of gender inequality, conceiving economy as a gendered structure (Cagatay/Elson/Grown 1995). If we look at economy as being socially and globally embedded (Lachenmann/Dannecker eds. 2001), we should abandon 'impact analysis' in favour of interaction and structuration.

The problem is less the transfer than the understanding of these globalisation processes, implying active diversity. Of course these processes often mean powerlessness in the sense of reduction of room to manoeuvre. This is exemplified with regard to all development issues such as economy, poverty, decentralisation, resource protection and gender, even knowledge. With globalisation, (mostly informal) economic patterns are travelling which implies the creation or destruction of (precarious) jobs as well as investments.

Observing Globalisation: Empirically Grounding Globalisation/Doing "Global Ethnography"

An important aspect which has changed the practice of adhering strictly to one country/society/community or ethnic group, is certainly the fact that more and more concepts of intercultural and especially translocal, transnational and also transcultural relevance are being developed in social science. This is probably an empirical feature of glocalisation. In our research project this has already proven to be very useful in terms of organising the empirical research around networking and discourses on development concepts in the different communities etc.

Stauth's (1995) concept of *"kulturübergreifende Sozialforschung"* – we call it trans-cultural social research – is absolutely pertinent. He criticises a concept he calls "comparative sociology of civilisations" for "assuming a homogenous, universalistic classificatory system of communication absent in multicultural societies" (ibid: 1995: 102). Within this framework our approach consists of looking at different dimensions relevant to our subject of engendering development and how they are situated within an Islamic cultural orientation.

Thereby, it is certainly useful to work out typologies. In our project we generate concepts of gender/social equality, types of gender constructs with regard to occupying public spaces and engaging in economic activities, concepts of poverty and wealth and societal obligations, types of NGOs and their closeness to the state and types of intensity of inward/outward looking social legitimacy of gender policies. Also female types of representing Islam, including local or popular forms, can be found, and of discourses regarding gender and development (see above), as well as intensity and type of transnational networking.

The comparative approach we follow does not aim at developing fixed indicators or categories for comparing the various cases focused on. Rather the comparative perspective is based on "comparing by contextualising" (Nageeb 2005) and explaining the ways in which the issues under study, be it the constitution of spaces, or the negotiation of development concepts, are embedded in specific local and trans-local contexts. Indeed the nature of the state, Islamisation processes, development institutions and policies, political and social structures have presented themselves in very decisive ways and influence our subject matter. It is clear, however, that the actors and arenas involved in the field of negotiating development, as well as the subjects of negotiation, are different in the three regions being studied. The comparative perspective is thus meant to reflect on the different nature of the actors involved and their modes of interaction in each context. The variation lies in the development concepts which are signified as subjects for negotiation in each case, and the kind of spaces and identities which are being constituted while negotiating development in the different countries being studied.

In our approach, the comparison takes place on a meso level using middle range theories and tries to explain the differences through contextualisation. This means that our methodology is interactive and cross-cultural diversity oriented. Our comparative approach therefore operates in the sense of explaining integration through difference, overcoming a dualistic approach, as well as through glocalisation and localisation, and perhaps hybridisation. The conventional comparative approach is outdated (Kaelble/Schriewer 2003; Kaschuba 2003) because of the ongoing processes of interaction, deterritorialisation etc.. Theoretical sampling within the countries and across our three countries is based on ideas of similarity or of difference. If we take grounded theory serious we can extend the outcome of empirical research to other contexts – which is not a comparison in the classical sense. Grounded theory generates theses which can be fed into further research. We very clearly realise that the relevance of our research subject for the context, i.e. adequacy regarding the object of research, has to be challenged in each and every case with regard to the relevance structure of the respective community or society when studying women's rights conventions and politics with their completely different histories and backgrounds of the women's movement and political struggle.

Complex or thick methods of empirical research are being used to structure the analysis of data (Geertz 1983; Elwert 2003). Design and theoretical sampling, always implying comparison, have been thoroughly developed for each country and mutually discussed. Methods which have been employed quite successfully were contrasting case studies, typologies (even trans-cultural), interfaces between different actors and knowledge systems, biographies and trajectories of activists in networking, event analysis especially of workshops and transnational conferences (who organises, invites, participates, excludes; major topics, discussions, conflicts, consequences), organisational analysis (leaders, discourses, networking.).

Marcus (1998: 10pp.), in his chapter on "ethnography of the world system" (ibid: 79pp.) stresses contextualisation; mobile ethnography according to him constructs "aspects of the system itself through the associations and connections it suggests among sites". He takes an interesting position regarding "the loss of the subaltern", thereby "also decentring the resistance and accommodation framework ... for the sake of a reconfigured space of multiple sites of cultural production". He claims that "comparison reenters the very act of ethnographic specification by a research design of juxtapositions in which the global is collapsed into and made an integral part of parallel, related local situations rather than something monolithic or external to them" (ibid: 80, 85p.).

Burawoy et al. (2000) pursue the explicit aim of linking critical ideas of globalisation theories (considered to be of "too high abstraction") and political economy with what they had called "ethnography unbound", asking whether their "extended case method...[was] flexible enough to link everyday life to transnational flows of population, discourse, commodities and power" (ibid: x, ix).

"We wondered whether exploring the global dimensions of the local changes the very experience of doing ethnography. The narrow boundaries of the traditional ethnographic 'site' as conceived by the Chicago school were, for us, permeated by broader power flows in the form of local racial and gender orders, free-flowing public discourses, economic structures...one of the questions facing us was whether globalisation had rendered ethnography, apparently fixed in the local, impossible or even irrelevant. Our experience...has suggested quite the reverse: ...ethnography's concern with concrete, lived experience can sharpen the abstractions of globalisation theories into more precise and meaningful conceptual tools" (ibid: xii).

Regarding contextualisation, Burawoy acknowledges that many ethnographers are "systematically incorporating historical and geographical context" (27). Pulling together "questions of power and reflexivity" is an important dimension to him, so are "extensions of observations over time and space", in order to understand "the succession of situations as a social process", demanding strongly more thorough historical work and asking for a "'structured' macro-micro link ... in which the part is shaped by its relation to the whole" (17).

And fortunately he does see that "constituting the extralocal as forces gives them a false sense of durability" (27), problematising "the concept of forces" by seeing themselves as "product of contingent social processes"; "they are examined as the product of flows of people, things, and ideas", and as "global forces and...connections [being] constituted imaginatively, inspiring social movements to seize control over their immediate but also their more distant worlds, challenging the mythology of an inexorable, runaway world". He sees the "locality fight back, adapt, or simply be destroyed" (ibid: 27, 17, 29).

We try to operationalise these ideas by an interface approach revealing power constellations and adding complex methods crosscutting communities, places, levels, time, space and social worlds, such as the analysis of trajectories. In our research field this applies to, over and beyond biographic research, persons whose personal history and career in different knowledge spaces, institutions and organisations we follow based on the narrative approach. Here we would complement it with an approach dealing with agency, knowledge, authority, and meaning. Also, combined with studies at the interface we very fruitfully practice multi-level analysis (see Lang 2005; Berg-Schlosser 2000) which can be applied in very different ranges studying concrete interactions and following movements and discourses.

Burawoy (2000: 28) promotes "the study of global connections" whereby "multi-sitedness becomes the object of theorisation". "Space and time, rather than being disembedded, are intensified by the global workplace". Therefore he wants to "demystify...globalisation as something given", to study "how different images of globalisation are produced and disseminated" as a resource of what is possible forming a "thickening global public sphere" (ibid: 30-32).

Research Questions, Process and Interpretation

A complex comparative design and interpretation has to appear in the research process on the basis of a mix of methods and ongoing new questions. We explicitly formulate dimensions of contextualisation which are directly relevant to the problem researched, thereby constituting an instrument of validation – and not, as is often done – just of background information.

After studying the relevant literature and the discussion of the empirical data collected, brainstorming on possible differences and similarities between the case studies took place and constantly became more analytical concerning different issues: Gender discourse is influenced in Malaysia by a high level of industrial participation of women, in Senegal by poverty and in Sudan (especially recently) by conflict and peace constituencies. Regarding local moral discourse on gender and religion, in Malaysia a clear instrumentalisation of the 'good Muslim woman' is taking place. In Senegal a conventional women in development approach is dominant, feminism is regarded as Western or non-African, or as non-religious. In Sudan complete othering is taking place, although more and more local NGOs have been created and are cooperating with external donors. In Malaysia ethnic and religious differences play an important economic, national and social role. In Senegal, these are of minor relevance although certain Islams are clearly linked to ethnic differences. In Sudan ethnic/identity discourses are highly political and conflictive as the current political situation shows.

Based on our empirical studies, concrete comparative questions have emerged to be asked for analysis. These questions include: How is Islam, religion, rules, religiosity addressed by the organisations researched? Is it addressed in texts, discourses, as well as in interviews/narratives/conversations, directly or indirectly, without or with explicit questioning by researcher? What are the ascriptions made by different types of religious women regarding the West and their religiosity and its connection to gender and development, economy, education and public sphere participation? When and how are certain issues taken up by the state, such as human rights, following (women's) civil society activities, especially their external visibility?

The instrument of conducting workshops turned out to be especially fruitful at first at a very small scale in the three countries studied, organised with the local community of researchers and activists, and then at the level of exchange between researchers and activists from each country as well as researchers working on relevant areas in Europe/the North (Nageeb/Sieveking/Spiegel 2005a, b). The debates on our work presented as well the (written) inputs of the participants took place on a very intensive, highly theoretical and methodological level. Thereby we produced or re-produced the object of our research, interpreting data and debating about conclusions, and showing how translocal spaces for negotiating knowledge are constituted.

The theoretical and political importance of networking, and of constituting and restructuring the public sphere, is evident. We think in both a methodological as well as empirical sense, and our approach is to look at interfaces between different female social spaces and cross-cutting national boundaries. But we also look at diversity and battles within national and transnational spheres. These interfaces of female spaces and public spheres permit to formulate conclusions concerning national societies and processes and the institutionalisation of globalisation.

Gendered social spaces can be seen as constituting a non-homogeneous public sphere, one that does not converge in one common public interest. We are using the concept of social space in the sense that it is a relatively non institutionalised and non delineating concept, going beyond community, place or territorial or physical space. The concept of social space is clearly linked to agency, to the production of gender specific and culturally defined meanings, and to the social construction of reality and the life-world (Spiegel 2005).

We wanted, in a common effort, to deepen our theoretical and methodological interest with regard to the dimensions of networking and of structuring the public sphere which had been introduced as main concepts in our research project and were empirically grounded. How far does the networking indeed take place so to be able to say that this is where glocalisation takes place? Do female spaces indeed intersect with a societal public sphere, or do we need to qualify this concept more for Muslim societies in the sense of gendered social structure. Does the state discourse still dominate, or would indeed the female social spaces and the interfaces they institutionalise be the relevant actors in civil society – as in Malaysia and Sudan. Are they as marginalised and reduced to a female vulnerability and rights discourse, restricted to gender specific difference or to women in development discourses as it seems to be the case in Senegal? I.e. does no engendering of development take place?

The result of our studies, however, seems ambivalent. The gender networks and public debates are indeed to be very diverse and relevant for constructing the global arena. At the same time we might question in how far the link to the national civil society and global public sphere does indeed take place as regards relevant issues of hegemonic concern, or whether it is a field tolerated and instrumentalised by global governance.

References

Albrow, Martin/King, Elizabeth (eds.) (1990) *Globalization, Knowledge and Society: Readings from International Sociology*, London etc.: Sage.
Appadurai, Arjun (1998) *Modernity at Large: Cultural Dimensions of Globalization*, Minneapolis etc.: Univ. of M. Pr.
Appadurai, Arjun (2000) "Grassroots Globalization and the Res Imagination." Public Culture: Soc. for Transnational Cultural Studies 12/1, Durham: Duke Univ. Press, pp. 1-19.
Berg-Schlosser, Dirk (2000) "Mehrebenen-Analysen." In: Dirk Berg-Schlosser/Norbert Kersting (eds.) *Armut und Demokratie: Politische Partizipation und Interessenorganisationen der städtischen Armen in Afrika und Lateinamerika.*, Frankfurt a.M./New York: Campus, pp. 251-270.
Berger, Peter L./Luckmann, Thomas (1966) *The Social Construction of Reality: a Treatise in the Sociology of Knowledge*, Garden City N.Y.: Doubleday.
Burawoy, Michael (2000) "Introduction: Reaching for the Global."; "Grounding Globalization." In: Michael Burawoy et al. (eds.) *Global Ethnography: Forces, Connections, and Imaginations in a Postmodern World*, Berkeley etc.: University of California Press, pp. 1-40; 337-350.
Cagatay, Nilüfer/Elson, Diane/Grown, Caren (1995) "Introduction." In: Nilüfer Cagatay/Diane Elson/Caren Grown (eds.) *Gender, Adjustment and Macroeconomics*, World Development, Special Issue 23/11, pp. 1827-1836.
Chaudhuri, Maitrayee (2005) "Betwixt the State and Everyday Life: Identity Formation among Bengali Migrants in a Delhi Slum." In: Meenakshi Thapan (ed.) *Transnational Migration and the Politics of Identity*, New Delhi etc.: Sage, pp. 284-311.
Dannecker, Petra (2005) "Transnational Migration and the Transformation of Gender Relations: The Case of Bangladeshi Labour Migrants." In: Current Sociology 53/4, pp. 655-674.
Dannecker, Petra (2007) *The Re-Ordering of Political, Cultural and Social Spaces through Transnational Labour Migration*, Working Paper 27, Bielefeld: COMCAD – Center on Migration, Citizenship and Development, www.comcad-bielefeld.de.
Denzin, Norman K./Lincoln, Yvonna S. (eds.) (1994) *Handbook of Qualitative Research*, London: Sage.
Elwert, Georg (2003) *Feldforschung. Orientierungswissen und kreuzperspektivische Analyse,* Sozialanthropolog. Arbeitspapier, H. 96, FU Berlin Inst. F. Ethnologie, Berlin: Hans Schiler.

Evers, H.D./Schrader, Heiko (eds.) (1994) *The Moral Economy of Trade. Ethnicity and Developing Markets*, London: Routledge.

Faist, Thomas (1998) "Transnational Social Spaces out of International Migration: Evolution, Significance and Future Prospects." Archives Européennes de Sociologie 39/2, pp. 213-247.

Faist, Thomas, (2007) *Transnationalisation and Development(s): Towards a North-South Perspective*, Working Paper 16, Bielefeld: COMCAD – Center on Migration, Citizenship and Development, www.comcad-bielefeld.de.

Fischer-Rosenthal, Wolfram/Rosenthal, Gabriele (1997) "Narrationsanalyse biographischer Selbstpräsentationen." In: Ronald Hitzler/Anne Honer (eds.) *Sozialwissenschaftliche Hermeneutik*, Opladen: Westd. Verlag, pp. 133-164.

Flick, Uwe/von Kardoff, Ernst/Steinke, Ines (eds.) (2004) *A Companion to Qualitative Research*, London etc.: Sage.

Freitag, Ulrike/Oppen, Achim von (2005) *Translokalität als ein Zugang zur Geschichte globaler Verflechtungen*, Forum (http://hsozkult.geschichte.hu-berlin.de/forum/type=artikel&id=632).

Geertz, Clifford (1983) *Local Knowledge*, USA: Basic Books.

Glick Schiller, Nina (2007) *Beyond the Nation-State and Its Units of Analysis: Towards a New Research Agenda for Migration Studies: Essentials of Migration Theory*, COMCAD Working Paper 33, Paper presented at the conference on 'Transnationalisation and Development(s): Towards a North-South Perspective', Center for Interdisciplinary Research, Bielefeld, Germany, May 31 – June 01, 2007.

Glick Schiller, Nina/Basch, Linda/Szanton Blanc, Cristina (1992) *Towards a Transnational Perspective on Migration: Race, Class, Ethnicity and Nationalism Reconsidered*, New York: New York Academy of Sciences.

Gupta, Akhil/Ferguson, James (1997) "Culture, Power, Place: Ethnography at the End of an Era." In: Akhil Gupta/James Ferguson (eds.) *Culture, Power, Place: Explorations in Cultural Anthropology*, Durham, London: Duke Univ. Pr., pp. 1-29.

Hannerz, Ulf (2000) "Transnational Research." In: H. Russel Bernard (ed.) *Handbook of methods in cultural anthropology*, Walnut Creek etc.: Altamire Pr., pp. 235-256.

Harcourt, Wendy (ed.) (1999) *Women @ Internet: Creating new Cultures in Cyberspace*, London: Zed Books.

Harcourt, Wendy (2000) "Rethinking Difference and Equality: Women and the Politics of Place." In: Roxann Prazniak/Arif Dirlik (eds.) *Places, Identities and Politics in an Age of Globalization*, New York: Rowan and Littlefield.

Inda, Jonathan Xavier/Rosaldo Renato (eds.) (2002) *Anthropology of Globalization*, Maiden MA, Oxford: Blackwell.

Kaelble, Hartmut/Schriewer, Jürgen (eds.) (2003) *Vergleich und Transfer: Komparatistik in den Sozial-, Geschichts- und Kulturwissenschaften*, Frankfurt a.M.: Campus.

Kaschuba, Wolfgang (2003) "Anmerkungen zum Gesellschaftsvergleich aus ethnologischer Perspektive." In: H. Kaelble/J. Schriewer (eds.) *Vergleich und Transfer: Komparatistik in Sozial-, Geschichts- und Kulturwissenschaften*, Frankfurt a.M.: Campus, pp. 341-350.

Knoblauch, Hubert (ed.) (1996) *Kommunikative Lebenswelten. Zur Ethnographie einer geschwätzigen Gesellschaft*, Konstanz: Universitätsverlag.

Lachenmann, Gudrun (1993) "Civil Society and Social Movements in Africa: The Case of the Peasant Movement in Senegal." The European Journal of Development Research 5/2, pp. 68-100.

Lachenmann, Gudrun (1997) "Intervention, Interaktion und Partizipation – zu einigen Methodenfragen der empirischen Entwicklungsforschung." In: Manfred Schulz (ed.) *Entwicklung: Theorie – Empirie – Strategie – Institution*, Münster: Lit, pp. 99-114.

Lachenmann, Gudrun (1998a) "Strukturanpassung aus Frauensicht: Entwicklungskonzepte und Transformationsprozesse." In: Ruth Klingebiel/Shalini Randeria (eds.) *Globalisierung aus Frauensicht: Bilanzen und Visionen*, Bonn: Dietz, pp. 294-329.

Lachenmann, Gudrun (1998b) "Frauenbewegungen als gesellschaftliche Kraft des Wandels: Beispiele aus Afrika." In: Uta Ruppert (ed.) *Lokal bewegen – global verhandeln: Internationale Politik und Geschlecht*, Frankfurt a. M.: Campus, pp. 208-232.

Lachenmann, Gudrun (2004a) "Weibliche Räume in muslimischen Gesellschaften Westafrikas." Peripherie 95/24, pp. 322-340.

Lachenmann, Gudrun (2004b) *Gendered Spaces: Translocality and Migration – Methodological Issues*, paper given at Expert Workshop 2004 on Engendered Migration in Transnational Spaces, Ahfad-Humboldt-Link Programme, organised by Parto Teherani-Krönner, Berlin.

Lachenmann, Gudrun (2005) *Introduction: Methodology and Comparison – Embedding the Research Project*, Paper presented at the Workshop "Negotiating Development: Trans-Local Gendered Spaces in Muslim Societies" 13th – 15th of October 2005 in Bielefeld, (www.uni-bielefeld.de/tdrc/projects).

Lachenmann, Gudrun (2007) *Transnationalisation and Development – Methodological Issues*, Working Paper 19, Bielefeld: COMCAD – Center on Migration, Citizenship and Development, (www.comcad-bielefeld.de).

Lachenmann, Gudrun/Dannecker, Petra (eds.) (2001) *Die geschlechtsspezifische Einbettung der Ökonomie. Empirische Untersuchungen über Entwicklungs- und Transformations-prozesse*, Münster etc.: Lit.

Lang, Andrea Marianne (2005) *Das Ineinanderwirken von Aushandlungen in und zwischen sozialen Räumen: Forschung auf der Meso-Ebene. Eine Methodikreflektion*, Working Paper 349, Univ. Bielefeld: Forschungsschwerpunkt Entwicklungssoziologie/Sozialanthropologie, (http://www.uni-bielefeld.de/tdrc/homesdrc).

Long, Norman (1992) "Introduction: From Paradigm Lost to Paradigm Regained?"; "The Case for an Actor-Oriented Sociology of Development."; "Conclusion." In: Ann Long/Norman Long (eds.) *Battlefields of Knowledge: The Interlocking of Theory and Practice in Social Research and Development*, London: Routledge, pp. 3-15; 268-277; 16-46.

Long, Norman (2000) "Exploring Local/Global Transformations: A View from Anthropology." In: Alberto Arce/Norman Long (eds.) *Anthropology, Development and Modernities: Exploring Discourses, Counter-Tendencies and Violence*, London/New York: Routledge, pp. 184-222.

Mahler, Sarah/Pessar, Patricia R. (2006) "Gender Matters: Ethnographers bring Gender from the Periphery toward the Core of Migration Studies." International Migration Review 40/1, pp. 27-63.

Marchand, Marianne H./Parpart, Jane L. (eds.) (1995) *Feminism, Postmodernism, Development*, London: Routledge.

Marcus, George E. (1998) "Ethnography through Thick and Thin." In: *Ethnography in/of the World System: The Emergence of Multi-Sited Ethnography*, Princeton, N.J.; Chichester WS: Princeton Univ. Pr., pp. 79-104.

Nageeb, Salma (2005) *Negotiating Development: Trans-local Gendered Spaces in Muslim Societies: A Methodology Paper*, Working Paper 354, Univ. of Bielefeld: Sociology of Development Research Centre.

Nageeb, Salma/Sieveking, Nadine/Spiegel, Anna (2005a) *Engendering Development in Muslim Societies: Actors, Discourses and Networks in Malaysia, Senegal and Sudan*, Working Paper 353, Univ. of Bielefeld: Sociology of Development Research Centre, (www.uni-bielefeld.de/tdrc/projects).

Nageeb, Salma/Sieveking, Nadine/Spiegel, Anna (2005b) *Negotiating Development: Trans-Local Gendered Spaces in Muslim Societies*, Report on Workshop 13-15 October 2005, Working Paper 355, Univ. of Bielefeld: Sociology of Development Research Centre, (www.uni-bielefeld.de/tdrc/projects).

Nederveen Pieterse, Jan/Parekh, Bikhu (eds.) (1995) *The Decolonization of Imagination: Culture, Knowledge and Power*, London: Zed Books.

Peleikis, Anja (2003) *Lebanese in Motion, Gender and the Making of Translocal Village*, Bielefeld: Transcript.

Pries, Ludger (2001) "The Approach of Transnational Social Spaces: Responding to New Configurations of the Social and the Spatial." In: Ludger Pries (ed.) *New Transnational Social Spaces: International Migration and Transnational Companies in the Early Twenty-First Century*, London: Routledge, pp. 3-29.

Robertson, Roland (1995) "Glocalization: Time-Space and Homogeneity-Heterogeneity." In: Mike Featherstone/Scott Lash/Roland Robertson (eds.) *Global Modernities*, London etc.: Sage, pp. 25-44.

Saloma-Akpedonu, Czarina (2006) *Possible Worlds in Impossible Spaces: Knowledge, Globality, Gender and Information Technology in the Philippines*, Manila: Ateneo de Manila Univ. Pr.

Schlee, Günther (1985) "Mobile Forschung bei mehreren Ethnien: Kamelnomaden Nordkenias." In: Hans Fischer (ed.) *Feldforschungen: Berichte zur Einführung in Probleme und Methoden*, Berlin: Reimer, pp. 203-218.

Schrader, Heiko/Kaiser, Markus/Korff, Rüdiger (eds.) (2001) *Markt, Kultur und Gesellschaft: Zur Aktualität von 25 Jahren Entwicklungsforschung*, Festschrift zum 65. Geburtstag von Hans-Dieter Evers, Münster/Hamburg/London: Lit.

Spiegel, Anna (2005) *Alltagswelten in translokalen Räumen, Bolivianische Migrantinnen in Buenos Aires*, Frankfurt a. M.: IKO-Verlag für interkulturelle Kommunikation.

Spiegel, Anna, Nadine Harig (rapporteurs) (2002) *Gender and translocal networking through information technology*, Working Paper 342, Univ. of Bielefeld, Sociology of Development Research Centre, www.uni-bielefeld.de/tdrc/

Stauth, Georg (1995) "Globalisierung, Modernität, nicht-westliche Zivilisationen." In: Josef Langer/Wolfgang Poellauer (eds.) *Kleine Staaten in großer Gesellschaft*, Eisenstadt: Verl. f. Soziologie u. Humanethologie, pp. 89-107.

Stauth, Georg (1998) "Introduction."; "Islam and Modernity: The Long Shadow of Max Weber." In: Georg Stauth (ed.) *Islam – Motor or Challenge of Modernity*, Yearbook of the Sociology of Islam 1, pp. 5-14; 163-186.

Strauss, Anselm (1987) *Qualitative Analysis for Social Scientists*, Cambridge: Cambr. Univ. Pr.

Strauss, Anselm/Corbin, Juliet (1998) *Basics of Qualitative Research: Techniques and Procedures for Developing Grounded Theory*, Thousand Oaks: Sage.

Thapan, Meenakshi (2005) "'Making Incomplete': Identity, Women and the State." In: Meenakshi Thapan (ed.) *Transnational Migration and the Politics of Identity*, New Delhi etc.: Sage, pp. 23-62.

Thapan, Meenakshi (ed.) (2005) *Transnational Migration and the Politics of Identity*, New Delhi etc.: Sage.

World Bank (1999) *Knowledge for development. World Development Report 1989/99*, New York: Oxford Univ. Pr.

World Bank, infoDev (2000) *The networking revolution. Opportunities and challenges for developing countries*. Global Inform. and Comm. Techn. Dept., WP, June.

Yurkova, Irina (2004) *Der Alltag der Transformation: Kleinunternehmerinnen in Usbekistan*, Bielefeld: Transcript.

World Society, Transnationalism and *Champs Migratoires*: Reflections on German, Anglo-Saxon and French Academic Debates

MONIKA SALZBRUNN

Rescaling Processes and Transnationalism across Academic Borders

This chapter aims at elaborating a genealogy of academic debates and research on migration in different academic contexts. The differences between German, Anglo-Saxon and French academic worlds are not only a reflection of language problems. The organisation of academic disciplines, the relationship between academics and politics, and finally the way scientific categories are elaborated in each context, explain remaining differences and a lack of dialogue, especially between French and German references. My aim is not to go back to national histories, but to analyse specific ways of doing academics, from an epistemological point of view developed in the *Histoire croisée* approach.[1] The latter includes a transnational analysis of cross-cutting ties and shifting intellectual borders that can be observed in contemporary academic work. German and English speaking scholars have inspired each other for a long time, thanks to academic exchange programs and cooperation. Although these academic fields have their own developments and specific terms, they are capable of reaching similar views in practice. However, the concepts that were used and translated for the purpose of cooperation are not necessarily understood in the same way by scholars. There are also French speaking researchers on migration who have cooperated with English-speaking colleagues, but these exchanges are often limited to particular dynamic research groups or institutes. Besides these exceptions, more common anti-American and anti-Liberal (in the negative French understanding of the term) intellectual barriers have caused misunderstandings or rejection on the

---

1 The *Histoire croisée* approach, developed by Michael Werner and Benedicte Zimmermann (2002), includes a systematic reflection on the semantic evolution of categories used in social sciences.

French side. On the other hand, the representatives of what the English-speaking authors call "French Theory" (Derrida, Deleuze, Foucault) are not necessarily the main references for those who write contemporary French theory in France. However, they remain the main authors translated into English. It is not easy for French-speaking and German-speaking scholars to be cited by American colleagues who do not read these languages. Other examples for limited exchange due to language problems could easily be cited, but I chose to concentrate on the German-, English- and French-speaking scientific communities because the largest part of the world's scientific production is written in these languages and because I know them much better then others.

Finally, I will look at Franco-German cooperation and mutual intellectual inspirations. I see that entangled as well as parallel and isolated tracks lead to similar conclusions in contemporary research on migration, transnationalism and urban rescaling processes.[2] The analysis of festive events in a context of migration will be used to provide examples for these intellectual dialogues. Thus, I have developed an approach that takes festive events as an entry point for the analysis of migrant dynamics in urban contexts. Focusing on these events in New York and Paris, I can observe the emergence and dynamics of group building, the development of new hybrid references (to music, food, clothing, political cultures etc.), and the impact of the particular dynamics of these places, namely the very local urban environment on these social and political practices. I use political and cultural events in these spaces as the entry points for understanding different pathways of migrant urban incorporation. Finally focusing on events in New York and Paris allows me to analyse the local embeddedness of transnational networks and thus to overcome certain critiques of transnationalism mentioned below. Glick Schiller's and Çağlar's concept of rescaling processes (2006; forthcoming) is a result of their critical reflection on transnationalism that I will present below and apply in order to analyse these festive events.

Localising Transnational Networks

Migration studies have extensively dealt with networks, transnational spaces and migration fields during the last 15 years and the term transnational social space has even become part of the common vocabulary in migration studies. Recently, researchers concerned with transnational migration have once again expressed a concern with "the local". Ludger Pries (1996; 2008) links geographic and sociological aspects by analysing the spatial spanning of the social; Nina Glick

---

2   The notion of rescaling processes is discussed below. Following Glick Schiller's and Çağlar's definition (forthcoming), the term "scale can be defined as the summary assessment of the differential positioning of cities determined by the flow and control of capital and structures of power as they are constituted within regions, states and the globe".

Schiller and Ayse Çağlar (2006; forthcoming) develop a "theory of locality in migration studies". In francophone social geography there is a similar research agenda influenced by Gildas Simon's poly-centred and multi-polarised migratory spaces (1996) and in migration sociology there is growing interest in researching local-global embedding processes, such as Alain Tarrius' "La mondialisation par le bas" (globalisation from below) (2002). In their own ways, each of these authors and the literature on transnational migration in general represents an effort to move beyond the methodological nationalism that posited the nation-state as the unit of analysis for migration studies (Smith 1983; Beck 2000; Wimmer/Glick Schiller 2002). However, contained within a shared interest in transnational process and apparently a similar perspective focus on place and space, there are different perspectives that are worth distinguishing. In addition, by positing a transnational space bounded by a shared national origin or ethnicity, many of the studies actually reinforced the notion of the naturalness of nation-based identities, reinvigorating methodological nationalism but in a new form, according to Glick Schiller, Caglar, and Guldbrandsen (2006).

I mention the history of French migration research now because the perception of immigrants by research and public policy has an impact on their self-definition and on the way they behave within public space. I will show later how the production of alterity is shaped by the existence or the ignorance of individual difference in the concept of a nation (as an assimilating Republic or a State as a salad bowl, to put it briefly). None of these authors cites world-society as a relevant reference for the immigrants or as a theoretical concept. The French-speaking migration studies rather refer to interethnic relations, to co-presence or to world-wide networks. Globalisation phenomena, if they are researched as such in France, are described as "mondialisation", but in general, French sociologists and anthropologists put into question the innovative character of this concept, arguing that world-wide exchanges of goods, knowledge or people have existed for centuries. I will give an overview of French migration research and divide the numerous schools and approaches into roughly three groups in order to make my argument clear. It would certainly be possible to go into the distinctions further but the main argument would remain the same.

The migration research carried out in France until the 1990s can roughly be divided into three tendencies: 1. Research conducted by Alain Tarrius and his PhD students at University of Toulouse, 2. Research projects hosted by university research institutes like URMIS in Paris and Nice that were deeply involved with political consulting and public demands from Ministries, 3. Research influenced by geographers and sociologists from MIGRINTER research group Poitiers or INED in Paris, which are part of international networks like IMISCOE. Furthermore, there are numerous researchers working at Universities that are not specialised in migration studies but include migration in area studies or general sociology like in Strasbourg or Lyon.[3]

1. The sociology of migration developed at the University of Tours did not refer to transnational social spaces or to residence places, but focused on circulation. One of its representatives, Alain Tarrius (2002: 18), stresses the primary role of the migration process itself. He speaks of the emergence of a "capacity to circulate." By this he means a new capacity of being here and there at the same time, and not being here or there.[4] The interesting point of Tarrius' approach is that he posits that the experience of circulation creates new cosmopolitanisms and the consciousness of a new identity. However, Tarrius' focus on circulation leads to a problematic understanding of the migrant experience of localities of settlement. He speaks of a nomadic identity, assuming that these new nomads remain economically dependent exclusively on their place of origin.[5] This assumption is shaped by a part of the French migration literature. Therefore, despite any reference to the local, the thrust of Tarrius' research and the literature it reflects has failed to examine migrants multiple ties to and participation in local institutions and social, economic, political, and cultural processes. However, Tarrius made an important point by underlining migrants' capacity for self-organisation and entrepreneurship, underestimated by other sociologists.

2. Other researchers are shaped by their engagement with French public policy debates and tend to interpret their empirical material according to the demands of the Ministry of Social Affairs or public institutions that pay them for consulting. In this case, lower social classes within the migrant population were researched and often considered as being dependent on the French State. Women are particularly concerned by a research perspective that sees them as victims and economically dependent on men. However, the average economic activity rate of migrant women is higher than that of the French women (Cahiers du CEDREF). Although the working class composes the majority of first generation immig-

---

3 Catherine Delcroix is Professor of Sociology at Marc Bloch University of Strasburg and member of the research group Cultures et Sociétés en Europe. Laurence Roulleau-Berger is member of the Laboratoire Interdisciplinaire pour la Sociologie Economique and of the Institut des Sciences de l'Homme Lyon. Both have done extensive research on migration and are board-members of the Research Committee on Sociology of Migration of the French Association of Sociology. Laurence Roulleau-Berger and Monika Salzbrunn are speakers of that committee.
4 Tarrius (2002: 18): "Une capacité inédite d'être d'ici, de là-bas, d'ici et de là-bas à la fois se substitue à la vieille opposition entre d'ici ou de là-bas".
5 Tarrius (2002: 18): "Ces étonnants territoires circulatoire confèrent de la sorte une identité nomade à des dizaines de milliers de migrants...Les nouveaux nomades, par contre, restent attachés à leur lieu d'origine et demeurent économiquement dépendants de lui seul" ("These surprising circulation territories produce in a way a nomadic identity for ten thousands of migrants. In contrast, the new nomads stay attached to their place of origin and remain economically dependent exclusively on the latter"; translated by M.S.).

rants, there are also highly skilled immigrants, to which much less attention has been directed.

3. Other representatives of French social sciences have been concerned with independent migrant self-organisation, assuming this indicated a form of empowerment and a political consciousness that was independent of the French nation-state and/or directed towards the home country.[6] These aspects are lacking in the work of the representatives of French migration sociology who are part of the second group mentioned above: Focusing on immigrants who are part of the working class and who are geographically excluded by residing in rundown suburbs, some of the sociologists influenced by Marxism and structuralism drew a general picture of immigration that victimised the immigrants. The social and economic structure was over-emphasised whereas the migrants' agency was underestimated.[7] Moreover, individual identification processes remained hidden behind the collective categories used in research settings, which lead to a reproduction and essentialisation of categories.

Contemporary migration research in France[8] tries to overcome these differences and takes into consideration transnational social spaces and interethnic relations in the sense of Barth (1969). In a recent work on the migrant's contribution to urban changes in Sofia, Bulgaria and Alicante, Spain, Lamina Missaoui and Alain Tarrius develop the concept of "circulation territories" (Missaoui/Tarrius 2006: 64). They assume that this is a new form of migration which differs from diaspora[9] configurations, and reveals networks, "bound by word given and honour, stretching beyond the boundaries, and social norms of the various nation-states they pass through or live in" (ibid.). This "spatio-temporal topic [...] covers all transactions and interactions, all symbolic and concrete relations, which express those international forms of mobilisation, and [...] are likely to produce or harbour new types of social relations" (ibid.). Missaoui and Tarrius do not cite any of the German-speaking or English-speaking theorists of transnationalisation processes, but refer to the French social geography of migration developed at Migrinter research group in Poitiers and their own works in sociology of migration at the University of Toulouse (which is inspired by the early Chicago school of urban sociology and by Georg Simmel's work). However, they end up with a definition of circulation territories that comes close to the notion of transnational

---

6   This perspective was developed over the past twenty years by geographers from the "Migrations internationales" research group in Poitiers. As most of their members are geographers, they have very early linked geographical space to social space in their fieldwork but also in their conceptual reflections (cf. Simon 1996).
7   This research perspective can be explained by the strong involvement of these research groups, mainly from University Paris-VII and Nice, with public policies and research programs financed by the State or the Region.
8   See the websites of the Migration Section of the French Association of Sociology for an overview: http://www.afs-socio.fr/rt2.html and www.migrations.ouvaton.org.
9   For the use of the term diaspora cf. Dufoix 2003; Berthomière/Chivallon (eds.) 2006.

social spaces developed by Ludger Pries (1996, 2008) and Thomas Faist (2000; this volume). Finally, despite the fact that this is not expressed explicitly, the idea of social change in urban spaces inspired by migrant's social and spatial practices shares commonalities with Nina Glick Schiller's and Ayse Caglar's innovative approach on rescaling processes in cities (2006; forthcoming). Both approaches focus on gentrification processes within cities and amongst cities. I offer several examples based on my own research on the cities of Paris and New York, which illustrate these ongoing rescaling processes resulting from gentrification.

William Berthomière and Marie-Antoinette Hily (2006: 67-82), both members of the French research group Migrinter, provide a critical review of transnationalisation theory on the occasion of the 20th anniversary of this research group and of its review, the *Revue Européenne de Migrations Internationales*, which has become a major reference in the French-speaking scientific community specialised on migration processes. Berthomière and Hily provide a rich critical analysis of the Anglophone and Francophone approaches in transnationalisation theory[10]. They come to the conclusion that the notion of multiple belongings in pluri-directional settlement processes can provide a useful concept for the analysis of migration paths. Their own research, grounded on action-theory, is also based on fieldwork in urban spaces and focuses the "organisational modes of collectives in co-presence". Hence, they focus on "the manner in which collectives seize 'opportunities' when they meet in non-set social spaces" (Berthomière/Hily 2006: 82). Their fieldwork on neighbourhoods in Beirut and Tel Aviv also provides examples of opportunity structures and rescaling processes within cities that are subject to a dynamic migration process.

Ludger Pries and Thomas Faist also see the emergence of social experiences and identities that are created, that are more than the sum of their parts, and generate new identities or practices. However, they concentrate not on the process of circulation but on what they posit as transnational space. The term is used as a geographic metaphor for the connections, processes, and identities created by people who live across borders. They describe the ways in which cross border locations are connected through the social networks of migrants, building on a seminal analysis of the transnational social networks of "transmigrants" (Glick Schiller/Basch/Blanc-Szanton 1992: 2). Studying migration between Mexico and the United States, Pries (1996, 2008) identified as the transmigrant, a working migrant who is situated in plurilocal social spaces. Transmigrants interact in highly complex transnational networks that provide information about employment, facilitate the transfer of money to family in the home village, and offer a means of identification with the home country by network members' sharing everyday practices like the action of preparing food and organising social gatherings according to well-established patterns. Networks are structured by mutual obligations and are the result of a complex system of loyalties. The positions and

---

10 The French researchers do not always refer explicitly to the term "transnationalism", but Marina Hily and William Berthomière (op. cit.) use the term.

identities created in this way are hybrid because they take into consideration elements of the original and host countries. These transnational social spaces are the result of new forms of delimitation and differ from geographic or national boundaries, transcending a simple coexistence of the two systems of reference (Pries 1996: 456). However, this concept does not yet take into consideration the specific aspects of the localities in which migrants settle (temporarily or permanently). Even though Pries included the importance of elements of the new environment within the transnational social space, the reference to the home country seems to be the most important part in the reference system. Pries speaks about pluri-local frames of reference and a relational social geographic space. He is close to geographers' approaches with his focus on place-making and on the geographic-spatial dimension of the Social. In my own work on Senegalese political networks, I have shown how these networks go beyond ethnic or religious belonging by rooting themselves into local and national geographic and social spaces. This allows them at the same time to attain their transnational political goal: the victory of Abdoulaye Wade from the opposition party at the Senegalese presidential elections in 2000 (Salzbrunn 2002; 2004). Similarly, Glick Schiller and Fouron (2001) have given us an example of Haitian long-distance transnationalists who collaborated with US-American actors.

Caglar and Glick Schiller (2006, forthcoming) also speak of the local but their emphasis is not a general sense of multiple rootedness but a call for a specific investigation of the forces that shape the specific places. They are concerned with the localities from which migrants and their descendants leave, in which they settle, and to which they are connected by social fields, which often extend across the borders of nation-states. They build on Glick Schiller's (2005; Glick Schiller/Basch/Szanton Blanc 1992) concept of a transnational social field[11] as specific set of networks of ego-centred social relations that are linked to institutions located in specific places. These fields contain social relations of unequal power constituted by differential access to forms of capital, military force, and means of discursive representation. This approach focuses on social relations and institutions – workplaces, schools, religious social, financial and political organisations that differ in their functioning according to their location and that can be empirically studied. The theorisation of locality they express is influenced by the scholarship that uses a concept of rescaling to describe the contemporary neo-liberal restructuring of urban space.

---

11 Gildas Simon's concept of poly-centred and multi-sited migration spaces that emerge from world-wide networks (1996: 223) is, although not referring to the same literature, close to Glick Schiller's concept of transnational social fields. The latter goes further by emphasising the relations of unequal power constituted by differential access to (military, economic, political, discursive) resources.

Translocal Social Spaces: The Importance of the Local Living Conditions in the Process of Place-Making

Following L. Pries' concept of transnational social spaces which takes into consideration the spatialisation of the social, T. Faist's approach (in this volume), G. Lachenmann's methodological considerations (in this volume) and Schiller and Caglar's work on transnational social fields and localities which emphasises urban rescaling processes and power relations, I suggest emphasising the importance of the specific local living conditions and the process of place-making by adopting the notion of translocal social spaces. During my fieldwork among Senegalese migrants in Senegal, in Europe and the United States of America, I observed that the local economic, social and cultural reference systems became more and more important within the transmigrant's identification process. Their actions were only partly determined by their reference to their original nation, village or family. More and more, their actions referred to their new local and national environments. Understanding the local power relations, the processes and discourses of political lobbying and the concrete conditions of access to land, property, business, residence permits etc. is crucial in the rooting process of the network within different localities, reaching far beyond a dyadic relation between "home" and "host" countries. Their references and contacts went far beyond their ethnic or national peer group. The latter has often been the focus point of researchers wearing "ethnic lenses" (Glick Schiller/Çağlar 2006), and as a consequence of treating the ethnic group as the unit of analysis, the social configurations beyond ethnic/national lines within or beyond borders were ignored in migration scholarship. This is a general problem of migration research which concerns also certain religious groups which are constructed by the research focus, although the people concerned may declare neither that they are part of that group nor that they fit to the researchers' definition of belonging to it. Particularly after 09/11, public funding of studies on Muslim immigrants increased and contributed to establishing a distinction between immigrants according to their religion, without taking into consideration the whole range and diversity of religious practice.

Hence I suggest a definition of translocal social spaces as the result of new forms of delimitation that partly consist in, but also reach beyond geographic or national boundaries. These translocal spaces become the new sources of identification and action within specific local and global reference systems. However, this does not mean a local determinist position denying any agency to the migrants. It is the migrants which also shape the conditions of the local. Migrants contribute to rescaling of certain cities and certain urban districts and zones; for example the African migrants in Harlem in New York City are important part of the rehabilitation of housing there. Especially studies on gender and migration have underlined agency from an action-theory point of view (Lachenmann, in this volume).

An entanglement of various subjective and objective rescaling processes is taking place in the context of recent immigration from West Africa to Europe and North America. I develop below how the visible diversity has become an important point in city marketing and worldwide competition of global cities for tourists and investors attracted by this diversity. Furthermore, the migrants themselves are in a subjective rescaling process of different locations, and adapt their life projects and objectives to the new subjective scalar hierarchy. Potential highly skilled immigrants also choose a new place to work according to the criteria of whether there are open-minded citizens living in cosmopolitan cities or not.[12]

The importance of a whole city like Paris can change in a context of international competition amongst tourists who are in search of cultural diversity and cosmopolitanism: The official tourist guide of Paris nowadays includes districts with a variety of national and ethnic groups. Ten years before, these districts were not recommended for tourists because of criminality.[13] Furthermore, migrants often develop a subjective scalar perspective that creates a hierarchy of cities or countries based on their subjective references and criteria for the choice of a place of residence. Abdoulaye Gueye (2001) illustrates in his article the "relegation" of France to the benefit of the North American continent in general and New York, Washington or Montréal in particular. He expresses a subjective national and local rescaling process established by migrants. These processes have consequences for objective rescaling processes because New York has become an important financial platform for money transfer and investment thanks to the recently immigrated Senegalese and other highly skilled African workers. Thus subjective rescaling processes go along with the objective rescaling processes that are being researched. According to Saskia Sassen (2007a: 16),

"Existing theory is not enough to map today's multiplication of practices and actors contributing to these rescalings. Included are a variety of nonstate actors and forms of cross-border cooperation and conflict, such as global business networks, the new cosmopolitanism, nongovernmental organisations (NGOs), diasporic networks, and such spaces as global cities and transboundary public spheres".

In her latest book, Sassen (2007b: 7) explicitly includes local and translocal perspectives on rescaling processes:

---

12 The assumption that perceived respect or perceived disregard can influence a migrant's choice to move further is a result of my field work on Senegalese in New York and Paris. Abdoulaye Gueye (2001) has similar findings for Senegalese who move from France to Canada or plan to do so.
13 These districts suffered from an image of being central places for drug trafficking, although this was only true for a certain type of visible drugs. In other, more fashionable and richer districts, less visible drug traffic was also going on, but in chic discotheques rather than on the street.

"studying the global, then, entails not only a focus on what is explicitly global in scale. It also calls for a focus on locally scaled practices and conditions articulated with global dynamics; perhaps the most developed scholarships with this type of focus are those on global cities and commodity chains".

A concrete operational definition of scale is provided by Glick Schiller and Çağlar (forthcoming):

"the term scale can be defined as the summary assessment of the differential positioning of cities determined by the flow and control of capital and structures of power as they are constituted within regions, states and the globe".

By focusing on festive events in two global cities, I will show how rescaling processes are undertaken by various actors who have differential access to power. This is the result of a fruitful interaction between migration studies, transnationalism and social geography, as it is done by Glick Schiller and Çağlar, and by the discussion about the notion of scale offered by Neil Brenner in Anglophone academic circles. In France, the research group Migrinter (Migrations Internationales) at Poitiers, founded by social geographer Gildas Simon and still dominated by geographers who work together with sociologists like Marie-Antoinette Hily, have also combined urban sociology with social geography. As I mentioned above, Hily is the editor in chief of the important journal "Revue européenne des migrations internationals" (REMI). Together with William Berthomière, the director of Migrinter and former student of its founder Gildas Simon, he has recently given a critical overview of transnationalism in Anglophone and Francophone research (Berthomière/Hily 2006). They come to the conclusion that a description of the ways in which migrating collectives seize opportunities in a co-presence with other groups can lead to a better understanding of organisational modes of collectives than a search for causes of emigration.

The research group MTE (UMR 5045 MTE Mutation des Territoires en Europe) at the Universities of Montpellier and Nîmes provides also an interesting framework for the study of migration and transformation of rural or urban space. The members of MTE are dealing with festive events and their influence on the symbolic construction of territories (Catherine Bernie-Boissard and Dominique Crozat, forthcoming). I want to develop this approach further (Salzbrunn, forthcoming in Bernie-Boissard/Crozat) by underlining the migrants' impact on this transformation process.

The Incorporative Impact of Festive Events in a Migratory Context

Once we agree that it is necessary to go beyond an essentialisation of national states as the "natural" unit of analysis in global contexts and to turn from space as a metaphor to an examination of migrants in relationship to specific localities, we have to suggest an alternative approach and innovative methods (see Lachenmann and Pfaff-Czarnecka in this volume). I have developed an approach that takes festive events as entry point for the analysis of migrant dynamics in interaction with the urban context. Focusing on these events, I can observe the emergence and dynamics of group building, the development of new hybrid references or "hyphenated identities" (Çağlar 1997) and I can observe the impact of the particular dynamics of these places, namely the local urban environment on these social practices. I focus on political and cultural events in these two cities in order to understand the different pathways of migrant urban incorporation in these places. This chapter does not operate with *a priori*-defined ethnic or religious groups as the units of analysis; there is no assumption that people who share a religious or national origin settle together as a community and identify themselves in any situation as members of a community based on these elements. Both NY and Paris are global cities, and focusing on two such cities enables me to address the following questions: what are the differences among the rescaling processes experienced by both cities and neighbourhoods in these cities? What are the different impacts of these processes on the paths and trajectories of migrant transnationalism in these global cities? How do two specific global cities (Paris and New York) relate to migrants in different ways? How do the migrants themselves recognise their place in the city vis-à-vis their fellow city dwellers? How do they work out their ties to the city with the other neighbourhood dwellers? How do rescaling processes effect the representation of locality and identity in each city? How does the historicity of the neighbourhood (the places) shape the ways the migrants are being incorporated into the diversity[14] of the urban fabric? Putting my research questions this way helps to move the migrants, global cities and transnationalism debate beyond the current discussions, which are usually cast in cultural diversity[15], cosmopolitanism,[16] or

---

14 I do not mean cultural diversity here, but the diversity in terms of neighbourhoods.
15 Cf. the book on cultural diversity in metropolitan cities edited by Bernard Jouve/ Alain-G. Gagnon (2006).
16 Cf. Eleonore Kofman's critical analysis of John Urry and Ulrich Beck's notions of cosmopolitanism (2005). She argues that both have developed the notion of cosmopolitanism in a context of growing worldwide accessible reference systems. Their views are too narrow in scope because they are directed towards politically and economically privileged groups, leaving aside considerations about others. Kofman also criticises the optimistic view of cosmopolitans, arguing that independent cosmopolitan individuals or networks can also be perceived as being threatening in the eyes of representatives of the nation-State.

migrants' role in unskilled labour or as ethnic entrepreneurs in the labour economy.[17]

Translocality in Urban Spaces: Senegalese in New York

Paris, while marketed as quintessentially French, is not representative of France. Similarly, New York while serving as a cultural reference for the United States is an exception in comparison to other big American cities in multiple ways including the tremendous diversity of its migrant population and its long history of encouraging the identity politics of its newcomers. New York and Paris are both global cities in the sense of Saskia Sassen's (1991; 2007a; 2007b) definition. They emerge as one territorial or scalar moment in a transurban dynamic and each is a complex structure that can articulate a variety of crossboundary processes and reconstitute them as a partly urban condition. "At the same time there has been a sharpening inequality in the concentration of strategic resources and activities in each of these cities compared with that of other cities in the same country" (Sassen 2007a: 112). Global financial processes (see Hering in this volume) are concentrated in these cities and stretch beyond national borders within worldwide networks. The periphery (i.e. the poorer suburbs and the provincial towns in the Parisian case) is becoming increasingly marginalised and excluded from major economic processes. In both New York and Paris, spatial segregation processes are coinciding with social and cultural exclusion.

In France, closeness to the city centre of Paris reflects the closeness to power. Real estate prices are the highest in the districts where political, financial and cultural power is concentrated. Furthermore, Paris *intra muros* hosts the best secondary schools and some of the most prestigious universities and elite schools, with some exceptions in the western suburbs like Neuilly. A recent study on racism based on nationality and family name, financed by the French Prime Minister, has also shown the impact of the residence of a candidate on an employer's choice (Duguet/Leandri/Horty/Petit 2007). Here the position of Paris in France differs from any US-American city in that, in the United States, cities of differing scalar positions host the best ranked Ivy League universities and there are a number of intellectual centres. On the other hand, the segregation of migrants of different class backgrounds is sharper and more visible in New York than in Paris (Salzbrunn forthcoming in Glick Schiller/Çağlar). This is due to differences in international relations, immigration policy and local housing policy. Both cities contain not only diverse migrant populations but significant concentrations of West African migrants. The first West African immigrants came to Paris in a colonial context, particularly during World War I and World War II. They were fol-

---

17 For a critique of the notion of ethnic entrepreneurship cf. Thomas Lacroix, Leyla Sall, Monika Salzbrunn (forthcoming 2008).

lowed by low skilled workers who found work in the car industry from the 1950s until the 1980s. They resided in poor suburbs with other workers, but these neighbourhoods became more and more segregated in the 1990s. West African entrepreneurs, students and highly skilled workers arrived after World War II or they were French born children of immigrants from West Africa. The West African immigrants to the United States arrived much later, mostly in the 1990s, and were better educated than those who reside in Europe. New York (and the east coast of the US more generally) concentrates the largest part of West African migration to the United States and offers an important contact platform for these newcomers (Salzbrunn 2004; Stoller 2002).

In New York City, West African Muslim groups have successfully promoted their specific Islamic practices by connecting them to common American discourses on minorities. Making use of the available religious discursive resources in US and their prominence within the identity politics of New York City, Murid[18] organisations and movements have developed in a particularly successful way in New York. Although the migrants, notably the political and religious activists, follow strategies across their translocal spaces, they also take into consideration the cultural and political differences between their various places of residence. In New York City, they pay attention to the diverse inhabitants of Harlem[19] and its local geographical setting, to the state representatives and their immigration politics, as well as to the mayor and his political program. These actors are part of specific opportunity structures that interest groups can exploit when pursuing their goals in New York (Wilson/Rodriguez Cordero 2006; Furlong et al. 1996). By the end of the 1990s, the two week-long annual visit of the Murid Shaykh Mourtada Mbacke had become an important event, not only within the Murid transnational networks and in Harlem but within New York City. The Senegalese and New York press, as well as radio stations, regularly reported the news. Video producers filmed the whole event in order to market the tapes through retailers in the US, Europe and Senegal. The culminating point of the annual visit is the Murid parade, a march through the streets of Harlem that ends with several speeches held in Wolof, Arabic and English at a corner of Central Park, the southern boundary of Harlem.[20] Senegalese who participate in these

---

18 Murids are followers of a Sufi brotherhood founded in the 19th century by Shaykh Ahmadou Bamba in Touba (today's Senegal). Murid is derived from the Arab term for disciple within a Sufi-brotherhood, Murids are members of a tariqa (Arabic: brotherhood, pl. turuq).
19 Most of the Senegalese in New York live in Harlem and Brooklyn. Here, I concentrate on Harlem.
20 Wolof is one of the languages spoken in Senegal. As the dominant political groups come from Wolof-speaking regions, speaking Wolof here can signify an affirmation of these groups. French is understood by the elder generation and by people who have gone to school. English is now becoming a lingua franca for Senegalese residing in the US.

activities are becoming part of the landscape of Harlem through their religious expression and its visibility in public space.

Instead of feeling "marginalised" in a predominantly Christian country, through their religious organisations and presence in public sphere Senegalese migrants in New York City have become more and more incorporated into the city in the eyes of other residents, including black and white Americans. This acceptance allows the Senegalese in return to identify more with "American values" or political practices. One example of this ongoing identification process is the increasing use of the English language and the decreasing use of French and the presence of American flags, especially on T-Shirts, during religious demonstrations like the Murid parade. Another part of the Murid's strategy of becoming firmly rooted in the public space in Harlem is the translation of their values into a language and a social discourse understood by Americans. The representation of Murid economic and moral practices plays an important role in how they locate themselves vis-à-vis the other inhabitants of Harlem. The ideology of hard work and the ideal of a certain form of piety are welcomed by a section of American society, as represented by the mainstream press.[21] In his proclamation of Shaykh Ahmadou Bamba Day, 1988 the mayor of New York connected African roots and Sufism with a reference to "African personality and culture." Such connections enable the African American Muslims, searching for their African roots, to identify themselves with this spiritual leader. In the context of city officials' open battle against drugs and alcohol, the promotion of an ascetic lifestyle by the Murids is considered as a helpful initiative. The authorities trust the new migrants because of their Muslim ethics. Murids, in turn, underscored these social values in the course of their political lobbying and in public events like the annual Murid parade.[22] In this context, it is important to note that the local Murid networks in Harlem, as well as the Nigerian and Asian networks researched by Stoller (2002), have contributed to the transformation of the urban landscape of New York City and paved the way for the current gentrification of Harlem. Since the arrival of the first Senegalese migrants in the 1980s, the housing market within that area has considerably changed.

Murids declare also in their own discourse that they have reconstructed large parts of Harlem, fought crime and stopped the disintegration of the area. They see themselves contributing economically and morally to a decaying neighbourhood and helping to upgrade it. The administrative and economic support and encouragement provided to them by the federal government and by New York City and its borough of Manhattan facilitate Murid incorporation into economic networks and the administration structures of daily life. The public visibility of religious practices infuses Senegalese Muslims, and particularly the members of the

---

21 See the articles by Susan Sachs (2003) and Natalia Antelava (2002).
22 American researchers who are specialists on Muridism also express their fascination with the expression of these values.

Murid brotherhood, with a feeling of positive recognition by and acceptance in the United States (Salzbrunn 2004; forthcoming).

Although their positive roles in the neighbourhood, public recognition, and success making in converts give the Africans in the Murid networks self-esteem in their place of settlement, this self-perception is built at the expense of other groups in Harlem, especially African Americans. Murids have adopted the more general US negative prejudices against African Americans, particularly about their putative work attitudes and loose morals. However, Murid's self-representation did not go unchallenged and the apparent unity, which is cherished in the Murid parade, seems to be in contrast with everyday tensions between Afro-Americans and Africans in Harlem.[23] Like Pentecostalism, which 'has become a transnational phenomenon that, in its modern form, is locally expressed through a highly accelerated circulation of goods, ideas and people' (van Dijk 2002: 178), Muridism has also developed its own transnational social field (Riccio 2000, 2008). On the one hand, the local expression of Muridism changes according to the specific context and influences of the religious network as a whole. On the other hand, the local expression of Muridism contributes to the restructuring of a local territory including its social, economic and political practices. In the case of New York, I have shown the way the Murids make use of the available administrative opportunities, to have access to public space as a religious community and of the specific symbols of belonging to America (through the Proclamation of Shaykh Ahmadou Bamba day, etc.) in order to become a part of Harlem. This is also an example of poly-centred migration spaces linked to the development of world-wide networks as defined by Gildas Simon (1996: 263).

The success of New York in the world wide competition to attract highly skilled immigrants is also due to the Murid's experience of exclusion in Europe and particularly in France. Abdoulaye Gueye (2001) points out how the Senegalese in general have "downgraded" France after having felt downgraded by the French. His French expression "déclassement" expresses a subjective process of re-ranking of localities (in this case this ranking includes Paris as a node of the religious and political networks but also France and Europe in general as an immigration option) done by the migrants. This process is closely related to the Murids' experience of hostility to displays of any sign of particularity, especially religious, within the French public space. During the 2007 presidential election campaign, politicians both from left and right-wing parties were denouncing the "communitarianism" that, according to them, threatens Republic's unity and equality. Nicolas Sarkozy (the current President of France and member of the right wing party UMP) and José Bové (from the leftist alter-globalisation-movement) were among these politicians denouncing communitarianism. They fail to note that the republican ideal of equality isn't working in practice, and immigrants are increasingly aware of their exclusion from the job market and various

---

23 For example African Americans working in shops and restaurants recently opened by Murids view their new immigrant employers as exploitative.

spheres of social life. This subjective process of positioning of places is influenced by objective rescaling processes and has an impact on ongoing rescaling processes.

Belonging to Urban Spaces through Festive Events in Paris

In my second example, I move even further away from examining migration through an ethnic or religious lens and concentrate on the insertion of migrants from multiple backgrounds into a particular neighbourhood in the throes of gentrification processes. This gentrification is intensified by efforts of the city leadership to increase the city's competitiveness within the global tourist market. I examine an event as access to the local dynamics of the Parisian district of Sainte Marthe in order to understand how groups emerge or evolve in a migratory context.

In 2001, the global competition between cities contributed to the electoral victory of Socialist mayor Bertrand Delanoë and his allies from the Green party in Paris. This victory was a culmination of pressures to recognise, celebrate, and market the diversity of the city. The latest municipal elections in 2008 confirmed and reinforced the success of the ruling coalition between the Green party and the Socialist party lead by Delanoë. Efforts to highlight Parisian diversity began in 1995, with leftist parties' victory in municipal elections in the multiethnic neighbourhoods. In addition, a global marketing trend that highlighted cultural and geographical diversity, as seen in several carnivals that were initiated in European cities such as Berlin and London (Knecht/Soysal 2005), stimulated efforts to market Paris as a capital of international recreation. The invention of arts and crafts villages (such as a street of fashion in Barbès[24]) and several festive events, supported by the City of Paris, such as the Chinese New Year in 2007, were all products of this commitment to highlight diverse cultures (Raulin 2004) in order to reposition the city within the global tourist industry.

Sainte Marthe is the name of one of the two parallel streets in the district; it provides the name for the whole district. Most of buildings in the area now known as Sainte Marthe, were built in the 1860s as part of a former Parisian suburb (Faubourg) by the Comte de Madre, an entrepreneur whose utopian ideas lead to the invention of a new type of architecture for workers' homes. By the

---

24 The fashion street in the Northern quarter of Barbès contains a high percentage of West-African immigrants and was an invention that was criticised by a part of the African population. The stylists, despite their vaguely common West African origin were perceived as being sociologically (especially in terms of class) and culturally alien to the inhabitants of the quarter (including the tailors). The clients, mostly rich inhabitants or tourists, came to the fashion street in search of exoticism, which did not match the social and cultural realities of the largest part of the population in Barbès.

1980s the buildings were in danger of collapsing because of their poor quality and at the beginning of 1991, the mayor wanted to destroy the whole quarter in order to construct huge buildings, such as the ones on north and east of Sainte Marthe. The inhabitants were afraid of being expelled and developed various resistance strategies. The association "Village Saint Louis Sainte Marthe" organised banquets and festivals, as part of a major public relations and press campaign, in order to win public and political support. The village reference in the association's name alluded to a territorial identity within a big city. In the festivals and activities organised by the association, the architectural and aesthetic value of the houses and the cultural richness of the inhabitants were emphasised. The history of the place and an identity as the common enemy of right-wing and the real-estate speculators strengthened the inhabitants' sense of belonging to this particular neighbourhood. In 1994, the notion of its rehabilitation figured for the first time in the plan for new urban projects in Paris. During the municipal election campaign in 1995, opposition to real estate speculation and the restoration of this quarter were at the centre of the political campaign of the left-wing parties. Thanks to this platform in 2001, the left won the district elections and for the first time the whole city of Paris was conquered by the left. However, it was not until 2003 that the restoration/renovation project of the quarter was approved and the home owners were offered financial support.

A central point of interest in Sainte Marthe is the celebration of cultural diversity, which features its inhabitants from various backgrounds and origins. Today, the population includes working class migrants from North Africa and the former Yugoslavia who arrived in the 1960s, Chinese from three provinces, artists and musicians who have occupied the deserted ateliers of the artisans, and a middle class population attracted by the diversity and the village-like ambience of the place. The events are organised by the association "The Four Horizons", which was created in 1997 when the "Village Saint Louis Sainte Marthe" split. Their founder and president, Kheira, is a French woman of Algerian origin,[25] who has sought to provide activities to the inhabitants (especially to the youth) of the quarter, create links between different people and establish a meeting venue for the Algerian women who suffer from isolation. She works as a housekeeper in the district and serves as a mediator between people searching for housing and for sites for shops and the real estate agencies. Because of her involvement in real estate transactions in the district, she has been criticised by a number of inhabitants, even though she is engaged in saving the neighbourhood from destruction. "The Four Horizons" has organised cultural events like outdoor balls, public couscous banquets and carnivals, which have made Sainte Marthe more and more popular in the eyes of tourists, potential investors in real estate, local political representatives and a section of the inhabitants of the district. The organisation of festive events like the carnival has played a central role in shaping the inhabit-

---

25 I hereby thank the German Research Foundation for having supported this research in Paris with an Emmy Noether grant.

ants' identification with the quarter. The president of "The Four Horizons" also acts as a development broker (Bierschenk/Olivier de Sardan 1993) and, forms an interface (Long 1989) with other actors during municipal elections. In 2008, she invited the (successful) district candidate of the Socialist Party, Rémy Fereaud, to present his program during an informal meeting in the association's assembly hall.

The association receives public funding from the State Secretary of Urban Affairs to do community work, and from the district mayor to enable it to participate in the organisation of the annual multi-sited nationwide Fête de la Musique in the Sainte Marthe Square. Furthermore, the association earns money from their members' fees (30-40 members) and from their banquets and the food sold during the festivals. In the course of building and conducting these events, the association interacts with various key persons in the district: the mayor and the elected deputies, the presidents of other associations (especially the Association for Local History). Others, such as local artists and craftswomen, participate in and benefit from these festive events. For the first time in 2003 several inhabitants of the quarter participated in a new type of summer carnival inspired by the London Notting Hill Carnival. They named it "Barbès Tour" in allusion to a popular quarter in the Northern Paris (Barbès) where migrants from Sub-Saharan Africa and North Africa have settled and where a large part of the participants reside. The year 2003 was declared the official year of Algeria in France; the President of The Four Horizons and its other members acknowledged this in the festival by wearing Berber costumes and walking in front of a banner with "Algeria my love", written on it in Arabic. In 2004, the "Barbès Tour" took place in Barbès and Sainte Marthe, where a music concert featuring a variety of styles was hold. During the carnival, the Four Horizons offers crêpes to the children of Sainte Marthe and prepares a Moroccan dish (*Tajine*) on Mardi Gras, the day before Ash Wednesday, in a local restaurant run by a community organisation. Similarly Four Horizons celebrated Halloween and the beginning of Ramadan in 2004 together at a restaurant. All these references and the activities exemplify the cultural *bricolage* that marks the neighbourhood. The conscious cultural creolisation carried out by the Four Horizons and the inhabitants of the neighbourhood draw attention to the emergent place-based belongingness of the district inhabitants. Despite the power asymmetries within this common place-based field of identification, the local political identity construed through festive events has led to the emergence of a we-group. It is a belonging that extends beyond ethnic and/or religious origin and identity.

It is important to note that if I had focused on the members of the district who were of Algerian descent, I could have told a story of an ethnic or transnational network: there are indeed connections between the President of The Four Horizons, her nephew in Great Britain and her uncles in Algeria. To begin instead with neighbourhood ties, and the evolving sense of local community, does not deny the fact that this *communitas* evolves within the context of the political situation faced by North Africans. Living within transnational social fields, North Africans in Paris are very sensitive to France's attitude to colonial history. They also face increasing daily restriction of access to public space especially around Belleville and Sainte Marthe because of a rise in identity checks by the police, which are justified by concerns about illegal migration.

However, these cultural practices and alliances can best be analysed in the context of specific local political, social and economic living conditions and understood as produced within space and time (Barth 1969; Cohen 1991). Actors' identities are "partial, multiple and fractured by cross-cutting alliances" (Werbner 1997: 265). The local dynamics of Sainte Marthe were shaped by the struggle to restructure the neighbourhood as part of broader globe-spanning forces that are repositioning cities. The residents, partly resisting the gentrification of the neighbourhood, were able to find support for their cause from the district authorities because of the increasing value placed on cultural diversity (best displayed in the neighbourhood) in the marketing of cities within the global tourist industry. By restoring most of the buildings instead of rebuilding them, most of the actual inhabitants could remain at home. However, the numerous reports on the public conflict in the media, particularly in writings covering the festive events, made the district famous and contributed to the gentrification process.

The appropriation of the urban space by the migrants in this case and its repositioning locally and globally were partly the outcomes of the subjective rescaling of the place from the local inhabitants' perspective (both migrant and native), as well as of local politicians' recognition of this neighbourhood's marketable value for the repositioning of Paris as its neighbourhoods are restructured within global flows of capital and the marketing of cultural difference. As Bodaar and Rath (2005: 4) point out, city

> "boosters increasingly acknowledge that urban diversity is a vital resource for the prosperity of cities and a potential catalyst for socio-economic development, particularly since business investors consider this diversity as one of the factors determining the location of businesses. The commodification and marketing of diversity, through the commercial use of the presence of the ethnic 'others' or their symbols, fits in well with this process, and this helps explain the growing enthusiasm for 'interesting' landscapes that have the potential to draw tourists...".

Consequently, in Sainte Marthe the response to the surveillance of migrants has been local rather than solely ethnic or religious. Surveillance has led to the development of solidarity networks for the protection of political and economic refugees. Several individuals have been supported by a network that extends beyond persons of Algerian descent. While in one case a family network was at the centre of the network, their ability to include other local residents and to extend into Paris was much more important for the support of this individual. Inhabitants of Sainte Marthe include these forms of solidarity among their reasons to be proud of their neighbourhood.

Conclusion: Rescaling Processes in Urban Spaces and Translocal Migrations

Although New York and Paris show common points in their marketing of cultural and spatial dynamics, there are still important differences between these two global cities in this regard. Paris is not only the biggest French city, but also the capital of France while New York City is not a political centre. Reflecting the differences between these two cities, the role, positioning and possibilities for the incorporation of migrants and for their transnational connections are different. I have illustrated the different positioning of migrants in these two global cities, which are subject to very similar dynamics, by using two festive events: the Murid Parade in New York and a neighbourhood festival in Paris as entry points for my analysis of translocal phenomena. In both cases, in Paris and to a lesser extent in New York, the mayors transgress national discourses that portray immigrants as a threat to the coherence of the national cultural and social fabric. It is noteworthy that while the mayor of Paris chose to send a positive message of belonging to the African residents of Paris by sponsoring a concert with the best known African musicians on the Bastille Day, (a French national holiday held on July 14th), the president of the country chose a French singer of popular but a bit old-fashioned chansons for the same occasion.[26] As local leaders of cities, who must constantly assure the continuing successful regional and global connectedness of their cities, mayors of global cities supported and celebrated the diversity of their urban space. They strive to facilitate continued global flows of capital, investments and high-skilled (migrant) labour force, as well as tourists. Placing my analysis on the local rather than the national level, allows me to note the situations in which urban discourses and policies may differ from those formulated by national leaders. It is noteworthy that the perspectives of the mayors of Paris and New York, as well as some of these cities local leadership, were closer to the sociological reality of immigrants and migrant incorporation than those espoused by the leaders of France and the United States who acted within national frameworks. The Borough President of Manhattan, NYC and the district mayors in the North-Eastern quarters of Paris generated responses to migration that reflected an awareness of competitive marketing of both particular cities and the contributions of migrants to both the restructuring and the marketing.

---

26 This choice, as well as the venue of the quite old-fashioned star Mireille Mathieu, singing the National anthem on the evening of Election Day, was interpreted by several journalists as an illustration of his political programme on "chosen migration" and expulsion, and his wish that migrants should identify with "French national identity".

However, the short-term success of the rescaling process both in New York and Paris can lead to mid-term social problems and increase inequalities in the city. The gentrification process in Harlem undertaken by Senegalese high skilled and/or middle class immigrants is to a certain extent built on the exclusion of the poorer Afro-American population from this area, as the latter can no longer afford the real estate prices. In Paris, the gentrification process as mediated through neighbourhood interventions and struggles reinforced the notion of belonging expressed by the inhabitants. The Parisian and the district mayors did not suffer electoral defeat in its wake, at least as long as they maintained a certain balance between different interest groups, in the voters' eyes.

In the analysis of the interplay between urban and migrants settlement dynamics in New York and Paris, it is important not to follow a common trajectory of migration scholarship in which social scientists build their nation-wide models on specific urban examples like Paris or New York. New York's ethnic politics have long been a product of New York and its particular relationship to national and global relationships of power. Conclusions drawn from studying New York are not reflective of the United States in general.[27] Similarly, Paris' late recognition of urban diversity was a product of the local context of Paris including its specific electoral politics, which was shaped in interface with the global and regional pressures asserted on that city and the way its leaders sought to reposition the city and themselves in urban politics and governance structures.

Although migrants' subjective ranking of places within transnational social fields may follow a logic different from the rescaling of cities within neoliberal restructuring, the New York case demonstrates that both processes are entangled with each other. In New York, Harlem has become a global platform for the Murid brotherhood and an imaginary centre for high skilled Senegalese and Murids residing in Europe who wish to migrate to a place that is most attractive within their own subjective rescaling. In Paris, rescaling processes within the city realised partly by migrants' activities and festive events place the city on a different scale for an emerging type of tourist who travels in search of sociologically dynamic quarters like Notting Hill in London or Kreuzberg in Berlin. Nevertheless, it should still be noted that the highly skilled migrants and potential Murid investors' perceptions of France and the new restrictive (anti-) immigration laws are reflected in the transnational field of the Senegalese political and religious networks as a subjective rescaling in favour of New York.

Both New York and Paris share intensive gentrification processes where spaces are globally marketed in ways that reflect the struggle of both cities to retain their dominant global positioning. Examining the relationship between urban rescaling processes and migration allowed me to reposition urban political economy within more global fields of capital, tourism, investment, and transnational

---

27 Paris can fruitfully be compared to London as a capital and global city with specific local policies under mayor Livingstone, although Great Britain is organised differently in national political terms than France.

social fields. It also places the restructuring of neighbourhoods and gentrification processes within globally extending markets in interaction with migrants' transnational social fields and settlement dynamics. Using festivals as entry points to analyse the interplay between migrant dynamics, transnational networks, global restructuring, and questions of political representation, this study allowed me to ask questions about the divergence of local political discourses on immigration from homogenised narratives of national policy.

Furthermore, focusing on localities rather than on a priori defined groups, based on national, ethnic or religious criteria, allowed me to go beyond methodological nationalism and to follow the actor's social practices, which extend beyond national and ethnic frameworks. This multi-sited fieldwork started by focusing on one predefined group of migrants, and then enlarged the transnational perspective to group-building processes around events in public space. Thereby, ethnic or national lenses were replaced by a place-based perspective in rescaling processes within urban spaces. It became clear that a systematic comparison of the rescaling and restructuring of localities was indispensable in order to understand how these processes interact with the migrants' activities. I suggest that a focus on events can avoid taking an a priori-defined ethnic, religious or sociocultural category as a key issue in the processes of communitarisation. This epistemological perspective with its comparative design reveals some surprising crosscutting local alliances which go beyond predefined categories. The history of transnationalism in different scientific communities shaped by linguistic areas presented in the first part of this chapter could be continued by this epistemological choice. This would allow researchers to overcome former disjunctions and to give a constructive answer to critiques of transnationalism research.

References

Antelava, Natalia (2002) "Feature: A different kind of Islam in NYC." United Press International (July 30).
Barth, Fredrik (ed.) (1969) *Ethnic Groups and Boundaries: The Social Organisation of Culture Difference*, Boston: Little Brown.
Beck, Ulrich (2000) "The Cosmopolitan Perspective: Sociology of the Second Age of Modernity." British Journal of Sociology 51/1, pp. 79-105.
Bensa, Alban/Fassin, Eric (2003) "Les sciences sociales face à l'événement." Terrain 38, pp. 5-20.
Bernie-Boissard, Catherine/Crozat, Dominique (forthcoming) *La fête au présent. Mutations des fêtes dans le champ des loisirs*, Montpellier: Université Paul Valéry Montpellier 3.
Berthomière, William/Chivallon, Christine (eds.) (2006) *Les diasporas dans le monde contemporain*, Paris: Karthala/MSHA, Hommes et Sociétés.

Berthomière, William/Hily, Marie-Antoinette (2006) "Décrire les migrations internationales. Les expériences de la co-présence." Revue Européenne des Migrations Internationales 22/2, pp. 67-82.

Bodaar, Annemarie/Rath, Jan (2005) "Cities, Diversity and Public Space." Metropolis World Bulletin 5, pp. 3-5.

Çağlar, Ayse S. (1997) "Hyphenated Identities and the Limits of 'Culture'." In: Tariq Modood/Pnina Werbner (eds.) *The Politics of Multiculturalism in the New Europe. Racism, Identity and Community*, London: Zed/The Postcolonial Encounter, pp. 169-185.

Cohen, Abner (1991) "Drama and Politics in the Development of a London Carnival." In: Pnina Werbner/Muhammad Anwar (eds.) *Black and Ethnic Leaderships in Britain: The Cultural Dimensions of Political Action*, London/New York: Routledge, pp. 170-202.

Dijk, Rijk van (2002) "Religion, Reciprocity and Restructuring Family Responsibility in the Ghanaian Pentecostal Diaspora." In: Deborah Bryceson/Ulla Vuorela (eds.) *Transnational Family: New European Frontiers and Global Networks*, Oxford: Berg, pp. 173-196.

Duguet, Emmanuel/Leandri, Noam/L'Horty, Yannick/Petit, Pascale (2007) *Discriminations à l'embauche. Un testing sur les jeunes des banlieues d'Île de France*, Paris: La documentation française.

Dufoix, Stéphane (2003) *Les diasporas*, Paris: Presses Universitaires de France, Que sais-je.

Faist, Thomas (2000) *The Volume and Dynamics of International Migration and Transnational Social Spaces*, Oxford: Oxford University Press.

Furlong, Andy/Biggart, Andy/Cartmel, Fred (1996) "Neighbourhoods, opportunity structures and occupational aspiration." Sociology 30/3, pp. 551-565.

Glick-Schiller, Nina/Basch, Linda/Blanc-Szanton, Suzanne (eds.) (1992) *Towards a Transnational Perspective on Migration: Race, Class, Ethnicity and Nationalism Reconsidered*, New York: New York Academy of Science.

Glick Schiller, Nina/Fouron, Georges Eugene (2001) *Georges Woke up Laughing. Long-Distance Nationalism and the Search for Home*, Durham/London: Duke University Press.

Glick Schiller, Nina (2005) "Transnational Social Fields and Imperialism: Bringing a Theory of Power to Transnational Studies." Anthropological Theory 5, pp. 439-461.

Glick Schiller, Nina/Çağlar, Ayse (2006) *Towards a Theory of Locality in Migration Studies: Migrant Incorporation and City Scale*, Paper delivered at Migrinter Colloque 1985-2005, Poitiers, 7th July.

Glick Schiller, Nina/Çağlar, Ayse/Guldbrandsen, Thaddeus C. (2006) „Jenseits der ethnischen Gruppe als Objekt des Wissens: Lokalität und Inkorporationsmuster von Migranten." In: Helmuth Berking (ed.) *Die Macht des Lokalen in einer Welt ohne Grenzen*, Frankfurt a. M.: Campus Verlag.

Glick Schiller, Nina/Çağlar, Ayse (forthcoming) "Towards a Theory of Locality in Migration Studies: Migrant Incorporation and City Scale." In: (id.) (eds.) *Rescaling Cities* (working title), Ithaca: Cornell University Press.

Guedj, Pauline (2003) "Des 'Afro-Asiatiques' et des 'Africains'. Islam et afrocentrisme aux Etats-Unis'." Cahiers d'études africaines 43/4, 172, pp. 739-760.

Gueye, Abdoulaye (2001) "Quand les Sénégalais s'organisent aux Etats-Unis: le déclassement de la France." Sociétés Africaines et Diaspora 12, pp. 121-137.

Jouve, Bernard/Gagnon, Alain-G. (eds.) (2006) *Les métropoles au défi de la diversité culturelle*, Grenoble: Presses Universitaires de Grenoble.

Knecht, Michi/Soysal, Levent (eds.) (2005) *Plausible Vielfalt. Wie der Karneval der Kulturen denkt, lernt und Kultur macht*, Berlin: Panama.

Kofman, Eleonore (2005) "Citizenship, Migration and the Reassertion of National Identity." Citizenship Studies 9/5, pp. 453-467.

Lachenmann, Gudrun (1994) "Social Security in Developing Countries: The Gender Perspective." In: Deutsche Stiftung für Internationale Entwicklung (ed.) *Social Security in Africa. Old Age, Accident and Unemployment*, Berlin: DSE, pp. 127-150.

Lacroix, Thomas/Sall, Leyla/Salzbrunn, Monika (forthcoming 2008) "Les Marocains et Sénégalais de France, permanences et évolution des relations transnationales." Revue Européenne des Migrations Internationales 24/2.

Long, Norman (1989) *Encounters at the interface. A perspective on social discontinuities in rural development*, Wagenigse sociologische studies 27, Wageningen: Agricultural University.

Missaoui, Lamina/Tarrius, Alain (2006) "Villes et migrants, du lieu-monde au lieu-passage." Revue Européenne des Migrations Internationales 22/2, pp. 43-65.

Olivier de Sardan, Jean-Pierre/Bierschenk, Thomas (1993) "Les courtiers locaux du développement." APAD Bulletin 5, pp. 71-76.

Petersen-Thumser, Jens/Salzbrunn Monika (eds.) (1997) *Libérer le potentiel d'auto-promotion en décentralisant les mesures de politique sociale*, Berlin: Deutsche Stiftung für Internationale Entwicklung.

Pries, Ludger (1996) "Transnationale soziale Räume. Theoretisch-empirische Skizze am Beispiel der Arbeitswanderungen Mexico-USA." Zeitschrift für Soziologie 25/6, pp. 456-472.

Pries, Ludger (2008) *Die Transnationalisierung der sozialen Welt* Frankfurt a. M.: Suhrkamp.

Raulin, Anne (2004) *Anthropologie urbaine*, Paris: Armand Colin.

Riccio, Bruno (2000) "Spazi transnazionali: esperienze senegalesi." Afriche e orienti 3/4, pp 17-25.

Riccio, Bruno (2008) "West African Transnationalisms Compared: Ghanaians and Senegalese in Italy." Journal of Ethnic and Migration Studies 34/2, pp. 217-234.

Sachs, Susan (2003) "In Harlem, a Link to Senegal." New York Times (July 28).
Salzbrunn, Monika (2002) "Hybridisation of Religious Practices amongst Westafrican Migrants in France and Germany." In: Deborah Bryceson/Ulla Vuorela (eds.) *The Transnational Family. New European Frontiers and Global Networks*, Oxford: Berg, pp. 217-229.
Salzbrunn, Monika (2004) "The Occupation of Public Space Through Religious and Political Events: How Senegalese Migrants became a Part of Harlem, New York." Journal of Religion in Africa 32/2, pp. 468-492.
Salzbrunn, Monika (2007a) "Lokale und globale Produktion von Alteritäten im Rahmen von Ereignissen – Wie ein heterogenes Pariser Stadtviertel seine Identität konstruiert." In: Elka Tschernokoshewa/Volker Gransow (eds.) *Beziehungsgeschichten. Minderheiten – Mehrheiten in europäischer Perspektive*, Bautzen: Domowina.
Salzbrunn, Monika (2007b) "Enjeux de construction des rôles communautaires dans l'espace urbain: le cas du quartier de Belleville à Paris." In: Ivan Sainsaulieu/Monika Salzbrunn (eds.) Esprit critique 10 "La communauté n'est pas le communautarisme." (www.espritcritique.fr.)
Salzbrunn, Monika (forthcoming) "Le carnaval de Paris: mise en scène de l'histoire et l'histoire de sa mise en scène." In: Bernie-Boissard/Catherine, Dominique Crozat (eds.) *La fête au présent. Mutations des fêtes dans le champ des loisirs*, Montpellier: Université Paul Valéry Montpellier 3.
Salzbrunn, Monika (forthcoming) "Rescaling Processes in two Cities: how Migrants are incorporated in Urban Settings through Political and Cultural Events." In: Glick Schiller, Nina/Ayse Çağlar (eds.) *Rescaling cities* (working title). Ithaca: Cornell University Press.
Sassen, Saskia (1991) *The Global City: New York, London, Tokyo,* Princeton/NY: Princeton University Press.
Sassen, Saskia (2007a) *A Sociology of Globalization*, New York: Noton & Company.
Sassen, Saskia (ed.) (2007b) *Deciphering the Global. Its Scales, Spaces and Subjects*, New York/London: Routledge.
Simon, Gildas (1996) "La France, le système migratoire européen et la mondialisation." Revue européenne de migrations internationales 12/2, pp. 261-273.
Smith, Anthony (1983) "Nationalism and Social Theory." British Journal of Sociology 34, pp. 19-38.
Stoller, Paul (2002) *Money Has No Smell. The Africanization of New York City*, Chicago: The University of Chicago Press.
Tarrius, Alain (2002) *La mondialisation par le bas. Les nouveaux nomades de l'économie souterraine*, Préface de Michel Wieviorka, Paris: Balland.
Werbner, Pnina (1997): "Afterword: Writing Multiculturalism and Politics in the New Europe." In: Tariq Modood/Pnina Werbner (eds.) *The Politics of Multiculturalism in the New Europe. Racism, Identity and Community,* London: Zed/The Postcolonial Encounter, pp. 261-267.

Werner, Michael/Zimmermann, Bénédicte (2002) "Vergleich, Transfer, Verflechtung. Der Ansatz der *Histoire croisée* und die Herausforderung des Transnationalen." Geschichte und Gesellschaft 28, pp. 607-636.

Wilson, Bruce M./Rodriguez Cordero, Juan Carlos (2006) "Legal Opportunity Structures and Social Movements. The Effects of Institutional Change on Costa Rican Politics." Comparative Political Studies 39/3, pp. 325-351.

Wimmer, Andreas/Glick Schiller, Nina (2002) "Methodological Nationalism and Beyond Nation-State Building, Migration and the Social Sciences." Global Networks 2/4, pp. 301-34.

– Transnationalism,
Political Participation and
New Forms of Belonging

Euro-Alevis: From *Gastarbeiter* to Transnational Community

BESIM CAN ZIRH

Introduction: "Non-Sunni-Muslim-Minority" as a New Label for Alevis

After a long period of silence and invisibility, Alevis of Turkey have dramatically become one of the controversial issues of Turkish politics in the last two decades. This is the phenomenon known as *Alevilik Uyanışı* (the Alevi Revival) (Çamuroğlu 1998) and popularly named as *Alevilik Patlaması* (the Explosion of Alevism) (Vorhoff 2003: 91). These gripping concepts refer to a dramatic and almost unexpected increase in the socio-political visibility of Alevism. Hundreds of books published, dozens of Alevi associations and new radio stations established appeared as the indicator of this phenomenon. Although some researchers had forecasted the nearly inevitable disappearance of this particular culture in the beginning of the 1980s (Vorhoff 1998: 31), the silence was broken when an open letter, the Alevi Declaration, signed by numerous intellectuals was published in 1990. With this 'coming out', constitutional recognition of Alevis, as a particular but integral component of the nation, was explicitly demanded for the first time in Turkish history.

Nearly 15 years after the Alevi Declaration, another phase in this revival was reached when a second declaration was jointly issued by *Avrupa Alevi Birlikleri Konfederasyonu* (the Confederation of European Alevi Unions – the CEAU)[1] and *Alevi Bektaşi Federasyonu* (the Federation of Alevi Bektashi – the FAB)[2] on 7th of October 2004. This declaration was actually a response to the EU Regular Re-

---

1 The CEAU has been established in 2000 as an umbrella organisation so as to represent Alevi associations on European scale. Presently, hundreds of Alevi associations from 10 European countries such as France, the Netherlands, Austria, and Norway are represented under this organisation.
2 The FAB has been established in 2004 in cooperation with the CEAU so as to supply a similar umbrella function for Alevi associations in Turkey.

port 2004 on Turkey's progress³ which defined Alevis as a "Non-Sunni Muslim Minority" (Regular Report 2004: 44-45) instead of using the concept of "Non-Sunni Muslim Community" or "Alevis" employed before 2004. Having endorsed this new conceptualisation without reservation, this declaration indicated a dramatic shift in the discourse of the Alevi movement⁴ as the decade long agenda of Alevi movement shifted from the "right to be equal" as citizens to the "right to be different" as a minority group.⁵ Furthermore, the declaration also revealed a publicly unknown fact, namely that the concept was able to find a place in the report as a result of a five-year-long lobbying campaign by CEAU at the EU Parliament.

The concept of "minority" was removed from the Regular Report 2004 as a result of immediate reaction by Turkish state and replaced with that of "community" again in the subsequent years.⁶ Even in the absence of the concept, it would not be wrong to argue that the question of Alevism has begun to be appraised as another painful task in Turkey's yellow-brick road to Europe.⁷ Some red-blooded words from the declaration may well indicate this forthcoming 'political danger': "Although solving these problems through impositions by the Eu-

---

3   The EU Regular Reports on Progress are prepared by the European Commission for each candidate country during the process of accession. The first Regular Report on Turkey's progress was issued in 1998 followed by the reports prepared in 1999, 2000, 2001, 2002, 2003, 2004, 2005, 2006 and 2007. For more information, http://www.avrupa.info.tr/AB_ve_Turkiye/Muzakereler,Regular_Reports.html.
4   By the Alevi Movement, I refer to the socio-political awareness appeared at the end of 1980s firstly in Germany. In 1988, a small group of Alevi immigrants from different German cities gathered in Hamburg under the name of Alevi Kültür Grubu (the Alevi Culture Group). In addition to their associational title which overtly voices the name Alevi, the group differentiated itself from the previous Alevi associations by directly referring to the question of Alevism from a new approach.
5   It is impossible to discuss the Alevi movement as a monolith entity. Apart from the main stream divisions, there are also many localised forms of the movement in Turkey and Europe. To illustrate, in spite of its prominent position in the CEAU, the Berlin Anatolian Alevi Culture Centre (BAAC) responded to the definition of Alevis as a belief out of Islam very critically. When I was coincidentally in Berlin on the day the declaration was issued in 2004, the members of the BAAC were discussing about suspending their membership to the CEAU.
6   Alevis in the EU Progress Reports, 1998: Turkey's Alawi Muslims with non-Sunni background. 1999: the Alevis. 2000: the non-Sunni Muslim communities. 2001: the Alevis. 2002: the non-Sunni Moslem/religious communities and the Alevis. 2003: the non-Sunni Moslem communities and the Alevis. 2004: the non-Sunni Muslim minorities and the Alevis. 2005: the non-Sunni Moslem/religious communities and the Alevis. 2006: the Alevi community/the large Muslim Alevi community. 2007: the Alevis and the Followers of Alevism. Main concerns about Alevis in the Reports are mainly about legal and socio-political difficulties of expressing and practising their belief and identity.
7   German Green Party MP, Cem Özdemir stresses this vital importance of the question of Alevism in EU accession process by saying "Türkiye'nin AB'ye giden yolu cemevlerinden geçer" (The path of Turkey to EU passes through cemevis [Alevi religious centres]) (Alevilerin Sesi, July 2004: 83).

ropean Parliament annoys us, the assimilationalist approach of the Turkish government in power leaves us with no alternative than EU" (CEAU – FAB, Manuscript – 2004). Additionally, the ensuing outcry from populist political groups blaming Alevis for "betraying" Turkey by cooperating with the EU indicates nothing but the ambiguous position of Alevism in Turkey. Needless to say, as we will see in the following section, such disagreements bear close resemblances to the political prejudices which stigmatised Alevis as an "inner-enemy" during the 1960s and 70s.

Considering the interaction and cooperation between the CEAU and the FAB, I prefer to approach this case as an appropriate example indicating the process of transnationalisation through migratory experiences in a historically specific context. In this sense, I claim that this is not a spontaneous 'revival/awakening' of what was going to sink into oblivion two decades ago. On the contrary, I suggest that 'Alevi Revival' should be understood as a 'reconstruction/recapture' on the basis of a new context that emerged as a result of migratory experiences. In other words, I basically claim that Alevism has become able to exceed the limitations of its historically rooted geographical, social, political, legal and economic marginality by establishing extensive social networks linking distant locales in the processes of internal and external migration. Alevi identity has been redefined and restructured on the basis of various restraints and opportunities and as a result of diverse struggles and negotiations on local, national and transnational levels. In this article I attempt to analyse the transnationalisation of Alevis in the process of migration to Germany/Europe so as to understand the appearance of the concept of "Non-Sunni-Muslim Minority".

What is Alevism? A Perpetual Working Definition

Any attempt to define Alevism has to deal with two main difficulties. On the one hand, as Sökefeld mentions, "the answer is neither clear nor self-evident; the question is not a rhetorical one" (2004a: 1). On the other hand, the question of Alevism has always been wrapped in political concerns. Two separate sources of literature can be mentioned to exemplify this complexity.[8]

8   John Shindeldecker (2001) notes that he located all these following definitions about the question of what is Alevism during his research: (1) "An Alevi is any Muslim who loves the family of the Prophet Muhammad", (2) "An Alevi is simply any democratic, tolerant, human rights-promoting, modern-thinking person, whatever his religious background", (3) "An Alevi is a filthy, immoral person who is so far from religion that he must first become a Christian before he can become a Muslim", (4) "Alevism is the original, true essence of Islam", (5) "Alevism is a heterodox sect within Islam", (6) "Alevism is the most authentic expression of Turkish Anatolian Islam", (7) "Alevism is a philosophy, a 'way of life'", (8) "Alevism is pure Sufism", (9) "Alevism is pure Shiism", (10) "Alevism is simply Sunni Islam with an extra emphasis on Ali", (11) "Alevism is so syncretistic that it can't be counted as Islam at all", (12) "Alevism is an alternative to orthodox Islam", (13)

The literature on "the people of Asia Minor" from the late 19th century mainly focuses on the question of origin of certain communities such as *Tahtacı* and *Kızılbaş* which are identified as Alevi today.[9] Although many European scholars have reached a consensus on the idea that such heretical communities represent the survival of pre-Islamic beliefs (Crowfoot 1900), the question is still loaded with "very considerable confusion" for Hasluck (1929: 311). De Planhol offers his "resignation" referring to "the complexity of the issue." To conclude his literature review, Grønhaug cites De Planhol's resignation and says "I feel no incentive to go further than that" (quoted in: Grønhaug 1974: 9, 189).

The question of what is Alevism has become very popular with the emergence of the 'Revival' at the end of 1980s and, since then, hundreds of books in Turkish have been published on the question which Alevis themselves are trying to answer (Vorhoff 1998: 31). However, this extensive literature blended with various political concerns does not supply more definite answers.[10] I would mention only some of the main exemplars of such definitions and their relation to certain political agendas (Okan 1999; Göker 1999):[11]

1. Having originated from Avesta and Zoroasterian, Alevism is an ethno-religion as a part of Kurdish Culture (Algül 1999).
2. Having originated from Middle Asian Turkic paganism, Alevism is an ethno-religion as a part of Turkish Culture (Türkdoğan 2004).
3. Alevism, as a syncretic belief, originated from Middle Asian Turkic paganism but also blended with many other different cultures during the process of Islamisation of the region (Ocak 1996).
4. Alevism is a branch of Islam specific to Anatolia (Sezgin 1998).
5. Alevism is a form of primitive communalism specific to Anatolia and the product of "class struggle" of early medieval period (Yürükoğlu 1990).

The first two definitions try to channel Alevism into Kurdish or Turkish national political movements. Various forms of the syncretism thesis, exemplified here in reference to Ocak (1996), are widely used by urbanised Alevis to celebrate Alevism as a secular culture rather than a belief system. The fourth thesis tries to loc-

---

"Alevism is an example of the classic Marxist struggle by an oppressed minority", (14) "Alevism is a mixture of the best elements of Islam, Christianity, Judaism, Manichaeism, Zoroastrianism, Shamanism, and 20th century humanism".

9 See also Footnote 15.

10 One of the prominent historians, Reha Çamuroğlu, who is Alevi himself and works on Alevism, concludes the discussion on the question of definition by referring to a Tao master who says: "Tao tanımlamaz, tanımlanırsa Tao olmaz" (Tao cannot be defined. If it is defined, it would not be Tao) (Çamuroğlu 2000: 10).

11 In his book titled as "What is Alevism?" in Turkish, Baki Öz, who is a retired high-school teacher and one of the "new Alevi intellectuals" himself, categorises such attempts to define Alevism under 32 different statements (Öz 1996).

ate Alevism in the circle of orthodox Islam, whereas the last praises as a proto-communist philosophy by indicating its non-conformism.[12] Massicard (2003: 3) employs the concept of "framing contest" to analyse this divergence in the definition of Alevism as a reflection of the political struggle between different parties over Alevism.

In light of these difficulties, my attempt to define Alevism should be understood as a working definition specific to this very moment of history. In other words, instead of trying to reach a static definition of Alevism, I focus on some essential symbols and institutions which are indispensable components of Alevism. Although their applications may differ in nuance for one or another reason, almost all Alevi communities share these institutions regardless of the question whether they are still in use or not.

To begin with, Alevi, as a contemporary concept, was popularised at the beginning of the 19th century, and refers to groups of people who have a particular belief system and set of practices which are different from that of Sunni Islam in Anatolia.[13] The concept derives from Alawi, and etymologically means the follower of Ali, the son-in-law and cousin of the Prophet Mohammed. His assassination in 680 in Kufa resulted in the first and main division in Islam. This is specifically important for understanding Alevism since they comprehend their collective history of victimisation as a fate beginning with the murder of Ali. This event functions as a "chosen trauma" for Alevis by combining "their loss of col-

---

12 During the visit by German-Turkish Joint Seminar group to an Alevi organisation in Ankara in 2005, an "Alevi intellectual" translated the historical position of Alevism in Anatolia in reference to the German Peasant War in 1524/5. He also urged the audience not to consider Alevism in reference to Martin Luther what he has all done is "temporising such a great revolt by creating a new religion for bourgeoisie classes": the Protestantism. Instead, he suggested another name, Thomas Munzer. Such a nuance could only been understood by those who already read The Peasant War in Germany by Friedrich Engels (Engels 2000).

13 The concept of 'Alevi' did not take place in the official documents of the Ottoman Empire until the 19th century (Ortaylı 1997: 120). These communities that we identify today with the name of Alevi, as the "umbrella term", were known by their tribal names such as Tahtaci, Abdal, Cepni, and Zaza (Eickelman 1989); or by imposed pejorative labels such as Rafizi, Zındık and Mülhid which means unbeliever, infidel and non-Muslim (Melikoff 1998: 5); or by the name of Kızılbaş (red-heads) which referred to the insubordinate attitude of heretical communities especially in the eastern part of Anatolia (Birge 1965: 67). Much more importantly, many historical resources have been re-written following the popularity of this "new" concept. The memoirs of İbrahim Ethem Begh who was a governor in Gallipoli regions during the War of Independence (1919-1923) may be presented as a proper example of such re-writings. In its 1936 version, "A lady informed that an old kızılbaş Çetmi came and ask for irregulars" (Ethem 1936: 164) re-published as "there is Çetmi, namely, an Alevi in the village asking for irregulars" in its 1989 version (Ethem 1989: 289) (I should thank Mehmet Demiray for this last quotation about İbrahim Ethem Begh. He noticed this nuance in the period of literature review for our joint research on Alevism in 2002).

lective self-idealisation and the emotional burdens of historical grievances" and allows them to "act as ready victims of circumstances" (Volkan 1997: 48).[14]

Alevism may roughly be defined as a belief which has its own specific "secrecy of Gnostic forms and esoteric teaching" (Erdemir 2005: 938) and claims "to posses the inner/esoteric meaning of Islamic revelation" (Kehl-Bodrogi 2003: 53). According to Melikoff, the formation of Alevism is rooted in the 11 – 12th century following the Islamisation of Mesopotamia which caused the convergence of pre-Islamic beliefs with Islam (Melikoff 1998). Tord Olsson portrays the Ali-oriented belief communities in reference to (1) the priority of oral over written culture, (2) the principal of takiye (dissimulation)[15] and (3) the insubordinate and non-conformist characteristic in opposition to any kind of political centrality and institutionalised orthodoxy (Olsson 1998).

Alevis, in their traditional settings, organise themselves in the form of endogamous and closed communal units. Membership can only be achieved through cognation but it is also needed to be upgraded with a special ceremony conducted by a *dede* (spiritual leader). Alevism may properly be defined by referring to what it is not, namely, its essential differences from orthodox-Islam. They do not observe any of the core rites of Islam such as practising *namaz* (Sunni prayer),[16] or fasting during the Ramadan.[17] *Saz* (Turkish lute) and Semah (ritual dance) occupy a central position in their rituals during which men and women gather under the same roof. In some communities, a symbolic amount of alcohol, *dem/dolu*, is consumed at the opening part of rituals. Lastly, Alevi women, mainly in the urb-

---

14 As Vorhoff writes, Alevis usually define their historical origin in a very pronounced dualism with Sunni-Islam by referring to Kerbela where Huseyin, son of Ali, and his followers were killed. The Alevis as "the people of Ali", "the descendants of Kerbela", "the adherents of the Ehlibeyt [the family of Mohammed]" oppose the Sunnis as "the people of Ebu Bekir, Ömer and Osman [first three caliphates]" or "the followers of Yezid [political rival of Ali during his caliphate]" (Vorhoff 2003: 103).

15 In Alevi tradition, the takiye principle refers that Alevis may dissimulate their belief and identity in the presence of non-Alevis so as to conceal the "secrecy" of the belief and to avoid possible discriminations by orthodox-Islam (Zeidan 1999: 2).

16 Unlike the followers of orthodox Islam, Alevis do not attend mosques, and consequently their settlements in rural Anatolia are known as Camisiz Köyler (the villages without mosques).

17 However, this non-practicing should not be considered as a denial of Islamic rites. The main structure of Alevi cosmology is described as a path though the four doors which are hierarchically ordered as Şeriat (the Sheri'a), Tarikat (Mysticism), Marifet (Ingenuity), and Hakikat (the Truth). Islamic rites are required by the first door. Since Alevis accept that their belief system has already passed through this very first door, they do not need to practice these core rites (Shankland 2003: 85).

an context, usually do not wear headscarves[18] (Shankland 1993; Hasluck/Hasluck 1929: 153).

In modern Turkey Alevis constitute the second largest religious community. According to some estimates, the population of Alevis fluctuates between ten and twenty-five per cent of the total population of Turkey (70 million 2006 est.). Additionally, twenty per cent of the Alevi population is also Kurdish (Vorhoff 1998, Zeidan 1999). Regional, linguistic, ethnic, and ritual differences draw historical borders among Alevi communities (Aktaş 2000; Kehl-Bodrogi 1997). Nevertheless, these differences among the communities are not as vital as the difference between Alevism and Sunnism. As Geaves mentions, "otherness [in Alevism] is more a religious term rather than tribal" (2003: 61).[19]

Three social institutions, which have indispensable importance in the reproduction of Alevism, can further be focused to discuss Alevism. First of all, *dedelik* as a spiritual leadership has a unique role which cannot be compared with the role of imam in Sunni-Islam. Each Alevi community consists of *talips* (the followers) who are organised under the leadership of a *dede* who needs to be committed to specific spiritual centres, *ocaks* (heart) and is also supervised by a *pir* (grand-master) who resides in these centres (Shankland 2003). It is believed that each *dede* comes from the holy lineage of Ali which is the main sources of their spiritual charisma. *Dedes* also have absolute judicial roles.[20] In the special inter-

---

18 In Turkey, the difference between Türban and Başörtüsü is needed to be mentioned specifically. According to the republicans and secularist, although Başörtüsü as a rural and folkloric way of veiling does not have any political connotation; Türban is used by political Islam as a symbol of their movement. In light of some critiques to earlier versions of this paper where I used the concept of 'headscarf,' I prefer to use Türban to indicate the form of more urban and contemporary veiling – if it is not political – to stress the difference between Alevism and Sunnism. In this sense, my claim here does not apply to veiling in rural contexts where Alevi women may traditionally veil their heads.
19 The historical relation between Kurdish-ness as an ethnic identity and Alevi-ness as a spiritual/religious identity also highlights another difficulty about Alevism. On the basis of historical evidence, it would not be wrong to argue that Kurdish-Alevis and Turkish-Alevis can get together around the Alevi-ness much easier than Kurdish-Shafis and Kurdish-Alevis make a coalition on the basis of the Kurdish-ness. In this sense, Alevi and Kurdish organisations today constitute a strong neither/nor alternative to each other. A Kurdish-Alevi has to choose either an Alevi or a Kurdish organisation if he or she needs to participate in one. This choice also determines which part of his/her identity is going to be emphasised. During my pilot research, I came across many examples of this situation. Although they can use the Zaza/Kurdish language as the everyday language among family members, some people prefer to identify themselves only as 'Alevi'.
20 According to many sources, Alevis especially in rural settings did not apply to the official judicial system. Any kind of intra-communal problems was preferred to be solved under the supervision of dedes. This principle has gradually dissolved since the 1950s when the internal migration began (Demir 1999: 24). On the other hand, it would not be wrong to argue that respected dedes have still some level of judicial authority to solve certain disputes in modern Alevi associations.

rogation ritual, *görgü cemi*, which is performed only once a year, the *dede* examines his *talips* as to whether or not they behaved in a morally up-right manner according to Alevi doctrine.[21] In the case of being found guilty, a member can be required to compensate his/her fault in accordance to varying degrees of penalty. In much more extreme cases such as murder and adultery, the dede has the authority to label a guilty member as a *düşkün* (shunned) which implies a total excommunication from the community (Zeidan 1999; Geaves 2003: 63).

The main ritual in Alevism is *cem*, a nocturnal ritual constituting the main platform for Alevis to congregate under the supervision of a *dede*. Etymologically, *Ayin-i Cem* means gathering at the core of existence, namely, great integration (Bal 1997: 82). In Alevi cosmology, every human, *can* (life), is a form of energy which comes from and goes through the *hak* (God). In this sense, *cem* means glorification of the only sacred thing on this earth, namely, human beings (Shankland 1998: 20). *Musahiplik* is the third important social institution which is a prerequisite for entering into *görgü cemi* in some communities. *Musahiplik* is a kind of kinship relation which one can not be born into such as kirvelik (godparenthood of circumcision) (Kieser 2001: 5). The concept etymologically means the fraternity of path/world which refers to making two males socially responsible to each other about their way of life and commitment to the doctrine (Kaygusuz 1991: 11).

As a conclusion, these three institutions have critical importance for the reproduction and transmission of Alevism through generations. Some scholars stress this importance by claming that Alevism cannot be imagined in the absence of these institutions (Yörükhan 1998: 35; Yaman 2000: 5). For anyone studying Alevism, especially in the urban and migration context, it is very difficult to locate 'proper' applications of these institutions.[22] In this sense, first of all, I prefer to understand Alevism on the basis of these institutions. Secondly, I claim that focusing on the evolution of these institutions is important to understand the transformation of Alevism.

Historical Background: Alevis of Turkey: From "Non-Person" to "Inner-Enemy" – *Leaving* and *Losing Home*.

In the long history of the Ottoman Empire Alevi communities known by their tribal names and affiliations were treated differently in accordance with the politic-

---

21 These manners are understood in reference to the motto of "eline, beline, diline sahip olmak". Be Master your hand, tongue, and loins; namely, do not take what is not yours, do not lie, and do not commit adultery (Tur 2002: 451).
22 Sökefeld, for instance, quotes on a dede living in Hamburg who says "Cem [which he is conducting in Hamburg] is a game, it is a drama because a deep, spiritual involvement of all the participants is missing" (2004b: 147).

al tensions of specific periods and regions. Their position in this long history has always been ambivalent. Although, they were often labelled as 'non-believers' or 'out-of-Islam', they were never recognised as "non-Muslim" within the Ottoman Millet system which entitled non-Muslim communities such as Jews and Christians to have particular rights and duties. In this sense, as Vergin argues, in addition to suffering from suppression and pressures over their belief and ways of life, Alevis, then and now, have a kind of "non-person" public persona which enhanced their public invisibility (2000: 76).

During the disintegration period of the Empire, especially at the very beginning of the 20th century, newly emerging nationalists approached Alevis from a different angle. This 'disrespected' and 'ignored' culture began to be esteemed in the search for an alliance during the War of Independence and then it was also socially mobilised in the frame of the new national identity (Küçük 2002: 165). During this period, certain literary components of Alevism such as folk lyrics and poets (Kehl-Bodrogi 2003: 57) were utilised as the culture of "true Turks" in order to purify the new official Turkish language in opposition to the Ottoman language (Karpat 1976: 120). With reference to this flirtation as opposed to their disadvantaged position during the Ottoman period, Alevis are usually presented as strong adherents of secular republicanism since the very beginning of the Republic. Alevis' sympathy for the republic derives from both myth and reality which is a phenomenon that should also be contextualised to understand Alevism in Turkey (Öz 2000: 35, 45).

It would not be appropriate to understand this convergence as an attempt to open a new space for Alevis on the grounds that all these cultural elements were "neutralised" before being utilised for national identity building (Massicard 2003: 6). Once again, "the existence of Alevis in the state was covered in silence" (Sökefeld/Schwalgin 2000: 11). Since the Republic "did not discriminate [Alevis] in favour of Sunnis" (Ahmad 1994: 167), this new period has opened the door to social, economical and educational mobility for Alevis but only if they abondon their particularity (Alevi identity) to melt into the republican commonality (national identity). In this sense, I suggest that this "republican socialisation" has enabled Alevis to leave their geographically isolated locations and socially marginalised position.

In the 1940s, considerable inner-migration flows appeared in Turkey as a result of rapid industrialisation as well as modernisation. Considering their communal structure, Alevis were both the 'victors' and the 'victims' of this new period. They were victors because they were able to break free from violence and repression of the centuries under the Ottoman the Empire. They were victims because this liberation required them to keep a very low-profile in terms of displaying their identity in public life. They could be a part of newly emerging world by jumping on the bandwagon going to the cities, but their well-preserved communal structure also receded in their memories with every kilometer traveled.

In the same decade, the multi-party system was announced and the *Demokrat Parti* (the Democratic Party – DP) achieved a victory against the founding *Cumhuriyet Halk Partisi* (the Republican People Party – RPP) in 1950. In the political atmosphere of the period, Alevis were also among the supporters of 'democracy', however, they turned to the RPP as the DP's discourse shifted from liberal-democratic to conservative-Islamist which reminded them of repressive days during the Ottoman Empire (Karpat 2004: 91). With the military coup in 1960, Turkish socio-political life entered a new phase in which socio-political organisations mushroomed in accordance with the new constitution. This has brought the freedom of association. In this context, the first "Alevi Revival" came to fruition parallel with the urbanisation of Alevism which is the process increased their social and economic visibility especially in previously Sunni-dominated Anatolian city and town centres (Kaplan 2000: 246). The main motivation in this period derived from the necessity of responding to reactions by conservative-Islamists against the increasing visibility of Alevis. This process concluded with the establishment of *Türkiye Birlik Partisi* (the Turkish Union Party – TUP)[23] in 1966 (Şener/İlknur 1995: 77).

Although this first initiative managed to utter the name of Alevi publicly, Alevism remained invisible during the period between 1960s and 1980s. The reason of the invisibility in this period derived from another flirtation which was between Alevism and the leftist-secular politics. In the beginning of 1960s, quite a considerable number of Alevis had already been urbanised. As a result, in addition to legal and social difficulties, preserving and practising Alevism became nearly impossible as the organic relationships with three institutions mentioned above heavily dissolved.

In this sense, Alevism is now inadequate for helping Alevi youth to understand the new contradictions they have encountered in the highly-politicised urban context. In the wake of this 'forgetting', Alevi youth began taking part in the secular-leftist organisations against the raising rightist-Islamist hostility (Kehl-Bodrogi 1997: 11). In other words, as seen from this perspective it would be reasonable to argue that a historical enmity between Sunnism and Alevism emerged from the political polarisation of the period in the form of an antagonism between leftist and rightist groups (Neyzi 2003: 113). As one of initial outcomes of this process, Alevism was altered and transferred from the field of belief into that of politics as a "folk-socialism" (Koçan/Öncü 2004: 476).[24]

This logical marriage of secular-leftist politics and Alevism also had some negative outcomes for the latter. First of all, this articulation reinforced the pro-

---

23 The TUP could never gain real political power. Especially after the national election in 1972, it turned into a more secular-leftist party by embracing a socialist agenda. It was abolished by the Military Coup in 1980.
24 For instance, a traditional motto of Alevi cosmology, "En'el Hak" (I am the God) was phonetically rewritten as a political slogan of "Emek-Hak" (labour-right) (Çoşkun 1995: 274) as "the untrimmed moustache of the Alevi becomes the distinctive features of all Turkish revolutionist" (Kehl-Bodrogi 1997: 11).

cess of forgetting by rendering Alevism as a local-symbolic component of a universal ideology inasmuch as Alevi youth in this period abandoned Alevism "in favour of the new secular ideologies" (Çamuroğlu 1998: 80). At the risk of oversimplification, it is possible to claim that sheltering in secular-leftist politics was the only way for Alevis to participate in the new social and political life of Turkey during this period. This sheltering may also be seen as a modernised version of the traditional dissimulation strategy by which Alevis were able to keep their identity invisible. Secondly, Alevism was identified with secular-leftist politics, and slightly with Kurdish separatism in the eyes of the rightist-Islamist groups which treated Alevism as an "internal enemy".[25] This political polarisation culminated as a result of several armed attacks in a number of central and south-eastern Anatolian cities, such as Çorum, Sivas, Malatya, and Kahramanmaraş, between 1978 and 1980. Hundreds of people were killed in these attacks and most of them were Alevi (Sinclair-Webb 2003: 220-216). These events were very traumatic for Alevis who had become an integral part of social and economic life in these cities (Kaleli 2000: 102-103). Eventually, they started fleeing to Turkish and European metropolises and Alevis in Europe decided to stay instead of returning to insecure "home on fire". In other words, "The homeland Turkey, which has become a land of repression and sorrow, has turned into a 'lost homeland'" (Rigoni 2003: 164).

The military coup in 1980 constituted another turning point for Alevism. Initially, the tragic social extermination of secular-leftist politics in Turkey has left Alevis voiceless once again. With the emergence of "Turk-Islam synthesis" as a new *cementing ideology*, public life was radically reconsolidated on the basis of more nationalist (Turkish) and more religious (Sunni-Islam) ideology (Jongerden 2003: 71). This reconsolidation inevitably brought an end to *sui generis* neutrality of the Turkish state. Turkification and/or the Sunnification of the official persona of the state did not only ignore but also pushed sub-national identities into the category of "lesser Turks" (Kosnick 2004: 990).

Furthermore, the rise of the Kurdish armed struggle of the Kurdistan Worker's Party (PKK) also heightened the situation of Alevis since they were caught in the crossfire between the Turkish state and the Kurdish separatism both of which attempt to redefine and mobilize Alevism for the sake of their own political agenda (Çamuroğlu 1998: 80; White 2003: 17). Another significant outcome of this period had to do with Alevis living in European countries. Before the military coup, they had already organised under highly home-land-oriented secular-leftist political organisations which were usually sister chapters of Turkey-based organisations. In this sense, the abolishment of all social and political organisations in the home-land drove them into a political vacuum which was hard to fill again.

---

25 During the period, 3K Doctrine appeared as an unofficial internal security doctrine, which indicates all "internal-enemies" of Turkish sate: Kızılbaş-Kürt-Kommünist (Kizilbas-Kurd-Communist).

Alevis of Germany: From "Institutions of Alevis" to "Alevi Institutions" – *Desiring Home*

In the Turkish case, international migration basically refers to the process of labor migration from Turkey to Western Europe, especially to Germany, which began in 1961 in the frame of bilateral agreements. Secondly, although Turkish immigrants share certain social and cultural similarities, "it is impossible to talk about 'the Turkish-German transmigrant' as a homogeneous ideal type" (Jeffrey 2001: 107). In other words, Germany has a unique role in the story of Turkish immigration and the case of Alevism has its own particular chapter in this story. There are 2.5 million Turkish immigrants in Germany. Of those 600-700 thousands, about thirty per cent are Alevis (Rigoni 2003: 166). In Germany, Alevis have organised in the form of home-town and/or worker charity associations since the early days of immigration. In accordance with the changing political climate in both, the home- and host-land, previous "home-away-home" organisations have been gradually superseded by political and ideological ones. At the beginning of 1970s, secular-leftist organisations, which were usually official or unofficial sister chapters of home-land based legal or illegal political organisations, have appeared as the dominant form of organisation (Şahhüseyinoğlu 2001: 250). Despite a changing political climate, the political mobilisation of Turkish immigrants has remained as highly home-land-oriented. Consequently, it is not surprising that political organisations abroad inherited the home-made blindness to the question of Alevism. In this sense, as Sökefeld and Schwalgin claim, they were "institutions of Alevis" but the socio-political networks they established gave birth to "Alevi institutions" at the end of 1970s (Sökefeld/Schwalgin 2000: 12).

During this period, Alevis in Europe usually gathered at private meetings which were only open to acquaintances and compatriots who knew each other personally. These private meetings mainly resembled social chatting. Although the question of transmission of Alevism to next generations was a burning issue of these meetings, they were not able to perform even basic rituals due to difficulty of finding a learned *dede* in the context of migration. (Sökefeld/Schwalgin 2000: 12). On the other hand, a significant level of discrimination by Turkish Sunni immigrants constituted another difficulty for Alevis in expressing their identity during this period (Naess 1990: 188; Østergaard-Nielsen 2003: 28). Just as in Turkey, most of Alevis felt uncomfortable expressing Aleviness overtly.[26]

Consequently, Alevis abroad had also remained "unorganised and invisible in secular-leftist organisations/associations" (Sökefeld/Schwalgin 2000: 12). In other words, the modernised dissimulation strategy has been imported to Europe

---

26 One of the most frequent examples of this dissimulation strategy appeared during the holy month of Ramadan. During this long period of silence, although they do not practice this core rite of Islam, Alevis in Europe pretend to be fasting to avoid humiliating discrimination by Sunni Turkish immigrants.

along with the arrival of the home-based antagonism and conflicts. Since they kept such a low profile, even in Germany, Alevis were almost invisible to academic research as well as to official reports until the end of 1980s (Thomä-Venske 1990: 83). The idea of discarding the cover of leftist-secular politics as a home-land custom appeared in the wake of the bloody attacks of the late 1970s. In this period, Mustafa Timisi, the leader of the TUP, visited Germany and toured several cities to seek for cooperation. As a result of his encouraging visit, a new association was established by Alevis who left secular-leftist political organisations to be part of this first independent initiative of their own. *Yurtseverler Birliği* (the Union of Patriots – UP) established as a sister chapter of the TUP to support the struggle for the rights of Alevis in the home-land. In a short period of time, the UP had organised in several German cities and they united under the roof of *Yurtseverler Birliği Federasyonu* (the Federation of Union of Patriots – FUP) with the participation of twenty-five local UPs. This first independent initiative also encountered depressing criticism from ex-comrades who accused Alevis of becoming "factionalist", "religiously oriented" and "fickle".[27]

Even though they continued to use a social-democratic (right to be equal) instead of an ethno-religious (right to be different) discourse in the political context of the period, they were able to courageously reveal Alevism by mobilising and liberating their cultural symbols. For instance, one of the first organisational activities was an amateur play, *Türkiye Gerçeğinde Kerbela* (*Kerbela* in the Reality of Turkey), which attempted to inform Turkish and German audiences about the bloody conflicts in Turkey (Şener/İlknur 1995: 116). In spite of its organisational power, members of the FUP were easily de-motivated after the military coup in 1980 due to the fear of being investigated in Turkey because of their political activities in Germany. As noted earlier, the military coup caused a political vacuum for Alevis at home and abroad. Under this circumstance, the FUP could survive only up to the mid-1980s by gradually losing its organisational influence. In my opinion, the period between 1980 and 1988 can be conceptualised as "reconsideration period" in which Alevi leaders and intellectuals considered former political strategies and searched for a new road map to overcome this political vacuum. As an outcome of this period, in the late 1980s some ex-leaders of the FUP and exiled leftist Alevi youth established a new social-democratic organisation which would be more concerned with problems of "being immigrant" in Germany rather than with the issues of their country of origin (Sökefeld/Schwalgin 2000: 13).

Towards the end of this period, in 1988, the most crucial point was reached when an independent small circle, *Alevi Kültür Grubu* (the Alevi Culture Group – ACG), gathered in Hamburg to discuss possible strategies to reveal *Alevi*

---

27 In the May Day demonstration in Germany in 1990, for example, a group of Alevis who want to participate in the demonstration with a placard which said "Freedom for Alevi Doctrine" was blocked by members of a Turkish leftist organisation (Tosun 2000: 113).

Gerçeği (the Alevi Reality) at home and abroad. Almost all the members were ex-members/leaders of the FUP. At the same time, some of them were also members of the Association of Turkish Social Democracy and volunteers for the *Deutsch-Ausländische Begegnungsstätten* (the German-Foreign Association of Cultural and Social Exchange – GFA) founded by the city council of Hamburg (Sökefeld/Schwalgin 2000: 15).

In the light of their experiences in the GFA, they noticed that the newly emerging multicultural context in European allows a particular identity to become a form of positive social capital.[28] With this inspiration, as a first step for revealing the question of Alevism in the home-land and Europe, they drew up a bi-lingual declaration which would clearly give voice to their demands on behalf of Alevism. This declaration was announced on the opening day of the first Alevi Culture Week organised by the ACG in December 1989. During this week, they also announced the establishment of the Hamburg Alevi Culture Center (HACC) as a new organisational model which focuses on the question of Alevism and migration. This was also the first association which used the name of "Alevi" as an organisational title in the history of Alevism. Some sentences from the declaration may be enlightening for understanding their initial motivation:

Alevism, nearly with 20 million participants, is a branch of living Islam in Turkey… Alevis disguise their identity because of anxieties about being excluded by Sunnis… Alevism is not a new trend; it is a cultural heritage hundreds of years old… A foreign worker is able to be a migrant worker in the case that both his/her society and German society accept the phenomenon of migration. This is the same for Alevis. It is necessary that he/she should accept him/her self as Alevi and the others should be acquainted with their Aleviness… We understand differences in society as dynamic of society… In the country that we are living in, fragments of Christianity, Catholicism and Protestantism, are living in harmony and even in solidarity. We believe that Alevis and Sunnis, one day, will reach this kind of tolerance (Manuscript[29] – 1989).

With these words, Alevis, as citizens of Turkey and as immigrants in Germany, proclaimed their problems in their home and host-land by directly referring to their particular identity which was invisible on these national spaces. Moreover, this declaration also points to their position of "double liminality" in the sense that they have certain difficulties because of their identity as Alevi in Turkey and as Alevi and immigrant in Germany (Mandel 1989). Another significance of this declaration is its transnational characteristic. After being announced in Germany,

---

28 For instance, the S.O.S Rassismus and the Beur is Beautiful movements of the 1970s are frequently mentioned by the current leaders of the Alevi Confederation to indicate their source of inspiration for a new strategy to reveal Alevi identity in Europe.

29 By 'manuscript', I refer to announcements and press releases issued by the organisations mentioned. To the best of my knowledge, the content of these documents were only partially and indirectly covered by the media, so I have quoted directly from the sources I have collected.

the declaration was 'exported' to Turkey through personal networks and published in *Cumhuriyet* newspaper with some retouches at the beginning of 1990. In this sense, although it is rarely known, the declaration written by ACG was the first version of the "Alevi Declaration" which is recognised as the milestone of the Alevi movement in Turkey (Kaleli 2000: 174).

This first phase of 'revival' ended with an unexpected incident. A mob, provoked by Islamist-fundamentalists, attacked the *Pir Sultan Abdal* commemoration festivals on the 2nd of July, 1993 in Sivas. In this incident, thirty-seven people died and of those thirty-three were Alevi. Alevis perceived this attack as another 'massacre' in reference to the bloody conflicts at the end of 1970s. The Sivas is a very critical turning point for the Alevi movement both in Turkey and abroad reinforcing the feeling that Turkey has become a "lost home-land" (Kaya 2000: 102). Under this extraordinary circumstance, Alevi Cultural Centres (ACC) could establish a complete hegemony over Alevism in opposition to some local and highly religiously-oriented Alevi initiatives.[30] On October 30th 1993, ACCs convened the 2nd General Assembly with the participation of 36 sister chapters from Germany and changed the name of FAC to *Avrupa Alevi Birlikleri Federasyonu* (the Federation of European Alevi Unions – the FEAU).[31] After the Sivas, transnational cooperation between the European and Turkish Alevi movement has also become much more institutionalised.

Transnational Cooperation between Turkish and German Alevi Associations – *Transforming Home*

During the long decade of the Alevi movement in the 1990s, the newly emerging Alevi movement managed to generate a powerful discourse serving to uncover the question of Alevism both in Turkey and Europe. The main fields of associational activity in this period can be categorised under six interrelated topics:

- *Defining and Framing Identity*: As an initial outcome of the 'forgetting' in the 1960s, one of the most urgent tasks was to define Alevism in order to answer the question of "who are we?" In view of the complexity of the question, the Alevi movement inevitably drifted into a "framing

---

30 In contrast to new Alevi intellectuals of the period arguing "Alevis should turn their faces toward Europe" (Sökefeld 2004: 11), these local initiatives were in favour of keeping a low-profile to avoid the politicisation of Alevism.
31 The FEAU was established in Germany in 1994 with the participation of 140 Alevi associations represent 30,000 Alevis from all over Europe. Many of these associations were established just after Sivas. This is the process which is known as the 'mushrooming period'. By this concept, I refer to a five-year-period between 1993 and 1998 in which a remarkable increase in the numbers of Alevi associations experienced. In this period, the number of Alevi associations in Germany increased from 20 to 140.

contest" (Massicard 2003: 3). In opposition to Turkish and Kurdish nationalists attempting to redefine Alevism ethnically, political Islamists tried to inject/eject Alevism into/from Islam, Kemalists desired to mobilize Alevism against a rising political Islam, leftists expected to take advantage of being linked to Alevism, and religiously-oriented *dede*s looked forward to restoring their status in the community.

- *Organising Panel Discussions*: In relation to "framing contest", panel discussions on theological, historical, ethnic, and even political origins of Alevism were the most frequent and prestigious activity. Especially during the early period of the 1990s, a number of intellectuals were invited from Turkey on the basis of their expertise on Alevism.
- *Organising Cultural Courses*: Almost all associations tended to hold a variety of courses such as *saz* (musical instrument) and *semah* (ritual dance) to transfer the Alevi culture to new generations. Organising a course, however, has never been an easy task due to the lack of local expertise and of financial resources to invite professionals from Turkey.
- *Organising Religious Rituals*: Due to rising demands for religious services, almost all associations tend to organise *cem ayini*s and to employ a *dede*. At the beginning of 1990s, European associations invited *dede*s from Turkey through personal networks. However, as a result of disharmony between 'Turkish' *dede*s and 'European' audiences, associations have turned to European *dede*s who are much more familiar with the expectations of Alevis in Europe (Sökefeld 2002; Dumont 1997: 146).[32] Due to the seriousness of the problem of defining and framing Alevi identity, employing a *dede*, who would be able to be flexible in adapting his view of Alevism in accordance with the association's approach, became a very important asset for new Alevi leaders who need to gain a secular control over religious issues.
- *Organising Concerts*: Concerts are specifically useful for raising funds to buy a new building, to support sister associations in Turkey and to improve infrastructures and/or building *cemevi* in home-villages in Turkey (Rittersberger-Tılıç 1998).
- *Issuing Reports*: Especially in the mid-1990s, some Alevi villages experienced brutal treatment by Turkish Special Forces operating against the Kurdish separatists in Sivas, Erzincan, Tokat and Ordu. The FEAU from Germany and *Pir Sultan Abdal Kültür Derneği* (Pir Sultan Abdal Cultural Association – the PSKAD) from Turkey issued several reports on these events in the framework of human right violations. The FEAU also con-

---

32 For instance, in a cem ritual that he participated in 1986 in Strasburg, Dumont witnessed that a dede needed to be prompted to complete the ceremony since it was one of the first rituals he was invited to supervise after many years (Dumont 1997: 144).

veyed these reports to the European Court of Human Rights (Şahhüseyinoğlu 2001: 385, 391).
- *Organising Burial and Funeral Services*: Funerals of Alevis were among the most traumatic experiences in Europe. Contrary to the situation in Turkey, where religious institutions were under the control of the state, in Europe, each Islamic community can establish a religious centre based on their particular understanding of Islam. Due to lack of their own centres, Alevis had to apply to Sunni-owned centres for having burial services. This situation renders them open to pejorative discriminations. One frequently hears sad stories of the rejection of an Alevi funeral by Sunni-owned centres on the grounds that Alevis do not attend mosques.[33] Consequently, establishing their own internment and funeral centres is always very important for Alevi associations in Europe (Gül 1999: 115).

These associational activities can be summarised as an attempt to redefine and reframe Alevism as a particular identity based on the new context of immigration. In addition, European and Turkish Alevi associations also have been working to institutionalize transnational relations between the home and host-lands. *Alevi Bektaşi Temsilciler Meclisi* (the Council of Alevi-Bektashi Representatives – the CABR) was established in 1994 as an initial result of this search for transnational cooperation. In its statutes, the CABR was defined as the only organisation which is authorised to speak on behalf of Alevis both in Turkey and abroad (Şahhüseyinoğlu 2001: 294).

Another remarkable cooperation between European and Turkish Alevi associations was the establishment of *Barış Partisi* (Peace Party, PP) in the mid-1990s. This project was actually advocated by Germany-based Alevi federation so as to proclaim the demands of Alevis in Turkey.[34] In fact, they were aiming to apply a well-known political strategy which is commonly practiced in Europe. This political party would be established in order to withdraw just before the election, or members of this party would participate in the election as independent candidates. In both cases, their demands would be raised on the national level by taking advantages of the election period.[35]

---

33 During my field research, I was told at many times that one of the most common expressions Alevis encounter is "diriyken gelmezsiniz anca ölünce gelirsiniz" (you don't come [to mosque] when you are alive but only when you die).
34 For example, the chairman of the FEAU (then he was elected as a MP from the Republican Party in Turkey), Ali Rıza Gülçiçek, says "If we have had eighty MPs in the parliament [in Turkey], we could have expressed our demands by shouting [not by murmuring]" (Şahhüseyinoğlu 2001: 328).
35 This joint project concluded with a discouraging conflict between Turkish and European Alevi associations when the Turkish side of the project attempted to act independently. The Alevi Federation in Germany constituted an inspection committee to investigate this process.

The FEAU also attempted to establish cooperative relations among Alevi associations on the European level. They invited leading Alevi associations from all over Europe to the 7th General Assembly on November 28, 1998, in Cologne (Kaleli 2000: 76). With the participation of Alevi associations from Austria, France, Denmark, England, Switzerland, the Balkans and the Netherlands, they agreed on the establishment of a federation in each participant country which would also be organised under the European Alevi Confederation. This was done in order to coordinate the struggle to raise the issue of Alevism on the European level in 2000. Parallel to the establishment of the Confederation in Cologne, in 2002 the CARB was transformed into a new organisational body, the *Alevi-Bektaşi Federasyonu* (the Federation of Alevi-Bektashi – the FAB), with the participation of hundreds of local or national associations from all over Turkey. The most remarkable outcome of this process appeared as the first transnational and multi-lingual campaign, "Yes to a Democratic Turkey on the Way to the European Union", organised to state the Alevi views on Turkey's accession process to the EU. The campaign was started at the European Parliament in Brussels on May 5, 2004 by the CEAU and the FAB (Alevilerin Sesi, May 2004: 14-15). It was signed by ten member federations: Austria, Belgium, Denmark, England, France, Germany, Norway, Switzerland, Sweden and the Netherlands, and Turkey as a representative of the home-land. In the proclamation, they declare their support for the accession of Turkey to the EU with a 'big but' which demands official recognition of Alevis in Turkey as a particular identity (Manuscript – 2004).

In conclusion, the confederation can be considered as an example of "an affirmative 'politics of recognition', voicing demands in order to be recognised as a specific group and to obtain equal participation" (Massicard 2003: 91). It "serves as a bridgehead between political parties or movements in Turkey and organisations in other European Countries" (Østergaard-Nielsen 2003: 81). In this sense, the CEAU can be seen as a proper example of a transnational (immigrant) organisation. Østergaard-Nielsen states that "political institutions in the sending state" and "the receiving country's particular political institutional context […] has been heralded as central actors in shaping the field of transnational political practices" (2003: 20, 23). In this sense, to understand the transnationalisation of Alevi communities in the form of the CEAU, Turkey as a sending country, Germany as a receiving country, and Alevis as an immigrant group, all these should be considered as a single unit of analysis.

Fields of Transnational Alevi Community: Turkey and Germany

Living in Turkey has always held specific difficulties for Alevis in terms of expressing and practising their belief and identity. In accordance with the constitutive principles of the Republic, Turkish socio-political life has been closed to any particular identity rather than "Turkish" since the very early days of Modern Turkey. As we have seen, Alevis could participate in Turkish public life by articulating their demands through secular-leftist politics during the period of silence until the late 1980s. These demands were basically to push for proper application of the secularism principle, to have the "right to be equal" before the constitution and to gain protection against rising nationalist-Islamist threats. Furthermore, a considerable rupture in the relationship with "authentic" Alevism and its social institutions has also left Alevi communities voiceless in answering the question of "who are we?" especially for the younger generations born in new urban contexts.

In contrast to Turkey, where the "non-person" status of Alevis was maintained, Germany has provided Alevis with significant opportunities for expressing and practising their belief and identity especially after the 1980s (Schiffauer 1995). In other words, "had there been less restriction on freedom of thought, expression, and organisation in Turkey, Turkish society might have looked politically more like its simulacra in Europe today" (Ercan-Argun 2003: 30). From a different and plainer angle, Europe means liberation of all kinds of "anthropological diversity" from any suppression and restriction of the home-land (Kastoryano 2000: 127). In this sense, the socio-political context of Germany plays a unique role in the formation of immigrant transnationalism, especially for those suppressed in Turkey.

To understand this role, certain particularities of the German context should be mentioned. First of all, based on the *ius sanguinis* principle, German citizenship is defined as an "ethno-cultural exclusionist" regime in which "foreign migrants find it difficult to obtain full citizenship rights and thereby join the national community" (Koopmans/Statham 1999: 661). In other words, since the concept of *gastarbeiter* (guest-worker) refers to a temporary stay (Kastoryano 2000: 27), German immigration policy indirectly causes institutional marginalisation for immigrants. They can be a part of the labor market but, at the same time, they are also excluded from the political and social spheres (Wilpert 1990: 90). As a result of this institutional marginalisation, immigrants "remain strongly tied to their homelands which might in turn strengthen the position of home-land based organisation" and "they organise and identify themselves on the basis of their national origin" and "the politics of homelands" (Koopmans/Statham 1999: 667, 691). At the same time, the "formalistic inclusion" system of Germany channels immigrant communities to restructure their organisational model and redefine the way of defining their identity so as to have access to certain legal rights and public resources to perform and practise their beliefs (Koopmans et al. 1992). For instance, the highest legal status for the religious communities, *Körperschaft des öffentlichen Rechts*, has remarkable importance as such, any community aims to benefit from certain rights and social funds has to be recognised with this status (Massicard 2003: 19).

During the 1980s, traditional "neutrality towards all different religions and denominations" overlapped with rising multiculturalism (Massicard 2003: 7-9) and opened a new space for immigrants in Germany. In contrast to the well-known motto of German immigration policy, *Deutschland ist kein Einwanderungsland* (Germany is not a country of immigration), Castles considers this articulation as the emergence of de facto multiculturalism on the basis of an ethnically defined national citizenship (*ethnos*) and a democratic state (*demos*) (2000: 136). In this context, the concept of *Gemeinde* (community) does not just refer to a kind of social network among immigrant communities but also to a kind of identification tool for carving out a niche for one's group in host-societies. This means that the only condition for claims-making appears as to define their position as a minority community in Germany (Kastoryano 2000: 53; 96). The modification of the association constitution of Berlin Anatolian Alevi Culture Centre can be given as an example to illustrate how this challenging functions. When the directors of the association decided to apply for the right of denominational religious instruction at Berlin schools, the title of the association was needed to be changed from a secular one to *Glaubensgemeinschaft* (religious community) so as to be eligible to apply for this right (Sökefeld 2004a: 14-15).

In conclusion, institutional socio-political marginalisation in addition to German-type multiculturalism blended with a bi-denominationalist tradition "has resulted in policies that favoured and encouraged ethnic and religious differentiation among migrants" and "heterogenisation and deprivation of religion and ethnicity" among Turkish immigrants in Germany (Ercan-Argun 2003: 69). Thus, Alevism has been transformed "by Alevis themselves into a kind of denomination on the Christian model" by underlining the differences between Alevism and Sunni-Islam (Massicard 2003: 12). In other words, Alevism has gradually been repositioned by new Alevi intellectuals on the model of Protestant-Catholic dichotomy to emphasize their difference from Sunni-Islam during the 'revival' period in Germany.[36] For instance, Alevism has begun to be represented as a "humanitarian face of Islam" (Çakır 1998: 63), especially, with the rise of Islamophobia in Europe (Halliday 1999) which also overlapped with an increasing concern about the rise of political Islam in Turkey. Consequently, the Alevi movement in Germany is organisationally less divided and is discursively more inclined to define Alevism as a belief out of the circle of Islam (*İslam dışı*) than the Alevi movement in Turkey (Massicard 2003: 13) because this difference (or *différance*) is the *raison d'être* of their legal existence in the German context.

---

36 Turgut Öker, the chairman of the confederation, states that "Alevism is a bridge for peace between Islam and Christianity". (Alevilerin Sesi, February 2004: 32). Actually, the identification of Alevism with Protestant Christianity is not new or rare. As Baykurt quotes, when an Alevi immigrant woman decided to get married with a Protestant Greek man, her family introduced their Protestant son-in-law to their relatives in the village in Turkey by saying "He is not a stranger, he is a Greek Alevi" (Baykurt 1998: 174).

The changing nature of global context has also played a certain role in the transnationalisation of Alevi communities. The appearance of new advancements in transportation and communication technologies has enabled more intensive and constant engagements among immigrant and non-immigrant communities which are scattered over distant locales (Portes et al. 1999; Foner 1997; Vertovec 2004: 220). In this shrinking world, the restructuration of the global economic system on the basis of neo-liberalism, de-industrialisation and the withdrawal of welfare state increased the vulnerability of immigrants. As a result, they became much more dependent on their social networks as an economic survival strategy (Basch/Glick Schiller/Szanton Blanc 1992; Faist 2000). The emergence and the empowerment of international and supra-national institutions, such as the UN and EU, enabled previously disadvantaged groups to proclaim their particularistic demands by by-passing national border and categories (Kriesberg 1997: 4). As a result of these transformations in the global context, as Nuhoğlu-Soysal indicates, immigrants can "make particularistic claim through universalistic discourse" and "mobilisation of claims takes place at different levels" such as local, national and transnational (Nuhoğlu-Soysal 2000: 7; Faist 2000: 240).

As a result of these transformations, the question of locality in the age of globalisation has become fragmented as "the circulation of interaction, goods, and populations" (Appadurai 2003: 338) gaining a transgressive momentum "through a static and unchanging notion of space" (Kaplan 1996: 146) and "in the midst of these displacements, new concerns over borders, boundaries, identities, and locations arise" (ibid. 101). The main outcome of this process appears as the locales "substantially divorced form their national context" resulting from new forms of practices and relations such as marriages and exchanges in the migratory context. These "divorced" single locales, however, fused into a new embeddedness what Appadurai calls "translocalities" (2003: 339). Ong conceptualises the condition of this emergence as "the processes of disembedding from a set of localised relations in the homeland nation and re-embedding in new overlapping networks that cut across borders" (ibid. 2003: 87).

Conclusion: From the Invisibility of Locales to the Visibility of the Transnational

The unexpected appearance of the concept of "Non-Sunni Muslim Minority" in the Regular Report 2004 is interwoven into the matrix of a multifaceted historical background in which Alevism has been redefined and restructured on the basis of certain restraints and opportunities in relation to various struggles and negotiations on local, national and transnational levels. This concept, however, refers to a striking increase in the (trans-)national visibility of Alevis in the last two decades which is usually understood as the "Alevi Revival". Instead of backing this essentialist approach of 'revival', which tells a story about the spontaneous return of what was forgotten, I propose to understand this phenomenon as a 're-capture' of what has already been there. Speaking concretely, it is possible to assume that Alevism has been reconstructed as a new social identity during the long historical period which began in the 1950s. During this period, Alevis played the most important role by shuttling their life and culture, ideas and stories, identities and labels, fears and expectations, money and goods back and forth between Turkish and German contexts which are also subject to the spirit of our age – globalisation. Therefore, it seems quite reasonable to argue that the reconstruction of Alevism is inscribed in the transnationalisation of Alevi immigrant communities.

The appearance of the concept of "Non-Sunni Muslim Minority" is a direct outcome of this process.[37] In this sense, I also propose to understand the Germany-based Alevi movement as a transnational organisation of Euro-Alevis. From the same point of view which Europeanises Islam and Turks, Alevis can also be portrayed as a group of people who came from outside and stayed inside with their distinctive identity which has also been "culturally adjusted to the civic culture of modernity" (Tibi 2002: 37). Alevi organisations in Germany found a very fertile ground for gaining an important experience of the new global political climate in which immigrant communities have unexpectedly become an active actor in international as well as domestic politics (Shain 2005). As a result of their superiority arising from this spectacular experience and financial well-being, the Germany-based Alevi movement has also become the "agenda-setter" for Alevi associations in Turkey and Europe (Avcı 2005: 204).

In conclusion, it can be argued that Alevism has been transformed by Euro-Alevis from a locally invisible *Gemeinde* into a transnationally visible *Glaubensgemeinschaft* after several phases of their history. These phases are first, leaving home parallel to modernisation and industrialisation processes in which Alevis were subjected to inner or outer migration flows beginning in the 1950s, secondly, losing home in which Turkey as the home-land became 'lost' as a result of political polarisation and bloody conflicts which victimised Alevis at the end of the 1970s, thirdly, desiring home during the reconsideration period of the 1980s in which they searched for a new road map to uncover the question of Alevism in both Turkey and Europe, and fourthly, transforming home in which Alevis appear in the form of new social movements with wide transnational networks so as to struggle for the rights of Alevis in Turkey and to increase their visibility in Europe since the beginning of the 1990s.

---

37 It should also be mentioned that it is impossible to discuss the Alevi movement as a monolith and static entity. Apart from the main stream divisions, there are also many localised forms of the movement in Turkey and Europe. All these parties have very dynamic relationships with each other. Additionally, recent political developments in Turkey also make the emergence of a unified Alevi quite difficult. The "agenda-setter" characteristic of Germany-based Alevi movement is specifically focused in this paper to portray the historical background of the process. But, it is not easy to claim that this position would continue in the following years.

References

Ahmad, Feroz (1994) *The Making of Modern Turkey*, London: Routledge.

Aktaş, Ali (2000) "Kent Ortamında Alevilerin Kendilerini Tanımlama Biçimleri ve İnanç Ritüellerini Uygulama Sıklıklarının Sosyolojik Açıdan Değerlendirilmesi." *Alevi-Bektaşi*, August 14, 2001 (http://www.alevibektasi.com/tkent.htm).

Algül, Rıza (1999) *Geçmiş ve Gelecek Gözüyle: Alevilik İnsandan Başka İnsandır*, Istanbul: Can Yayınları.

Appadurai, Arjun (2003) "Sovereignty without Territoriality: Notes for a Postmodern Geographies." In: Setha M. Low/Denise Lawrence-Zúñiga (eds.) *The Anthropology of Space and Place: Locating Culture*, Oxford: Blackwell, pp. 337-349.

Avcı, Gamze (2005) "Religion, Transnationalism and Turks in Europe." Turkish Studies 6/2, pp. 201-213.

Bal, Hüseyin (1997) *Alevi-Bektaşi Köylerinde Toplumsal Kurumlar, Burdur ve Isparta'nın İki Köyünde Karşılaştırmalı Bir Araştırma*, İstanbul: Ant Yayınları.

Basch, Linda/Glick Schiller, Nina/Szanton Blanc, Cristina (1992) "Transnationalism: A New Analytical framework for Understanding Migration." In: Linda Basch/Nina Glick Schiller/Cristina Szanton Blanc (eds.) *Towards a Transnational Perspective on Migration: Race, Class, Ethnicity, and Nationalism Reconsidered*, New York: New York Academia of Sciences, pp. 1-10.

Baykurt, Fakir (1998) "Ege'de Bir Tahtacı Köyü: Alamut." Alevilik Araştırmaları 1/1, pp. 168-174.

Birge, John Kingsley (1965) *The Bektashi Order of Dervishes*, London: Luzae & Co. Ltd.

Çakır, Ruşen (1998) "Political Alevism versus Political Sunnism: Convergences and Divergences." In: Tord Olsson/Elizabeth Özdalga/Catharina Raudvere (eds.) *Alevi Identity: Cultural, Religious and Social Perspectives*, Istanbul: Swedish Research Institute, pp. 63-98.

Çamuroğlu, Reha (1998) "Alevi Revival in Turkey." In: Tord Olsson/Elizabeth Özdalga/Catharina Raudvere (eds.) *Alevi Identity: Cultural, Religious and Social Perspectives*, Istanbul: Swedish Research Institute, pp.79-84.

Çamuroğlu, Reha (2000) *Değişen Koşullarda Alevilik*, İstanbul: Doğan Kitapları.

Castles, Stephen (2000) *Ethnicity and Globalization*, London: Sage.

Crowfoot, J.W. (1900) "Survivals Among the Kappadokian Kizilbash (Bektash)." The Journal of the Anthropological Institute of Great Britain and Ireland 30, pp. 305-320.

Demir, Murtaza (1999) "Anadolu Aleviliği ve Pir Sultan Abdal Kültür Derneğinin Konumu." Pir Sultan Abdal Kültür Sanat Dergisi 35, pp. 19-26.

Dumont, Paul (1997) "Günümüz Türkiye'sinde Aleviliğin Önemi." In: İlhan Cem Erseven (ed.) *Tuttum Aynayı Yüzüme Ali Göründü Gözüme: Yabancı Araştırmacıların Gözüyle Alevilik*, Istanbul: Ant Yayınları, pp. 141-161.

Eickelman, Dale F. (1989) *The Middle East: An Anthropological Approach*, Englewood Cliffs: Prentice-Hall.

Engels, Friedrich (2000) *The Peasant War in Germany*, New York: International Publishers.

Ercan-Argun, Betigül (2003) *Turkey in Germany: The Transnational Sphere of Deutschkei*, London: Routledge.

Erdemir, Aykan (2005) "Tradition and Modernity: Alevis' Ambiguous Terms and Turkey's Ambivalent Subjects." Middle Eastern Studies 41/6, pp. 937-951.

Ethem, İbrahim (1936) *İstiklal Harbinde Demirci Akıncıları (Gerilla)*, İstanbul: İstanbul Askeri Matbaası.

Ethem, İbrahim (1989) *Demirci Akıncıları, İbrahim Ethem Akıncı*, Ankara: Türk Tarih Kurumu Basımevi.

Faist, Thomas (2000) *The Volume and Dynamics of International Migration and Transnational Social Spaces*, Oxford: Oxford University Press.

Foner, Nancy (1997) "What is New about Transnationalism? New York Immigrants Today at the Turn of the century." Diaspora 6/3, pp. 355-376.

Geaves, Ron (2003) "Religion and Ethnicity: Community Formation in the British Alevi Community." *Koninklijke Brill NV* 50, pp. 52- 70.

Göker, Emrah (1999) *Reconstructing the political: A study on contemporary Alevi politics from a generative structuralist perspective*, unpublished MSc Thesis, Bilkent University, Ankara.

Grønhaug, Reidar (1974) *Micro-Macro Relations: Social Organization in Antalya, Southern Turkey*, Bergen Studies in Social Anthropology 7.

Gül, Zeynel (1999) *Dernekten Partiye: Avrupa Alevi Örgütlenmesi*, Ankara: İtalik Kitapları.

Halliday, Fred (1999) "'Islamophobia' reconsidered." Ethnic and Racial Studies 22/5, pp.892-902.

Hasluck, Frederick William/Hasluck, Margaret Masson Hardie (eds.) *Christianity and Islam under the Sultans*, Oxford: The Clarendon Press.

Jeffrey, Jurgens (2001) "Shifting Spaces: Complex Identities in Turkish-German Migration." In: Ludger Pries (ed.) *New Transnational Social Space: International Migration and Transnational Companies in the Early Twenty-First Century*, London: Routledge, pp. 94-109.

Jongerden, Joost (2003) "Violation of Human Rights and the Alevis in Turkey." In: Paul J. White/Joost Jongerden (eds.) *Turkey's Alevi Enigma: A Comprehensive Overview*, Leiden: Brill, pp. 71-89.

Kaleli, Lütfi (2000) *Alevi Kimliği ve Alevi Örgütlenmeleri*, Istanbul: Can Yayınları.

Kaplan, Caren (1996) *Question of Travel: Post-modern discourses of displacement*, London: Duke University Press.
Kaplan, İsmail (2000) "Avrupa'daki Alevi Örgütlenmesine Bakış." In: İsmail Engin/Erhard Franz (eds.) *Aleviler/Alewiten, Vol: 1, Kimlik ve Tarih/Identität und Geschichte*, Hamburg: Deutsches Orient-Institut, pp. 241-260.
Karpat, Kemal (1976) *The Gecekondu: Rural Migration and Urbanization*, Cambridge: Cambridge University Press.
Karpat, Kemal (2004) "Turkish Democracy at Impasse: Ideology, Party Politics and the third Military Intervention." In: Kemal Karpat (ed.) *Studies on Turkish Politics and Society*, Leiden: Brill, pp. 272-336.
Kastoryano, Riva (2000) *Kimlik Pazarlığı: Fransa ve Almanya'da Devlet ve Göçmen İlişkileri*, Ankara: İletişim Yayınları.
Kaya, Ayhan (2000) *Berlin'deki Küçük İstanbul: Diyaspora Kimliğinin Oluşumu*, Istanbul: Büke Yayınları.
Kaygusuz, İsmail (1991) *Aleviliğin İnançsal ve Toplumsal Yol Kardeşliği*, İstanbul: Alev Yayınları.
Kehl-Bodrogi, Krisztina (1997) "Introduction." In: Krisztina Kehl-Bodrogi/ Barbara Kellner-Heinkele/Anke Otter-Beaujean (eds.) *Syncretistic Religious Communities in the Near East*, Leiden: Brill, pp. 11-18.
Kehl-Bodrogi, Krisztina (2003) "Atatürk and the Alevis: A Holly Alliance?" In: Paul J. White/Joost Jongerden (eds.) *Turkey's Alevi Enigma: A Comprehensive Overview*, Leiden: Brill, pp. 53-70.
Kieser, Hans-Lukas (2001) "Muslim Heterodoxy and Protestant Utopia. The Interactions between Alevis and Missionaries in Ottoman Anatolia." Die Welt des Islams, New Ser. 41/1, pp. 89-111.
Koçan, Gürcan/Öncü, Ahmet (2004) "Citizen Alevi in Turkey: Beyond Confirmation and Denial." Journal of Historical Sociology 17/4, pp. 464-489.
Koopmans, Ruud/Kriesi, Hanspeter/Duyvendak, Jan Williem/Giugni, Marco G (1992) "New Social Movements and Political Opportunities in Western Europe." European Journal of Political Research 22, pp. 219-244.
Koopmans, Ruud/Statham, Paul (1999) "Challenging the Liberal Nation-State? Postnationalism, Multiculturalism, and the Collective Claims Making of Migrants and Ethnic Minorities in Britain and Germany." American Journal of Sociology 105/3, pp. 652-696.
Kosnick, Kira (2004) "'Speaking in One's Own Voice': Representational Strategies of Alevi Turkish Migrants on Open-Access Television in Berlin." Journal of Ethnic and Migration Studies 30/5, pp. 979-994.
Kriesberg, Louis (1997) "Social Movement and Global Transformation." In: Jackie Smith/Charles Chatfield/Ron Pagnucco (eds.) *Transnational Social Movements and Global Politics: Solidarity Beyond the State*, New York: Syracuse University Press, pp. 3-18.
Küçük, Hülya (2002) *The Roles of the Bektashis in Turkey's National Struggle*, Leiden: Brill.

Mandel, Ruth (1989) "Ethnicity and Identity among Migrant Guestworkers in West Berlin." In: Nancy Gonzales/Carolyn McCommon (eds) *Conflict, Migration, and the Expression of Ethnicity*, Boulder: Westview Press, pp. 60-74.

Massicard, Elise (2003) "Alevis Movements at Home and Abroad: Mobilization Spaces and Disjunction." New Perspective on Turkey 28, pp. 163-188.

Melikoff, Irene (1998) *Hacı Bektaş Efsaneden Gerçeğe*, Istanbul: Cumhuriyet Kitapları.

Naess, Ragnar (1990) "Being an Alevi Muslim in South-Western Anatolia and in Norway: The Impact of Migration on a Heterodox Turkish Community." In: Thomas Gerholm/Yngve Georg Lithman (eds.) *The New Islamic Presence in Western Europe*, New York: Mansell, pp. 174-195.

Neyzi, Leyla (2003) "The Alevi renaissance, Media and Music in the Nineties." In: Paul J. White/Joost Jongerden (eds.) *Turkey's Alevi Enigma: A Comprehensive Overview*, Leiden: Brill, pp. 111-124.

Nuhoğlu-Soysal, Yasemin (2000) "Citizenship and Identity: Living in Diasporas in Post-War Europe?" Ethnic and Racial Studies 23/1, pp. 1-15.

Ocak, Ahmet Yaşar (1996) *Babailer İsyanı: Aleviliğin Tarihsel Altyapısı Yahut Anadolu'da İslam-Türk Heterodoksisinin Teşekkülü*, İstanbul: Dergah Yayınları.

Okan, Murat S. (1999) *Etnisite, din ve kültür ilişkisi: Aleviliğin tarihsel boyutu ve Cem Vakfı örneğinde bugünü üzerine sosyal antropolojik bir değerlendirme*, unpublished MSc Thesis, Hacettepe University, Ankara.

Olsson, Tord (1998) "Epilogue: Scriptualizations of Ali-oriented Religions." In: Tord Olsson/Elizabeth Özdalga/Catharina Raudvere (eds.) *Alevi Identity: Cultural, Religious and Social Perspectives*, Istanbul: Swedish Research Institute, pp. 197-184.

Ong, Aihwa (2003) "Cyberpublics And Diaspora Politics Among Transnational Chinese." Interventions 5/1, pp. 82-100.

Ortaylı, İlber (1997) "Les Groupes Heterodoxes et L'administration Ottomane." In: Krisztina Kehl-Bodrogi/Barbara Kellner-Heinkele/Anke Otter-Beaujean (eds.) *Syncretistic Religious Communities in The Near East*, Leiden: Brill, pp. 203-225.

Østergaard-Nielsen, Eva (2003) *Transnational Politics: Turks and Kurds in Germany*, London: Routledge.

Öz, Baki (1996) *Alevilik Nedir?*, İstanbul: Dergah Yayınları.

Öz, Baki (2000) "Cumhuriyet'in Kuruluşunda Dersim Olayı Sonununa Kadar Alevilerin Durumu." In: İsmail Engin/Erhard Franz (eds.) *Aleviler/Alewiten Vol: 1, Kimlik ve Tarih/Indentität und Geschichte*, Hamburg: Deutsches Orient-Institut, pp. 35-62.

Portes, Alejandro/Guarnizo, Luis E./Landolt, Patricia (1999) "The Study of Transnationalism: Pitfalls and Promise of an Emergent Research Field." Ethnic and Racial Studies 22/2, pp. 217-237.

Rigoni, Isabelle (2003) "Alevis in Europe: A Narrow Path towards Visibility." In: Paul J. White/Joost Jongerden (eds.) *Turkey's Alevi Enigma: A Comprehensive Overview*, Leiden: Brill, pp. 159-173.

Rittersberger-Tılıç, Helga (1998) "Development and Reformulation of a Returnee Identity as Alevi." In: Tord Olsson/Elizabeth Özdalga/Catharina Raudvere (eds.) *Alevi Identity: Cultural, Religious and Social Perspectives*, Istanbul: Swedish Research Institute, pp. 69-78.

Şahhüseyinoğlu, H. Nedim (2001) *Alevi Örgütlerinin Tarihsel Süreci*, Ankara: İtalik Yayınları.

Schiffauer, Werner (1995) "From Exile to Diaspora: Transnational Islam in Europe." In: Aziz El Azmeh/Effie Fokas (eds.) *Euro-Islam at the Turn of the Millenium: Present Conditions and Future Perspectives*, London: Ashgate.

Şener, Cemal/İlknur, Miyase (1995) *Şeriat ve Alevilik: Kırklar Meclisi'nden Günümüze Alevi Örgütlenmesi*, Istanbul: Ant Yayınları.

Sezgin, Abdülkadir (1998) "Osmanlı ve Cumhuriyetin Kuruluşunda Bektaşiler ve Günümüzde Bektaşilik." Köpru 62, pp. 99-112.

Shain, Yossi (2005) *The Frontier of Loyalty*, Ann Arbor: University of Michigan Press.

Shankland, David (1993) *Alevi and Sunni in Rural Turkey: Diverse Paths of Change*, Unpublished PhD dissertation, Darwin College, Cambridge.

Shankland, David (1998) "Anthropology and Ethnicity: The Place of Ethnography in the New Alevi Movement." In: Tord Olsson/Elizabeth Özdalga/ Catharina Raudvere (eds.) *Alevi Identity: Cultural, Religious and Social Perspectives*, Istanbul: Swedish Research Institute, pp. 15-22.

Shankland, David (2003) "Social Change and Culture: Responses to Modernization in an Alevi Village in Anatolia." In: Paul J. White/Joost Jongerden (eds.) *Turkey's Alevi Enigma: A Comprehensive Overview*, Leiden: Brill, pp. 33-52.

Shindeldecker, John (2001) *Türkische Aleviten Heute*, Istanbul: Şahkulu Sultan Külliyesi Vakfi (also http://www.alevibektasi.org/john_almanca.htm).

Sinclair-Webb, Emma (2003) "Sectarian Violence, the Alevi Minority and the Left: Kahramanmaraş 1978." In: Paul J. White/Joost Jongerden (eds.) *Turkey's Alevi Enigma: A Comprehensive Overview*, Leiden: Brill, pp. 215-235.

Sökefeld, Martin (2002) "Alevi Dedes in the German Diaspora: The Transformation of a Religious Institution." Zeitschrift für Ethnologie 127, pp. 163-189.

Sökefeld, Martin (2004a) *Alevis in Germany and the Question of Integration*, paper presented at the Conference on the Integration of Immigrants from Turkey in Austria, Germany and Holland, Boğaziçi University, Istanbul, February 27-28, 2004.

Sökefeld, Martin (2004b) "Religion or Culture? Concepts of Identity in the Alevi Diaspora." In: Waltraud Kokot/Khachig Tölölyan/Carolin Alfonso (eds.) *Diaspora, Identity, and Religion*, London: Routledge, pp. 133-155.

Sökefeld, Martin/Schwalgin, Susanne (2000) *Institutions and their Agents in Diaspora: A Comparison of Armenians in Athens and Alevis in Germany*, paper

presented at the 6th European Association of Social Anthropologists Conference, Krakow, 26-29 July 2000.
Thomä-Venske, Hanns (1990) "The Religious Life of Muslim in Berlin." In: Thomas Gerholm/Yngve Georg Lithman (eds.) *The New Islamic Presence in Western Europe*, New York: Mansell, pp. 78-87.
Tibi, Bassam (2002) "Muslim Migrants in Europe: Between Euro-Islam and Ghettoization." In: Nezar al-Sayyad/Manuel Castells (eds.) *Muslim Europe or Euro-Islam*, Lexington Books, pp. 31-52.
Tosun, Halis (2000) *Alevi Kimliği ile Yaşamak*, İstanbul: İtalik Yayınları.
Tur, Derviş (2002) *Erkanname Aleviliğin İslam'da Yeri ve Alevi Erkanları*, İstanbul: Can (Adil ali Atalay) Yayınları.
Türkdoğan, Orhan (2004) *Alevi Bektaşi Kimliği*, Istanbul: Timas Yayınları.
Vergin, Nur (2000 [1981]) "Din ve Muhalif Olmak: Bir Halk Dini Olarak Alevilik." In: Nur Vergin (ed.) *Din, Toplum ve Siyasal Sistem*, İstanbul: Bağlam, pp. 66-83.
Vertovec, Steven (2004) "Cheap Calls: The Social Glue of Migrant Transnationalism." Global Networks 4/2, pp. 219-224.
Volkan, Vamık (1997) *Bloodlines: From Ethnic Pride to Ethnic Terrorism*, Boulder: Westview Press.
Vorhoff, Karin (1998) "Academic and Journalistic Publications on the Alevi and Bektashi of Turkey." In: Tord Olsson/Elizabeth Özdalga/Catharina Raudvere (eds.) *Alevi Identity: Cultural, Religious and Social Perspectives*, Istanbul: Swedish Research Institute, pp. 23-50.
Vorhoff, Karin (2003) "The Past in the Future: Discourses on the Alevis in Contemporary Turkey." In: Paul J. White/Joost Jongerden (eds.) *Turkey's Alevi Enigma: A Comprehensive Overview*, Leiden: Brill, pp. 93-109.
White, Paul J. (2003) "The Debate on the Identity of 'Alevi Kurds'." In: Paul J. White/Joost Jongerden (eds.) *Turkey's Alevi Enigma: A Comprehensive Overview*, Leiden: Brill, pp. 17-32.
Wilpert, Czarina (1990) "Religion and Ethnicity: Orientations, Perceptions and Strategies among Turkish Alevi and Sunni Migrants in Berlin." In: Thomas Gerholm/Yngve Georg Lithman (eds.) *The New Islamic Presence in Western Europe*, New York: Mansell, pp. 88-106.
Yaman, Ali (2000) "Anadolu Aleviliği'nde Ocak Sistemi Ve Dedelik Kurumu." Alevi Bektaşi, August 14, 2001, (http://www.alevibektasi.com/dedelik.htm).
Yörükan, Yusuf Ziya (1998) *Anadolu'da Aleviler ve Tahtacılar*, Ankara: Kültür Bakanlığı Yayınları.
Yürükoğlu, Rıza (1990) *Okunacak En Büyük Kitap İnsandır*, İstanbul: Alev Yayınları.
Zeidan, David (1999) "The Alevi of Anatolia." Middle East Review of International Affairs Vol: 3 No: 4, August 27, 2008, (http://www.ciaonet.org/olj/meria/meria99_zed02.html).

Periodics

"Milletvekilleri ile Buluşma." *Alevilerin Sesi* (February 2004, p. 32).
"Avrupa Birliği Yolunda Demokratikleşen bir Türkiye'ye Evet." *Alevilerin Sesi* (May 2004, pp. 14-15).
"Yeşiller Partisi Milletvekili Cem Özdemir ile Görüşme." *Alevilerin Sesi* (July 2004, p. 83).

Appendix

CABR: the Council of Alevi-Bektashi Representatives *(Alevi Bektaşi Temsil ciler Meclisi)*.
CEAU: the Confederation of European Alevi Unions *(Avrupa Alevi Birlikleri Konfederasyonu)*.
DPM: Democratic Peace Movement *(Demokratik Barış Hareketi)*.
FAB: the Federation of Alevi-Bektashi *(Alevi Bektaşi Federasyonu)*.
FEAU: the Federation of European Alevi Unions *(Avrupa Alevi Birlikleri Federasyonu)*.
FGAU: the Federation of Germany Alevi Unions *(Almanya Alevi Birlikleri Federasyonu)*.
FPR: the Federation of Populist Revolutionist *(Halkçı Devrimçi Feder asyonu)*.
FUP: the Federation of Union of Patriots *(Yurtseverler Birliği Feder asyonu)*.
HBVA: Hacı Bektaş Veli Associations *(Hacı Bektaş Veli Dernekleri)*.
PKK: the Kurdistan Worker's Party *(Partiya Karkerên Kurdistan)*
PP: Peace Party *(Barış Partisi)*.
PSKAD: Pir Sultan Abdal Culture Association *(Pir Sultan Abdal Kültür Dernekleri)*.
RPP: Republican People Party *(Cumhuriyet Halk Partisi)*
TUP: Turkey Union Party *(Türkiye Birlik Partisi)*.
UP: the Union of Patriots *(Yurtseverler Birliği)*.

Identity Politics as an Expression of European Citizenship Practice: Participation of Transnational Migrants in Local Political Conflicts

MICHAEL JANOSCHKA

Political Participation of Retired Migrants in Southern Spain and the Emergence of Local Political Conflicts

The increasing migration of retired northern Europeans to the coastal regions of the Mediterranean, mainly to Spain, is a remarkable phenomenon within the context of European integration. In contrast to traditional labour migrants, the key protagonists of these movements can be characterised as (mostly) affluent senior citizens, who migrate/move in order to fulfill a leisure- and outdoor-oriented lifestyle after retirement. Within the last decade, seasonal and temporary movements (to spend autumn and winter in Southern Europe) have been widely replaced by permanent migrations. Different statistical analyses give evidence that the coastal areas of Spain are the most important destination, followed by the French Riviera, Portuguese Algarve and Italian Tuscany (Casado-Díaz et al. 2004; Warnes 2001). Taking into account the various reasons for migration in Europe, this "amenity migration" of senior EU residents is a highly important and rapidly increasing practical experience of a borderless Europe.

Recent discussions concerning migration processes of (senior) EU residents have mainly been concerned with approaching the transnational social conditions of this specific type of migration (Ackers/Dwyer 2002; Casado-Diaz et al. 2004; O'Reilly 2000; Warnes et al. 2004). More than 750,000 of such migrants, coming principally from the EU-15 member states, are currently registered with coastal municipalities throughout Spain, and more than two thirds of them are within age of retirement (INE 2007). But the statistical data available do not track the record: Breuer (2003: 45) and Huber (2005: 328) confirm that a realistic estimation of northern European expatriates at least doubles the official data. Including the seasonal migrants, an estimated figure of two and a half to three million foreign senior residents live in Spain. Throughout Spain, many municipalities, especially in coastal areas of Andalusia, Valencia, the Baleares and the Canaries, count large numbers of foreign residents, in some case exceeding by far the figure for native inhabitants. These villages and towns are prototypes for wider areas of the Mediterranean coast and can be characterised as an important "social laboratory" for both the empirical study of senior migrations and a theoretically focused research approach regarding the outcome of the European political integration on a local and regional sphere. Given the fact that many of these "European residents", as they name themselves, belong to the economic elite and were successful professionals, they count on powerful tools, know-how and resources to integrate themselves and exercise leadership in a variety of areas within local politics, ranging from the formal representation in local parliaments to all kinds of informal participation settings, especially in areas or topics related to urban and regional planning (Durán 2004).

In an attempt to regulate urban development, the Spanish region of Valencia adopted a complex planning law in 1994 (the *LRAU*[1]). The stated purpose of the law was principally to give the municipalities in larger urban centres the legal authority to force reluctant, normally large-scale landowners to cede portions of their property, with the aim of providing space for low-cost housing (Sánchez de Madariaga 2003: 92pp). In summary, the law enables local authorities to change the assignment of land from agricultural use (where following national laws the construction of two-storey-houses on plots of at least 10.000 square metres is possible) to urbanizable land, whenever a developer wishes this. The promoters do not necessarily have to buy the future building plots, because a system of forced concessions lead to the situation where the private owner has to pay the investor all urbanisation and infrastructure costs deriving from urbanisation and concede additionally up to two thirds of the total area to the developer (Soriano/Romero 2004). However, in the last few years, it has become increasingly evident that the land laws, coupled with the expropriation powers, have been widely misused. Local councils are under pressure from promoters and developers who exploit the legal system to obtain land at low cost in order to build expensive holiday and retirement accommodation and get substantial economic returns. Many thousands of mainly foreign residents suffer under the consequences of this law. In 2002, some of the victims of the land law, decided to fight for their rights and founded an NGO named "*Abusos Urbanísticos No*[2]" with the aim of, via active political participation, achieving a moratorium against development plans in several municipalities and also in the region as a whole. As local and regional authorities did not show any cooperation or sympathy, they decided to de-localise this primarily local conflict and organised petitions directed at the European Commission, the European Parliament and the European Court of Human Rights. The embeddedness of several members of the NGO in important

---

1   LRAU is the Spanish abbreviation for "Ley Reguladora de la Actividad Urbanística".
2   This Spanish name means "No to urbanistic abuses".

networks of the transnational political elite led to success, and the queries were answered with frequent visits and reports by the Commission and the Parliament. A team of activists took up the challenge to fight for property rights as a full-time job and were able to convince several delegations from the European Union of the failures of the law. By vote of the Euro-Parliament on December 13, 2005, infringement proceedings against Spain were opened, and as a final consequence, a new law replaced the former Valencian land use law in 2006.

The case against the LRAU planning legislation and its local applications does not only show the political involvement and power of transnational elite migrants in political conflicts. European residents in Southern Spain were able to de-territorialize this local conflict and involve supranational institutions usually unknown in local conflicts, for instance making use of the formalised power of European institutions by exercising European citizenship rights. But the most important aspect, which will guide the conceptual discussion in this text is based on the fact that the foreign residents also managed to invent a commonly shared identity which is mainly based on "European" principles. Thereby, this paper will focus on the question of how identities are strategically used within the political conflict dealing with the local application of the land-use regulations. It will provide a conceptual analysis of the role of "European" identity politics and identification processes within this political conflict and discuss how identity politics can be evaluated as a practical resource in this specific and transnational struggle.

The Shifting Spaces of Citizenship and the Decisive Role of Identity Politics

Elite migrants, such as the amenity-seekers in Southern Europe, are often referred to as a living example of the embodiment of a new transnational world (Favell 2003: 397pp). In this new world, citizens increasingly escape from some of the constraints of the old national systems. Different authors integrate this observation in the conceptualisation of what is named transnational social spaces or transnational social formations (Faist 2000; Smith/Guarnizo 1998). Within the European Union, the ratification and implementation of the Treaty of Maastricht did not only expand the freedom of residence, mobility and labour, but also established new forms of citizenship which contest the common understanding of national citizenship (Wiener 1998: 7pp). Citizenship rights such as the possibility to vote and to be a candidate in municipal elections do not exclusively relate to a static national concept any longer (Day/Shaw 2002), but include political participation in different societal settings. As a consequence, authors such as Mitchell (2003: 397p) believe in a rising process of national de-consolidation and defend the de-territorialisation of democratic participation.

As Jackson et al. (2004) emphasise, in a globalising world many social relations are increasingly stretched out across the borders of nation states. Consequently, urban politics and social movements are also becoming more and more transnational. Following their main ideas concerning the geographies of transnationalism, three different perspectives on transnational studies (from "above", "below" and "between") can be differentiated. While studies of transnationalism "from above" are associated with the impact of supranational political institutions, transnationalism "from below" is commonly understood as the incorporation of different forms of local resistance, e.g. via grassroots activism (Jackson et al. 2004: 8p). According to Smith (2001), transnationalism "from between" is regarded as a permanently reconstructed product of political and cultural practices, involving transformations of individual and daily (political) practices. This approach can be evaluated as an effort to conceptualize the transformations within a global world, without the necessity to refer to Luhmann's conceptualisations of "world society" (Luhmann 1991). Despite its inspiring analysis of social systems, recently interpreted within the framework of geography and geographical migration studies (Pott 2005; Goeke 2007), adaptations of system theory still mainly focus on macro-scales and a systemic perspective. As discussed in the introduction to this volume, process-oriented approaches, which concentrate on the analysis of individual constructions such as this contribution, may better fit into a conceptualisation which is based on the broader debate on transnationalism.

In this regard, recent discussions from Global City research and political theory concentrate on the changing role of the national state in a transnational world (cf. Barnett 2003; Davidson 2000; Low 2004; Vandenberg 2000). One of the central arguments is that the growing importance of transnational European economic, cultural and political interaction is leading to a post-national era with the subsequent formation of a European civil society through daily practices and routines (Finke/Knodt 2005: 11pp). Post-national power positions include different forms of governance, ranging from the local up to the transnational levels, which may contest institutionalised links between social power positions and the nation state (Held 1995; Mann 1993). Cosmopolitan individuals like elite (senior) migrants with a wide variety of lifestyles, political ideas and options, are the prototypes of a new "transnational citizen", disintegrate nationally-confined organisational spheres, both from "above" and from the "bottom", and establish new forms of flexible social control and power (Faist 1998).

Lepofsky and Fraser (2003: 127) argue that the rising flexibility in practical uses of citizenship goes hand in hand with a transformation of its theoretical conception. Post-modern or post-national citizenship includes more than just only a collection of rights, but is also a powerful discursive mechanism which articulates identities and which has shifted from a given status to being a performative act. This idea leads to the question discussed in this paper of how citizenship may be important for claiming the rights to the city, the production of space and the participation in (local) political conflicts about urban space. According to Rose (2001: 474), citizenship is currently shifting from being a possession towards being a capacity of "citizenship practice" (Wiener 1998: 7). Considering citizenship as a practice, it includes the connotation of increasing flexibility in identity. Postnational or European citizenship as an expression of the rising role of Europe also causes potential problems with identities, which traditionally were discussed as bound to the invented community of a nation (Anderson 2006).

In a transnational world with multiple migration patterns, cultural and political identities are a commonly shared social construction which is constantly destabilised (Hall 1996). All social subjects are constituted through cultural hybridisation (Bhabha 1996). At the same time meanwhile they refer to a strategic use of essential cultural concepts, e.g. within political resistance. Essentialisation with the use of empty signifiers is a necessity within hegemonic relations, in order to establish the possibility of representation (Mouffe 2002). Stuart Hall (1997) offers two possible reactions of identity politics in response to the weakening of the national state. One possible response regresses towards a defensive and aggressive nationalism, which searches for the establishment of new social power relations through the essentialisation of cultural identities. The other way of dealing with the menace of loss of stable identities implies an integrative action with the strategic application of new cultural patterns. Identity politics, by means of contesting traditional identification processes, is the base for social and political innovation. This is despite the fact that all political actions, for instance, require temporary fixations of our flexible identities (Krauß 2001: 21pp). Within political activities in a globalised environment with a wide variety of transnational ties and meanings, questions of cultural identity play an increasing role in political action. Identity politics, as representations of social and spatial meanings, offer the opportunity for political coalitions and a commonly shared basis for action in political conflicts.

The Social Construction of Europe and European Identities

Following Benedict Anderson (2006: 15pp), each community with a larger scope than face-to-face groups, has to be conceptualised as an imagined community. That is the reason why communities should not be differentiated by their authenticity but rather through the hegemonic way in how they are imagined (Wodak et al. 1998). In contrast to many European nation states, Europe can be neither clearly recognised – nor can its geographical borders even be defined. As a consequence, the hegemonic discourse about Europe and European identity is still widely contested (Quenzel 2005: 5pp). Different authors argue that this aspect contains the problem of Europe, as a discursive product without complete national functions (Wiener 1998: 8pp). Different and partly exclusive dimensions and ideas about Europe and its identity are being negotiated within the media and the political system and involve a variety of controversial debates. Authors such as Nissen (2006: 155pp) understand the European identity as the collective identity of EU citizens in relation to the Union institutions, while Loth (2002: 93pp.) interprets European identity as one flexible possibility of identification based on shared traditions. In his conceptualisation of Europe, Bach (2000) refers mainly to the bureaucratic elite located in the administrative and political institutions and provides a conceptual analysis of the transnational networks of administrative restructuring processes resulting from the proliferation of European institutions. Puntscher Riekmann and Wodak (2003) propose the theoretical argument that any politcies which refer to Europe and its identity, simply make strategic use of the same theoretical constructions as used in national discourses. From this point of view, European identity is just one layer between many others, which can be used to unify any kind of community. For the political utility of collective representations of (European) identities, as is the case in the political participation of foreigners in Southern Spain, two aspects should be considered: First, collective identities cannot be thought of without the existing power relations and can be interpreted as expression of or protest against them. Secondly, identities should be evaluated as politically motivated engagement and representation, which regularly build on a commonly shared emotional basis and which activate the integration of the group itself.

Any construction of European identities always contains positive and negative aspects, as identity must always be thought of as the binary opposition of identity and difference. Every process of identification always comes back to an inscribed difference, which is constitutive of every positive statement. Following Stuart Hall (1996: 4), "identities are constructed through, not outside difference", which implies that any positive identity is only possible "through the relation to its Other". This theorem is deducted from Derrida's radical de-constructivism (Derrida 2004), political thoughts about social power (Laclau/Mouffe 1985) and feminist theory of Judith Butler (1990). It is also the basic starting point for the possible use of European identities in political conflicts such as those foreign residents are engaged in Southern Spain. In this context, Gudrun Quenzel (2005) offers an interesting overview of the different possibilities of Europeanness. Her contribution applies Stuart Halls' ideas of the constructive Other (1997: 223pp) in order to defend the position that Europe is constituted both through internal and external Others. Aspects, which derive from positive identity constructions such as "Civilisation and technical advancement", "Christendom", "European values" or "Aesthetic community always imply an inscribed difference to internal and external Others, who are marked as less or not European. These constructions establish the analytical framework for the empirical discussion of the strategic use of identity politics and "Europeanness" as the expression of a commonly shared identity in the conflict over land use and the expropriation powers of local authorities in Southern Spain.

Between Formal and Informal Forms of Political Participation: European Identities as a Practical Resource of (retired) Elite Migrants in Local Political Conflicts

A common hypothesis proposes that the recent strengthening of the European institutional frame, the increasing mobility of European citizens and the formal possibilities for transnational political participation within Europe develop automatically and result in European civil society. But different analyses of municipal data show, for instance, that the formal political participation of EU-citizens abroad is extremely low (Jacobs et al. 2004; Strudel 2004). Adrian Favell (2005), who conducted qualitative research on the political interests and involvement of highly mobile foreign professionals in London, Brussels and Amsterdam concludes that these "Eurostars" do not show no more major interest in the municipal voting rights granted to EU citizens, even if they are locally social active, possess social capital and have only minor language problems, than traditional labour migrants. Apparently, it is not the right to vote which encourages the political participation of foreigners. It seems instead that rather the symbolical signs and codes that control the access to local politics keep even foreigners with perfect language skills away from active interaction with the local political elites. In the words of Pierre Bourdieu, this exclusion means that the capital of cultural practices bound to the field of local politics are so restrictively controlled and monopolised by the traditional elites, that foreigners are discouraged from participating actively in political life abroad (Bourdieu 1989). Mahnig (2004: 35p) interprets this exclusion of migrants from political participation as a typical and systemic attitude of governmental structures and regimes. This poses the interesting question of why and how specific governance contexts give power to foreigners. Diehl (2002: 5pp) argues that within local politics, ethnicity may play a decisive role, although it is less relevant if it reflects symbolic, invented or even fictional ethnicity. If political integration follows ethnic topics and specific groups can identify the representation with shared cultural symbols, the establishment of ethnic motivations can be a successful way to gain influence in local politics.

Most of the ideas referred to are a helpful tool for the theoretical and empirical analysis of the political participation of foreign residents in the Mediterranean. But it is evident that other conditions also play a decisive role:

- In contrast to the centres of the European economy and administration such as London and Brussels which are a magnet for highly mobile urban professionals, the Mediterranean attracts mainly retired people who did not move as a step in their career, but came for the lifestyle maximisation.
- Elderly residents show a major interest in local and regional political questions, have more time to engage in local politics and count on knowledge and experience in organisational tasks. Age, gender and nationally

- bound behaviours are important factors in the daily practice of political participation of foreign EU residents in the Mediterranean.
- Political participation is evaluated as a form of formal and informal social engagement abroad, especially in cases including "interpretation" between communities, e.g. via the application of language skills.
- National, regional and especially local governance regimes play a key role in the motivation for the participation of foreign residents. In cases when the residents disagree with political regimes and the way decisions are taken or communicated, they are highly interested in taking an active role in their municipality. This explains the high regional variation in exercising the right to vote in local elections held in Spain in 2003 and 2007 respectively.
- Given the fact that many of the "European residents", as the senior migrants in Spain call themselves, belong to the economic elite and were successful professionals, they count on powerful tools, know-how and resources to integrate and assume leadership in local politics, ranging from formal representation in local parliaments to all kinds of informal participation settings. Migrants from northern Europe have founded their own parties in many municipalities and are currently active politicians in an increasing number of local councils.

Within the Costa Blanca region, which is the "home zone" of political participation of retired EU foreigners in Spain and the protest against the regional planning regulation, there are about two dozen municipalities. In these municipalities where European residents have taken an active part in the formal political system, being elected local councillors and playing a major role in the local political decision making. Cultural aspects and identity politics subsequently emerge as part of this participation, as the following statement from a councillor in a village with a vast majority of foreign residents, mainly Germans, shows: "Yes, I told our *Alcalde*[3] once, when he said to me: 'Hey, you must learn better Spanish!' So I told him: 'No – you must first learn German, don't you? (laughs) You are here mayor of mainly Germans.'" (Wilfried R.)

Although the statement sounds ironical, it also expresses the councillor's own desire for a greater role in all questions regarding the representation of German citizens in his village. On the other hand, there are other examples where the formal political scene reacted to the threats of foreign political participation. In Teulada-Moraira, an elite beach resort of about 12,000 inhabitants with more than 70 per cent foreigners, a new locally based party put in place a policy of full political integration of foreigners. "Europe" as a daily practice was the strategy to achieve a shared vision of a hometown with multiple transnational social ties. The participation of foreigners in important positions of the local council (e.g. vice Mayor, Head of the Department of Finance, Head of the Department of

---

3 Alcalde is the Spanish word for Mayor.

Ecology) led to a win-win-situation for both social and the administrative life, while local conflicts were subsequently de-escalated, by using a common "European" identity: "Here we have a Europe in a pocket design, and especially this European idea has been realised here. Total integration, no? And we all are working here to improve our place to live, our region. What we wanted, was exactly this. We are a little Europe here." (Sylvia T.)

The statement cited shows how actors in local politics try to realize an integrative vision of future local development through recourse to a "European" vision, although expressed as a fairly vague idea. Identity politics explicitly using the notion of an empty signifier called "Europe", helped to establish a basis for the political integration of various foreign groups. By strategically using this empty concept of a European identity, every individual can imagine different aspects of how this concept may be filled within a context. But an important aim was to eliminate all conflicts between foreigners and the native population. The strategic use of "Europeanness" does not only mean symbolic participation of foreigners, but also leads to a re-definition of local development strategies. In contrast to other villages, the actors involved in the local governmental institutions recognised early the social dynamite that was behind the cited land law application and had established as early as the year 2001 a moratorium on all building permits. Within a participative process of a Local Agenda, which was held in six different European languages, different development lines for the municipality were established, mainly focusing on upgrading the local development by the proliferation of primarily high quality housing. As a consequence, since 2002, no cases of abuses related to the application the LRAU land law were reported in this village – a very different and striking situation as compared with the surrounding areas.

European Identities as a Practical Resource of Elite (Senior) Migrants in Local Political Conflicts: The Case of Parcent

Although many studies focus on the formal political involvement of foreign residents in European cities, it is the "informalisation" of the contribution of foreigners which emerges as a recent "key policy issue in European cities" (Fennema/Tillie 2004: 85). Authors such as Salzbrunn (2001) show that the expression of the political interests of migrants is not reflected in the common and formal modes of participation. Especially, the possibility of internet based media use (e.g. blogs), enables and de-locates new forms of participation and identity politics. But how does this informal political participation work in different contexts, what can be learnt from the conflict over the abuse of the land use regulations in Southern Spain, looking again at the role of "Europe" and "European identities" in the conflict?

As mentioned in the introduction, February 1, 2006 was an important date for the tens of thousands of signers of the petition that was presented by the NGO *"Abusos Urbanisticos No"* at the European Parliament. By this date, the new land use regulations had been applied in the region of Valencia and the former LRAU was replaced. But promoters and developers were able to convince, in more than 120 cases, the municipal authorities to authorize new development projects by granting building permits for more than 60.000 new houses, chiefly through parliamentary decisions taken in the last days of January 2006. Three of these highly disputed decisions took place in Parcent, conceding a construction company owned by the Spanish music star Julio Iglesias, the right to construct more than 1,800 houses on a highly attractive hillside outside the current village of only 900 inhabitants, a fairly disproportionate size for such tiny village. Following LRAU land law application, more than 50 (mainly foreign born) neighbours living currently within the development area and also about 35 (mainly native) landowners, producing citrus fruits in the valley mainly on small agricultural plots, received the official claim for paying high fees to the developer and lose important parts of their land. The following quotation from one of the interviews explains how the law worked on a "micro scale":

"We had no letters, no notification, nothing, neither the Spanish landowners nor any of the mainly foreign owners of the 50 houses. We heard nothing. So, we pressed and got a meeting with the town hall, with the *alcaldesa*[4] and with the technical officer, Ignacio. In this meeting Ignacio, the architect, explained to us that this plan had been submitted on the LRAU. And he said, well, on the LRAU first of all, you will have to pay a contribution towards the infrastructure. And not just for my road, for my house. But as a proportion of the total area. So whatever the cost of the infrastructure is for the whole area, you must pay according to the size of your plot. And we asked him how much this might be. And he indicated with a shrug of his shoulders: Well, on a kind of rocky mountain side, a range of around about 75 Euros per m², is normal, you know. So, a very quick calculation: You know, I have got 1,500 m² here, that is gonna make a bill of over 100,000 Euros. Then he goes on to explain: On top of that, on the LRAU you must contribute...., all the landowners of the area, because the developer within the plan has to set aside 30% for public open space, for green space, a certain amount for public use, like a school or health centre or something. You must all contribute to that as well, as a proportion of the plot size. And that could be 30-40% of your plot. And I said, well, what is the use of me giving 300 meters in that corner of my garden, it is no use for anybody. And he said: No, no, not like that. But you have to pay if you want to keep it. So on top of the 100,000, I was gonna have to pay a lot of money to keep my own land. We protested, [...but], the mayor just shrugged and said: "*¡Es la ley!*"[5] – You understand Spanish? So we came away, very angry, very upset and the first thing we did was, get together, inform the residents." (Mark H.)

---

4   Spanish expression fort he mayoress of the village.
5   The Spanish expression means: "This is the law!"

Threatened with significant economic damage and the annihilation of the physical environment, the neighbours decided to set up a locally organised protest movement in order to respond to the publication of the plans in late 2004. The protest strategies of the association can be divided into two phases: Until the decision of the local government, all protest was locally based and tried to stop the project by convincing politicians to vote against the plans. After the decision in favour of the plan, the conflict was strongly de-localised, organising juridical and political protest in the provincial capital Alicante, the capital of the Autonomous region of Valencia, the national capital Madrid and at the European institutions in Strasburg and Brussels. It was exactly the combination of carefully designed protest strategies with legal actions, which finally led in October 2006 to a decision of the Supreme Court in Valencia, stopping the plan due to a number of illegal aspects in the whole procedure.

The following analysis centres on the local conflict and the strategic use or construction of an array of "differences" as expression of identity politics within the struggle against the planned urbanisation of the local hillside. Despite the fact that the protest movement was organised by foreign European residents (mainly British citizens), they achieved a broad coalition with native inhabitants, including local farmers, environmental organisations and even a xenophobic movement of the nationalist regional party. The analytical aspects are derived from a series of interviews with local citizens, activists, and politicians and also consider information available in published newsletters, flyers, websites and newspaper articles. But the main arguments will be presented in the words of the leader of the local neighbourhood association. His interpretations and representational schemes are key elements for the development of this conflict, as it was him who was constantly negotiating with the potential investors and the local administration over many months.

All the arguments of the protest movement are based in a permanent process of identification, which has a typical pattern. Following Stuart Halls' perspectives on identity politics, it is important to consider that, within the discursive action, constructions of different elements of European identity are contextualised through the constitutive "Other" of the protest – which is mainly the coalition of municipal leaders and land developers. Following this perception, different identity politics – mainly centred in the dichotomy Europe vs. Spain:Valencia: Parcent – can be identified and will be discussed.

One central interpretation of this conflict, being highly representative of similar situations in other villages, takes into consideration the question of how democratic participation and the will of the inhabitants are respected. The reference frame is always analogous to this statement and implies aspects such as corruption and non-participatory democracy, comparing local authorities and political structures with the Other which can be labeled as "British":

"I thought that this was really nice, that you could walk up to the town hall and you could ask for information, you could meet the mayor walking in the street. And for the first year or so, you know, I met the mayor a couple of times and *"Hola Mark. Como estás? Ah, muy bien..."*[6] uh, and I thought, this is really nice. What a nice way to run a village. But of course once you get involved in something like this and you realize just how devious they are, how uh, undemocratic they are, you suddenly realize that actually, a lot of the problems here stems from the fact, that there are just so few people who run the council. When there is only four people against three people on the council, if those four people get together and decide on a particular course of action, or, as if some of those are corrupted in whatever way by developers or anything else, uh, then you suddenly find that, that democracy just doesn't exist at all." (Mark H.)

At this point and without mentioning any directly European aspect, it is clearly understandable that normative concepts of how democracy should work within Europe are implicitly engaged in the meaning of his statement. The prototypical situation of many small villages is reflected in the following statement of another foreign resident who is politically active in a local government.

"In this government with seven seats, we own four of them. That also means that I had to take my responsibility in participating in governing. And that was a desolation to be honest. Just because you became aware how poorly it was organised. How it is a matter of, uh, "be nice to friends and be hard to the other half". That's not my system. Democracy doesn't mean dictatorship of the majority. That's not my view. Democracy is not-, I always say it's not *la dictadura de los quatros*[7]. It's not fair. You need to listen to the others and really consider what they say and if they have better ideas, implement the better ideas but do not create another dictatorship." (Jan T.)

The expressions give clear hints that local politics in the region do not reflect what the self-identified group of European residents considers as proper democracy. The retired elite migrants, many of them with experience in local politics in their home countries, have clear ideas of the local failures due to their well established internal principles of how democracy should work:

"I retired from local government in Southeast London when I was 50 years old. I was part of the chief executive department of a big council in Southeast London. I studied law, though I wasn't a lawyer, I just studied law at university and then became an administrator really. And, I was very involved in the political processes. One of my jobs was to provide the services to the council for meetings, the committees and the council itself. I also did a lot of work on public consultations over new policies, new programs, part of my job was as head of public relations as well. So I was constantly familiar with organising meetings for the public, informing public, providing information to the pub-

---

6 Imitation of a prototypical situation, when meeting someone on the street, saying: "Hello Mark, how are you? Fine, everything okay?".
7 In English, this statement means "the dictatorship of the four (governing politicians)".

lic, dealing with the press, dealing with the media, all that kind of thing. So, I came with this background of understanding the way that democracy works. [...] When I came to Spain, I very quickly found that certainly in Parcent, and I suspect in a lot of the little villages, it doesn't work anything like that." (Mark H.)

The sequence from the biographical story shows two of his personal principles in relation to public administration: (i) confidence in the procedures of state action based in the laws and (ii) confidence in trustworthy public relations and participatory commitment at a local level. This normative concept of democracy, in the light of his professional career, is the interpretational basis for his valuation of the democratic system in Spain and explicitly in the village in question. His hegemonic normative point of view, his Londoner perspective, is loaded with aspects such as development versus backwardness and leads to a negative evaluation of everything which is different from his own cultural background – conceptualised as "British" and "European". The following statement develops this argument:

"It is taking me a long time to realize and understand what goes on in a village like Parcent. But as someone coming from Britain and someone who used to work in local government in Britain, you bring with you a kind of European concept of democracy and fairness and consultation and honesty and trust with politicians and all of those. Even in Britain, Politicians aren't always a 100 per cent trustworthy. But when you deal with them here long enough, what you realize is, that you have to clear your mind of any ideas that you brought with you from England or Germany or Holland, wherever you might come from. And start thinking Spanish because they just don't accept or understand any of those principles." (Mark H.)

The culturally interpreted discrepancies that lie behind this interpretation lead to a wide essentialist point of view: (Political) values defined as typically British, Western European or cosmopolitan become the "European" standard and are used as the reference point for all criticism of the local politics. The argumentation is based on the superiority of his point of view and the resemblance between the British and European identities. The expression of his identity politics gain importance through the discursive unification he applies by combining the concept of "European democracy" with aspects such as fairness, honesty and trust within politics. In order to express his ideas of European identity, he refers to a spatially defined "core of Europe", formed by countries such as Britain, Germany or The Netherlands. This implies a location of Spain as the constitutive internal Other of his identity construction. Whoever comes to Spain, has to re-program his understanding of politics, because the usual "European" values do not work there. From the point of view discussed by the activists, the reason seems to be easy: Spaniards do not respect the European way of governing. This is his central argument for discursively excluding Spain from any kind of European identity and values. But where does he locate Spain and Spanish democracy?

"The problems here stem not just from the political situation but from the structure of the council and the way these councils operate. In Britain, and I am sure it is the same in Europe, there is a separation of power, even in local government. There you have professional paid officers of the council. And then you have the politicians. The politicians take the policy decisions, but the officers operate the law and tell the politicians what they can and can't do within the law. What happens here is, that distinction doesn't exist at all. The mayor in the town hall and the councillors basically see themselves as the bosses of the offices. If an officer says, by law you really should be doing this, the mayor just says: Oh, we are not interested! Forget it, we are doing it this way! You know, I was often in this position with politicians in England, I would sit with the politicians and I would say: I don't give a damn, if you are the leader of the council, the mayor or anyone. I am the paid officer, I am telling you legally you cannot do that and you will not do it. But here, that doesn't exist. (…) The people in power run the town hall as if it was their own little empire. You know, the mayor is treated like a god-type figure. And it is almost as if Franco was still here." (Mark H.)

Following his reasoning, a central aspect of the deficiencies of the "non-European" Spanish democracy is concerned with the role of politicians and officers. He draws an image of the Spanish administration that indicates the lack of separation of powers such as established since the French revolution, trying to exclude again Spain from a supposed European way of governing. The image is one of the remarkable and essential differences in local politics between the village he lives in and his reference frame, which is the city council of Greater London. Beyond the absence of separation of powers, he describes an image of quasi-dictatorship and links this to "Spanish" political thinking and actuality that implies a belief in the absolute authority of the mayor as the local leader. He describes Spanish administration in a pitiful condition and links it to the dictatorial past of the country, when the mayor was installed by the central government. Again, this argument points to an essential European value, which is proper democracy. As not being fulfilled in the particular village government, he constructs an image of dictatorship in order to strip the local politicians of all possible moral legitimacy.

The examples quoted demonstrate that any use of identity politics within this local conflict takes three important dimensions into consideration: (i) the discursive construction of a commonly shared identity using "Europe" as the central positive identification, (ii) the discursive construction of Spanish politics as the internal Other which contests the positive identity through an inscribed difference and (iii) the discursive construction of a geographical representation of normative ideas through its location at the "core" of Europe, where Spain is excluded twice through the combination of cultural values with spatial aspects. This arrangement offers a highly coherent frame for the constitution of an interest group that acts on the local political scene.

Conclusion

The political conflicts over land use regulations in Southern Spain, analysed in this text, show the different meanings of transnational political action and the flexibility of belonging. Supranational institutions such as the European Parliament or the European Court of Human Rights, which represent new possibilities for an activation of transnational power structures in local conflicts within Europe, play a decisive role in the struggles against local politicians. Institutional power is accompanied by the array of citizenship rights granted to foreign residents in Spain as a result of the enlargement of the European Union. Rights to appeal at the higher European institutions as well as the right to an active and passive vote in local election, transform the legal starting point for any protest movements by European residents living abroad. It is only the legal framework, which constitutes European citizenship rights and allows for the de-localisation of the conflict over misuse of local planning laws. But it is important that, considering the political involvement and the activation of individuals, it is not the formal European frame that is considered as a major resource in identity politics. Although legal, the European institutions and possibilities for political participation are constantly applied, the central discursive references and the social construction of conflict strategies, however, regard European values as a practical resource to activate citizens and form pressure groups. These "European" identity politics play a decisive role in all aspects concerning social mobilisation in relation to the conflict.

Regarding broader theoretical discussions of the dissemination of "transnational" values, lifestyles or political culture within different migration settings, the conclusions remain less optimistic: It is important to consider that, with exception of the discussion presented in the elite beach resort Teulada-Moraira, all analysed identity politics are not developing towards any kind of transnational political culture. Moreover, the political activism can be evaluated primarily as protest against traditional local politics in Spanish municipalities by means of the organisation of a lobby group. This group makes use of the transnational power relations established by the EU legal framework and the interconnection of the political activists with the EU framework, but they do not extend to other spheres of public life. Any transnationalism regarded in this chapter is highly selective: While the personal sphere and daily organisation of the amenity migrants is clearly located within each language group (e.g. British, Dutch or German), "transnational spaces" occur or are organised around certain, well established values of civil society and political organisation. But the example also shows that discursive mechanisms including "Europe" are one important reference scheme primarily that arise in conflicts and include the "education" of the regional social and political setting, emphasising a "colonial" aspect of European structures and values.

In consequence, transnational political practices arise both around official structures and concepts of any transnationally interpreted identities and identification. They set up a flexible framework for the discussion of European citizenship which can be evaluated as a practical resource or capacity of certain subjects. Both the daily practice of "Europe" and the conceptual discussion within social sciences assign to provide European identity a prominent place in order to respond to flexible conceptualisations of citizenship and identities. Such approaches and empirical conclusions coincide with some of the principal ideas of transnationalism theories, in this case primarily in the political sphere, and express the necessity of the transnational framework in order to re-consider the practical implications of European citizenship which was observed in political struggles.

References

Ackers, Louise/Dwyer, Peter (2002) *Senior Citizenship? Retirement, Migration and Welfare in the European Union*, Bristol: The Policy Press.

Anderson, Benedict (2006 [1983]) *Imagined Communities: Reflections on the Origin and Spread of Nationalism*, London: Verso.

Bach, Maurizio (2000) "Die Europäisierung der nationalen Gesellschaft? Problemstellungen und Perspektiven einer Soziologie der europäischen Integration." In: Maurizio Bach (ed.) *Die Europäisierung nationaler Gesellschaften*, Wiesbaden: Westdeutscher Verlag, pp. 11-35.

Barnett, Clive (2003) *Culture and Democracy. Media, Space, and Representation*, Edinburgh: Edinburgh University Press.

Bhabha, Homi (1996) "Culture's In-Between." In: Stuart Hall/Paul Du Gay (eds.) *Questions of Cultural Identity*, London/Thousand Oaks/New Delhi: Sage Publications, pp. 53-60.

Bourdieu, Pierre (1989) *La noblesse d'Etat: grandes écoles et esprit de corps*, Paris: Editions de Minuit.

Breuer, Toni. (2003) "Deutsche Rentnersiedlungen auf den Kanarischen Inseln." Geographische Rundschau 55/5, pp. 44-51.

Butler, Judith (1990) *Gender Trouble: Feminism and the Subversion of Identity*, London/New York: Routledge.

Casado-Diaz, María Angeles/Kaiser, Claudia/Warnes, Anthony (2004) "Northern European retired residents in nine southern European areas: characteristics, motivations and adjustment." Ageing & Society 24/3, pp. 353-381.

Davidson, Alastair (2000) "Fractured Identities: Citizenship in a Global World." In: Ellie Vasta (ed.) *Citizenship, Community and Democracy*, Houndmills: Basingstoke/London: Macmillan Press, pp. 3-21.

Day, Stephen/Shaw, Jo (2002) "European Union Electoral Rights and the Political Participation of Migrants in Host Polities." International Journal of Population Geography 8/2, pp. 183-199.

Derrida, Jaques (2004 [1972]) *Die différance. Ausgewählte Texte*, Stuttgart: Reclam.

Diehl, Claudia (2002) *Die Partizipation von Migranten in Deutschland. Rückzug oder Mobilisierung?*, Opladen: Leske+Budrich.

Durán, Rafael (2004) "Political Involvement of Older European Migrants in Southern Spain." In: Anthony Warnes (ed.) *Older Migrants in Europe. Essays, Projects and Sources*, Sheffield: Sheffield Institute for Studies on Ageing, pp. 47-50.

Faist, Thomas (1998) "International Migration and Transnational Social Spaces." Archives Européennes de sociologie/European Journal of Sociology 39/2, pp. 213-247.

Faist, Thomas (2000) "Transnationalization in International Migration: Implications for the Study of Citizenship and Culture." Ethnic and Racial Studies 23/2, pp. 189-222.

Favell, Adrian (2003) "Games without Frontiers? Questioning the Transnational Social Power of Migrants in Europe." Archives Européennes de Sociologie/ European Journal of Sociology 44/3, pp. 397-427.

Favell, Adrian (2005) "European Citizenship in Three Eurocities", January 26, 2006 (http://aei.pitt.edu/3096/02/austin2.doc).

Fennema, Meindert/Tillie, Jean (2004) "Do Immigrant Policies Matter? Ethnic Civic Communities and Immigrant Policies in Amsterdam, Liège and Zurich." In: Rinus Penninx et al. (eds.) *Citizenship in European Cities. Immigrants, Local Politics and Integration Policies*, Aldershot: Ashgate, pp. 85-106.

Finke, Barbara/Knodt, Michèle (2005) "Einleitung: Zivilgesellschaft und zivilgesellschaftliche Akteure in der Europäischen Union." In: Michèle Knodt/Barbara Finke (eds.) *Europäische Zivilgesellschaft. Konzepte, Akteure, Strategien*, Wiesbaden: VS Verlag für Sozialwissenschaften, pp. 11-28.

Goeke, Pascal (2007) *Transnationale Migrationen. Post-jugoslawische Biografien in der Weltgesellschaft*, Bielefeld: transcript.

Hall, Stuart (1996) "Introduction: Who Needs 'Identity'?" In: Stuart Hall/Paul Du Gay (eds.) *Questions of Cultural Identity*, London: Thousand Oaks/New Delhi: Sage Publications, pp. 1-17.

Hall, Stuart (ed.) (1997) "The Spectacle of the Other." *Representation. Cultural Representations and Signifying Practices*, London: Sage, pp. 223-290.

Held, David (1995) *Democracy and the Global Order. From the Modern State to Cosmopolitan Governance*, Cambridge: Polity Press.

Huber, Andreas (2005) "La migración de retirados entre culturas. El caso de los jubilados suizos en la Costa Blanca." In: Tomas Mazón/Alejandro Aledo (eds.) *Turismo residencial y cambio social. Nuevas perspectivas teóricas y empíricas*, Alicante: Editorial de la Universidas de Alicante, pp. 325-340.

Instituto Nacional de Estadísticas, Spanish National Statistical Institute (INE) (2007) "Padrón Municipal al 1 de enero del 2006. Madrid." April 10, 2007 (www.ine.es).

Jackson, Peter/Crang, Philip/Dwyer, Claire (2004) "Introduction. The Spaces of Transnationality." In: Peter Jackson/Philip Crang/Claire Dwyer (eds.) *Transnational Spaces*, London/New York: Routledge, pp. 1-23.

Jacobs, Dirk/Phalet, Karen/Swyngedouw, Marc (2004) "Associational Membership and Political Involvement Among Ethnic Minority Groups in Brussels." Journal of Ethnic and Migration Studies 30/3, pp. 543-559.

Krauß, Andrea (2001) *Einwürfe. Identität und Identitätspolitik bei Judith Butler*, Berlin: Stiftung Sozialpädagogisches Institut Berlin.

Laclau, Eernesto/Mouffe, Chantal (1985) *Hegemony and Socialist Strategy: Towards a Radical Democratic Politics*, London: Verso.

Lepofsky, Jonathan/Fraser, James (2003) "Building Community Citizens: Claiming the Right to Place-Making in the City." Urban Studies 40/1, pp. 127-142.

Loth, Wilfried (2002) "Die Mehrschichtigkeit der Identitätsbildung in Europa. Nationale, regionale und europäische Identität im Wandel." In: Ralf Elm (ed.) *Europäische Identität: Paradigmen und Methodenfragen*, Baden-Baden: Nomos Verlaggesellschaft, pp. 93-110.

Low, Murray (2004) "Cities as Spaces of Democracy: Complexity, Scale and Governance." In: Clive Barnett/Murray Low (eds.) *Spaces of Democracy. Geographical Perspectives on Citizenship, Participation and Representation*, London: Sage Publications, pp. 129-146.

Luhmann, Niklas (1991) "Die Weltgesellschaft." In: Niklas Luhmann (ed.) *Soziologische Aufklärung 2. Aufsätze zur Theorie der Gesellschaft*, Opladen: Westdeutscher Verlag, pp. 51-71.

Mahnig, Hans (2004) "The Politics of Minority-Majority Relations: How Immigrant Policies Developed in Paris, Berlin and Zurich." In: Rinus Penninx et al. (eds.) *Citizenship in European Cities. Immigrants, Local Politics and Integration Policies*, Aldershot: Ashgate, pp. 17-37.

Mann, Michael (1993) *The Sources of Social Power*, Cambridge: Cambridge University Press.

Mitchell, Katharyne (2003) "Educating the National Citizen in Neoliberal Times: from the Multicultural Self to the Strategic Cosmopolitan." Transactions of the Institute of British Geographers 28/4, pp. 387-403.

Mouffe, Chantal (2002) "Which Kind of Public Space for a Democratic Habitus?" In: Jean Hillier/Emma Rooksby (eds.) *Habitus: A Sense of Place. Second Edition*, Aldershot: Blackwell, pp. 109-116.

Nissen, Sylke (2006) "European Identity and the Future of Europe." In: Maurizio Bach/Christian Lahusen/Georg Vobruba (eds.) *Europe in Motion. Social Dynamics and Political Institutions in an Enlarging Europe*, Berlin: edition sigma, pp. 155-174.

O'Reilly, Karen (2000) *The British on the Costa del Sol. Transnational Identities and Local Communities*, London: Routledge.

Pott, Andreas (2005) "Kulturgeographie beobachtet. Probleme und Potentiale der geographischen Beobachtung von Kultur." Erdkunde 59/1, pp. 89-101.

Punscher Riekmann, Sonja/Wodak, Ruth (2003) "Europe for all – diskursive Konstruktionen europäischer Identitäten." In: Monika Mokre/Gilbert Weiss/ Rainer Bauböck (eds.) *Europas Identitäten. Mythen, Konflikte, Konstruktionen*, Frankfurt/New York: Campus, pp. 283-303.

Quenzel, Gudrun (2005) *Konstruktionen von Europa. Die europäische Identität und die Kulturpolitik der Europäischen Union*, Bielefeld: transcript.

Rose, John (2001) "Contexts of Interpretation: Assessing Immigrant Reception in Richmond, Canada." The Canadian Geographer 45/4, pp. 474-493.

Salzbrunn, Monika (2001) "Transnationale soziale Räume und multidimensionale Referenzsysteme westafrikanischer MigrantInnen in der Pariser Region." In: Alexander Horstmann/Günther Schlee (eds.) *Integration durch Verschiedenheit. Lokale und globale Formen interkultureller Kommunikation*, Bielefeld: transcript, pp. 95-112.

Sánchez de Madariaga, Ines (2003) "Aktuelle Tendenzen in der spanischen Raumordnung." Planungsrundschau 3/6, pp. 92-105.

Smith, Michael Peter (2001) *Transnational Urbanism: locating globalization*, Oxford: Basil Blackwell.

Smith, Michael Peter/Guarnizo, Luis (1998) "The Locations of Transnationalism." In: Michael Peter Smith/Luis Guarnizo (eds.) *Transnationalism from below*, New Brunswick: Transaction Publishers, pp. 3-34.

Soriano, José/Romero, Carlos (2004) *El Agente Urbanizador*, Madrid: Iustel Publicaciones.

Strudel, Sylvie (2004) "La participation des Portugais aux élections européennes et municipales en France." Cahiers de l'Urmis 9, pp. 69-76.

Vandenberg, Andrew (2000) "Contesting Citizenship and Democracy in a Global Era." In: Andrew Vandenberg (ed.) *Citizenship and Democracy in a Global Era*, London/New York: MacMillan Press, pp. 3-17.

Warnes, Anthony (2001): "The international dispersal of pensioners from affluent countries." International Journal of Population Geography 7/6, pp. 373-388.

Warnes, Anthony/Friedrich, Klaus et al. (2004) "The Diversity and Welfare of Older Migrants in Europe." Ageing & Society 24/3, pp. 307-326.

Wiener, Antje (1998) *"European" Citizenship Practice. Building Institutions of a Non-State*, Oxford/Boulder: Westview Press.

Wodak, Ruth/Cillia, Rudolf de et al. (1998) *Zur diskursiven Konstruktion nationaler Identität*, Frankfurt: Suhrkamp.

Mothering in Migration: Transnational Strategies of Polish Women in Italy

GERMANA D'OTTAVIO

Polish women have established a long-standing and steady migratory flow in Italy that has mainly, but not only, met the demand for care and domestic workers in the country. While providing support mostly for the elderly, numerous migrant working mothers have to leave their children in Poland in order to find employment as care workers. Therefore, it is significant to analyse East-West European female mobility in order to understand its specific patterns, and how they modify mothering arrangements and their perception in emigration and immigration societies.

This article is based on qualitative research conducted between 2003 and 2005. It analyses the strategies of mothering in migration adopted by Polish care workers, and it explores intergenerational relationships in the household, articulating a theory concerning a double international presence of transnational migrant mothers.

International Transfer of Caretaking and Intra-European Migration during the EU-Enlargement Process

Migratory patterns have been developing steadily and rapidly in post-cold war Europe, shaping new and diverse pathways capable of triggering crucial social phenomena. In the last twenty years, the balance between the sexes in labour migration has shifted decisively towards women. Empirical studies have challenged the idea of a predominantly male migration associated with labour in a booming industrial sector during the 1950s and the 1960s. Sociological literature analysed the growth of a predominantly female migration especially from Central-Eastern European Countries (cf. Morokvasic 1983, 1984, 1991, 1992, 2004; Phizacklea 1983, 2003; Anthias/Lazaridis 2000; Friese 1995; Kofman et al. 2000). The service economy of the "global cities" (cf. Sassen 1998, 2002) has attracted and absorbed those migratory flows. Recently, this phenomenon has also become noticeable in towns, villages, and non-urban areas. This is especially true in Southern-European states (cf. King/Zontini 2000) where welfare policies are chronically inadequate to meet the increasing rate of women's participation in the labour market, and where household arrangements between the sexes have not modified the unequal burden of domestic chores shared between men and women. In a system marked by social and gender inequalities, polarisation processes are growing between an upper or middle-class in need of household assistance, and a migrant class that is willing to accept low income, time consuming, and emotionally demanding jobs. Moreover, ongoing intra-European migrations are adjusting the demographic balance in sending and receiving migrants' societies, and are increasingly connecting those areas by means of transnational mobility strategies. These are "occupations and activities that require regular and sustained social contacts over time across national borders for their implementation" (Portes et al. 1999: 219).

Eastern and Western Europe were separated but not definitely divided by the so-called "Iron Curtain". Therefore, new relations between areas previously unconnected fuelled an era of mass transportation on wheels. During the fall of the Soviet regime and in the post-1989 private business rush, many companies were been created to meet the cheap transport demand which is typical of a growing *migratory industry* (cf. Castles/Miller 1998) that brought thousands new economical opportunities in Western Europe (Okólski/Stola 1999; Okólski 2001; Wallace/Stola 2001; Wallace 2002). Political processes also are influencing the composition and direction of these migratory flows. The enlargement of the European Union (EU) is a contradictory process of which the long-term effects are still unknown. In the short term, citizens of the new member States[1] of Central Eastern Europe were granted the right to move freely across European borders. Nevertheless, the governments of many 'old' EU members have been concerned with the impact of workers' mobility on national social welfares systems and employment rates, to such an extent that EU institutions approved a discipline of transitory regimes, which divided the enlarged Union into three main areas.[2]

In Italy, among so-called neo-communitarian citizens, only tourists and autonomous workers have achieved a real freedom of movement, as it is still necessary to be included in the national quota system to have a salaried job.[3] The government decides every year how many people for each State or group of

---

1 In 2004 Poland, Czech Republic, Slovak Republic, Slovenia, Hungary, Lithuania, Latvia, Estonia, Malta and Cyprus; in 2007 Romania, Bulgaria.
2 It is a free movement zone, extending over Great Britain, Ireland, Sweden; a two years restricted zone, extending over Italy, France, Spain, Portugal, Greece, Norway; finally, a seven years restricted zone, extending over Germany, Austria, Belgium, Holland, Luxembourg, and Denmark. For more info: Accession Treaty signed on 16 April 2003 "Freedom of movement for workers after enlargement", July 29, 2007 (http://europa.eu/scadplus/leg/en/cha/c10524.htm).

States are able to work legally in the country and in what occupations they are entitled to work. Among those occupations, care and domestic work have been assigned an important share. In 2002 an amnesty law,[4] that paved the way for the new immigration regulations, showed the professional niche to which Polish migrants are confined: 75,8 per cent out of 25,002 requests were related to domestic labour (INPS 2004), a job that is mostly feminised, and where private families are employers. In 2003, Polish migrants were granted 34.980 residence permits, 25.282 to women and 9.698 to men.[5] The same year, 10.905 women and 6.453 men were entitled to work legally in Italy (ISTAT 2007). Despite the amnesty, the incidence of informal jobs is still very high, also because according to the last immigration law, only people with a contract can receive a residence permit; undocumented migrants therefore represent high numbers.[6]

This article focuses on circular migratory projects of Polish care workers who find new arrangements for mothering and who negotiate new meanings, and identities in the context of the international division of labour. The increasing demand for migrant women to help alleviate the reproductive labour of the growing number of working women in post-industrial nations provokes the formation of an international division of reproductive labour (Parreñas 2001a: 369) that is shaped by "[...] global capitalism, gender inequalities in the sending country, and gender inequalities in the receiving country." (Parreñas 2000: 569).

The international transfer of caretaking is a facet of the division of reproductive labour, and it refers to three groups of women in two different nations: middle-class women in receiving countries, migrant care workers, and other women (relatives or local domestics) in the sending country too poor to migrate.

In Central-European countries, as was stressed for the Philippines (Lindio-McGovernor 2003: 513), the economical measures imposed on the governments by the World Bank and International Monetary Fund affected local communities in the form of more austere social policies (cf. Deacon/Hulse 1997). This

---

3 "Documento programmatico relativo alla politica dell'immigrazione e degli stranieri nel territorio dello Stato per il 2004-2006", July 29, 2007 (http://www.governo.it/ Presidenza/DICA/ docprogrammatico_immigrazione.html).

4 Decreto-Legge 9 settembre 2002, n. 195 "Disposizioni urgenti in materia di legalizzazione del lavoro irregolare di extracomunitari" (issued after the immigration law L. 189/2002, so-called "Bossi-Fini", July 29, 2007 (http://www. stranieri.it/ attualita/ dl_migr/dl02_195/dl02_195.htm).

5 In 2001, Italian government issued 1.379.749 residence permits, 745.836 to men and 633.913 to women; Polish people received 30.419 residence permits, specifically 8.844 to men and 21.575 to women; working permits were 11.092 for women and 5.917 for men (ISTAT 2007).

6 Since the EU enlargement process, Eastern and Central European citizens cannot be considered undocumented migrants anymore, since a valid identity document is sufficient for internal border-crossing; however, the working permits are granted only to a limited number of people, thus the combination of documented legal status and employment in the informal sectors create new tensions and disadvantages for newcomers.

triggered new mobility flows. Women have emigrated from economical peripheries to the cores, contributing to a "global care chain" this means

[...] a series of personal links between people across the globe based on the paid or unpaid work of caring. A typical global care chain might work something like this: an older daughter from a poor family in a third World country cares for her siblings (the first link in the chain) while her mother works as a nanny caring for the children of a nanny migrating to a first world country (the second link) who, in turn, cares for the child of a family in a rich country (the final link). Each kind of chain expresses an invisible human *ecology of care*, one care worker depending on another and so on. A global care chain might start in a poor country and end in a rich one, or it might link rural and urban areas within the same poor country. More complex versions start in one poor country and extend to another slightly less poor country and then link to a rich country (Hochschild 2000:32).

However, the present study discloses a different aspect of the transnational transfer of care taking since the core's strategy is a continuous pattern of emigration, immigration, return, and re-immigration, wherein women attend to two households and two families in an alternate way. Therefore, the present study reveals how Polish women tend to be in "two places at the same time".

Why are those strategies necessary, and how are they organised? In the present case study, women in Poland seldom rely on paid care givers to attend to their families. In most case it is responsibility of other household members. Therefore, we analyse only two of the links forming the care chain model.

Moreover, many women are unable to migrate with their children because care and domestic workers face enormous difficulties in the host country living together with their sons and daughters, especially in the early years. This is because of intense working hours, lack of public or affordable social services, difficulty in finding accommodation, poor economic conditions, weak or nonexistent familiar social networks. As a result, other members of their families (mostly female) will attend to transnational domestic workers' children. A research on Latino migrants in Los Angeles (Hondagneu-Sotelo/Avila 1997) shows that also Latino immigrant domestic workers are transforming their own meanings of motherhood to accommodate spatial and temporal separations: "[...] many of these domestic workers care for the homes and children of American families while their children remain 'back home' in their societies of origin. This latter arrangement, which I call transnational motherhood, signals new international inequalities of social reproduction." (ibid: 24).

Mothering in Migration

We can define mothering in migration as a set of possible arrangements taking place whenever a mother lives in a different country than her child or children; it refers also to connotations associated to *places* where she is present or absent, to *meanings* attached to her identity, to *representations* related to her role.

Mothering is a historically and culturally variable relationship, in which one individual nurtures and cares for another. It occurs within specific social contexts that vary in terms of material and cultural resources and constraints. "[...] Mothering is constructed through men's and women's actions within specific historical circumstances. Thus agency is central to understanding of mothering as a social, rather than biological, construct." (Glenn et al.1994: 3).

Therefore, we can draw a distinction between mothering and motherhood where the latter, as Adrienne Rich (1995) wrote, refers to an institution in a male-defined site of oppression. On the other hand, mothering represents a form of maternity that can be a possible source of empowerment.

The transnational arrangements of mothering are rooted in what Helma Lutz calls "a jointly operated informal commuter network" (2002: 91). The existence and endurance of these networks allows migrant mothers to alternate their presence between two households, where they attend to both the productive and reproductive role. They exchange job information in a restricted network, usually formed by close relatives (mothers, sisters, cousins, aunts, sisters-in-law) and friends, as to alternate their presence in two places by means of long and exhausting travels by bus and, more recently, by plane. In Italy, they are often responsible for the seriously ill, the handicapped, or elderly who need an accompanying person. They do domestic chores, frequently also in some neighbours' houses; they buy food and prepare the meals. The vast majority of the women met during the research share a house with the person they take care of. While they are in Italy, their mothering role is temporarily transferred to another woman, usually their own mother, sisters, mother-in-law, and sometimes to the husband or the children's father. The present study stresses the importance of special arrangements between female cohabitating relatives that allow both women to have their work abroad, providing material resources for maintaining the household, at the same time guaranteeing a constant care for their children. From the interviewees' point of view, the choice to rear sons and daughters in Poland refers to practical exigencies, such as being able to live in a peaceful and healthy environment, especially when homes are located in rural or semi-rural areas. Indeed, the mothers are very concerned about the education and freedom of movement their children will have, and also about the language and the transmission of their own culture.

In the Field: Methodological Approach

The present study is based on qualitative research that took place in Italy and in Poland from February 2003 to October 2004, and it was initially not aimed at analyzing mothering in migration. Instead, the topic emerged as relevant during the interviews and fieldwork. Following a grounded theory approach, I started the field research in central Italy in the provinces of Chieti and Teramo (Italy) where the presence of informal care workers is significant, since demand for their work is high not only in metropolitan areas, but also in provincial towns and in non-urban areas.

The research is composed of twenty-four interviews with Polish household members; the interviews were conducted in Italian and in Polish, then fully transcribed and translated with the help of a research assistant; their length span is from one hour to three hours. I applied an unsystematic sampling using a snowball process, starting with an acquaintance of mine in the city of Chieti. To diversify the sample I have been travelling regularly between Italy and Poland (around 350 hours in six months) on the buses used habitually by Polish commuters. Altogether, I gathered twenty-five background questionnaires and did a period of observant participation.

Ten women were interviewed in-depth; they are from non-urban areas of the Sub Carpathian and Little Poland voivodeships[7]; three of them are in their twenties, three in their thirties, four in their forties and fifties. The majority received secondary education (five), while three went to high school and two were completing their university studies. Only two among them were not married and one is a widow. Eight out of ten have their sons and daughters in Poland; in one case, the daughters are working in Italy as well. Subsequently I have interviewed three sons and three daughters of migrant care workers, age 22 to 24, and all of them are attending university. Two are working students. Finally, I interviewed other cohabitants (mother, father, sister, brother-in-law, daughter-in-law) of migrant women in order to have a wider perception of their household arrangements.

"I'm My Grandma's Son": Strategies of Transnational Mothering and Shared Mothering

In narratives about maternity, I have rarely encountered any positive aspects of simultaneously managing parental duties and care work. Not only live-in workers, but also women who have their own (shared) apartment and who work on an hourly basis recounted these difficulties. In fact, one of the main conditions of having and maintaining a job in the care sector is to be free from family responsibilities. Sometimes, fearing unemployment, live-in care workers decide to terminate a pregnancy, while others who do become mothers have to face a number of difficulties, especially in the early years. Efficient public services that are able to provide continuous support to mothers of young children are difficult to find, therefore the absence of a wide social and familiar network is not compensated by affordable private care. Frequently the only viable option for these mothers is to entrust the care of the children to a member of their family, usually to their own mothers. As a matter of fact mothering in migration is deeply influenced by

---
7 This is an administrative division of the State similar to a region.

the condition in which it takes place, for instance whether the woman is a single mother, has a working contract, or has valid residence papers. It is therefore important to also analyse the children's father's position, which may be difficult because of a number of factors: whether he knows about the pregnancy, if he agrees to it, his civil status, his nationality, his occupation, and his relationship to the children's mother.

The present study, which focuses on care and domestic informal workers, observed a major strategy[8] that allows women to manage maternity transnationally. Care workers who are already mothers themselves when going to work abroad usually decide to leave their children in care of their own kin, or with the husband and his relatives, or less often with friends. Women who become pregnant in Italy, especially single mothers or who are in relationship with a Polish man, entrust their baby to the care of relatives or friends in Poland. In those cases, it is relevant to analyze the role of commuting strategies between Italy and Poland in the work and life arrangements of migrant mothers. Before Poland joined the EU in 2004, circular migration usually took place every three months, since informal care workers used to request a tourist permit which is only valid for three months. On the other hand, women working with a regular contract were able to visit their family only once or twice a year, usually for a period of one month. For this reason many migrant care-workers, I met during the fieldwork, rejected regular employment opportunities. They preferred to work illegally because they have more flexibility in their movements and work arrangements via an informal system of job exchange.

In Germany, domestic migrant workers use a similar system of rotation to exchange work information and to organise transnational households:

"Polish women have themselves set up a system of rotation so that they can go home at regular intervals, while their female substitute assume their cleaning or other jobs in Germany in the meantime. They are usually a group of 4-5 women sharing both employers and housing. This reduces the costs incurred by double residence. The regularity of their commuting seems to be determined by their care for the family remaining in Poland. In the case of the males whom I interviewed, working mainly in construction or in agriculture, commuting takes place at less regular intervals and is determined by the seasonal nature of their jobs and by the needs of the employer. Women engaged in 'self managed rotation' also avoid being captured in an institutionalised form of dependency. Not only they are not dependent on one employer, but their employers become dependent on their 'self-managed' rotation system. Their constant mobility also enables them to avoid illegal status" (Lutz 2002: 6).

---

8   The present research did not consider cases of family reunion since before the entry of Poland in the EU, in May 2004, a minority of migrant workers were able to obtain it.

Malina's[9] migratory experience will help us understand how these migratory strategies and social networks are organised. She is a grandmother of two and both mother and daughters are working in Italy. In their household they established a rotation system that allows the three women to work in Italy, while at the same time the children can grow up in Poland. Her daughters are domestic workers, while Malina takes care of an old man. In Poland they all live in the outskirts of a small town, in a big house that symbolises an important knot in a network linking two mountain areas in Poland and in Italy. For the women who live in the neighbourhood and are looking for a job, their house telephone is a precious means of connection with people in Italy who need assistance for a close relative and who will often accept care workers with little or no knowledge of the language. Although she knows women who are exploiting these *weak ties* (cf. Granovetter 1983) to earn money by selling job information (D'Ottavio 2005), she deplores doing it for profit. She expresses a proactive stance in a form of empowerment associated with her role as an informal community leader. She is a widow and the two other members of her household are her son and her partner. She is over fifty and achieved economical independence and autonomy for her and her children by means of her migratory work. After her husband died, she had to work in Italy during the summer holidays in order to sustain her family, as her salary was insufficient. She received job information via her sister-in-law. Her grandparents looked after the children, and afterwards she went to different Italian cities more and more often. As a result, she has been able to renovate her house and afford the cost of education for her children. At present, she cohabitates with her partner who is younger than she is and in a traditional country such as rural Poland, to be tolerated by the local community is highly significant.

One of her daughters alternates her presence in the household. At irregular intervals, every six months or more, she enjoys her life in Italy, finding the life in Poland too quiet for her. But she also enjoys living with her daughter, who is nearly a teenager, preparing preserves for the winter and sewing. The daughter's husband also works abroad and they rarely see each other. The other daughter, who is a single mother, gave birth to a baby in Italy, but she could not arrange mothering and a steady cleaning job at the same time, although her sister and friends supported her. She was living with three flatmates in a small apartment where the space was inadequate. Working on an hourly basis, as house-cleaner, she had to rely on a local kindergarten to look after her baby.[10] Her child was often ill, and she was under emotional pressure since she could not cope with working full-time and taking care of the baby at the same time. Finally, she decided to bring the child to Poland, to Malina's place, where he could live with his cousin and uncle. In this peaceful environment, the child regained his health and a

---

9 I used pseudonyms to protect the anonymity of my informants.
10 According to the previous national category contract, a working mother does not have any special rights or protection after the baby's third month of life.

strong bond developed between the boy and his grandmother; indeed, he used to say: "I am my grandma's son".

The Ideology of Mothering and Emotional Distress

For the mothers, the need to leave their children "back home" in other people's care can cause great emotional distress. Also a source of distress is a public discourse that tends to criticise women who choose or have to emigrate. The loss and grief the women deplore in their interviews are often related to what Rachel Salazar Parreñas called the ideology of mothering (2001a: 381).

In Poland, Catholicism and the Marian cult have deeply influenced the representation of the mother's role, especially in relation to the importance of women's domesticity. The nationalistic myth of Matka Polka (Hauser/Heyns/Mansbridge 1993; Delsol et al. 2002; Heinen 1995; Marody/Giza-Poleszczuk 2000), popular in nineteenth century Poland and still present nowadays, is germane to the cult of St. Mary. It gives power to women as the protector and reproducer of the nation but, at the same time, it demotes the woman's role to that of a powerless mother devoted to self-sacrifice and martyrdom for the sake of the nation's children.

Social transformations taking place during post-communism deeply challenged these processes of de-individualisation. A study of women's magazines published in Poland from 1974 to 1994 (Marody/Giza-Poleszczuk 2000) analysed a change in the representation of women and the stereotypes associated with the idea of femininity. This new idea implies a persuasive emphasis on individualism, on consumerism and on the image of a "self-investing" woman who has esthetical and physical features to be attractive to men. Nevertheless, the stereotypical idea of the "winning woman" is appealing only to the tiny elite who have been able to exploit new possibilities in the free market economy (Baer 2003).

In a society suspended between traditional and progressive values, the ideas of good and bad mothering are also linked to these conflicting ideas of femininity. Dominant ideologies of the family stress the importance of the mother-child dyad (Zontini 2004: 1118) and this privatised, intensive idea of motherhood contrasts with the reality of migrant mothers who opt for a shared and extensive form of mothering. The following interview was recorded with a 43-year-old mother of a care worker who has been in Italy since 2002. She is taking care of her nephew, who was four years old at the time of the interview:

"The first time she came back she was so scared...I remember it was after she stayed away for ten months, a very long time. The child was already three years old. He is now four. I told her that I was telling to the baby that his parents were not with him because they had to earn some money and that afterward they would come back...but she was scared that he wouldn't recognise her as his mother anymore. I always told the child that I was his grandma. One day [when his mother was back] he suddenly woke up staring at the couch where we were sitting, and he was looking at my daughter and at me. He didn't know what to do, so I told him: "Look, mommy is here" and he said: "Ooh!" and he ran to hug her. [...] Now everyone is saying that it is bad to leave little babies, but he managed. Now it's getting worst. Recently, his father came back in December and my daughter in January, then they left together... He suffered a lot, because now he understands more."

Economic necessities are the main discourse that women choose to legitimise their decision to migrate. This is because in times of need mothers are expected to find a way to insure economic security for their children. The conflicting interests between a mother as nurturer or as breadwinner provoke great emotional distress. Rumianek is a 46-year-old mother of three children who are already in their twenties. She has been a circular migrant care and domestic worker since 1996. She said:

"When I am here [in Poland] already after one month I start to think that we need more money... The girls are already grown-up, they can manage without me, they are very good in taking care of the house... But then I realise that I am not aware of many things, like...if the girls are in trouble, or if something happens, I am not with them, and I feel sorry about this. But you cannot have everything."

The last sentence highlights what an interviewee called "a dilemma between brain and hearth". This is a central dimension influencing the decision to migrate, especially for young mothers, since it entails a difficult choice between the pain of an immediate separation or a life in poverty for her and her children. It means, indeed, to renounce to the rearing of her children intensively and trying to assure them a better future with better chances for education. An alternative is to choose a traditional model of motherhood, which guarantees a stable mother's presence, but is lacking in the material means for social mobility. In periods of economic hardship, Polish women have arranged a different way of mothering in order to be able to overcome this dilemma. They do this by means of circular migratory projects and close-knit social networks aimed at job sharing.

Intergenerational Relations in the Household and Shifting Meanings of Maternity: Mothers as Breadwinners

In Poland, fathers do not commonly look after their children, since mothers are usually expected to do so. Whenever the woman works abroad, however, the couple has to rearrange the division of household labour, a process that is often marked by conflict. During fieldwork it emerged that Polish fathers, mostly those who are unemployed, take care of the children, often helped by their own mothers or by other close kin (sisters or brothers). Nevertheless, some of them cope poorly with domesticity, and often get depressed or develop alcohol problems.

Grandparents on both sides of the family are frequently responsible for their grandchildren's care, as it is unusual to hire local domestic workers in a Polish household, especially in rural areas. Moreover, fathers appeared less active and in some cases simply unable to positively modify their behaviour towards the children, and acquire those attributes considered conventionally female. These attributes include willingness to listen, compassion, and understanding. As a result, they struggle to invent a new model of fatherhood able to provide support to their family in modified circumstances. These processes are transforming household roles and are posing fresh challenges to the new generation. The following is from an interview with a 22-year-old male university student, son of a woman who has been migrant care worker since 2000:

"The most important thing for me is that mother is able to create a cosy atmosphere. You know, with two men around, me in one room, father in the other...when mother is home, she understands immediately when I have a problem...when I go home [and I am worried] she notices it as soon as I step into the house. She comes to hug me and I [say to her]: "Mom, I'm twenty years old now!" [annoyed] and she says: "What's wrong?" [sadly], and so she starts tickling me and she says to me: "Tell me about your problem"...it's obvious that I miss such an atmosphere, it really affects me. When mother is not at home, first thing I do when I come back home is to switch on the TV set or the stereo, and I do different things to avoid thinking. I want to hear sounds, like if someone is in the house."

In this interview it was possible to also analyse his perception of his mother's role in sustaining potential pathways for social mobility:

"The first time mom went to work abroad, I was living with my father and I did not suffer too much since we were living apart, she was already living in another city [in Poland]. During that period, I was attending the third class in high school, and I didn't feel the consequences of it, but only later...it became important only later, since my mother changed a lot after the divorce, she became more a friend to me than a mother, she took me more seriously. Then, when she left again, I had really a good relationship with her. But when I was in the first year at the university, the situation was awful, and I have suffered from her absence a lot. Now since I moved and I'm not living with my father anymore, if it was not for her I wouldn't know how to survive. She sent me money for six months, while my father didn't give me even "half grosz" [nothing]."

Interviews with migrant care workers' sons and daughters are valuable for investigating the perception of their mothers' migratory pathways through a generational lens. Such interviews are important in order to understand how transnational mothering strategies reflect upon the perception of the mother's role. A 24-

year-old daughter of a woman who has been working in Italy since 1998 said in an interview:

"When someone is missing so suddenly, afterward you realise many small details that normally you don't take into account, but that later you miss…yes, it's like that...
– What details do you mean? –
Chatting, listening to the music, having a homemade meal...you could go out together, talk, ask for an advice...things like that, normal ones, that you miss afterward...little details even hard to recall."

Migrant care workers' children are suspended between a traditional idea of motherhood, like "the angel of the fireside", and a "pro-active" idea of maternity where mothers' material support for their children is able to create greater spaces of autonomy and more opportunity for their sustenance and social mobility, as expressed by this 23-years-old daughter:

"My mother went to Italy because we have a big house, and we had to renew a part of it, since we didn't want to sell it. In addition, we had to pay for our university studies and even though in the past we had a good financial situation, lately it was not like that. So it was important for us to pursue our university degrees and now my brother and I live in the centre of the city, I cannot complain...but this has a cost. Finally, I think it is worth it since the education is important. You have more possibilities guaranteed for the future."

Opinions about the decision taken by their mothers to migrate have been generally positive and they refer to important developments taking place in the household. In first place, it is important to underline that the willingness to challenge assumptions and conventions their mothers showed, represent for them a constructive encouragement. They do not consider their mothers as passive victims of unemployment and/or of unhappy marriages, but as brave women who are able to improve their lives and social condition. Therefore, their mothers' proactive stance often provided daughters and sons with a source of strength and self-esteem.

We can analyse a sense of discovery of hidden resources expressed by a 24-years-old daughter who communicates her amazement in relation to her mother's deeds:

"At the beginning, I was very emotional about it, I was sad. Maybe my father and my sister they spoke more often about it, but practically nobody mentioned it to me when I was back home for Easter [she studies in another city]. I was really astonished when she left…for me it has been shocking. I thought she could not manage there, since she did not know the language, but then I went to Italy to visit her I was really impressed…I went in September, and she was already able to speak Italian! I was really surprised."

From an interview with a 24-years-old man who was eighteen when his mother went to Italy for the first time:

"First time she left, it was like "Ooh!" [a surprise]...I was feeling kind of weird, because she was going somewhere else, and we didn't know how it was over there, and so I was feeling anxious, but now it is ok, I feel more calm. Actually, she is more spirited, she has more energy; maybe doing a physical job is better for her, it has to be different from the one she used to have here, an office job. When she comes back, she just wants to go out, to do something together...to live. It has influenced her outfit also. Before she used to wear suits, high heels, and jackets, now she wears jeans and training shoes."

Communication media are also transforming mothers' moral and emotional support. The availability of new technologies allows migrant mothers, while they are abroad, to redefine their role by means of strategies of virtual mobility that allow the carrying on of an intimate relationship "from a distance" and which are able to provide support, guidance and assistance to their children in Poland.[11] These strategies are possible given a set of conditions in emigration and immigration areas, like the availability of a computer and the ability to use it, an Internet connection, and sufficient free time. Especially younger mothers use these means to keep up a constant relationship with their sons and daughters, for instance organizing virtual rendezvous on the net among two or more people in order to "chat" via text messages or VOIP[12] to discuss daily activities, in particular about school, friends and family.

Conclusion

Mothering in migration refers to *places* where mothers are present or absent, to *meanings* attached to their identity, to *representations* related to their roles.

Circular migration connects two places, creating a mother's double presence and absence in two different households where they perform a productive and reproductive role in the international division of caretaking typical of global capitalism and post-industrial societies. The process of European Union enlargement modified those migratory paths since family reunions are now less troublesome; moreover, a new law on domestic workers in Italy[13] allows job sharing thus allowing the emergence from informal work.

As to the meanings, it has been stressed how transnational mothers construct "new measures to gauge the quality of mothering" (Hondageu-Sotelo/Avila 1997: 26). The "commodification of love" occurs whenever providing children with material goods, in the attempt to substitute for mothers' presence, is an im-

---

11 This analysis refers to teenagers and adult sons and daughters.
12 Voice On Internet Protocol.
13 Cfr. Contratto Collettivo Nazionale Di Lavoro Sulla Disciplina Del Rapporto Di Lavoro Domestico 13 Febbraio 2007 (valid from 1/03/2007 to 28/02/2011)

portant aspect of our narratives. Nevertheless it is important to underline that is mostly education and social mobility that migrant mothers strive for.

Therefore, the representation of a domestic maternity is increasingly challenged by a positive representation of breadwinner mothers who are able to fulfil their parental role even when the household arrangements break up, and the family is scattered.

Migration can turn into a painful process because of work exploitation, social isolation and demotion of social status. On the other hand, it is important to underline the agency and role of women in migration who are catalysts for important changes.

In Poland, gender relations inside the household are in a state of tension as a direct consequence of migratory experience and, indirectly, as result of social processes connected to the economic transition. Moreover, life conditions in the context of immigration are deeply influencing the extent and the intensity of those modifications inside the household. Young women who have been interviewed are not willing to accept the traditional lifetime phases composed of rigid temporal ladders stipulating that at a certain age it is appropriate to study, to have a job, to marry and to have children. These steps correspond to *passage rites* towards adulthood that an increasing number of women are rejecting. Thus, the possibility to emigrate represents a way of decreasing tension and of lowering the pressure to conform, coming especially from rural areas. Migration allows women to achieve economic independence and, therefore, to emancipate themselves from the family. As a result, they can avoid strict social control and can gain emotional autonomy. Some of them mostly spend what they earn on commodities and trips abroad, while others prefer saving in order to buy a house in Poland, with the intention of going back one day. In this framework, new familiar models are arising in the transnational space; for instance, cohabitation of unmarried couples is a widespread condition, or multiple families in emigration and immigration areas are (silently) tolerated since in many cases divorce is not accepted and it is preferred to maintain the legal married status, even if the spouses are managing different lives. This context might create difficult situations for transnational children living in a complex setting but, on the other hand, the possibility to receive support socially and economically by a "pro-active" mother might imply several benefits.

The present case study is based in the Polish-Italian migration system typical of a transition period that took place during the European enlargement process in 2004. It analyses transnational motherhood arrangements as deeply interconnected to continuing commuting movements, which imply "going and coming back" between societies, spaces, networks and households, and it therefore underlines how migrant women are inventing for themselves a condition of *double presence*.

References

Anthias, Floya/Lazaridis, Gabriella (eds.) (2000) *Gender and Migration in Southern Europe: Women on the Move*, Oxford-New York: Berg.

Baer, Monika (2003) *Women's Spaces: Class, Gender and the Club. An Anthropological Study of the Transitional Process in Poland*, Wroclaw: Wydawnictwo Uniwersytetu Wroclawskiego.

Castles, Stephen/Miller, Mark (1998) *The Age Of Migration*, Basingstoke: Macmillian.

Deacon, Bob/Hulse, Michelle (1997) "The Making of Post-communist Social Policy: The Role of International Agencies." Journal of Social Policy 26, pp. 43-62.

Delsol, Chantal/Maslowski, Michel/Nowicki, Joanna (2002) *Mythes Et Symboles Politiques En Europe Centrale*, Paris: Presses Universitaire De France.

D'Ottavio, Germana (2005) "Migrant Women and 'Black Agencies': Polish Domestic Workers in Some Italian Provinces." Studi Emigrazione 159, pp. 547-560.

Ehrenreich, Barbara/Hochschild, Arlie Rusell (eds.) (2002) *Global Woman: Nannies, Maids, and Sex Workers in the New Economy*, New York: Metropolitan Books.

Friese, Marianne (1995) "East European Women as Domestics in Western Europe: New Social Inequality and Division of Labour among Women." Journal of Area Studies 6, pp. 194-202.

Funk, Nanette/Mueller, Magda (eds.) (1993) *Gender Politics and Post-Communism. Reflections from Eastern Europe and The Former Soviet Union*, New York-London: Routledge.

Glenn, Evelyn Nakano/Chang, Grace/Forcey, Linda Rennie (eds.) (1994) *Mothering: Ideology, Experience and Agency*, New York: Routledge.

Granovetter, Mark (1983) "The Strength of Weak Ties: A Network Theory Revisited." Sociological Theory 1, pp. 201-233.

Hauser E., Heyns B., Mansbridge J. (1993) "Feminism In The Interstice Of Politics And Culture: Poland In Transition." In: Nanette Funk/Magda Mueller (eds.) *Gender Politics And Post-Communism. Reflections From Eastern Europe And The Former Soviet Union*, New York/London: Routledge, pp. 257-273.

Heinen J. (1995) "La Nation, l'Eglise Et Le Mythe De La 'Matka Polka.'" In: M. Hoock-Demarle (eds.) *Femmes, Nations, Europe*, Paris: CERIC, Publications De l'Universitè Paris 7- Denis Diderot.

Hochschild, Arlie (2000) "The Nanny Chain." The American Prospect (January 3, pp. 32-36).

Hondagneu-Sotelo Pierette and Ernestine Avila, 1997, "'I'm Here, but I'm There': The Meanings of Latina Transnational Motherhood." Gender and Society, 11/5, pp. 548-571.

Hondagneu-Sotelo, Pierette (2001) *Doméstica: Immigrant Workers Cleaning and Caring in the Shadows of Affluence*, Berkley and Los Angeles: University of California Press Ltd.

Istituto Nazionale di Statistica (ISTAT) (2007) "Permessi di soggiorno al 1° gennaio 2006", July 29, 2007 (http://demo.istat.it/altridati/permessi/index.html).

Istituto Nazionale Previdenza Sociale (INPS) (2004) "Immigrazione e Collaborazione Domestica: I Dati del Cambiamento." In: *Monitoraggio Flussi Migratori Caritas/Migrantes*, Roma: INPS.

King, Rusell/Zontini, Elisabetta (2000) "The Role of Gender in the South European Immigration Model." Papers 60, pp. 35-52.

Kofman, Eleonore/Phizacklea, Annie/Raghuram, Parvati/Sales, Rosemary (2000) *Gender and International Migration in Europe. Employment, Welfare and Politics*, London-New York: Routledge.

Lindio-Mcgovern Ligaya (2003) "Labor Export In The Context Globalization, Experience Of Filipino Domestic Workers." International Sociology 18/3, pp. 513-534.

Lutz, Helma (2002) "At Your Service Madame! The Globalization of Domestic Service." Feminist Review 70/1, pp. 89-104.

Marody, Mira/Giza-Poleszczuk, Anna (2000) "Changing Images of Identity in Poland: From Self-Sacrificing to Self-Investing Woman?" In: Susan Gal/ Gail Kligman (eds.) *Reproducing Gender: Politics, Publics, and Everyday Life after Socialism*, Princeton: Princeton University Press, pp. 151-175.

Morokvasic, Mirjana (1983) "Women in Migration: Beyond the Reductionist Outlook." In: Annie Phizacklea (ed.) *One Way Ticket*, London: Routledge & Kegan, pp. 13-31.

Morokvasic, Mirjana (1984) "Birds Of Passage Are Also Women." International Migration Review 18/4, pp. 886-907.

Morokvasic, Mirjana (1991) "Fortress Europe and Migrant Women." Feminist Review 39, pp. 69-84.

Morokvasic, Mirjana (1992) "Une Migration Pendularie: Les Polonais En Allemagne." Hommes Et Migration 1155, pp 31-37.

Morokvasic, Mirjana (2004) "'Settled In Mobility': Engendering Post-Wall Migration In Europe." Feminist Review 77, pp. 7-25.

Okólski, Marek (2001) "Incomplete Migration: A New Form of Mobility in Central And Eastern Europe. The Case of Polish and Ukrainian Migrants." In: Claire Wallace/Dariusz Stola (eds.) *Patterns of Migration in Central Europe*, Houndmills/Basingstoke: Palgrave Macmillan, pp. 105-128.

Okólski, Marek/Stola, Dariusz (1999) "Migrations between Poland and the European Union: The Perspective of Poland's Future Membership Of EU." Prace Migracyjne 25, p. 28.

Parreñas Salazar, Rachel (2000) "Migrant Filipina Domestic Workers and The International Division Of Reproductive Labor." Gender & Society 14/4, pp. 560-580.

Parreñas Salazar, Rachel (2001a) "Mothering from a Distance: Emotions, Gender, and Intergenerational Relations in Filipino Transnational Families." Feminist Studies 27/2, pp. 361-390.

Parreñas Salazar, Rachel (2001b) *Servants of Globalization: Women, Migration And Domestic Work*, Palo Alto: Stanford University Press.

Phizacklea, Annie (ed.) (1983) *One Way Ticket*, London: Routledge & Kegan.

Phizacklea, Annie (2003) "Gendered Actors in Migration." In: Jacqueline Andall (ed.) *Gender and Ethnicity in Contemporary Europe*, Oxford-New York: Berg, pp. 23-37.

Portes, Alejandro/Guarnizo, Luis Eduardo/Landolt, Patricia (1999) "The Study of Transnationalism: Pitfalls and Promise of an Emergent Research Field." Ethnic and Racial Studies 22/2, pp. 217-237.

Rich, Adrienne Cecile (1995) *Of Woman Born: Motherhood as Experience and Institution*, New York-London, Norton.

Sarti, Raffaella/Andall, Jacqueline (2004) "Le Trasformazioni Del Servizio Domestico In Italia: Un'Introduzione." Polis 7/1, pp. 5-16.

Sassen, Saskia (1998) *Globalization and Its Discontents: Essays on the New Mobility of People and Money*, New York: The New Press.

Sassen, Sasakia (2002) "Global Cities and Survival Circuits." In: Barbara Ehrenreich/Arlie Rusell Hochschild (eds.) *Global Woman: Nannies, Maids, and Sex Workers in the New Economy*, New York: Metropolitan Books, pp. 254-275.

Stola, Dariusz (1998) "Migrations in Central and Eastern Europe." International Migration Review 32/4, pp. 1069-1072.

Stola, Dariusz (2001a) "Two Kinds of Quasi-Migration in the Middle Zone: Central Europe as a Space for Transit Migration and Mobility for Profit." In: Claire Wallace/Dariusz Stola (eds.) *Patterns of Migration in Central Europe*, Basingstoke-New York: Palgrave, pp. 84-105.

Wallace, Claire (2002) "Opening and Closing Borders: Migration and Mobility in East-Central Europe." Journal of Ethnic and Migration Studies 28/4, pp. 603-625.

Wallace, Claire/Stola, Dariusz (eds.) (2001) *Patterns of Migration in Central Europe*, Basingstoke-New York: Palgrave.

Zontini, Elisabetta (2004) "Immigrant Women in Barcelona: Coping with the Consequences of Transnational Lives." Journal of Ethnic and Migration Studies 30/6, pp. 1113-1144.

Transnationalism and Development

Opening to the World: Translocal Post-War Reconstruction in Northern Sri Lanka

Eva Gerharz

The world turned its attention to Sri Lanka when the Government and the Liberation Tigers of Tamil Eelam (LTTE) decided to sign a ceasefire agreement in February 2002. The peace process, brokered by facilitators at the initiative of the Norwegian government, gave rise to a glimmer of hope that a lasting solution might be found for the almost twenty year old conflict. It opened up new perspectives for the entire country in political, social, and economic terms. The Ceasefire Agreement brought about considerable prospects for relief and reconstruction in the war-devastated North and East of the country.

The Jaffa peninsula in the far North deserves special attention among the war-affected areas in the North and East of Sri Lanka. For the first time after twelve years, this almost exclusively Tamil-inhabited region regained a connection to the world. Linked to the mainland by only a small strip of land called "Elephant Pass", the peninsula was isolated in terms of infrastructure. For civilians, Jaffna remained inaccessible and people living there had to face severe troubles when leaving the peninsula. Ship and flight services sometimes operated only to a very limited extent, and illegal land/sea routes were extremely dangerous. Telecommunication and electricity were defunct for several years. After the Ceasefire Agreement, the parties decided to open the land route. This was the A 9 highway crossing the LTTE-controlled Vanni region. Despite several security-related obstacles civilians were able to travel between Jaffna and Sri Lanka's South and all kinds of essential and luxury goods could be transported into the devastated peninsula.

The reopening constituted a unique momentum in Jaffna's history. Access to Jaffna was regained, and translocal relations that made Jaffna a space for social change and development were established. This reopening constituted the moment at which Jaffna began to have access to all kinds of globalised knowledge. Of outstanding significance were the various efforts made by various actors with regard to post-conflict reconstruction and development. The need to rebuild and "develop" the peninsula activated different actors in the realm of formal development cooperation and reinforced the massive commitment of the globally dispersed Tamil diaspora.

This chapter aims at exploring the various dimensions of translocal interactions related to post-conflict development. It attempts to show how the reopening has intensified translocal interactions which constitute an important feature of Jaffna's integration into world society. With "world society" I refer to the integratedness of the world as a whole, as a single social system which is thought of as one single entity (Wobbe 2000: 10). The peace process in Sri Lanka marks an event in the world society (*Weltereignis*), because it was recognised globally and the relevant actors in Sri Lanka were well aware of this. There has been a reciprocal recognition of the event and its protagonists on the one hand, and the global public (*Weltöffentlichkeit*) on the other. On this basis I argue that the development and reconstruction process in Jaffna led to its re-integration into world society. This re-integration was realised through the proliferation of flows of goods, knowledge and information, images, and people between Jaffna and other parts of the world. At the same time, these flows lead to processes of closure and a reaffirmation of boundaries, localities and identities (Meyer/Geschiere 1999). These processes of closure will be discussed in the latter part of this article.

I first present a rather general introduction into the background of the conflict. The recent history of Jaffna will be followed by a description of the main actors and of their commitment to Jaffna's reconstruction. This leads us to the analytical framework, which helps me to explore the inclusion of Jaffna's reconstruction and development process into world society. The concept of the arena, as it has been used in development sociology (Long 2000, 2001), is a useful tool to capture the various relationships between localised settings, and a place targeted by development efforts certainly is a locality.[1] Secondly, I will map the positions of the various actors who participate in the localised development project. The Tamil diaspora has emerged as a considerably strong and diversified actor. Various organisations, associations, and individuals interact with local stakeholders according to different rationalities. These actors have their own ideas and aims, and they use diverse networks, relationships, organisational belongings, and so forth for the realisation of initiatives and projects. Another cluster of very important actors are those representing international development cooperation. All kinds of multilateral, bilateral, and non-governmental organisations (funded by governments in the so-called developed world) contribute to the process in different ways. Here I will limit myself to a rather narrow introduction into their positions within the arena of Jaffna. Finally, I will show how these diversified in-

---

1 A number of scholars have argued that localities are relational and contextual categories and are constructed according to the very different rationalities of those involved in the process (Appadurai 1996; Pfaff-Czarnecka 2005) How Jaffna is constructed as a locality by various actors is beyond the scope of this paper and is explored elsewhere (Gerharz 2007; 2008).

teractions lead to local processes of social change which are beyond the rather technical aims of reconstructing and developing.

The Field: A Translocal Development and Reconstruction Arena in Sri Lanka's North

Almost 20 years of war (1983-2002) between the Sinhala-dominated government and the Liberation Tigers of Tamil Eelam (LTTE) were mainly justified on the basis of insurmountable boundaries between different groups. Sinhala, Tamils, Muslims and Burghers[2] speak different languages and belong to different religions such as Buddhism, Hinduism, Islam and Christianity.[3] Consecutive ethnicisations in the process of state and nation building before and after independence can be regarded as the main trigger for the bloody ethnic conflict. Fernando (1999: 77) notes in this context that "the state has become not only a field of ethnic conflict but also its main instrument". Resulting from unequal access to education and administrative posts during colonial rule, which benefited the Tamil minority, the Sinhalese majority collectively suffered from a minority complex (Wilson 2000: 5). Thus, immediately after independence, ethnic difference was already a decisive identity marker in politics and everyday-life. This led to an increasing polarisation between Sinhalese and Tamils. Different exclusionary political moves by the Sinhala-dominated government, such as the "Sinhala Only Policy" introduced in 1956, reinforced anti-state resentments among the Tamil minority living predominantly in the northern and eastern parts of the island. The LTTE emerged out of a youth movement based in Jaffna as a result of increasing marginalisation and frustration over limitations of their rights as citizens and as a minority.

Three so-called Eelam Wars were fought between the government forces and the LTTE between 1983 and 2002. Various aspects, such as its initially productive relationships to various important supporters in neighbouring India, intensified relationships with other insurgent groups worldwide and a strong, autocratic leadership allowed the LTTE to grow into a mature military force. Most supportive has probably been the formation of a globally dispersed Tamil diaspora consisting of those who emigrated for educational and economic reasons before the war and those who have left Sri Lanka as refugees since the early 1980s. At least 400,000 Sri Lankan Tamils live in European countries and North America[4]

---

2   Burghers are Sri Lankans supposedly of European descent.
3   According to the census of 1981 Sri Lanka's population consists of 74 per cent Sinhala, 12.7 per cent Sri Lankan Tamils. 5.5 per cent Indian Tamils, and 7 per cent Moors. The rest constitute Burghers, Malays and others. A more recent census for Sri Lanka including the war-zones is not available.
4   Gunaratna states that the Sri Lankan Tamil population living in North America, Europe, India, Africa, Middle East and Australasia numbers an estimated 770,000 people (Gunaratna 2001: 2).

(Cheran 2000: 186) and Oceania, Africa, the Middle East and India. The LTTE and its various aligned organisations have created a global support network. They have done so by exploiting and perpetuating the collective consciousness of being a Sri Lankan Tamil on the basis of language, ethnicity, caste and religion (Cheran 2001: 9). Constructing history and memory through practices such as media work, public meetings, rallies, and ritual performance, the LTTE could exert social and political control in the diaspora communities (Cheran 2001: 15). This opened up the possibility of interlinking these practices with fundraising for the war activities, but also for humanitarian purposes and relief. Apart from these so-called collective remittances, sending individual remittances to relatives at home was an essential practice making survival possible. In Northern Sri Lanka, especially Jaffna, large parts of the population depended on remittances. According to Sri Lankan government estimates, LTTE overseas fundraising amounts to 80 million US$ annually (Wayland 2004: 421). But the process of diaspora formation has not only led to effective funding, it has also reinforced a collective feeling of emotional attachment and shared responsibility for the "homeland". As we will see later, this is an important prerequisite for translocal development initiatives.

By the end of 1999, the arms race among the Sri Lankan Army (SLA) and the LTTE led to a no-win-situation. Both sides, and the international community observing the conflict, realised that no military solution is possible. Norwegian mediators supported the negotiation of the Ceasefire Agreement of February 2002. The international community greatly appreciated the newly opened space for a peaceful settlement and attempted to support this by providing positive incentives. Various multi- and bi-lateral development cooperation partners provided huge amounts of money for reconstruction and development in order to create a "peace-dividend" for the war-affected Sri Lankan populations. This, however, aimed at stabilising the ground situation for sustainable peace.[5] As a result, the CFA period saw ample planning and implementation efforts in the field of development cooperation especially in the North and East, but also in other parts of Sri Lanka. Unfortunately, this strategy did not prove successful. The initial enthusiasm for peace declined and from 2004 onwards a "shadow war" determined the fragile situation (Hellmann-Rajanayagam 2007: 124). The space for sustainable peace diminished successively and fighting broke out alongside a number of political killings. The road to Jaffna was closed again in August 2006. In January 2008 the government unilaterally declared the Ceasefire Agreement to be defunct.

Within the period of the Ceasefire, the peninsula Jaffna was regarded as a prime location for development and reconstruction efforts for various reasons. First, the towns and villages of the peninsula were severely damaged during the conflict and large parts of the infrastructure, including schools, health facilities,

---

5 This strategy was called "Kilinochchi consensus" by Sriskandarajah (2004) who argued that the idea was also to demonstrate international support.

public building, power and telephone supply were destroyed. The local economy was in a state of almost complete ruin. About 80,000 houses were damaged or completely destroyed (Halbach 2003: 171). Large parts of the population suffered and still suffer from war-related trauma (Somasundaram 1998). There was an urgent need to start reconstruction, rehabilitation and development as soon as possible. Secondly, the peninsula inhabited almost entirely by Tamils has always been the capital of Sri Lankan Tamil culture and heritage. It was, at the same time, the centre of advanced education from which the Tamils have benefited since colonial times. This reinforced the emergence of Jaffna as the centre of a Sri Lankan Tamil educated class and, in the light of increasingly limited minority rights and access to resources, as the place of origin of about 90 per cent of the Tamils living abroad (Gunaratna 2001: 2). Thirdly, due to its isolation, Jaffna was difficult to access for the humanitarian and development organisations operating in the other parts of Sri Lanka. After 1995, a UN Emergency Task Force was established to monitor the situation. In 1996, there was a major initiative to provide assistance to Jaffna (Foster 2003: 157). At that time, donors pledged a lot of money for humanitarian assistance. Only after 1999 did intensified fighting break out again in Jaffna and most organisations withdrew from the peninsula. The re-opening in April 2002, however, offered the possibility of operating in Jaffna relatively unhindered.

Jaffna's situation after the 2002 CFA, however, was characterised by very particular conditions. The interplay between previous isolation for twelve years, its significance as the main locality of reference for the globally dispersed Tamil diaspora and its prominence among the donors invites us to investigate the emergence of translocal interactions. The fact that these interactions were made possible "all of a sudden" creates an interesting research perspective. This appears to be especially true considering that Jaffna was cut off from the processes of globalisation which the other parts of Sri Lanka have faced from the late 1970s onwards (Hettige 2000).[6] Since the 1990s the lives of most Sri Lankans have changed with the import of fridges, washing machines, computer facilities, satellite TV, tourists, and associated globalised culture and lifestyles. Jaffna remained almost untouched by this integration into world society. The re-opening created a fascinating situation of catching up with the rest of the world. Very soon after April 2002, mobile phones were operating in Jaffna, satellite TV was broadcast, internet cafes mushroomed, globalised brands like Coca Cola, Nestle and Maggi were available everywhere. The first supermarkets emerged next to shops for computers and electronic devices. People were talking about the latest events in the war against the Iraq in 2003. Huge crowds of foreigners entered the peninsula

---

6   In the 1977 elections the United National Party with its liberalisation programme came into power. The related economic reforms led to the intensification and diversification of Sri Lanka's external links which affected the significance of the nation-state as the dominant framework for identification and ideological orientation for many people (Hettige 1998: 8).

which led to the growth of guesthouses and hotels. Not just researchers, but also journalists, business people, and tourists started to travel to Jaffna. The 2004 edition of the "Lonely Planet" even promoted Jaffna as the latest hottest spot in the Sri Lankan tourism paradise and provided an extra section on it. Apart from the changes related to everyday-life, contact with foreigners, consumption and access to globalised media, a number of significant changes in the field of development took place.

Given this diverse landscape of the actors shaping the process of integrating Jaffna into world society, it is necessary to define a clear analytical framework which enables the observer to understand the complex dynamics of interaction leading to various societal changes. The concept of an arena as developed by development sociologist Norman Long (2001: 59), appears to be useful:

"arenas are social locations or situations in which contests over issues, resources, values, and representations take place... That is, they are social and spatial locations where actors confront each other, mobilise social relations and deploy discursive and other cultural means for the attainment of specific ends, including that of perhaps simply remaining in the game".

The concept of arena allows us to take a look at social relations and interactions. It provides an analytical tool for ordering the material, for setting action into context. It is open enough to bring very different dimensions into focus. Goetze (2002: 58) argues in this context:

"it is the notions of domain and arena that permit the analysis of the processes of ordering, regulating and contesting social values, relations, resource utilisation, authority and power".

Recognising the fact that we are particularly interested in interactions which transcend the boundaries of the locality of Jaffna, it is necessary to re-think the nature of the interactions since these are embedded into the context of world society. We regard world society as a global space because world society refers to a perspective which encompasses the totality of all social relations[7] and it is constituted by all kinds of flows of commodities, people, capital, technologies, information and images (Long 2001: 214). These flows cross territorial boundaries. This entails constant processes of social change on a global scale.

At the same time, it is important not to forget that the "local" dimension is still highly relevant when analysing the development and reconstruction processes in Jaffna: Development is regarded as a local project because it is the local infrastructure which has been destroyed and it is the local "Jaffna Tamil society" who are the beneficiaries of this project. It is the clearly defined locality of Jaffna

---

7   See the introduction of this volume for a more concise discussion of the term world society.

which is the reference point for everything, the Tamil diaspora coming from Jaffna and calling themselves "Jaffna Tamil" (Wilson 1994) and the development organisations which contribute to the construction of the locality by defining their project as locations and naming their projects. All activities taking place in the realm of development and reconstruction target concrete, localised objects, be it schools, hospitals, roads, and NGOs members as areas of intervention. Therefore, it is necessary to look at interactions as inter-linkages between global and local spaces. Robertson (1995) introduced the term "glocalisation", which nicely captures the interrelatedness of the local and the global scale. This also means that the local is to a large extend shaped by flows at a translocal or super-local level (Robertson 1995: 26).

Using the concept of "translocal" rather than the more familiar and well elaborated concept of the "transnational" (Bash/Glick Schiller/Szanton Blanc 1994; Faist 2003; Pries 2001 among others) has several conceptual advantages in this specific case. It also diverts our attention to a slightly different perspective (see Gudrun Lachenmann's contribution in this volume). Instead of highlighting the significance of flows transcending the boundaries of the nation-state, I see the locality as the major unit of analysis. This is of special importance in the context of Jaffna, because the integration of the peninsula into the nation-state remains contested, even after the CFA (Ceasefire Agreement). The translocal perspective also takes into account the critique of methodological nationalism elaborated by Wimmer and Glick Schiller (2002).[8] Translocality, however, opens up the possibility of applying a more encompassing research perspective but allows us to focus on a specific object of research. These phenomena transcending all kinds of boundaries are at the centre of attention (Freitag/von Oppen 2005).

Focussing on development and reconstruction efforts Jaffna, the concept of arena has great analytical value. The arena is a space for interactions between all the kinds of actors who participate in the project of reconstructing and developing Jaffna. This arena is embedded into translocal space, because it is constituted by negotiations of a variety of actors who are not confined to the locality. In focus, however, are the relational and processual aspects which cross the territorial and symbolic boundaries of the locality. We can thus speak of a translocal development arena which is constituted by flows, interactions and negotiations of whatever the actors consider to be development.

Diaspora Commitment to Development

Research on diaspora-local relations before the CFA has shown that the Tamil diaspora was organised systematically with the goal of supporting the armed resist-

---

8   The focus on national societies as it has been applied in social sciences has also been especially criticised by those who have worked on the notion of world society in the German context. See for example Schimank (2005).

ance of Tamil organisations fighting for the Tamil cause (Radke 2004: 248). Fundraising and actions expressing solidarity were at the core of these transnational activities and were centralised by the LTTE especially. At the same time, various scholars have described how organisations and groups were formed by members of the diaspora. Some of them provided humanitarian assistance to the Tamils remaining in the homeland and who were being affected by the war.[9] The landscape of these organisations is quite diverse. Individuals and organisations concerned with development and reconstruction of the homeland can be categorised according to different dimensions of interaction.

The first dimension consists of interactions in the field of religious institutions. Not all Sri Lankan Tamils believe in Hinduism. Some follow different forms of Christianity, particularly Catholicism. Christian Tamils have formed groups which raise funds and generate support for the physical reconstruction of religious institutions and development of related social institutions such as orphanages or other organisations aiding weaker segments of the local society. By interacting closely with religious institutions, such as the local branch of Caritas for example, development projects are financed by diaspora members. Research has shown that personal contacts play a very important role in the manifestation of such projects, but belonging to the Church as a global institution is also very relevant. There are examples of Christian Tamils living abroad who have established contact with churches in their town of residence. In these cases "native" volunteers work together with Tamils to provide assistance for the reconstruction of social institutions in Northern Sri Lanka.

These established structures did not change much after the Ceasefire. At the same time it could be observed that, among the Hindu communities, practices of exchange and support were transformed considerably. Hindu Tamils in the diaspora formed associations to support temples in their home villages. These contacts link them to those who have stayed behind as well as to those who have migrated. After the Ceasefire, such spontaneous initiatives greatly increased. Diaspora members collected money to aid the reconstruction of temples and related social projects. This increase can partly be explained by the rise of communicative linkages between the homeland and the diaspora. After 2002 it was possible to communicate via media such as telephone and internet. The hope, that the peace process would be successful, created the impression that the invested resources would not get lost in renewed fighting. Religious events like festivals also attracted diaspora Tamils to make personal visits. The temple festival in Jaffna's most important temple in Nallor was attended by thousands of visitors during the Ceasefire. Transport facilities to Jaffna were fully booked far in ad-

---

9   These activities are strongly tied to processes of safeguarding memory and preserving identity, which have been analysed for the Canadian Tamil diaspora by Cheran (2001; 2000), the Swiss Tamil diaspora by McDowell (1996) and for the Norwegian context see Fuglerud (2001). As such, these processes are a feature of "diaspora" itself (see for example Clifford 1994 and Brubacker 2005).

vance. Temple festivals are always fundraising occasions. Another important temple attracting diaspora members was the one in Tellipillai. This temple is devoted to Durga Devi and said to help in cases of infertility and in finding suitable marriage partners. After the Ceasefire, the numbers of visitors and the funds donated on these occasions rose considerably. Although the temple always had an extraordinarily good income due to its multiple translocal linkages to diaspora groups[10] worldwide, its financial situation was greatly enhanced and various new projects were initiated during the time of this research.

Diaspora support for school reconstruction was a second important dimension in the reconstruction process. Education has a high value among the Jaffna Tamils. This can be explained by the peninsula's historical position as Sri Lanka's educational centre.[11] So-called Old Boys Associations (OBA)[12] for almost all higher level schools follow the British tradition of maintaining contact with one's school by forming alumni networks. OBAs provided primarily financial support. Especially the OBAs bigger schools have become translocal and maintain branches in Colombo and overseas. Some Old Boys are so numerous in particular places that they form networks and comprise branches in several different countries. Others are quite dispersed and primarily maintain contact with their school without relying on institutionalised structures in their country of residence. After the CFA the commitment of OBAs to support Jaffna's schools exploded. Having the opportunity to visit Jaffna primarily for family reunions, many Old Boys also paid visits to their former schools. Confronted with the large-scale destructions and the many shortages, Old Boys immediately organised financial and material support. Several schools received IT equipment, sports kit, funds for re-building class rooms, science labs, sports grounds, and scholarships for individual students. One school received money to buy the land necessary for expansion. Several schools discovered the potential of the internet and other forms of long-distance communication. Numerous web-pages can be found introducing the schools, their OBAs, the persons involved in these as well

---

10 I had the chance to interview the management president and chairperson of the temple society intensively and learned that she used to travel to different diaspora centres in Australia, Great Britain and Canada to deliver speeches and to network with Tamil Hindu communities.

11 Various authors have shown that education has great significance in Jaffna. This is a result of the impact of Christian missionaries during the colonial period. These missions started to establish a high-quality school system, which let to the emergence of competition between Christians and Hindus (Gunasingham 1999; Hellmann-Rajanayagam 1990). The importance of education was also emphasised by numerous interviewees during fieldwork.

12 I use the term Old Boys Associations because it was used by the interviewees and is, in many cases, also the official designation used by the associations themselves. There are also Old Girls Associations, but only from a very few schools. Most schools have been mixed and the old girls have been absorbed under the term "old boys".

as their projects.[13] Although a "jungle" of internet-based presentations has emerged during recent years, the main goal seems to be the initiation of support and finance from other globally dispersed Old Boys and Girls. This is done through spreading information, announcing events, telling stories about the school's history, providing photo-galleries, and discussion forums. This process of networking has strengthened the bargaining position of the local actors in the reconstruction processes. In some cases, overseas OBAs were formed at the initiative of the school principal who visited the community abroad. In other cases, local OBAs and School Development Societies actively encouraged funding by sending "wish-lists" to Tamil organisations abroad.

So-called home village associations (HVA), having gained much attention in the current debate about migration and development (Guarnizo/Smith 1998), function according to a similar logic. Like diaspora branches of OBAs HVAs are formed as an expression of solidarity. Cheran describes how charity and philanthropy are the main motivation for establishing Canadian Tamil HVAs. Many started to function as social clubs and were transformed into development organisations after the Ceasefire Agreement (Cheran 2007: 288). Some of these organisations, which quite often employ the suffix "friendship society" in addition to the village's name, use print and electronic media to inform others about their activities and to network. They use funding strategies similar to those of OBAs and temple societies. In practice they sometimes overlap, but since they are not related to a particular type of insitution, they can easily switch roles depending on the needs in the respective village. Examples of HVA support which I came across during fieldwork, were based on fisherman societies and rural development societies, the organisation of private tuition classes, provision of scholarships for students, and the reconstruction of community centres. Like OBAs HVAs mainly rely on personal networks. Following the CFA, solidarity with the village was expressed through personal visits, even if no family members were living in the village any longer. This resulted in many initiatives by diaspora Tamils.

The forms of translocal interaction established by institutions such as Home Village Associations, Old Boys Associations and Temple Societies were highly localised and place-based. They were rooted in the maintenance of emigrants' solidarity with their place of origin, which might be related to a sense of nostalgia and the desire to assist people in the villages back home who struggle during and after war (Cheran 2007: 288). This is in contrast to the LTTE-dominated development initiatives, which are rooted in translocal interaction as well, but which follow a different rationale.

Support for local NGOs is a widespread phenomenon among the Tamil diaspora, but very much dominated by a particular organisation. Nevertheless, it could be observed that representatives of local NGOs in Jaffna attempted to raise

---

13 See for example the very detailed page of the Jaffna Hindu College, December 10, 2007 (http://www.jhcobajaffna.com).

funds in the diaspora. All the representatives interviewed reported that this is a difficult task. As a result, they developed innovative strategies to realise diaspora commitment either by utilising personal networks, or by linking these to other fields. One NGO representative reported that she utilises the yearly temple festival for fund-raising, which was easy for her as a member of the temple society in her village. After the CFA many villagers living in the diaspora visited the temple festival and it is compulsory in these circumstances to donate money. Since the temple had already been rebuilt, this NGO representative campaigned for her organisation's projects by arguing that the temple was rich enough at that point and that people should do something for children and the other beneficiaries of the NGO. This empirical case shows religious based charity becomes interlinked with "professional" development work of NGOs which is rather uncommon. Though several NGOs tried to gain access to diaspora funds, they faced severe difficulties because this particular field had already been occupied by the Tamil Rehabilitation Organisation (TRO).

Established as the LTTE's developmental and humanitarian wing, TRO is the largest NGO in Sri Lanka's North-East and the organisation with the best translocal organisational set-up. According to Gunaratna (2001) there are fifteen TRO offices throughout the world, the headquarter in Kilinochchi and a branch in Colombo. The overseas offices provide information about the situation in Sri Lanka and raise funds for TRO's development and reconstruction projects. According to TRO's Annual Report of 2002 the organisation received more than half of its budget, a share which is labelled as "foreign income", in the form of material and financial donations. TRO organises a range of activities in the receiving countries in order to attract Tamils to donate for community work in the North-East. These activities are strongly influenced by LTTE's political ideology (McDowell 1996). At the same time, TRO pioneered a new development in the translocalisation of development and reconstruction which has been discussed as knowledge transfer in the recent migration-development debate. Diaspora volunteers helped in various fields such as management and capacity-building of the organisation and engineering in infrastructure projects. Social skills and language skills for translation purposes were also in demand. Other local NGOs discovered the usefulness of diaspora knowledge. In some interviews I was told that networking aids local NGO workers in asking diaspora Tamils for advice in questions related to the implementation of projects where engineering skills for example are required.

Another phenomenon which emerged after the CFA is comparable, and closely related to the integration of skilled migrants in the reconstruction work of NGOs. Diaspora professional have formed networks and organisations on the basis of their profession and support local institutions. The most significant are diaspora Tamils who are medical professionals. Organisations like the Tamils

Health Organisation (THO), the Medical Institute of Tamils (MIOT)[14] and the Tamil Medical Institute (TAMMED) encourage Tamil medical doctors in diaspora countries to network.[15] MIOT, for example, has branches in Canada and the UK. These associations collect money and other donations in the countries were diaspora Tamils live through charity events, or other forms of fund-raising and they support medical institutions in Sri Lanka's North and East by providing cash and material donations. They also send members to different places in North East Sri Lanka (see also Cheran 2007: 291). During fieldwork I met several medical doctors who spent their holidays working as volunteers in Sri Lanka's North. These professionals help to reduce waiting lists for surgeries in existing hospitals, provide training for local staff in specialised areas in which local capacities are lacking or are engaged in developing new or rebuilding old medical institutions which have been destroyed during the war.

Although these medical associations also function like HVAs and OBAs on the basis of solidarity and commitment to Sri Lanka's war-ravaged North-East, there are certain important differences. Medical associations may network with local actors in Sri Lanka on the basis of personal and professional relationships. One example was cooperation between MIOT and a local NGO, which came into existence because the NGO director's sister worked at the MIOT office in London. But generally, I observed that the medical associations paid little attention to their members' place of origin. This may be related to the fact that they were formed by professionals and not on the basis of common roots in one locality. This makes them more flexible in choosing their project locations and is also related to political loyalties. Attracting these non-locality based associations is important for the LTTE which attempts to integrate diaspora development initiatives into their nation-building project. Since Jaffna did not belong to the LTTE-controlled area and it was unlikely that it could be regained, the LTTE concentrated on the Vanni located south of Jaffna in their state-building efforts. But because most diaspora members come from Jaffna and concentrate their commitment on projects in Jaffna, the LTTE faces the challenge of attracting diaspora funding for the Vanni. OBAs and HVAs have been formed on the basis of memory of their members' sensory experience in the place and childhood memories. Often a feeling of obligation to the institution where the individual gained the opportunities which enabled him/her to become successful after migration also plays a role. One interviewee for example expressed: "I love this place although I have lived abroad for 34 years. I got free education here from kindergarten onwards and I need to give something back". With regard to temples interviewees also mentioned that the obligation derives from the hope

---

14 For detailed information see MIOT's webpage December 12, 2007 (http://www.miotyf.org/contents).

15 There are many other organisations based in different diaspora countries. Some are more specialised like the Cancer Aid in North & East (Sri Lanka) UK, and the Jaffna General Hospital Development Organisation (which is based in Jaffna).

that donating to the temple is thought to aid personal salvation. Networks and organisations like those run by medical doctors under contract are less motivated by the importance of a specific place or the place based institution, but rather related to the ethos of professionals in the field of medicine combined with a non-place-based Tamil identity. This also explains the strong emphasis on the TRO as a dominant NGO in translocal networking, which is also related to the fact that the LTTE, as a non-state actor is not eligible to receive funds for donor organisations directly because it is not an officially recognised partner.

The analysis so far has been concentrated on flows of financial support, know-how, people, and ideas, but this does not mean that the interactions were always smooth and uncomplicated. Although the transfer of funds was largely unproblematic, there were also disappointed local actors who felt deprived, and there were conflicts over priorities chosen. The NGO representative, who diverted the funds meant for the temple, to the NGO projects managed to avert conflict over the deployment of resources.

In other cases local actors were discouraged by the ideas of their diaspora counterparts. Several interviewees complained that diaspora Tamils had counter-productive plans and were not sensitive to the needs of the people. One person complained about diaspora plans to construct a swimming pool for the school, although Jaffna is surrounded by beaches where the students could go to swim and enjoy recreation opportunities. In hospitals, local staff complained that diaspora doctors would occupy their time unnecessarily. Quite often, it became clear that diaspora Tamils had different visions of what was meant by development and the local actors felt that their priorities were wrongly set. Another dimension in which processes of resistance and closure took place as a result of flows was the realm of identity and cultural practices. Especially the "Westernisation", that many locals observed among diaspora Tamils, caused resentments. This became particularly obvious in inter-generational encounters. Many children had been born in the diaspora, and some of them did not speak proper Tamil any longer. Some of them were regarded as behaving like Westerners, especially when girls wore blue jeans or tight clothes. This led to processes of closure and reinforced alienation among those who were committed to sharing an inclusive, common Tamil identity.

Increased diaspora-local cooperation in the realm of development marks an important step in Jaffna's reintegration into world society. By analysing the various dimensions and fields of interaction, a number of negotiation processes takes place, which reflect Jaffna's positioning vis-à-vis the world. The interactions lead to the formation of translocal spaces in which globalised ideas of development are negotiated and in which the different actors shape the local development and reconstruction process. The formation of migrant-local relations in translocal spaces enable them to jointly organise, plan and implement reconstruction and development measures in different fields while they remain in contact. As a consequence, local reconstruction becomes a project embedded into the ideas and norms perpetuated within world society through translocal flows. At the same time the formation of translocal spaces allocates agency to local actors to understand themselves as being part of an integrated world society. Through reflecting their own identity and their localised development project against the background of their images of the world, local development also means that normative ideas such as modernity and identity are negotiated at the interface with diaspora Tamils. But this is also strongly related to the increased significance of formal development cooperation after the Ceasefire. Not only the flow of large sums of money, but also the presence of a large number of international staff has reinforced renewed negotiations of local identities and development in the context of an integration into world society.

Development Cooperation in Jaffna

Hoping to support the peace process through initial and immediate reconstruction efforts, the "donor community" pledged immense sums for Sri Lanka in two donor meetings. After the second meeting in June 2003 in Tokyo, the donor community stated that a sum of US$ 4.5 billion would be allocated over a four year period. Jaffna, which is formally controlled by the Sri Lankan government and which suffered severe destruction became subject to extensive reconstruction efforts. Many organisations, like the so-called UN family, had already initiated support after 1996 but were forced to withdraw during a major military offensive in 2000. Most of these came back after the Ceasefire Agreement in 2002 and re-established offices and relationships with local institutions. As a result, donor agencies attend to a broad variety of these fields ranging from demining and assistance for returning refugees and IDPs, to aspects of food security, employment generation, education, health, housing, water and sanitation and transport, infrastructure reconstruction. Agencies involved are among others: various members of the UN family, the World Bank, the Asian Development Bank, different bilateral agencies such as British DIFD, Japanese JICA, USAID and German GTZ. There is a broad variety of strategies for providing assistance, ranging from basket funding, implementation via national or international NGOs, implementation via state institutions such as local government or ministries to, in a few cases, implementation in cooperation with local community groups or local NGOs.

Apart from enabling finance to flow, the bi- and multilateral cooperation was especially oriented towards globalised strategies of conflict management.[16] As part of a larger policy formulation based on structural stability within the coun-

---

16 Different, rather confusing terminologies exist with regard to interventions in (post)conflict settings. See Reimann (2004) for an extensive discussion of the various approaches related to the terminologies. For simplification I use the term conflict management because it seems to be the most comprehensive term in this context.

tries of intervention, conflict management and related terms pinpoint, among many other aspects, the establishment and consolidation of stable institutions within the state. These function in order to avoid the outbreak of violence and hence stabilise the ongoing development process. Behind this logic rests the assumption, that violent conflict obstructs development and that inadequate development perpetuates conflict.[17] Therefore, development cooperation attempts to contribute to both: on the one hand, it needs to reinforce societal and economic development processes, on the other hand conflict prevention measures have to be employed in order to stabilise a post-conflict society. According to the most important policy document of recent years, the "DAC Guidelines on Conflict. Peace and Development Cooperation on the Threshold of the 21st Century", two major pillars are at the core of conflict preventive development policy. First, "structural stability" is based on the presumption of good governance, democracy and decentralisation, which can be ensured through reforms of state and bureaucracy. Second, a strategy called "local capacities for peace"[18] should ensure that civil society actors gain competence to enhance peace on the level of society.

The policy for mainstreaming conflict management as formulated in the DAC guidelines, however, suggests a two-fold approach, including partners in the civil society as well as governmental institutions. In Jaffna, this policy was implemented in the rather peculiar situation in which civil society (in this case, NGOs) and governmental institutions are embedded. There has been a shift in the global development debate from supporting civil society to institutions and public goods, especially those of the state, since the state is regarded as the most "neutral" actor in development. This is in contrast to civil society actors who may follow particularistic interests. The highly contested nature of Jaffna in the course of conflict has reinforced an anti-NGO policy on the part of the state. NGOs have always been considered as under LTTE control and generally sympathetic with the movement. The two aspects, that NGOs in Jaffna are considered to be politically non-neutral and that global development policy is based on an emphasis of the state as a partner in development, have reinforced cooperation with state-institutions.

Development cooperation is concentrated basically on infrastructure reconstruction and development. The bigger multi-lateral agencies have pledged large sums for water and irrigation (World Bank), and community restoration (Asian Development Bank) including construction of small roads, schools, community centres and private housing. The various UN agencies have been engaged in the tasks for which they are specialised. Various bilateral donors participated in joint

---

17 The conflict development nexus was discussed extensively during the 1990s both in academia and practice (for Sri Lanka see Sriskandarajah 2004; Culbert 2005). The relationship between conflict prevention and development strategies including institutional capacity building was also intensively discussed by von Braun/Grote/Jütting (2000).
18 This term is strongly related to the "do no harm" approach as developed by Anderson (1999).

basket-funding or channel funds through international non-governmental organisations which established their own structures for reconstruction and development. The German Technical Cooperation (GTZ) had implemented a rehabilitation project since 1996 and changed its focus to support for the institutional capacity building of local governance institutions after 2002.

Setting up development cooperation with state institutions, local institutions and also through their own implementation structures reinforced the formation of translocal space at yet another level which is embedded into the everyday-lives of the people in Jaffna. This dimension beyond professional working relationships is comprised of the various ways in which foreign employees of development and relief agencies interact with the local population. As soon as the isolation was lifted, herds of consultants and new foreign staff entered the peninsula. The devastated infrastructure was not able to accommodate the needs of all these foreigners, who were lodged in guesthouses run by the offices of the agencies. The UN and GTZ ran their own guesthouses, which provided accommodation for many of these foreigners. The UN also started to provide an internet connection by establishing the first internet café for locals and foreigners in Jaffna. Local stakeholders reacted quite quickly to the influx of foreigners. Local entrepreneurs established guesthouses and hotels to meet the exploding needs. Persons started businesses serving foreigners, such as renting cars. Local shopkeepers enlarged their range of products and sold imported products to attract foreign consumers. Also quite soon the "Palm Beach Restaurant", opened by some returned migrants, was offering pizza, ice cream and other Western-style food. This restaurant was among the most popular lunch places for foreign visitors. Some UN employees established a bar to meet the recreation needs of the international staff. Similarly, employees of international organisations organised parties at their homes. Such occasions alerted more conservative Jaffna residents to the fact that the Western visitors might expose local people to immoral behaviour. It was reported that some locals threw stones over the courtyard walls of the bar, when the music was too loud. Others reported that they found it funny when girls drank beer and danced with men at the parties.

Local people also reported that they found the impact of foreign agencies' capital on the local economy disturbing. The offices and residences of the agencies were mainly located in Jaffna's suburb Chundukuli, especially in and around Temple Road. In this suburb, virtually every second house had a signboard placed in front, indicating the office of a foreign or, in a few cases, local organisation. Some of the foreign organisations rented several houses as offices, and as accommodation for the international staff. Illustrative in this regard was the junction of Temple Road and Racca Road, which was dominated by ICRC buildings and facilities at each corner. Locally, this junction has become known as "ICRC junction". The international organisations did not pay much attention to the local prices for housing. Quite often they paid exacerbated rents to the owners who either live in other, often smaller, houses or abroad. Several interviewees claimed that they did not appreciate this impact of international organisations because it caused a horrendous rise in the cost of renting houses in the area. Local people were almost unable to afford living in these areas, which is especially critical considering the large numbers of displaced people and others who lost their homes during the periods of fighting.

Re-negotiating Local Development and Identity

Jaffna's integration into global development has led to a number of significant and complex local changes in the developmental, economic and cultural sphere. The analysis has shown that interactions between local actors and international actors produced increased efforts to reconstruct Jaffna and support the rehabilitation of its infrastructure in various ways. But the increased interactions also led to significant changes in the images Jaffna Tamils have of the foreigners representing the Western world for them since they are located within their local context and thus, subject to direct relationships and face-to-face contact. At the same time, it could be shown that the flow of international agencies and their staff also had, apart from being subject to moral critique, unintended consequences on local economic relations as well as on the already severe housing situation of Jaffna's inhabitants. These different aspects of interactions came together in the Jaffna arena and produced new images of the world. These were represented by the foreign visitors. These images were not only taken over but became subject to renegotiations and re-positionings at the levels of localisation and local identity.

In globalisation studies it has been pointed out that globalisation, in the sense of continuous global flows, reinforces the constitution of boundaries on various levels. These scholars contributed a great deal to a rather flawed debate about homogenisation through the diffusion of globalised goods, commodities, ideas and values. Notable in this context are Appadurai's works on the production of locality (1995; 1996), and also on the relationship between global processes and ethnic violence described in his article on dead certainty (Appadurai 1998). These ambivalent and complex processes of inclusion and exclusion, which seem to be inherent in the constitution of world society result from what Meyer/Geschiere (1999) called "dialectics of flow and closure". Although focusing predominantly on the relationship between globalisation and identity, the dialectic moment they seek to capture is rather broad in analytical scope. However, it captures the entire uneasiness we have with processes of globalisation and translocalisation based on the popular misconception that these processes might lead to the constitution and integration of a more or less uniform world society.

Jaffna's experience of being re-opened and becoming subject to development and reconstruction efforts is illustrative because it is such a particular case of globalisation. Through the constitution of a translocal arena, space for negotiating the local vis-à-vis the world has been created. All of a sudden Jaffna saw itself exposed to the flows from outside which led to demarcations in the realm of culture and identity. Through the influx of foreign visitors a space emerged, in which local Tamils could reflect upon their own moral norms and cultural particularities and reaffirm these by degrading the behaviour of immoral Westerners. Jaffna Tamils faced similar experiences, when their relatives from abroad visited them after an absence of several years, when they discovered that their Tamil relatives' daughters wore tight blue jeans and drove cars by themselves. The re-integration into world society through flows and the formation of translocal spaces constituted by face-to-face contacts and proximity reinforced local "closure" and the fixing of a local, authentic culture.

Similar processes happened in the realm of development. Through the constitution of the development arena, a number of different development ideas came together. Development agencies tried to implement their recently developed policies of sustainable development, in the sense of enhancing capacity and building state institutions, while diaspora Tamils transported their lived personal experience of Western economic wealth and values into the development arena. As part of the negotiation of an appropriate notion of development people in Jaffna (and to a certain degree also diaspora Tamils) discovered their own ideas of how Jaffna should be reconstructed and developed. The import of new ideas of development and visions of society reinforced processes of closure at yet another level and led to an accentuation of specifically local development ideas, constituted by a glorification of the pre-war past and a return to Jaffna Tamil "culture" and "tradition". What has been understood as a project of development and inherent betterment of the state of the post-war society by those living on the outside, has produced sentiments of alienation, boundary-drawing and closure.

In this article I attempted to show that translocal flows and interactions are features of and processes leading to the constitution of world society in a sense that makes it possible today to think of the world as one single construct. As Appadurai (1996) points out, the world is an interactive system with strikingly new features such as mobility of goods and information. Against this background, my aim was to investigate social interactions and processes in order to make contributions to how this world (society) might look like in a particular context. Or, in Appadurai's words: "we will need to ask not how these complex, overlapping, fractual shapes constitute a simple, stable (even if large-scale) system, but to ask what its dynamics are" (Appadurai 1996: 46). Therefore I have drawn together various dimensions of interaction between development actors in the context of Jaffna's reconstruction. By showing the different patterns of negotiation I argued that the embeddedness of these leads to both, to an integration but also to demarcation and localisation. Only through detailed empirical research is one able to draw assumptions on social realities and continuous processes of social change which characterise and shape world society in both, a structural and processual sense. From this perspective, Jaffnas reconstruction and development process appears to be embedded into world society and, at the same time, as happening in very specific locality which is constantly reproduced by the actors constructing it.

References

Anderson, Mary B. (1999) *Do no Harm. How Peace can Support Peace – or War*, Boulder/London: Lynne Rienner Publishers.
Appadurai, Arjun (1995) "The Production of Locality." In: Richard Fardon (ed.) *Counterworks: Managing the Diversity of Knowledge*, London: Routledge, pp. 204-223.
Appadurai, Arjun (1996) *Modernity at Large. Cultural Dimensions of Globalization*, Minneapolis/London: Minnesota University Press.
Appadurai, Arjun (1998) "Dead Certainty. Ethnic Violence in the Era of Globalization." Public Culture 10/2, pp. 225-247.
Basch, Linda/Nina Glick Schiller/Christina Szanton Blanc (1994) *Nations Unbound. Transnational Projects, Postcolonial Predicaments, and Deterritorialized Nation-States*, Langhorne PA: Gordon & Breach.
Braun, Joachim von/Grote, Ulrike/Jütting, Johannes (2000) „Zukunft für Entwicklungszusammenarbeit." In: Rolf Kreibich/Udo E. Simonis (eds.) *Global Change – Globaler Wandel. Ursachenkomplexe und Lösungsansätze. Causal Structures and Indicative Solutions*, Berlin: Berlin Verlag, pp. 237-254.
Brubaker, Rogers (2005) "The 'diaspora' diaspora." Ethnic and Racial Studies 28/1, pp. 1-20.
Cheran, R. (2000) *Changing Formations: Tamil Nationalism and National Liberation in Sri Lanka and the Diaspora*, Toronto: York University, Toronto, unpublished PhD Thesis.
Cheran, R. (2001) *The Sixth Genre: Memory, History and the Tamil Diaspora Imagination*, Colombo: Marga Institute.
Cheran, R. (2004) "Diaspora Circulation and Transnationalism as Agents for Change in the Post Conflict Zones of Sri Lanka." In: Jörg Calließ (ed.) *Wenn es in der Heimat um Krieg und Frieden geht. Die Rolle der Diaspora in Krisenentwicklung und ziviler Konfliktbearbeitung*, Rehberg-Loccum: Evangelische Akademie Loccum, pp. 263-280.
Cheran R. (2007) "Transnationalism, Development and Social Capital: Tamil Community Networks in Canada." In: Luin Goldring (ed.) *Organising the Transnational*, British Columbia: UBC Press.
Clifford, James (1994) "Diasporas." Cultural Anthropology 9/3, pp. 302-338.
Culbert, Vance (2005) "Civil Society Development versus the Peace Dividend: International Aid in the Wanni." Disasters 29/1, pp. 38-57.
Faist, Thomas (2003) "The Border-Crossing Expansion of Social Space: Concepts, Questions and Topics." In: Thomas Faist/Özveren Eyüp (eds.) *Trans-*

national Social Spaces. Agents, Networks and Institutions, Hauts: Ashgate, pp. 1-34.

Fernando, Laksiri (1999) "Ethnic Conflict and the State in Sri Lanka: A Possible Solution?" In: Siri Gamage/I. B.Watson (eds.): *Conflict and Community in Contemporary Sri Lanka. 'Pearl of the East' or the 'Island of Tears'?*, New Delhi/Thousand Oaks/London: Sage Publications, pp. 77-88.

Foster, Yolanda (2003) "Jaffna – The Context of Development in a War for Peace." In: Markus Mayer/Darini Rajasingham-Senanyake/Yuvi Thangarajah (eds.) *Building Local Capacities for Peace. Rethinking Conflict and Development in Sri Lanka*, Delhi: Macmillan India Ltd., pp. 152-166.

Freitag, Ulrike/Oppen, Achim von (2005) "Translokalität als ein Zugang zur Geschichte globaler Verflechtungen", http://geschichte-transnational.clio-online.net/forum/id=879&type=diskussionen.

Fuglerud, Oivind (2001) "Time and Space in the Sri Lanka-Tamil Diaspora." Nations and Nationalism 7/2, pp. 195-213.

Gerharz, Eva (2007) *Translocal Negotiations of Reconstruction and Development in Jaffna, Sri Lanka*, Bielefeld: University of Bielefeld: unpublished PhD Thesis.

Gerharz, Eva (2008) *Translokale Aushandlungen von Entwicklung. Eine akteurszentrierte Analyse des Wiederaufbauprozesses in Jaffna nach Sri Lankas Waffenstillstandsabkommen von 2002*, Working Paper Series des FSP Transnationalisierung und Entwicklung, Universität Bielefeld, http://www.uni-bielefeld.de/tdrc/publications/working_papers/WP359.pdf.

Goetze, Dieter (2002) *Entwicklungssoziologie. Eine Einführung*, Weinheim/München: Juventa Verlag.

Guarnizo, Luis/Smith, Michael Peter (1998) "The Locations of Transnationalism." In: Luis Guarnizo/Michael Peter Smith (eds.) *Transnationalism from Below*, New Brunswick/London: Transaction Publishers, pp. 3-34.

Gunaratna, Rohan (2001) *International Dimension of the Sri Lankan Conflict: Threat and Response*, Colombo: Marga Institute.

Gunasingham, Murugar (1999) *Sri Lankan Tamil Nationalism. A Study of its Origins*, Sydney: MV Publications.

Halbach, Eberhard (2003) "Rebuilding Lives in Times of Conflict in Sri Lanka: The Contribution of Jaffna Rehabilitation Project." In: Markus Mayer/Darini Rajasingham-Senanyake/Yuvi Thangarajah (eds.) *Building Local Capacities for Peace. Rethinking Conflict and Development in Sri Lanka*, Delhi: Macmillan India Ltd., pp. 167-176.

Hellmann-Rajanayagam, Dagmar (1990) "The Politics of the Tamil Past." In: Jonathan Spencer (ed.) *Sri Lanka. History and the Roots of Conflict*, London/ New York: Routledge, pp. 107-122.

Hellmann-Rajanayagam, Dagmar (2007) "Wer und was ist die LTTE?" In: Thomas Kolnberger/Clemens Six (eds.) *Fundamentalismus und Terrorismus. Zu Geschichte und Gegenwart radikalisierter Religion*, Essen: Magnus Verlag, pp. 118-141.

Hettige, S. T. (1998) "Introduction: Youth, Nation-State and Globalization." In: S. T. Hettige (ed.) *Globalization, Social Change and Youth*, Colombo: German Cultural Institute, pp. 1-10.

Hettige, S. T. (2000) "Globalisation and Local Culture: The Case of Sri Lanka." In: S. T. Hettige/Meyer Mayer (eds.) *Sri Lanka at Crossroads. Dilemmas and Prospects after 50 Years of Independence*, Delhi: Macmillan Publishers, pp. 169-205.

Long, Norman (2000) "Exploring Local/Global Transformations. A View from Anthropology." In: Alberto Arce/Norman Long (eds.) *Anthropology, Development, Counter-Tendencies and Violence*, London: Routledge, pp. 184-201.

Long, Norman (2001) *Development Sociology. Actor Perspectives*, London/New York: Routledge.

McDowell, Christopher (1996) *A Tamil Asylum Diaspora. Sri Lankan Migration, Settlement and Politics in Switzerland*, Providence/Oxford: Berghahn Books.

Meyer, Birgit/Geschiere, Peter (1999) "Globalization and Identity: Dialectics of Flow and Closure." In: Birgit Meyer/Peter Geschiere (eds.) *Globalization and Identity: Dialectics of Flow and Closure*, Oxford: Blackwell Publ., pp. 1-16.

Pfaff-Czarnecka, Joanna (2005) "Das Lokale als Ressource im entgrenzten Wettbewerb: Das Verhandeln kollektiver Repäsentationen in Nepal-Himalaya." Zeitschrift für Soziologie, Sonderheft "Weltgesellschaft", pp. 479-499.

Pries, Ludger (2001) "The Approach of Transnational Social Spaces." In: Ludger Pries (ed.) *New Transnational Social Spaces. International Migration and Transnational Companies in the Early Twenty-First Century*, London/New York: Routledge, pp. 3-33.

Radtke, Katrin (2004) "Diaspora und Konfliktfinanzierung. Die moralische Ökonomie des Bürgerkrieges in Sri Lanka." In: Jörg Calließ (ed.) *Wenn es in der Heimat um Krieg und Frieden geht. Die Rolle der Diaspora in Krisenentwicklung und ziviler Konfliktbearbeitung*, Rehburg-Loccum: Evangelische Akademie Loccum, pp. 245-262.

Reimann, Cordula (2004) "Assessing the State-of-the-Art in Conflict Transformation." In: Alex Austin/Martina Fischer/Robert Ropers (eds.) *Transforming Ethnopolitical Conflict. The Berghof Handbook*, Wiesbaden: VS Verlag, pp. 41-66.

Robertson, Roland (1995) "Glocalization: Time-Space and Homogeneity-Heterogeneity." In: Mike Featherstone/Scott Lash/Roland Robertson (eds.) *Global Modernities*, London/Thousand Oaks/New Delhi: Sage Publications, pp. 25-44.

Schimank, Uwe (2005) "Weltgesellschaft und Nationalgesellschaften: Funktionen von Staatsgrenzen." Zeitschrift für Soziologie, Sonderband "Weltgesellschaft" pp. 1-21.

Somasundaram, Daya (1998) *Scarred Minds. The Psychological Impact of War on Sri Lankan Tamils*, New Delhi/Thousand Oaks/London: Sage Publications.

Sriskandarajah, Dhananjayan (2004) "Closing the Circle. The Tamil Diaspora's Involvement in Sri Lanka." In: Jörg Calließ (ed.) *Wenn es in der Heimat um Krieg und Frieden geht. Die Rolle der Diaspora in Krisenentwicklung und ziviler Konfliktbearbeitung*, Rehburg-Loccum: Evangelische Akademie Loccum, pp. 191-210.

Wayland, Sarah (2004) "Ethnonationalist Networks and Transnational Opportunities: The Sri Lankan Diaspora." Review of International Studies 30, pp. 405-426.

Wilson, A. Jeyaratnam (1994) "The Colombo Man, the Jaffna Man, and the Batticaloa Man: Regional Identities and the Rise of the Federal Party." In: Chelvadurai Manogoran/Bryan Pfaffenberger (eds.) *The Sri Lankan Tamils. Ethnicity and Identity*, Boulder/San Francisco/Oxford: Westview Press, pp. 126-142.

Wilson, A. Jeyaratnam (2000) *Sri Lankan Tamil Nationalism. Its Origins and Development in the 19th and 20th Century*, New Delhi: Penguin Books.

Wimmer, Andreas/Glick Schiller, Nina (2002) "Methodological Nationalism and Beyond. Nation-State Building, Migration and the Social Sciences." Global Networks 2/4, pp. 301-334.

Wobbe, Theresa (2000) *Weltgesellschaft*, Bielefeld: transcript.

Transnationality, Translocal Citizenship and Gender Relations: Transformation of Rural Community Organisation, Local Politics and Development[1]

GILBERTO RESCHER

Transnational Rurality

Rural areas in developing countries are often seen as traditionalist, isolated and backward. This is also the case in Mexican discourses on underdevelopment. Such preconceptions are aggravated where indigenous communities are concerned. In such discourses, the region I am conducting research in, the *Valle del Mezquital*,[2] has been the example par excellence of an underdeveloped region.[3] Due to experiences from other rural areas and especially because of the existence of undocumented labour migration to the USA as a mass phenomenon (cf. Quezada 2004; Serrano 2006) it is obvious that such a vision of the communities studied is erratic, because it is based on a conceptualisation of them as enclosed communities in the sense of social formations "boxed" in territorial containers.[4] The case of the *Valle del Mezquital* is an excellent example to highlight the way in which even, or better said especially, such regions and communities, seen as remote and backward, actually have access to important transnational links. Such communities are able to manage processes of glocalisation (Robertson 1995) employing them as resource for their own reproduction and continuity, thus merging the so called traditional with relatively new elements of social life. Transnationality forms an important dimension of the rural communities and their social organ-

---

[1] This paper is based on empirical data that I have collected from 2005 during fieldwork in Mexico as part of my ongoing doctoral project on local political transformation in rural areas. I applied an ethnographic methodology based on the grounded theory and Long´s interface analysis (cf. Glaser/Strauss 1967; Strauss/Corbin 1998; Long 1989, 2005; Long/Long 1992; Arce/Long 2000)

[2] This region is part of the state of Hidalgo in central Mexico. It is located about 80 kilometres north of Mexico-City. *Valle del Mezquital* means "Valley of the Mezquite Grove".

isation, giving evidence of how global and local processes are interwoven in the social spaces of these supposedly remote and secluded communities. Furthermore, this everyday transnationality is related to processes of transformation of communitarian self organisation and its internal rules, the so called *usos y costumbres* (ways and customs). Taking into account that the community is an important arena for the negotiation of local politics and development, this social change ultimately relates to transformation in these fields (cf. Besserer 2006; Lisbona 2005; Rescher 2006).

There are only a few studies that put a focus on two important aspects of this kind of community transformation. These elements, in the forefront of the observed change, are the local concept of citizenship (*ciudadania*) and gender issues. Citizenship is a central point in which the transformation of the community organisation becomes visible. This is especially true concerning gender relations (cf. Rivera 2006; Mendoza 1999). Thus, I will discuss more thoroughly the relation between transformation in community organisation and its central elements, gender relations in- and outside the community and, as mentioned before, some links to the fields of local politics and development. My interest in this transformation arises out of its relations to the field of development. Political negotiation, as a facet of multilevel and multilocally negotiated development processes, is especially intriguing. We have to take into account the interwoveness of transnational everyday practices, and corresponding lifeworlds (Schütz/Luckmann 1974), with political aspects at all levels of policy making and political negotiations.

---

3   For a long time The *Valle del Mezquital* was seen as marginalised, poor and underdeveloped and it has been the target of a large number of development interventions and experiments of the Mexican state. The reason for this is the fact that, of the regions declared as underdeveloped, it is the closest to Mexico City. Thus, for the members of the urban middle class "poverty" became visible in the region and was considered a source of shame because it is so close to the capital. Nonetheless, since the 1960s, social movements have been active in this region, often drawing on ethnic discourses. The social pressure which manifested itself in those movements was mitigated through developmental programs and projects. For this a specialised organisation, the *Patrimonio Indigena del Valle del Mezquital* (Indigenous Patrimony of the *Valle del Mezquital*), was founded. It was intended to be an institution to represent and assist the rural population. At the same time, according to Mexican paternalistic ideas of politics, this aimed at their cooptation into the political system. The *Valle del Mezquital* eventually gained an image as a region extremely loyal to the (former) state party PRI and most throughly penetrated by clientelistic networks. Even the boundary of the region is related to disputes over development. (cf. Martínez/Sarmiento 1991)

4   According to Pries the term container was first used by Albert Einstein in his criticism of mechanistic visions of space (Pries 2001: 5).

The Case of Doña Clara and Don Raimundo[5]

In my fieldwork I came across the case of two informants that perfectly exemplifies the processes mentioned above. This is the case of Doña Clara and her husband Don Raimundo.

Doña Clara and Don Raimundo are native to El Thonxi a small village in a mountainous part of the *Valle del Mezquital*. Both of them grew up in peasant families and they "own" some land in the local *ejido*[6] along with an amount of small private property. Like most of the couples in the village they based their livelihood on a mix of diverse economic activities among which peasant agriculture, day labour and handicraft were the most important. This kind of market-oriented subsistence economy[7] was amplified when Don Raimundo migrated for the first time to the USA in the early 1990s in search of work. He started to work there in the agricultural sector and later on found a relatively stable, though irregular, job in a bean-packing-plant. Actually, he has been working there for more then ten years and has established a rather good relationship with his boss. During this period Doña Clara began to represent her husband in all domains. In addition to the activities she had been responsible for, she learned to manage the agricultural activities all by herself. She did all of the reproductive work and began to act as a representative of her domestic unit in dealing with the community. Thanks to his situation, Don Raimundo is able to visit his wife and his family without being afraid of losing his employment. These visits take place annually or every two years, mostly in winter, when important local holidays and festivals are held. However since he recently became ill, he is currently back in his village, trying to regain his health.[8]

During his periods of absence in the USA Don Raimundo always remained a full member of the community and was thus treated as a citizen. This meant that he could vote in the village assembly and had to pay financial fees as well as doing his share of

---

5   The names of persons and villages were changed to allow informants to remain anonymous.
6   *Ejido* is a common form of collective land ownership in Mexico. It was established after the Mexican Revolution and, as there are distinct types of *ejidos,* this does not necessarily imply that all the land belongs to everyone. Instead in this *ejido* it means that every member has got a share of land, but the overall organisation of this shared land ownership is collective. So there is an elected board with a representative, the *comisariado ejidal*, who is the link to institutions of agricultural extension services etc. In these communities the ownership of land is still very important, probably not just in terms of economy but also of identity, as common disputes over land show (in respect to the *ejido* and the relevance of land ownership from an ethnographic perspective cf. Nuijten 1998; for *ejido* in general cf. Eckstein, Florescano, Rivera).
7   Concerning the merging of distinct incomes and economic strategies cf. Evers (1985) and Elwert et. al. (1983) and for subsistence economy as related to market activities see Bennholdt-Thomsen (1984) and Bennholdt-Thomsen/Mies (2000).
8   This pattern of migration is common in the village. So is the fact that most reproductive work having to do with illness and aging is externalised from the productive process in the USA and left to "homestaying" family members in Mexico.

community work. As he is an experienced member of the community he was elected to community positions during his absence and never lost the esteem of other community members. Correspondingly he and his family always tried to fulfill these duties. Doña Clara and her sons carried out his communitarian labour obligations and represented Don Raimundo in the village's assemblies. His contribution was to send money to pay the communitarian fees. In time, with the migration of the older sons, Doña Clara gradually took over all of her husband's duties and became increasingly experienced and confident in community affairs. The apogee of her engagement was when she stood in for her husband in the fulfilment of his duties as *delegado*, the community's highest authority, an elected office. Although her activity was formally as a substitute for Don Raimundo she was, de facto, the first woman who filled the post of village head. In this function, she acquired more experience, especially on the level of the municipality, a political sphere which was in these days nearly out of the reach of women.

The villagers relate that there were some inconveniences during her administration. They usually expect the *delegado* to "work for the community". This means that at the end of the one year tenure there should be visible changes in the village normally achieved through the realisation of communitarian projects. This idea commonly refers to visible manifestations of progress or development[9] like the construction of new public works and buildings or at least the renewal of previous ones.[10] Obviously, owing to limited material resources, this can not be achieved during every term of office. In general it is important to negotiate with funding institutions, especially the municipality, to gain support for projects. But this implies the support of the community in constructing the image of a well organised group. Doña Clara's term was probably difficult due to a lack of confidence in her ability by male citizens, resulting in a kind of boycott. As a result she may have gotten less support than usual, in terms of the communitarian work itself or her duties of negotiation with the municipal administration. Nonetheless some people state that even if it was not the best of all tenures at least it was not the worst. But more importantly for our analysis, she insisted on trying to actively fulfil her responsibilities despite many odds and so managed to learn a lot about the modes of communitarian and local politics and was able to make some (personal) contacts in the municipality. After leaving the position she kept her interest in these spheres alive and felt the desire to continue her commitment "in support of her community" as she says. Thus, she started to "lobby" without a mandate on the municipal level. As a result she was elected a substitute counsellor and at present she is trying to collaborate with a NGO. Although several persons have criticised this dedication as a sign of Doña Claudia's supposed conceit she carries on with determination.

---

9 The most common emic expression for or reference to development is "so that the community advances" (*"para que la comunidad avance"*). Whereas the term development (*desarrollo*) is nearly never used.

10 This coincides with the vision of development in various parts of the world. An example is Benin where development is seen as manifested in prestigious buildings, named *réalisations,* which are supposed to exemplify progress irregardless their actual "usefulness", cf. Elwert 1991, 336pp.

In spite of the problems mentioned she can be seen as a pioneer within the community. Nonetheless this does in no way lead to recognition by the community's women. Instead there is a great rivalry among the women of the community and Doña Clara is constantly criticised, stressing the discourse already mentioned. It seems that especially other women consider her to be arrogant and claim that her administration and her commitment led to nothing. This constitutes a very common criticism of women who step out of their supposed domain. This attitude can be analysed as a reflex of the prevailing gender order in the community. Nobody is supposed to leave her social position and to act in violation of local rules.[11] Nonetheless following her term the participation of women as representatives in the assembly and the fulfillment of elected posts gained a different status and was more accepted. Surely, Doña Clara's tenure served as an example that other women could relate to.

Based on this case I am going to discuss these phenomena in relation to the dimensions of the rural community organisation in the *Valle del Mezquital* mentioned above.

Transnationalised Communities

The rural communities in this Mexican region are characterised by a specific form of social organisation. They are relatively small, of approximately 400 to 1000 inhabitants, and possess several semi-autonomous institutions through which the communities' internal affairs are dealt with. This kind of social organisation is often associated with the indigenous background of its members, although it can also be found in other non-indigenous rural communities. In this case the people belong to the ethnic group Hñähñu. I am going to briefly discuss the migration history of the *Valle del Mezquital* and the communities' pattern of social self-organisation and then discuss the transformation related to the rise of transnational migration. I will show how the villagers are able to adapt their social organisation, rules and institutions to broader transformation, repositioning themselves in the diverse fields they interact with.

Migration in the *Valle del Mezquital* is relatively new as a mass phenomenon and has recently resulted in undocumented labour migration to the USA. As a consequence, the region has been only lately considered a so-called "expulsing area". Migration research on Mexico still has a strong focus on the supposed 'traditional' migration states, like Oaxaca, Michoacan, Zacatecas and Jalisco.[12] However, there is actually a large history of migration and of translocality in the

---

11 Probably some of the women were also envious of the room to manoeuvre that Doña Clara gained and of her achievements.
12 This is reflected in anthologies like Fox/Rivera 2004 and Lanly/Valenzuela 2004. This is certainly owed to their prominence in pioneering studies on transnational migration spanning Mexico and the USA .

state of Hidalgo, especially in the *Valle del Mezquital*. (Martínez/Sarmiento 1991) Starting in the mid 20th century there has been an extended period of internal migration for work in the cities of Mexico as construction workers or housemaids. Everyday life even then seemed to have involved a certain level of translocality.[13] This shows the continuous flexibility and mobility of these rural people in the quest for their livelihoods. Some features of this mobility seem to have been translated to transnational migration. Migration to the USA surged in the 1980s and turned into a mass phenomenon in the 1990s. The actual commitment to this process varies from village to village, but currently all villages of the *Valle del Mezquital* witness considerable migration flows to the USA. In the communities I have studied there is no household without family ties in the USA, mainly in the states of North and South Dakota, Tennessee, Georgia and Florida. A fair amount of migrants were able to benefit from the 1984 amnesty, obtaining legal residence and thus accelerating the process of transnational community building (cf. Álvarez 1995; Schmidt/Crummett 2004).

As a result of the massive migration to the USA, several changes to the social organisation of communities in the *Valle del Mezquital* can be observed. One of the most important is, as in Doña Clara's case the admittance of women, normally migrants' spouses, to the community organisation and to formal positions as representatives of their husbands, or sons. This has resulted in an ongoing renegotiation of the community's gender relations leading to internal conflicts but bringing certain gains for some women as I shall discuss later. Transnationalisation is not the sole element in this transformation but it occurs in combination with several others. This shows that the transnational dimension of these communities is, in various ways, strongly related to diverse processes of current social and political transformation.

The key to the local organisation is the emic concept of citizenship (*ciudadania*). This concept is different from the legal and constitutional concept of citizenship, and has a peculiarly local character. Thus, it differs from the concept of transnational citizenship currently discussed in transnationalisation literature (Kivisto/Faist 2007; Smith/Bakker 2008). It is an emic term which makes reference to a social status inside the community which enables different persons to take part in community assemblies, where local affairs are discussed, as voting members. This means that they are enabled to formally take part in the communities' decisions. At the same time citizens have to fulfil collective work obligations in so called *faenas,* and to pay yearly contributions for the community projects. Furthermore citizens are eligible to fill community positions. These in-

---

13 In contrast to terms like transnational the term translocal refers to the fact that most social processes are not taking place in reference to a nation but are very localised. Thus the importance of the analysis lies not in the crossing of a national border but more generally in the spanning of social textures between distinct localities, be they border crossing or not (cf. for translocal as analytical category Peleikis 2003; Lachenmann/Dannecker 2008; Burawoy 2000 and for the discussion of locality, Pfaff-Czarnecka 2005).

clude the membership in committees, for example for the water supply, schools and public works, as well as the highest local authority, the *delegado*. He acts as a justice of the peace, forms the link to governmental institutions and is more generally the community representative to the outside world.

In the past citizens were supposed to be representatives of their family in the sense of family patriarchs. According to this conceptualisation, it is still assumed that the supposed "male breadwinner" is the spokesperson of a household. Nonetheless over the last few years the social embodiment of this concept has undergone severe modifications through diverse processes of negotiation, which finally converted it into a kind of transnational citizenship with a strongly gendered background. It is important to note that the transnationalisation of this local concept has only become possible through the commitment of women like Doña Clara in the realm of community organisation.

The weight of transnational citizenship is seen in the continuous reference to the community as a collective and to the ongoing fulfilment of citizen duties, even in cases of migrants who are away from home for years, despite the relatively huge expenses this implies. In a certain way this can be seen as coercion, because those who won't contribute lose all their rights in the community, e.g. to community based services like access to water supply or even the right to be buried in their home village. This shows that identity as a community member is an important aspect as well. No one would ever dare to be excluded beyond death from his village.

Thus another fundamental feature of the community is its importance in the villagers' identity formation. The community is a we-group in the classic sense (Elwert 1997, 2002). The villagers feel themselves to be part of a certain community, despite all conflicts. It is nearly unimaginable to live outside a community. Certainly there is certain pragmatism about this, as the community is needed for the provision of specific services and for the execution of projects. But deeper than this the community is a social construct every villager can relate him/herself to. This is even true in cases in which some people feel confronted by the community, (temporarily) cease to carry out their duties and speak about the community in an alienated way. In the end, these disputes demonstrate their commitment and their identification with the community. The members feel a strong sense of belonging (Cohen 1982) to this we-group which is reflected in their day-to-day relevance structures. So the rise of a transnational dimension is based on this deep identification with the community, finally enabling it to transform into a transnational formation.[14] As in every construction of identity the process itself is dynamic and negotiated through self and external ascriptions (cf. Schlee/Werner 1996; Schlee 2002). Through the interactions between the community and the outside world the visions and perceptions of the "indigenous community" are in constant transformation on both sides.

It is noticeable that these communities do not have the kind of migrant associations that a considerable part of the migration and transnationalisation literature concerning Mexico frequently refers to.[15] Neither have the migrants established formal organisations nor have they attempted to create informal equivalents with the goal of developing their communities or municipalities or to influence local and regional politics in their places of origin. This fact is based in the form of social organisation, to which the migrants are attached to. In transnational citizenship especially I see the reason why these types of migrant associations, like hometown associations, have not been developed in these communities. Migrants have to cooperate and their interest in helping and developing their community is thus satisfied, so there is no need for separate organisations. The outcome is a basically transnational community organisation in which so called traditional elements are well adapted to these new circumstances. We can see this phenomenon as exemplifying a strong transnational link between actors in their places of origin and the migrants. This kind of transnational organisation should not be overlooked due to an intense focus on formal migrant institutions. It could be a feature of transnationality as common as formal institutions are.[16] In my cases the relative informality of organisational patterns is essential for transnationality. In contrast to the stereotypic perspective on rural indigenous communities above mentioned, their organisation is very flexible and capable of coping with diverse changes. In this respect, my analysis points to the *"usos y costumbres"* (ways and customs), which are often perceived as traditionalistic, strict and rigid,[17] as being the basis for the communities' flexibility and ability to adapt to new circumstances. They ultimately assure the survival of the villages and of their form of organisation. As a matter of fact, most customs and 'traditional' institutions seen as a legacy of precolonial times, are of relatively recent origin. In

---

14 This sense of belonging and the correspondent relevance structures in identity formation are reflected in an often cited anecdote from El Thonxi. One villager was apprehended by the US Immigration Authority. When he was asked about his place of origin for deportation he answered "I am from El Thonxi." "Where is that?" asked the officers. "Next to Iglesia Nueva." the closest village. "And where is that?" "Close to Ixmiquilpan." the regional centre. This went on until the migrant finally said that he was from Mexico, the information the immigration officers were intending to find out. This shows that identity construction is not primarily related to Mexico as nation but to the local community.
15 Examples for this focus on formally established hometown associations are Goldring 2002, 1998 and Lanly/Valenzuela 2004.
16 This aspect will be discussed in detail in my forthcoming dissertation.
17 This vision is, on the one hand, present in some academic work and, on the other hand, in public discourse.

many cases for example, the *faenas* as an institutionalised form of community work, seem to be an recent reinvention of local traditions arisen in response to emerging necessities. This means that the community members have always been flexible enough to adapt themselves and their organisation to external changes. This has always been achieved through the interaction with the "outside". Since even the internal rules are based on constant renegotiations the community actors are able to achieve further transformation through this highly dynamic process. The everyday interactions in- and outside the community are ultimately the basis for the communities' flexibility.

These communities are basically transnationalised communities. I call them transnationalised in contrast to the concept of transnational community, which refers to broader communities that are formed in the process of transnationalisation (cf. Glick Schiller et al. 1992; Basch et al. 1993; Pries 2008). These consist mainly of transmigrants and persons related to them through regular interaction like their family members and other persons who stay in the places of origin as well as those who live in places of arrival. These formations are located in or encompass transnational social spaces (cf. Pries 1999; Faist 2000) that are plurilocally grounded crossborder social formations. In my cases I refer to already existing communities that developed a transnational dimension mainly through processes of migration and, as a result, became transnationalised. Thus, in this case the transnational space does not encompass the whole of the community but just a facet of it. The transnationalised community can be understood as part of transnational fields (cf. Glick Schiller et al. 1999) to use a more comprehensive concept.

Due to its manifestation of global and local processes this kind of transnationality could be understood as a feature of a world society in an open and inclusive sense. This specific transnational formation is part of larger border crossing societal arrangements. However this example exposes the lack of utility of those world society approaches that are based on systems theory for explaining processes related to (transnational) migration. In that mindset it is frequently assumed that, as Stichweh (2005) states, migration is going to disappear. In this view migration will be superseded by communication technologies because the relevance of face to face communication in social systems is declining. Moreover, supposed global world society structures are seen as influencing local formations. The independence of local formations, like communities, from global ones and their relevance in the shaping of global processes, where local agency is prominent, is deliberately omitted (cf. Lachenmann 2007). My case demonstrates that social formations depend upon a common ground which is constantly reaffirmed and renegotiated through personal interactions, this means by processes which depend upon face to face encounters. Communication technologies are employed in the transnational processes described but they are in no way making personal interactions obsolete. They are just an additional feature of the transnational social space that rather stimulates and assists the physical mobility of persons. In the communities studied, migration and the related symbolic flows are fundamental for the existence of a transnational social formation which can be part of broader global societal formations. Accordingly a world society concept has to take into account the localisation of world society based on encounters of social actors in localised formations. Only in this manner can it embrace significant parts of social realities.

Thus instead of leaving aside the analysis of interactions these should be the focus of study. The best way to analyse the dynamics of such processes is the analysis of the correspondent interfaces in the interactions between different social actors. According to Long, interface

"conveys the idea of some kind of face to face encounter between individuals with differing interests, resources and power. Studies of interface aim to bring out the types of discontinuities that exist and the dynamic and emergent character of the struggles and interactions that take place, showing how actors' goals, perceptions, values, interests and relationships are reinforced or reshaped by this process" (Arce/Long 1992: 214).

"Such an analysis stresses the reproduction and transformation of social discontinuities inherent in interface encounters [...]" (Long 1992a: 6).

and he states that

"studies of interface should not therefore be restricted to observing what goes on during face-to-face encounters, since these interactions are in part affected by actors, institutional and cultural frameworks, and resources that may not actually be physically or directly present. Hence [...] the analysis should situate these within broader institutional and power fields" (Arce/Long 1992: 214).

Thus, the positions of social actors are never stable but always transformed through interactions. This means that social processes, like in our case, are very dynamic because they are based on interactions forming the foundation for social change. At the same time the interface is just the point where the diverse logics, perspectives and resources of actors based in their specific lifeworlds, become visible. As in the case of transnational formations interfaces have to be analysed within broader fields.

In the case of the transformation of the community organisation an important interface exists between those "staying home", the supposedly less mobile villagers, usually considered equivalent to the community as an institution, and those citizens who have migrated. The main arenas in which the encounters take place are the village assembly and related institutions in the community organisation. I could observe in the assemblies how the logics of the main actors collided. Depending upon the concrete situation, the actors involved were the leaders of the community and its elected authorities, on the one hand, and the migrants or their representatives on the other. There were constant quarrels about the way in which repercussions of the physical absence of migrants could be remedied, exposing the distinct logics of the actors. Just one example is the migrants' goal of having more influence over the communitarian processes of decision making. This concern arises basically from the fear of not being taken into account in an appropriate manner and, due to the migrants' absence, not being able to argue in favour of their families needs. In this their increased self-confidence, owed to experiences, ideas and resources gained in the USA, forms a prominent part of the basis for the resulting interactions. The leaders and authorities, in contrast, are aiming at a smooth governing of the community. They often see themselves as owning the knowledge necessary for guiding village affairs and perceive the migrants' interventions as perturbing or even as threat to the "ways in which the community should work." Furthermore they are worried about maintaining their position in the internal power arrangements. In the end, this kind of negotiation at interfaces has led to the emergence of the transnational dimension of community organisation in its current pattern.

It is important to stress that the process of transnationalisation has reached impressive dimensions. The case of the village of Barranca Empinada it is especially striking. In a relatively short period this community and its migrants developed nearly the full "set" of features of transnationality, despite its being based mainly on undocumented migration. It can be stated that almost immediately, this community in Mexico has seen migrants as continuously participating in the community. There have never been tendencies towards separation or exclusion. Thus, the transnationalisation of this community took place faster than described for other Mexican cases. But more importantly it took a form of everyday practices of transnationality particular to these communities. Furthermore it has to be stressed that it is basically women's commitment and dedication to the community organisation that has facilitated the rise of and sustained the transnational dimension. At the core are changes to the ways and customs or better said, everyday practices of construction of citizenship and of the concept of citizenship itself. Thus, it can be affirmed that these rules, like community organisation as a whole, are constantly being renegotiated, which explains their flexible character. In this way transformation is achieved through interaction in a dynamic social field. The communities have developed their own specific transnationality through a dynamic process of interaction with diverse actors and groups. The change in gender relations is a prominent part of this process of transformation as I will analyse in the following.

Change in Gender Relations

Due to the growing incorporation of women into community organisation mainly as representatives of absent migrants, as in Doña Clara's case, spaces like the village assembly or the *faenas*, the community work, form the main arenas in which the negotiation of gender relations takes place. I am going to analise, as exemplarily, four arenas or sets of interfaces in which negotiations of gender relations take place, sketching briefly the distinct logics involved.

The first arena in which renegotiations occur are the formal public spheres of the communitarian organisation where interactions between participating women and male community members, especially the leaders and authorities, take place. Although the incorporation of women into the community organisation and work is fundamental for the survival of the community and in this sense, especially of the community in its transnational shape, this transformation is not fully accepted and has led to continuous subtle conflicts. In El Thonxi there is constant criticism about the women's participation in *faenas*. It is uttered in comments ranging from the supposed physical inability to do hard work well, accusations concerning their supposed unwillingness to work preferring to gossip, and claims that they don't even know how to do the work.[18] What underlies these statements is a lack of mutual understanding, and up to a certain degree, a wish to discredit women's participation. The same applies to women's position in the community assembly. Here, men's criticism is again that women gossip instead of participating constructively, that they don't pay attention, don't inform their husbands correctly and finally that they don't understand what is being talked about. These reproaches rise partially from a misinterpretation of the fact that some women need explanation or translation of certain aspects, which is given by other women and understood by some men as gossiping. Women who do actively participate in assemblies are criticised for being disrespectful, for criticising the men's proposals and for saying irrelevant things. In consequence, there are regular attempts to limit women's participation. Some *delegados,* for example, tried to forbid female work in the *faenas*, requiring them to pay fees, and the actual *delegado* didn't want to grant representatives of migrants the status of voting members in the assemblies. This never succeeded because women resisted and these restrictions would have ended up putting the community's functioning at risk.

We may see the attempts to restrict women's participation and to reverse their incorporation as a response to a feeling of discomfort and of threat felt by many men. In a certain way, they feel threatened by the growing presence and influence of women, and are afraid that women could start ruling the community. These general and diffuse fears are augmented by community leaders who fear that they could lose part of their power. Accordingly, especially old men and leaders feel that the established order or the customs are threatened. From their perspective, the community is no longer how it should be. And this fear is not just related to the women's participation, but also to a growing influence of male migrants. These attempts at restriction are accompanied and supported by a rising neotraditionalist discourse about community and its institutions, stressing collaboration and harmony as a result of "proper behaviour" in the community, especially concerning the positions of men and women. This is definitively to be seen

---

18 Obviously these reproaches stress classic preconceptions about female behaviour.

as a mix of prejudices and fear of losing power and control. It also concurs with statements that express the view that the community is going wrong, that the traditional order is affected, and that the village organisation, which from their perspective 'has been proven to work', should remain unaltered or be reinstated. Certainly, they also feel a risk of the community entering a state in which it would no longer work and thus disappear. For the leaders this involves the danger of losing the basis of their own political activities in the community and party politics. The resistance of women to these manoeuvres is quite inconsistent. Thus this neotraditionalist discourse is regularly supported by women. They often criticise in subtle ways the "inappropiate behaviour" of those women who take part in the community organisation.

In this context, the gendered power texture in the community and its organisation can be analysed where interaction between women is guided by gender rules, or in other words at the interface between different groups of women. Generally in the analysis of the gender relations in the communities it has to be taken into account that they are basically power relations. Nonetheless power should not be understood as something imposed on individuals and groups in an oppressive manner but as constantly constructed and renegotiated through interactions between diverse actors. As Foucault (1982: 225p.) states

"What makes power hold good, what makes it accepted, is simply the fact that it doesn't only weigh on us as a force that says no, but that it traverses and produces things, it induces pleasure, forms of knowledge, produces discourse. It needs to be considered as a productive network that runs through the whole social body, much more than as a negative instance whose function is repression."

Furthermore, as Abu-Lughod (1990: 41p.) suggests, power can be detected through the analysis of resistance. As Foucault (1978: 95p.) says

"Where there is power, there is resistance, and yet, or rather consequently, this resistance is never in a position of exteriority in relation to power."

In this sense the ongoing processes of renegotiation of women´s position in the communities points to the transformation of the gendered dimension of power relations. The challenging of established rules, supposedly ancient and traditional, by dedicated women is to be understood as a form of resistance inside the power texture of the community. But this is always related to power itself and in a certain sense implies a certain recognition and legitimation of the power relations themselves, perpetuating power and thus gender relations as a whole. So it is necessary to study in the long term whether or not the change in gender relations is nonetheless leading to a lasting transformation of the local gender orders.

As the example of Doña Clara reveals, women, as part of their involvement in the transnational community, are becoming more experienced in aspects of community organisation and some have even become politically active at the municipal level. This is in part a result of their involvement in community organisation but also of their increasing work and responsibility in all aspects of social life, in community, household, agriculture and waged labour. It also coincides with the migration experiences that many women have had on their own. Generally, this experience leads them to feel more self-assured and to be more independent, knowing that they can achieve goals by themselves. An important part, as these women often mention, is the feeling of earning their own money in the USA, which makes them more independent and 'equal' to their husbands. This change happens to an extent which leads the female villagers to categorise the older women as "women of the past" and the younger ones as "women of the present". This categorisation encompasses a vision of the younger women as having different values, attitudes and abilities based on their different education and experiences. This difference is marked and can be observed in everyday-life.[19]

In any case, there exists a marked difference between elder and younger women in questions of social control, an interface characterised by discontinuities (Long 1989). The relations of power in the negotiation of women´s positions and the existing ascriptions about what is defined as proper female behaviour imply a strong dimension of social control in the transnationalised community. This kind of control has always been common in the communities as social formations and refers widely to the control of women´s activities. This aspect has gained increasing importance in the realm of transnationality. Because married couples are often separated for long periods of time it is seen as important to assure the „good behaviour" of women by maintaining or even deepening the control over women's day to day activities. This is done especially to lessen the presupposed risk of infidelity. Thus in the transnationalised community the social control of women is stronger than before. It is mainly exerted through the instrumentalisation of gossip and rumour about the attitude of specific women. Actually an important part of the long-distance communication is related to gossiping and false rumours are used to intimidate women and to create an attitude of cautiousness. It is quite common that this social control is exerted through the mothers-in-law. This exemplifies the interface between women in which some uphold and enforce social rules, that are constituted by men as supposedly traditional, thus facilitating the social control of certain other women.

Nonetheless in addition to the upholding of power relations through women there are examples of hidden resistance in the sense of James Scott (1985, 1990). Often a visible subordination to the dominant rules and visions is just a strategy

---

19 It is striking that despite categorisation, and the discursive formation of two distinct groups there is no apparent generational conflict, no confrontation, at least among women. They often work together and help each other through well-defined ties of solidarity and reciprocity. Existing conflicts are related more to personal antipathy than to age based othering.

to defend existing particular spaces and room to manoeuvre. This properly describes the daughters-in-law's logic in coping with attempts at control. They cooperate up to a certain limit to avoid problems that could lead to stronger restriction. There are several other points in which this kind of hidden resistance can be seen in women's actions. Thus, Doña Clara almost always speaks Hñähñu, the local language, in the village assembly. Officially she states that this should be normal because they are an indigenous community. Nonetheless she told me that she does this to avoid being cheated by the leaders due to their eloquence in Spanish and to insure that the other women are able to understand the discussion.

There is a further point in which distinct visions of the internal rules of organisation could bring actual transformation to put a strain on the communities. The corresponding interactions take place in a more subtle and discursive way at an underlying all-embracing level in the communities. Although the transformation in the communitarian organisation leads to an increasing degree of incorporation of social groups that were formerly marginalised, it applies almost exclusively to male citizens. It is still very difficult for women to integrate themselves into the arenas in which such negotiations take place, and often they are not fully taken into account. Gender democracy is far from being achieved at all levels. This is especially problematic for the communities themselves, as currently the majority of villagers who go to university are young women receiving financial assistance from their migrant relatives, while young men prefer to migrate and work in the USA before even finishing secondary education. This causes a huge educational gap between younger men and women, but the main problem is that women, as they are not 'citizens', are not politically taken into account in their community. Thus, their potential is not used for the good of the community and in time, these women become alienated. As for the community, it is losing its educational elite in a context in which there are attempts by the leaders to instrumentalise village customs to maintain their position and power.

At the same time the physical mobility of women is seldom recognised in the communities. Even though very many of them actually have extensive migratory experiences, often made on their own, and an important share of the actual migrants in the USA are female, it is continuously assumed that women stay at home or migrate as a mere annex of their husbands and will return to the village after a short while.[20] Thus it is generally supposed that they will be present to cope with all of the responsibilities the migrating men leave behind. This causes problems for those women who live differently and are confronted with assumptions and demands based on this prejudiced attitude. This relates not only to migrants' spouses but also to the women who attend university. As they are not living in conformity with the local conception of a good women's life, especially by

---

[20] This corresponds to a widely shared view of female migration that fails to recognise women as autonomous and active migrants with their own strategies and objectives. For a discussion of academic blindness in relation to female migrants see Dannecker 2005.

not staying home, their reality is ignored in the communitarian self-organisation. Thus they drop below the authorities' horizon and their abilities are not used to benefit the community.

Looking at a fourth arena we can see that, despite the importance of transnationalisation for the transformation of gender relations in the communities, it is important to have a wider scope of analysis when taking into account other elements fostering their renegotiation. In this way it is possible to study transnationality in terms of the local context and to analyse how it relates to other distinct elements in the processes of transformation. This can be exemplified through the analysis of the community Barranca Empinada. Here the position of at least some women had already changed, mainly due to interaction at interfaces on the meso-level between the community and state institutions. In the 1990s this community had the reputation of being rebellious. This was due to its participation in a social movement which some say actually started in Barranca Empinada. The ground for this movement was a protest against local and regional politics especially concerning the disregard of the communities and the accusation of a clientelistic and unjust allocation of resources and assistance. As a result of these struggles, the autonomous status of the community was strengthened.[21] Although today a majority of the former activists feel that they were misused and their claims instrumentalised by the former leaders of the community and the movement, they seem to have enthusiastically participated at the time.[22] Several women also participated actively in the forefront of marches and other activities during this protest. Some say that this was a strategy by the leaders to draw attention to the mobilisation and to confuse the state forces. But even in that case these women gained experiences in the field of organisation and of local politics. This prepared them in the long run to take a more active and independent part in the community. Thus, this group of women formed part of the pool of persons who were entitled to occupy the most prestigious positions in the community.[23] In the same way they were always present as group in the discussions held to make decisions in the community. Although they were not formally entitled to be voting members their opinion was taken into account. When the community broke up due to its leaders' quarrels and split into two rival groups these women were, on the one hand, blamed for being responsible for the friction and, on the other hand, are frequently asked for supporting one of the sides.

Finally in this year, 2008, the community elected for the first time a *delegación* that is made up solely of women. This is presented as an attempt to overcome the two-year long friction in the community. Although most of these wo-

---

21 As mentioned before in this community nearly no interference of governmental actors from any level is accepted and state forces like police and military are not allowed to enter the community without having a permit obtained through the *delegado*.
22 This movement became famous in the region due to several roadblocks and the burning of the regional station of the federal police force.
23 Although none of them had been elected *delegada* before.

men are not formal citizens it appears that they were elected in their own right, this means elected as the persons they are and not as proxies of their husbands. I have come to this conclusion because of the fact that the most active women were already present in the community's organisation. In addition the *delegada* is the daughter of a previous informal leader of the community. That means that these women had to have a proper background and image in respect to organisational experience and their reputation inside the community.[24]

The analysis of this case shows that the involvement of women in arenas and spheres that were formally restricted to or at least mainly occupied by men has been achieved due to a combination of diverse aspects. In this the transformation related to the transnational dimensions of the social formations inside the communities, is not the sole cause although it is often an important aspect. Probably the most important point in reaching this goal of full participation is the continuous activity and insistence of these women. Thus it can be stated that they achieve a higher level of emancipation in this process. But at the same time the foundation for this seems to be really a previous emancipation which is then fostered. However these cases can not be understood as a compelling hint of a change in the gender order that goes beyond a mere change of gender relations in certain cases. Nonetheless an important change is definitively taking place.

Local Politics and Development

It is important to underline that these changes seem to be leading to more general change in various aspects. This transformation can not be discussed here in detail, but I will point briefly to some of them. Apart from the change described in gender relations and the renegotiation of belonging and of local institutions, there is a change going on in the local modes of political negotiation and even in the way state and national projects and programs are implemented. The formation of the transnational space seems to be leading, together with other national and global influences like political disappointments and discourses on democracy, human rights and ethnic identities, to more democracy in the sense of greater access to political decision making. Many persons in the rural communities are becoming increasingly interested in political decisions, starting in the community

---

[24] Generally women's position in the communities is also influenced by other aspects like their age or educational background. Elderly women have a distinct position which grants them freedom from certain expectations. They have, for example, more freedom of movement and can drink alcohol in public. Women with a formal education and often working as teachers have always had a distinct position in the community as they are citizens in their own right. This was due to their income but also to a respectful view of them as educated persons. Nonetheless this does not mean that they are fully exempted from rules and attempts at control. However the difference is that they always have been more self assured and devoted more effort to gain recognition by the community.

and reaching other levels. Based on experiences in the USA, a growing educational level and a far better economic situation, village dwellers are not as easy to manipulate as they were before. Many, and because of the concept of citizenship, mainly male migrants, are beginning to get actively involved in community affairs, claiming their right to be taken into account in decisions. This participation quickly leads them to take part in the discussion of aspects concerning the community's relation to various governmental levels and finally, as community representatives, in the corresponding negotiations. In certain cases their position is developing into what Bierschenk, Chauveau and Olivier de Sardan (2003) have conceptualised as one of development brokers. This means that the former community leaders' supremacy is being challenged, leading in some cases to a rupture and in other cases to the integration of the rising leaders. It can be also widely observed that the former local elites are being displaced or enlarged with migrants and younger professionals who are becoming politically active. As part of this process, a slight change in political logics and modes of negotiation can be observed. An example is the fact that governmental support granted to the community is no longer seen as personalised help in a clientelistic manner. Now, most citizens are aware of the impartial character of these benefits and of their right to receive them. Thus, the logic of clientelistic 'begging' is slowly changing to one of insisting on the right to support from public institutions.

As described before, migration to the USA and the formation of transnational social spaces has led, building upon former experiences of translocality, to the transformation of the communities' self-organisation. It is important to notice that communities' flexibility which I argue to be the basis of their survival despite all changes can even lead to a strengthening of the relative autonomy of the communities. This coincides with change in political logics and modes of negotiation and both processes seem to mutually reinforce each other. As a result of the remittances and local community organisation, which enables the villagers to undertake their own projects, the communities have become more independent of state projects and financing. This leads to a stronger position in negotiations with representatives of the state and its institutions. These villagers are conscious of being able to achieve something on their own and they are aware that the state projects would not work without their collaboration and especially without their financial cooperation. Although in the past, this fact has been neglected in designing their projects, over the last few years, communities are becoming more and more aware of the value of their own work and financial contribution. In consequence, the multitude of self-organised projects have enabled the communities to be more autonomous. They are no longer willing to accept every kind of conditions and "interference" from state institutions in exchange for a kind of assistance which is no longer seen as essential for achieving the development of their communities. At the same time, criticism and distrust of state agents has increased and this reinforces the caution about accepting interference in community affairs. This does not mean that the members of the communities would decline any kind of assistance. In fact they even ask for it, but basically the basis for the negotiation of benefits has changed. Parting from these interfaces can rise a new vision of the communities with a gradually more inclusive perspective on development.

Nonetheless, up to now state institutions have not nearly taken into account the existence of female migrants and professionals and their participation in the community decision making. So the general underestimation of rural communities is even worse in the case of their female members. The change in women's lives goes practically unnoticed by these institutions. Thus the planning of development programs and concrete projects remains rooted in a kind of artificial blindness to an inadequate image of rural women. If, nevertheless, change is noticed, it is only defined in negative terms, such as family disruption, etc. As a consequence development and social programs heavily emphasise women as being affected by migration, but the projects proposed are not adapted to women's social reality. Therefore, these programs often do not benefit women and even increase their work load as discussed before. This is a common outcome of development programs which are planned on the drawing board with too little contact with, and understanding of, the social reality of beneficiaries' everyday life. This is the case with several projects in the communities, e.g. the *oportunidades* programs and several projects which were planned to foster the local or "family" economy. Thus, women's work load, which is already increased due to the extra work in household, agriculture and community, is augmented by an extra-amount of communitarian work and of other duties as a result of programs implemented which do not take into account the transnational reality of their lives. A major problem in development planning is that these transnational aspects are not taken into account and therefore the programs and schemes offered do not fit into the social reality of most of the migrants and their family members.

Small Changes – Large Results

As I have analysed in this chapter there are several processes of transformation taking place in the central Mexican rural communities studied. There are changes in the communitarian self organisation and in gender relations and order which are related to transformation in other spheres like (local) politics and development. At a first glance this transformation may be seen as mere processes of emancipation giving rise to a more democratic and egalitarian social organisation. Nonetheless, as I have shown in my analysis, the underlying processes are very complex and diverse and have inconsistent outcomes. Thus certain phenomena concerning gender relations which could be seen as a gain for women in the communities can result in a higher burden and increased social control. For this reason it is important to continue studying the processes related to transnationality taking into account the relation and interwoveness of a variety of dimensions and processes.

The way in which the communities are transformed points to a particular type of transnationality. It is the way in which transnational phenomena are negotiated in those communities. An essential part of this social and political change is based on the activities of women. Nonetheless, instead the gendered dimension of physical mobility and thus of the rising of transnationality in the community organisation and its everyday life is frequently being overlooked. This refers as much to actors in the community itself as to relevant representatives of the state, especially in institutions concerned with development. Thus, even interventions which are meant to "support" women often have a contrary influence increasing their work-burden. It can be stated that the communities can not be simply developed and empowered from the outside. As Long (1992b: 275p.) shows, precisely the dynamics at the interfaces hinder such an emancipation driven from the outside. Such a deeper social change has to build on processes taking place inside the communities, gaining importance in interactions with (institutional) actors from the outside. As I have shown this is the case of the actual transformation that has led to a change of gender order, mainly due to the access to formerly restricted spaces. What is actually causing the problems discussed for the women actively engaged in community organisation and politics is the fact that their commitment is seldom formalised. As in the case of being informal proxies to their spouses, there exists no official manner of taking part in the relevant activities. A recognition of their commitment with a relative formalisation (at the community level) would enable them to combine their numerous duties and activities without being overloaded.[25] Up to now a subtle but considerable change in the gender order has taken place, not only due to transnationalisation but also to the growing education and formal employment of women. As I have shown this process is not just restricted to the communitarian level but reaches other spheres and levels as in the case of local politics. This exemplifies the opportunities for sustainable change through the interrelation with diverse processes of transformation.

---

25 This has already been achieved in few cases where couples have rearranged their duties. Thus when the husband is in the village they attend jointly the village assembly. These men state that the wife is better informed and more experienced in issues of community organisation. This happened with Doña Clara and Don Raimundo. Officially he is still the citizen but, de facto, the community considers her as a citizen.

References

Abu-Lughod, Lila (1990) "The Romance of Resistance: Tracing Transformations of Power Through Bedouin Women." American Ethnologist 17/1, pp. 41-55.

Alvarez, Juana (1995) "La Emigración Internacional en el Estado de Hidalgo." In: Pablo Vargas (ed.) *Hidalgo: Población y Sociedad al Inicio Siglo XXI*, Pachuca, pp. 243-264.

Arce, Alberto/Long, Norman (eds.) (2000) *Anthropology, Development and Modernities: Exploring Discourses Counter-tendencies and Violence*, London: Routledge.

Basch, Linda/Glick Schiller, Nina/Szanton-Blanc, Christina (eds.) (1993) *Nations Unbound: Transnational Projects, Postcolonial Predicaments and Deterritorialized Nation-States*, Amsterdam: Gordon and Breach.

Bennholdt-Thomsen, Veronika (1984) "Subsistence Production and Extended Reproduction." In: Kate Young/Carol Wolkowitz/Roslyn McCullagh (eds.) *Of Marriage and the Market: Women's Subordination Internationally and Its Lessons*, London: Routledge & Kegan Paul.

Bennholdt-Thomsen, Veronika./Mies, Maria (eds.) (2000) *Subsistence Perspective: Beyond the Globalized Economy*, London: Zed Books.

Besserer, Federico (2006) *San Juan Mixtepec: Una Comunidad Transnacional ante el Poder Clasificador y Filtrador de las Fronteras*, Mexico, D.F., UAM, Unidad Iztapalapa.

Bierschenk, Thomas/Chauveau, Jean-Pierre/Olivier de Sardan, Jean-Pierre (2003) "Local Development Brokers in West Africa: The Rise of a New Social Category." In: Journal of Development Studies.

Burawoy, Michael (2000) *Global Ethnography: Forces, Connections, and Imaginations in a Postmodern World*, Berkeley: University of California Press.

Cohen, Anthony P. (1982) *Belonging*, Manchester: University Press Manchester.

Dannecker, Petra (2005) "Transnational Migration and the Transformation of Gender Relations: The Case of Bangladeshi Labour Migrants." In: Current Sociology 53/4, pp. 655-674.

Elwert, Georg/Evers, Hans-Dieter/Wilkens, Werner (1983) "Die Suche nach Sicherheit: Kombinierte Produktionsformen im sogenannten Informellen Sektor." In: Zeitschrift für Soziologie, pp. 281-296.

Elwert, Georg (1991) *Mit den Augen der Beniner*, Dokumentation '90/Deutscher Entwicklungsdienst, Berlin: Dt. Entwicklungsdienst.

Elwert, Georg (1997) "Boundaries, Cohesion and Switching: On We-Groups in Ethnic National and Religious Forms." In: Hans-Rudolf Wicker (ed.) *Rethinking Nationalism and Ethnicity: The Struggle for Meaning and Order in Europe*, Oxford: Berg, pp. 251-272.

Elwert, Georg (2002) "Switching Identity Discourses: Primordial Emotions and the Social Construction of We-Groups." In: Günther Schlee (ed.) *Imagined*

Differences: Hatred and the Construction of Identity, Münster: Lit-Verlag, pp. 33-56.

Evers, Hans-Dieter (1985) *Wage Labour and Subsistence Production in the Shadow Economy,* Working Paper 73, Bielefeld: Forschungsschwerpunkt Entwicklungssoziologie, Universität Bielefeld.

Faist, Thomas (2000) *The Volume and Dynamics of International Migration and Transnational Social Spaces,* Oxford: Oxford University Press.

Foucault, Michel (1982) "Afterword: The Subject and Power." In: Hubert L. Dreyfus/Paul Rabinow (eds.) *Michel Foucault: Beyond Structuralism and Hermeneutics,* Chicago: University of Chicago Press, pp. 208-226.

Foucault, Michel (1978) *The History of Sexuality: Volume 1, An Introduction,* New York: Random House.

Fox, Jonathan/Rivera Salgado, Gaspar (eds.) (2004) *Indígenas Mexicanos Migrantes en los Estado Unidos,* México, D.F.: Porrúa.

Glaser, Barney G./Strauss, Anselm L. (1967) *The Discovery of Grounded Theory: Strategies for Qualitative Research,* New York: DeGruyter.

Glick Schiller, Nina/Basch, Linda/Szanton-Blanc Christina (eds.) (1992) *Towards a Transnational Perspective on Migration: Race, Class, Ethnicity, and Nationalism Reconsidered,* New York: New York Academy of Sciences.

Glick Schiller, Nina/Basch, Linda/Szanton-Blanc, Christina (1999) "From Immigrant to Transmigrant: Theorizing Transnational Migration." In: Ludger Pries (ed.) *Migration and Transnational Social Spaces,* Hants: Ashgate Publishing, pp. 73-105.

Goldring, Luin (1998) "The Power of Status in Transnational Social Fields." In: Michael Peter Smith/Luis Eduardo Guarnizo (eds.) *Transnationalism from Below,* New Brunswick: Transaction Publishers, pp. 165-195.

Goldring, Luin (2002) "The Mexican State and Transmigrant Organizations: Negotiating the Boundaries of Membership and Participation." In: Latin American Research Review 37/3, pp. 55-100.

Kivisto, Peter/Faist, Thomas (eds.) (2007) *Citizenship: Discourse Theory and Transnational Prospects,* Oxford: Blackwell.

Lachenmann, Gudrun (2007) *Transnationalisation and Development – Methodological Issues,* Working Paper 19, COMCAD – Center on Migration, Citizenship and Development (www.comcad-bielefeld.de).

Lachenmann, Gudrun/Dannecker, Petra (eds.) (2008) *Negotiating Development in Muslim Societies: Gendered Spaces and Translocal Connections,* Lanham: Lexington Books.

Lanly, Guillaume/Valenzuela, Basilia (eds.) (2004) *Clubes de Migrantes Oriundos Mexicanos en los Estados Unidos: La Política Transnacional de la Nueva Sociedad Civil Migrante,* Zapopan: Universidad de Guadalajara.

Lisbona, Miguel (ed.) (2005) *La Comunidad a Debate: Reflexiones sobre el Concepto de Comunidad en el México Contemporáneo,* Zamora: El Colegio de Michoacán.

Long, Norman (ed.) (1989) *Encounters at the Interface: A Perspective on Social Discontinuities in Rural Development,* Wageningse Sociologische Studies 27, Wageningen: Wageningen Agricultural University.

Long, Norman (1992a) "Introduction." In: Norman Long/Ann Long (eds.) *Battlefields of Knowledge: The Interlocking of Theory and Practice in Social Research and Development,* London: Routledge, pp. 3-15.

Long, Norman (1992b) "Conclusion." In: Norman Long/Ann Long (eds.) *Battlefields of Knowledge: The Interlocking of Theory and Practice in Social Research and Development,* London: Routledge, pp. 268-277.

Long, Norman (2005) *Development Sociology: Actor Perspectives,* London: Routledge.

Long, Norman/Long, Ann (eds.) (1992) *Battlefields of Knowledge: The Interlocking of Theory and Practice in Social Research and Development,* London: Routledge.

Martínez Assad, Carlos R./Sarmiento Silva, Sergio (eds) (1991) *Nos Queda la Esperanza: El Valle del Mezquital,* México, D.F.: Consejo Nacional para la Cultura y las Artes.

Mendoza, Silvia (1999) *Estructura y Relaciones Familiares ante la Migración de los Padres y Jefes de Familia a los Estados Unidos 1986-1997: Estudio de Caso del Maye Ixmiquilpan Hidalgo,* México, D.F.: UNAM.

Nuijten, Monique (1998) *In the Name of the Land: Organization, Transnationalism, and the Culture of the State in a Mexican Ejido,* Wageningen: The Netherlands.

Peleikis, Anja (2003) *Lebanese in Motion: Gender and the Making of a Translocal Village,* Bielefeld: Transcript.

Pfaff-Czarnecka, Joanna (2005) "Das Lokale als Ressource im entgrenzten Wettbewerb: Das Verhandeln kollektiver Repräsentationen in Nepal-Himalaya." In: Zeitschrift für Soziologie, Sonderheft "Weltgesellschaft" Stuttgart: Lucius & Lucius, pp. 479-499.

Pries, Ludger (2001) *Internationale Migration,* Bielefeld: Transcript.

Pries, Ludger (2008) *Die Transnationalisierung der sozialen Welt: Sozialräume jenseits von Nationalgesellschaften,* Frankfurt a. M.: Suhrkamp.

Pries, Ludger (1999) *Migration and Transnational Social Spaces,* Aldershot: Ashgate.

Quezada, Maria Felix (2004) *La Migración Hñähñu del Valle del Mezquital, Estado de Hidalgo: Tesis Presentada para Obtener el Grado de Maestro en Demografía,* master thesis, Tijuana, Colef.

Rescher, Gilberto (2006) "Ciudadanía Transnacional, Política Local y Desarrollo: El Caso de dos Comunidades en el Valle del Mezquital." In: Yolanda Lastra/ Ana María Salazar (eds.) *Estudios de Cultura Otopame,* México: Universidad Nacional Autónoma de México, Instituto de Investigaciones Antropológicas, pp. 229-247.

Rivera Garay, María Guadalupe (2006) "La Negociación de las Relaciones de Género en el Valle del Mezquital: Un Acercamiento al Caso de la Participación Comunitaria de Mujeres Hñähñus." In: Yolanda Lastra/Ana María Salazar (eds.) *Estudios de Cultura Otopame,* México: Universidad Nacional Autónoma de México, Instituto de Investigaciones Antropológicas, pp. 249-266.

Robertson, Roland (1995) "Glocalization: Time-Space and Homogeneity-Heterogeneity." In: Mike Featherstone/Scott Lash/Roland Robertson (eds.) *Global Modernities,* London: Sage Publications, pp. 25-44.

Schlee, Günther (ed.) (2002) *Imagined Differences: Hatred and the Construction of Identity,* Münster: Lit-Verlag.

Schlee, Günther/Werner, Karin (1996) *Inklusion und Exklusion: Die Dynamik von Grenzziehungen im Spannungsfeld von Markt, Staat und Ethnizität,* Köln: Köppe.

Schmidt, E./Crummett, M. (2004) "Heritage Re-created: Hidalguenses in the United States and Mexico." In: Jonathan Fox/Gaspar Rivera-Salgado (eds.) *Indigenous Mexican Migrants in the United States,* La Jolla: Center for U.S.-Mexican Studies, pp. 401-415.

Schütz, Alfred/Luckmann, Thomas (1974) *The Structures of Life-World,* London: Heinemann.

Scott, James C. (ed.) (1985) *Weapons of the Weak: Everyday Forms of Peasant Resistance,* New Haven: Yale University Press.

Scott, James C. (ed.) (1990) *Domination and the Arts of Resistance: Hidden Transcripts,* New Haven: Yale University Press.

Serrano Avilés, Tomás (2006) *Migración Internacional y Pobreza en el Estado de Hidalgo,* Pachuca: Universidad Autónoma del Estado de Hidalgo.

Smith, Michael Peter/Bakker, Matt (2008) *Citizenship across Borders: The Political Transnationalism of "El Migrante",* London: Cornell University Press.

Stichweh, Rudolf (2005) *Migration und Weltgesellschaft,* Working Paper 3/2005, Institute for World Society Studies, Bielefeld University, August 10, 2008 (http://www.uni-bielefeld.de/soz/iw/pdf/stw.migration.PDF).

Strauss, Anselm L./Corbin, Juliet M. (1998) *Basics of Qualitative Research: Techniques and Procedures for Developing Grounded Theory,* Thousand Oaks: Sage Publications.

Networks, Hubs, Localities

A Global City-State of Finance – the Staging of Singapore as Financial Hub between Global and Local Rhetoric

STEPHANIE HERING

Introduction

Singapore is a relative newcomer in the league of 'Global Cities'. Emerging like a shooting star, it grew within a short while not only into a regional hotspot but also to be a metropolis on global scale. The potency of its financial sector, its visibility and presence is rated by the Singaporeans as the most important push-factor for that status and is, therefore, highly cultivated and treated like a trophy. Much effort is spend on presenting Singapore as an investors' paradise, a little *Switzerland of Asia,* and of course a *vibrant Global City* to live in.

In so far as the image of globality is, per se, inherent in the public perception of finance, Singapore seems to provide an excellent object to investigate and display the universal mentality (or global mind set) of a whole nation. Like all sites of international finance and Global Cities, Singapore is concomitantly looking for and producing its specificity in order to demonstrate to the world the uniqueness of this location. Struggling with two opposed aspirations, there is no scarcity of pitfalls on the way. In the following article I will look at the *imagineering* of globality intertwined with locality in the Singaporean discourse about its status as a *Global City State of Finance.*

Firstly, I will summar the theoretical framework from which my considerations issue. Thereafter follows a short consideration of Singapore's spatiotemporal context. Finally, I shall present some key-notes from the Singaporean discourse[1] and discuss them within my theoretical framework. This paper's interest is in the flanking ideological arrangements around a self-perception as 'a Global City of Finance', not in the question of how this perception relates to the 'hardware' of the financial world. Economic sociology needs also to be concerned

---

1   Based on the material I gathered during a field-trip to Singapore in 2005.

with the analysis of the culture(s) and popular representations of finance, i.e. the public statements and the commonly held ideas about finance. The ideas of globality are not only enclosed in financial discourses but also in the visual and material statements of urban architecture which are widely neglected by the sociology of finance and/or globalisation. Of less interest are the market- (and world-) constructions of traders, generated especially through their interaction with the screen.[2]

Financial Flows, Financial Centres and Global Cities

Since the commencement of the discourse on globalisation, it is widely recognised that economy is its driving force. Finance, or more precisely the internationalisation of financial markets, is particularly relevant in this debate. Triggered by revolutionary advances in information technologies and wide-ranging liberalisation-policies by many states around the globe during the last decade,[3] monetary flows (or financial transactions) have risen enormously in volume and importance as has the public attention to, and awareness of, them.[4]

Finance seems to carry some qualities that are eminently associated with globalisation or globality. With the emancipation of (electronic) money from cash (or other forms of paper), financial products or instruments lack a material referent, visible beyond the screen. Now they can, at least potentially, travel unhampered around the globe, implementing an utopian notion of a world, where everything is free-floating. In this regard, the evidence of 'financial flows' perfectly confirms the observation of increasing disentanglement of space and time.[5] While past generalised concepts of economy were mostly concepts of national economies and hence contaminated with all the conceptual fallacies inherent in the notion of 'nation-sate' (now rather suspicious, and altogether unfashionable), the present financial system is usually perceived as a web of trans- or supranational circulations (Knorr Cetina/Preda 2005). Insofar, it is hardly astonishing that finance is sometimes celebrated as the avant-garde of globalism. Although, as a matter of fact, the financial policies of states and governments are still extremely important.

It is frequently argued (and dreaded) that due to disembeddedment, acceleration and dematerialisation, as inherent in globalisation, geographies will become obsolete or, at least, differences between specific venues will be levelled. Although there is a number of examples for a worldwide harmonisation of stan-

---

2   See Knorr Cetina (2005), Knorr Cetina/Bruegger (2002).
3   Which in effect meant opening their financial markets to plug into the world market.
4   Readily identifiable in the amount of information provided for, and news space occupied by financial markets in the media.
5   The term "time-space-compression" goes back to David Harvey's book *The condition of Postmodernity* (1989).

dards in some fields, the growing importance of local specifity conditioned by globalisation is as well attested. Not every aspect of social or individual life is swallowed by some abstract globality, and place does still matter. Far from being a paradox, this co-occurence can be perceived as two sides of the same coin. What is actually happening is a phase transition from one model of local and spatial order – that of the nation-state – to another world order in which regions and strategic cities are the nodal points for a new global map (Castells/Hall 1996).

Financial flows may seem to float freely and limitlessly across the globe, but in fact they are restricted in many ways. They are mediated by banks, transnational corporations, stock exchanges and governments; all of them are operating in a specific local business environment that is determined by laws, taxes, general infrastructure, stable or unstable political conditions and the trust solicited by the image of a particular financial site. These conditions are essential for the enablement (or disablement) of smooth financial flows, and these conditions are distributed unevenly around the globe. Some locations offer risks and raise barriers for global financial business while others are appreciated for their promise of chances and success. Thus, the more global financial flows animate phenomena of disembeddedness, their circulation effect more embeddedness in specific places at the same time (Thrift 1996: 231).

Here, the role of Global Cities (Sassen 2002) becomes crucial: Only these can provide a satisfactory milieu for financial business and offer financial flows an appropriate temporary home for investment. As Saskia Sassen (2005) and many others have pointed out for a long time, the social connectivity and central functions of a place are critical for the effective operation of the financial sector. Most characteristics of a Global City are also central requirements for a financial hub: An attractive infrastructure for the sophisticated demands of the highly educated transnational executive elite, a sense of cosmopolitanism, the availability of elaborated technologies and the (perhaps virtual) neighbourhood of other important strategic actors in the financial world.[6]

Success in soliciting global companies, especially banks or even a stock exchange, is highly profitable for a city and also for its environments. Increasingly and all over the world, Global Cities – as well as cities that aspire to this status – find themselves in the role of rivals in the business of attracting investors and in marketing themselves as perfect centres for global financial services. They all are driven constantly by the need to produce and display competitive advantages in the game of catching or channeling global financial flows.

Inasmuch as the global sector of finance is rated as a growing branch, and combined with the view that the accommodation of a flourishing financial sector will ensure an enhanced performance in other desirable and targeted develop-

---

6   Quite obviously, the meaning of these factors seems to be vague. But maybe it is exactly the stretchability of these factors that makes them so attractive and hard-fought in the Global Cities-game.

ments,[7] it is likely that competition of Global Cities for the status of prospective host-locality of international finance will intensify. Moreover, in a globalising world, in which distances between big cities are shrinking, there is no need to privilege locations in the Western world anymore. Cities and regions from other parts of the world in ascendance, starting with Asian localities, are now potent candidates with good prospects in this competition.

The following analysis is guided by the assumption that Global Cities are striving to stage themselves as attractive in accommodating financial nodal points of global significance as possible, thus shaping a specific image of the city. The self-projection must fulfil and display all the qualities that are required for a Global City. But just meeting the demands is not sufficient. The city must also imagine and project a specific 'otherness' or an aura of 'uniqueness'[8] that underlines the concrete locality and serves as an additional argument for a competitive advantage; in short: to signal why it is better to invest here than somewhere else.

Singapore: General Background, Economy and Finance

Singapore is hailed as a first rate achiever among the postcolonial states on the basis of its successful development. It has been rising like a phoenix within a few decades from the ashes of a poor run-down leftover of British colonial rule to become a hypermodern country that even performs better, in terms of most 'development-indicators',[9] than many Western states.

Following independence in 1965, development was announced as Singapore's primary objective. Lee Kuan Yew, the founding father of modern Singapore, accomplished this goal with firm, centralised and consistent leadership: He set the agenda for contemporary Singapore and invented (t)his particular Global City.

Development meant in the Singaporean context first and foremost economic development. The first step on that road was rapid industrialisation, mainly with electronic, chemical and petrochemical industries, followed quickly by a second step with priority given to the encouragement of increasingly specialised, highly professional and knowledge-based work. Aware of its dependency on the outside and its resulting vulnerability, Singapore tried to play a sustainable role in the world economic system by establishing the perfect pro-business environment with political stability and good governance. The strategic impact of the govern-

---

7   As the World Bank has been preaching for a long time: *World Bank Report* (2001).
8   Like the distinctiveness of a trademark or brand – this aspect is highlighted in the term "City-Branding".
9   Usually, such indicators can be divided in hard, economic indicators like the GDP or the rate of inflation and soft social indicators like life expectancy, infant mortality or health care facilities etc.

ment on the national economy cannot be overestimated. Developments are planned and always keenly observed by the government. Some evaluate the strong state-economy relationship pejoratively as a 'government driven economy' or even 'state-capitalism'[10] (Worthington 2003). The Economic Development Board (EDB) of Singapore[11] is one of the most powerful national institutions. It was set up in the 1960s as part of the national government with the agenda of creating the infrastructure which attracts multinational corporations to invest and start business in Singapore. The prime strategic purpose was to achieve full employment and to promote economic growth.

The creation of a stable and prosperous financial sector to facilitate, if not to stimulate further growth of the national economy has been a major strategic goal since independence. The plan to transform Singapore into a primary financial centre for East Asia was, however, not drafted before the late 1980s on the basis of observations of the increasing internationalisation of trade and finance, and the incipient discussion of globalisation (Koh Ai Tee et al. 2002). The Monetary Authority of Singapore (MAS), which was established in 1971 to conduct central bank functions, broadened its field of activity gradually and elaborated, in consequence, various financial instruments and institutions for the development of the financial sector. Extensive deregulation and liberalisation policies were introduced along with tax incentives. The plan accomplished its purpose in motivating foreign financial service firms to settle in Singapore and to mobil capital.[12] Since the 1990s finance has been one of the most intensively fostered branches of the service sector. The government places much emphasis on economic diversification. After even broader deregulation and liberalisation moves since the mid nineties and after the merger of the former stock exchanges SES and SIMEX to the new SGX in 1999, Singapore is now assessed as a major regional and international 'financial hub'.[13] Despite all the liberalisation and deregulation, Singapore still has effective supervisory instruments in order to contain risk; hence it was hardly affected by the recent Asian crisis.

Finance is rated as an increasingly important sector for the wealth of Singapore (Blomquist 2005; Das 2004; Koh Ai Tee et al. 2002; Tan Chwee Huat 2004). Therefore Singapore's planners[14] are doing what they can to provide a per-

---

10 Or, alternatively, a strange mix between socialistic and capitalistic practices.
11 http://www.sedb.com. Although its 'mission' changed enormously over the years, the EDB remains an important institution for Singapore's further strategic economic and financial goals.
12 Singapore is the destination of the highest foreign direct investment flows in Asia. Nevertheless, recently Singapore has also become an eminent source of outward investment (Blomquist 2005: 85pp.).
13 Singapore is ranked by the World Economic Forum Global Competitiveness Report (2004) among the top ten financial markets in the world. The term 'financial hub' is a recent catch-word used in the Global City-debate and -marketing; it describes financial sites with enormous economic impact on a global scale. It is often used in an affirmative way as self-description.
14 On the institutional level it is foremost EDB and MAS involved here.

fect general framework for the financial industry's boom. Singapore's proclaimed policy is not just to keep, but rather to expand its competitive advantage as a preferred location for global financial business for the foreseeable future. The Singapore government is pursuing this plan with amasing pragmatism and with great confidence in its feasibility. Taking into account research results on Global Cities, the internationalisation of finance and the increasing competition of financial sites worldwide, Singapore realised early that turning itself into a Global City would be essential for its future development prospects.

In a first step Singapore had to fulfill the seemingly universal requirements for Global Cities. Insofar as Global Cities are perceived as primary locations for key corporations, important institutions, prominent organisations and elite personnel, a salient infrastructure is needed. This includes on the one hand, e.g., a wide variety of opportunities for distinguished consumption, an airport, high-ranking educational facilities as well as, on the other hand, the provision for social, political, legal and economic stability. Singapore already offers all of this; it is famous for its advantageous business environment with low taxes and an efficient administration. In a second step all these amenities have to be communicated and displayed. They must be made visible and become obvious to the relevant audiences; this is meant and subsumed by the term 'city-marketing'. Rhetorical and visual strategies to demonstrate or point out the particular eligibilities as a global (financial) site go along with the agenda of transforming Singapore into a 'financial hub' in terms of the concrete business condition for finance in Singapore.

In addition to the 'hard amenities', a Global City must also engineer its image, i.e. imagineer its local peculiarities and stage them as unique qualities one will find nowhere but here in order to individual the locality and make it distinctive among its competitors. How is Singapore achieving that?

Some Features in the Making of Singapore as a 'Global City of Finance'

On 21 August 2005 Prime Minister Lee Hsien Loong ended his National Day rally speech[15] of two and a half hours on Singapore and its future with the invocation to build a '*vibrant Global City called home*' (Lee Hsien Loong 2005). A twofold claim is contained in this phrase: On the one hand the determination to live a global existence, on the other hand the compliance with the human need to construct a place one can identify with and even experience or 'feel' it as home. In the following paragraphs I shall take a closer look at the constituting myths at work here which put the idea of Singapore as a '*Global City called home*' into effect.

---

15 For the transcript of the speech, see: www.gov.sg/NDR06Engspeechtranscript.pdf

Singapore as Part and Parcel, or even the Avantgarde Location, of the Asian Renaissance

The success-story of Singapore, its prospering economy (and especially its financial sector) is often explained by the self-ascribed cultural distinctiveness of the place and the people.[16] This can be seen in the broader context of notions of a 'rising Asia' or an 'Asian come-back'[17] in the global networks of politics and economic power. Western countries perceive this image with a strange mixture of fascination and fear. When fear becomes dominant this perception is sometimes expressed as 'Asian *angst*'. In accordance with their economic success, potent Asian nations – at the moment especially China and India, in the 1990s rather the East-Asian 'tiger-states' with Singapore among them – have developed a new self-confidence. It is articulated in attempts to draw clear demarcation lines vis-à-vis 'the West'. In this context the term 'occidentalism' (Buruma 2004) was coined as an inversion of 'orientalism' (Said 1978).

In Singapore the official reinforcement of the so-called 'Asian values' reached its apex during the 1980s and 1990s. What 'Asian values' exactly means is not always clear, but a kind of Confucianism, i.e. a strong moral foundation of society, political organisation and even the economy and an emphasis on family, tradition and community is often associated with the term (Xinzhong Yao 2000; Oldstone-Moore 2002). The co-occurrence of this 'Asian values' debate and the successful story of the financial hub's performance serve as an argument for the supposedly obvious correlation between an Asian mindset and outstanding skills in economic matters, financial business in particular.

Organised as a parliamentary republic after the British Westminster model, Singapore's self-perception also contains the political concept of 'Asian democracy'.[18] This implies primarily putting 'community', not the individual, first. Arguments for political decisions are formulated according to the central requirements of: What is good for the development of the people? What is preferable for the development of Singapore as a whole? With this principle in the background, harsh political and social controls[19] can be justified. This leads some critics to see behind the glittering surface of Singapore's idiosyncratic style of democracy an authoritarian, if not totalitarian one-party state under a benevolent dictator. Look-

---

16 This is best observable in official and governmental documents in and about Singapore.
17 During recent years this debate has hit another peak of public dispute in Western media. Moreover there is also a growing academic debate; but there were also a few voices that highlighted the growing importance of Asia earlier, for instance André Gunder Frank in his ReOrient (1998).
18 Lee Kuan Yew often justified this with the argument that Western democracy would never work in Asia, because some of the inherent Western values would not fit with 'Asian culture' and 'Asian mentality'.
19 Visible for instance in the high degree of censorship and control of media, draconian punishments of deviant behaviour and the virtual absence of a civil society – in comparison with 'Western' democracies.

ing at it more sympathetically, Lee Kuan Yew and his PAP party achieved a high level of prosperity; critics also acknowledge the fast industrialisation and modernisation of the country, the speedy and continuous upgrading of infrastructure, the efficient administrative system without corruption[20] and the guarantees of stable political and economic terms and conditions. In its foreign affairs, Singapore has always acted quite pragmatically and maintained during the Cold War area a neutral openness to both sides. Some argue that the extremely output-oriented political system in Singapore can only work because of its small size (territorial and in terms of population) and that there is no magic formula, like an intrinsic supremacy of agents of Asian values or Confucianism, that might be applicable to other contexts.

There is much talk about Asian values, but in the case of Singapore the phenomenon would probably better be named 'Chineseness': the traditions, values and notions that are promoted in the Singaporean discourse are generally associated with Chinese culture. This pays tribute to the majority Chinese population in Singapore and – against all official declaration – its cultural and political dominance. In all these constructions the reasons and legitimacy of the location's success are, however, relocated to a long past and their roots in an (imagined) strong primordial identity of its people.

The Nation: 'Singaporean spirit' and a 'Long' History as a Trading Nation

Although in its self-perception clearly an Asian nation, Singapore has also generated a strong national identity, a factor X that makes it 'truly Singaporean' and glues people together. The social production of a Singaporean national spirit was challenged by the problem that Singapore did not really have a pre-colonial past to which the modern nation could trace back its roots. Not much is known about the early, pre-colonial history of Singapore (Hall 1999). Most historic narratives start with the arrival of Sir Stamford Raffles in 1819. By that time, the southern tip of the Malayan peninsula was part of the Johor sultanate, inhabited by only some 150 Malayan and Chinese fishermen, pirates and traders. Raffles, an explorer and scholar travelling on behalf of the British East India Company, played off the conflicting interests of local rulers and Dutch colonialists and established Singapore as a nodal trading station on the British East-Asian route to China. Subsequently large numbers of immigrants were attracted by the new hot spot. Traders and workers from different regions populated the island. Singapore (or this southernmost part of the former Malaya) represents an exceptional case in so

---

20 In publications of Transparency International Singapore is regularly ranked first as country with minimal corruption. Very early Lee Kuan Yew recognised corruption as a great problem, especially for developing countries, because it destroys trust – he stigmatised corruption as a "social disease" and implemented strong policies to inhibit and prosecute cases of corruption.

far as the colonised arrived after the colonisers. Raffles promoted free trade, blueprinted the whole city and errected buildings for the British government. The population grew rapidly, and only five years (1824) after the British takeover the first census counted 10.000 people.[21] Singapore was already quite cosmopolitan in composition and Malayans, Chinese, Indian, European, American and Arab people were registered.

The asserted Singaporean spirit is mainly based on the achievements of recent history since independence. In this respect Singapore is a *willensnation* par excellence. The national identity of Singapore consists of its very identity as the (global) city. As in many other ex-colonies 'nation' and 'nationalism' have different meanings than in European history: Nationalism was predominantly welcomed, being experienced as liberation from and counteraction to foreign rule.[22] Nationalism is still perceived as an important and admirable attitude.

On the other hand, the Singaporean expertise in economy, trade and finance is linked to its long history as a trading place and entrepot on the colonial East-Asian trading route which commenced shortly after the Napoleonic wars and ended with World War II. This 'long history' is, in fact, purely colonial – Singapore is effectively a product of European imperialism (Ferguson 2003). Interestingly and perhaps exceptionally, this colonial past is not loaded with negative connotations. It is used instead in an affirmative manner to communicate the advantage of location. Colonial rule and imperialism enormously increased the volume of trade and plugged Singapore into the world market. Singapore is a product of 19th century globalisation, a sort of 'Global City' since its very beginnings.

Consequently, the Singaporen national spirit is ambivalent. On the one hand it is based on the achievements after independence, on the other hand it is recognised that colonialism was a precondition for the nation and triggered its economic success.

The 'We can make it' – Attitude: Never say die!

The common attitude of the Singaporean people as publicly proclaimed is an important constituent of the city state's identity. The success-story '*from nothing to world-class*' is repeated at every possible opportunity – the story of a '*success beyond imagination*'. The predominant conviction is that 'we can do exceptional things although we are small' – this will work with discipline, hard work and perpetual learning processes. Every Singaporean can and should make his/her contribution to the continuous success of the nation, everyone has a place in it. Lee Hsien Loong epitomised this point in his speech with: "It's good luck, it's good government, it's strong people". He also mentions in this context Singapore's

---

21   50 years later there were more than half a million inhabitants. Today, ca. four and a half million people live in Singapore.
22   In other words, Singapore indulges in the nationalism of the American Revolution rather than the nationalism of ethnic groups in the Balkans.

Las Vegas-principle: innovation and enterprise, together with a fair portion of human imagination – that was seemingly all it took to shape Singapore, a productive re-invention of itself in perpetuity.

The most remarkable thing in the recent history of Singapore perhaps is the planning and implementing of a 'knowledge society' long before sociology discovered the topic and elaborated the concept. Given that the country has no natural resources, and abhorring the prospect of becoming a low-wage country or sweat-shop-nation and supplier of cheap and simple manufactured goods for the developed world (like so many other former colonies) after the breakdown of the shipping-and-harbour-industry during the first half of the 20th century, the government identified the people as its only valuable resource and placed a strong emphasis on education and human resource[23] development from the beginning. Consequently, capital investment in this sector since the 1970s has been immense.[24]

So far Singapore has experienced absolutely no trouble with this kind of social engineering: it just works fine. Success of the nation via its people functions as a unceasing confirmation of the much valued concepts of education and training. The belief in the power of education is omnipresent: Everything can be taught, everyone is educable, everyone can be trained, people are mouldable if they only receive the right education. For the same reason Singapore is the location of a extraordinary high frequency of public campaigns, that tell people how to behave, how to become a better citizen, and so forth.

This whole notion was called the *Las Vegas principle* by the Singaporean prime minister. The explicit reference to Las Vegas, the American gambling paradise and dream factory in the middle of nowhere (an inhospitable desert) is also a link to the more general myth of the American dream, the rise from rags to riches. The ideology that is behind this myth is the idea that everything is feasible if you really want and only try hard enough. The impossible is possible. The American dream, however, is organised around a strong individualism. In Singapore the American dream is transferred to a more communitarian level: Not the individual, but the society as a whole – according to the official values – is trained and educated in order to ensure long-term profit. The mindset of this declared official mentality is quite close to the ideas of neo-liberalism (Taylor 2004).

---

23 Or as Olds and Thrift note – not without a certain sense of admiration for the effective 'engineering' of a whole workforce: Singapore is "fashioning its citizens while considering them openly as a mineral resource with attitude." (2005: 275).

24 This was a apparently a profitable strategy – Singapore has today the best educated and strongest workforce in the world – in its own view but also something which is continuously attributed from outside.

The Sense of Cosmopolitism

The peaceful cohabitation of different 'races' and population groups in Singapore is frequently used as evidence for its cosmopolitan climate; it underlines its qualification as a truly Global City that is open to people from all parts of the world.

To be cosmopolitan is imperative for a Global City.[25] It must be stated that the concept of cosmopolitism is under-elaborated in the Global City literature – it remains nebulous. So possibly it is not Singapore's fault alone that in the discourses about self-perception it is not absolutely clear what cosmopolitism really means. Apparently the term is somehow used as a synonym for globality, as the opposite of localism or nationalism. But this ideal could be in conflict with the nationalism as it exists in Singapore. Because the city is the nation, there is no option to perceive the concrete city abstracted from the broader framework of the nation, as may work for other global cites and their relationship to the nations they belong to (e.g. New York City – United States, or Shanghai – China). Another general objection that can be raised: How can a city be cosmopolitan, when an attitude to the specific place is required, a sense of belonging (or non-belonging)?

As is the case with the term 'cosmopolitism' in the globalisation literature, it is probably more a diffuse but positive multiculturalism that is proclaimed here. The celebration of its multiculturalism, once again, Singapore owes to its colonial past. When the British were running short of low-skilled labour, they imported people from other colonies to Singapore. At first, the various ethnic groups produced various problems. Violent rivalries and even race riots were frequent. Being aware of the destructiveness of sub-group conflicts for an emerging nation, the officials of modern Singapore always observed that danger closely and tried to contain it with harsh anti-racism legislation. Paradoxically, this strong anti-racism policy keeps the basic problem alive which it pretends to combat. This is the conviction that human beings come in fundamentally different formats as ethnic groups. Still, Singapore lists in its population statistics Chinese, Indians, Malayans, etc. – although they are all Singaporean. Segregated ethnic districts were rebuilt (even if there was no surviving traditional structure at all, not a single brick), just for folkloristic and tourism purposes. Singaporeans are accommodated in HDB-flats, appropriately allocated to different race-groups to prevent segregation and dissociation of a single group from the national community.

So the ethnic groups preserve their differences partly by decree – but mainly those differences which can be consumed and enjoyed without causing too much trouble, for instance different clothing styles, different dances and music, different literatures and – very important in Singapore – different cuisines. Consequently the officially desired version of cosmopolitism or multiculturalism is reduced to a great diversity of available food.

---

25 See e.g. the Global City Forum, a network for urban decision-makers: www.globalcityforum.com.

To display openness, tolerance and an appetite for diversity is an essential factor of the marketing-strategy for Singapore. In addition to the importance of tourism, especially short-term shopping tourism during stopovers on the air-route from Europe to the Far East and Australia and vice versa,[26] it is increasingly dependent on immigration and a foreign workforce. Singapore has a great demand for highly trained employees. Because of a low birth-rate over decades and the fact that a number of highly qualified Singaporeans go abroad for work where some of them eventually stay, a growing demand in skilled labour is expected. Singapore is competing very hard with some other global locations for international elite-personnel in business and research. Singapore also seeks immigrants on a lower level, but always people who are capable of making a contribution to the nation, people with entrepreneurial spirit.

In this respect, it may be that cosmopolitism has always been an utopian as well as a pretended notion. In addition, a cosmopolitan ethos is also a perfect justification for Singapore's practice of exerting political and economic influence on the whole region and of viewing for dominance in ASEAN.

The Versatile Dwarf

Breaking with Malaysia in 1965, Singapore gained the status of an independent nation, but was now confronted with a number of problems and threats. It was still a third world country with bad infrastructure, little capital, only a few industries and a largely impoverished and uneducated population. At that time it appeared nearly impossible for such a small postcolonial country with no hinterland and without natural resources to survive. Against this background the government identified economic development as its prime ambition and central policy, a goal which persists to date. For this purpose, a strong outward orientation was unavoidable. Singapore's extreme dependence on its international and regional environment has appeared to be a critical factor ever since (Blomqvist 2005: 50 pp.). This implies that the importance of Foreign Direct Investment during the first decades of modern Singapore's existence was immense.

Singapore is small, but flexible. Involved in an unceasing coquetry with its smallness, Singapore celebrates its weakness as a strength: vulnerability and dependency on the world market are paradoxically the very qualities that facilitate a competitive attitude and inhibits inertia or stagnancy. Singapore is a versatile dwarf that always has to be watchful in a difficult and potentially hostile environment. It's a David-versus-Goliath story that Singapore retells, relying, once again, on its positive ending (for David). Inherent in this simile is a militaristic content. Singapore is in a constant war-like situation, always prepared for a fight, for self-defence. The status quo is always at risk.

---

26 Very much as, in the 19th century, when ships with the same destinations stopped here to unload or load coal.

A public advertisement for the Singaporean army popular in summer/ autumn 2005 provides an ironic validation of this assumption. In the middle of the poster, a handsome young man in army uniform is shouldering a gun, in the background lingers the scenery of downtown Singapore at night – high rise buildings fantastically illuminated. In huge white letters the message imprinted into this background reads: *Compromise is not an option*. The arguments are arranged around the soldier, in white letters and a relatively small type of why the army is so important for Singapore and why young men should join it – one of the arguments is: *Because investors' confidence is key*.

Conclusion

The case of Singapore shows very clearly that a Global City is not only defined by hard factors, but also invented and socially engineered on a grand scale. The making of Singapore as a 'Global City of Finance' is a process that consists of a number of different strategies and rhetorics and not just the evidences of social and economic hardware. Beside the hardware there is also adequate software required, consisting of everyday myths with an ideological driving force. In the staging of the city-state as a Global City specific local strategies and articulations of 'otherness' or 'uniqueness' are concomitantly inherent. The balancing of globality motifs and rhetoric of local specificity and cultural distinctiveness is not always possible without conflict. A closer look at some of the myths reveals quite antagonistic conceptions at their core. Behind the nice image of a Global City, a quite chauvinistic regionalism and local patriotism sometimes peeps up; which is never too disturbing as long as the image- and rhetorics-machine is well-oiled and works smoothly.

It seems as if the transformation of Singapore in a Global City-State of Finance works and continues to work. Singapore is doing fine, Singapore is prospering. And indeed: Nothing works better than success to stabil a (self-) invention.

References

Blomqvist, Hans C. (2005) *Swimming with Sharks. Global and Regional Dimensions of the Singapore Economy*, Singapore: Marshall Cavendish.

Buruma, Ian (2004) *Occidentalism. The West in the Eyes of his Enemies*, New York: Penguin.

Castells, Manuel/Hall, Peter (1996) "Technopoles: Mines and Foundries of the Informational Economy." In: LeGates, Richard T./Stout Frederic (eds.) *The City-Reader*, London/NewYork: Routledge, pp. 475-483.

Das, Dilip K. (2004) *Financial Globalization and the Emerging Market Economies*, London, New York: Routledge.

Ferguson, Niall (2003) *Empire. How Britain made the Modern World*, London: Penguin.

Frank, André Gunder (1998) *ReOrient: Global Economy in the Asian Age*, Berkeley: University of California Press.

Hall, Daniel George Edward (1999) *A History of South-East Asia, 4th Edition*, Basingstoke: McMillan.

Harvey, David (1989) *The Condition of Postmodernity. An Enquiry into the Condition of Cultural Change*, Oxford: Blackwell.

Koh Ai Tee/Lim Kim Lian/Hui Weng Tat/Bhanaji Rao/Chng Meng Kng (eds.) (2002) *Singapore Economy in the 21st Century*, Singapore: McGraw-Hill.

Knorr Cetina, Karin/Bruegger, Urs (2002) "Global Microstructures: The Virtual Societies of Financial Markets." American Journal of Sociology 107, pp. 905-950.

Knorr Cetina, Karin (2005) "How are Global Markets Global? The Architecture of a Flow World." In: Karin Knorr Cetina/Alex Preda (eds.) *The Sociology of Financial Markets*, Oxford: Oxford University Press, pp.38-61.

Knorr Cetina, Karin/Preda, Alex (eds.) (2004) *The Sociology of Financial Markets*, Oxford: Oxford University Press

Lee Hsien Loong (2005) *Speech at National Day Rally on 21 August 2005*, NUS University Cultural Centre, http://app.sprinter.gov.sg/ data/ pr/ 2005082102.htm.

Olds, Kris/Thrift, Nigel (2005) "Cultures on the Brink. Reengineering the Soul of Capitalism – On a Global Scale." In: Nigel Thrift (ed.) *Knowing Capitalism*, London: Sage, pp. 270-290.

Oldstone-Moore, Jennifer (2002) *Confucianism*, Oxford: Oxford University Press.

Said, Edward W. (1978) *Orientalism*, New York: Random House.

Sassen, Saskia (2002) *Global Networks, Linked Cities*, New York: Routledge.

Sassen, Saskia (2005) "The Embeddedness of Electronic Markets: The Case of Global Capital Markets." In: Karin Knorr-Cetina/Alex Preda (eds.) *The Sociology of Financial Markets*, Oxford: Oxford University Press, pp. 17-37.

Tan, Chwee Huat (2004) *Financial Services in Singapore*, Singapore: Ridge Books.

Taylor, Mark C. (2004) *Confidence Games. Money and Markets in a World without Redemption*, Chicago: University of Chicago Press.

Thrift, Nigel (1996) *Spatial Formations*, London: Sage.

World Bank Report (2001) *Finance for Growth: Policy Choices in a Volatile World*, Washington.

World Economic Forum (2005) *The Global Competitiveness Report 2004-2005*, Basingstoke: Palgrave Macmillan.

Worthington, Ross (2003) *Governance in Singapore*, London/New York: Routledge.
Xinzhong Yao (2000) *An introduction to Confucianism*, Cambridge: Cambridge University Press.

The Transnational Management of Hazardous Chemicals

ALEXANDRA LINDENTHAL

Introduction

Since the 1970s the number of environmental laws e.g. in the European Union (EU) has increased. Nonetheless an effective protection of the environment requires that societal actors assume responsibility and become active on this issue. In particular, corporations whose activities have an effect on the environment are brought to the fore, as is the case with those corporations that are involved in the production, trade, processing and application of chemicals. This is because, as chemical substances may have negative consequences for health and environment, it is necessary to handle them in a careful way. Harmful chemicals may cause environmental problems if they reach the ecosystem, e.g. via their use in consumer goods. Consequently, a safe management of chemicals is an important condition for a global protection of the environment. Against this background, this article concentrates on the corporation between the chemical industry – producers, distributors as well as consulting firms – and the automotive industry – car manufacturers and parts suppliers – which are linked by a value-added chain. Both industries are involved in the production of automobiles and have to deal with chemical substances. This value-chain section is not located in a single nation state, it even transcends the borders of trade-areas like the EU, and hence it could be regarded as a global production process.[1]

In the article at hand I will describe some common practices and cognitive structures in reference to the management or phasing out of hazardous chemicals that have emerged in the chemical and automotive industry.[2] Further, I will give

---

1 I would like to thank the editors as well as Martin Koch for helpful comments on an earlier draft of this article and Dörthe Hauschild and Tamara Brown for making the text more readable. The author bears responsibility for any shortcomings.
2 The empirical study is based on an analysis of documents as well as on interviews that were conducted with representatives of the automotive and chemical industry. The interviews were carried out together with Olaf Dilling in the context of the re-

some reasons for this emergence. Since the production process analysed reaches beyond the borders of nation-states, I regard these practices and cognitive structures as transnational. Of course, global business partners have to coordinate their behaviour in order to make the successful production and selling of goods possible; this includes the management of hazardous chemicals. Beyond this, I am interested in seeing if these transnational practices concerning the management of hazardous substances also add to the protection of health and environment.

This article is composed of three parts. First, I will give some examples of a transnational management of hazardous chemical substances appearing in the chemical and the automotive industry which illustrate the emergence of world society. Second, I will describe the extent to which these examples are indications of emerging and changing common practices and cognitive structures. Further, I will explain that these elements of a transnational management of chemicals can count as self-regulation. Then, I will give a short explanation for its emergence. Finally, I will conclude with the question of which other factors might explain the emergence of a transnational management of chemicals and in how far these factors contribute to the protection of health and environment.

The Transnational Management of Hazardous Chemicals in the Automotive Industry and the Chemical Industry

As denoted in the introduction, there are a lot of European laws concerning the protection of the environment. With reference to the regulation of chemicals, the European Economic Community adopted the first directive on classification, packaging and labeling of dangerous substances in 1967. Currently, chemicals are a field of activity of the European Unions' environmental policy. The directive on the management of end-of-life vehicles stipulates that vehicle manufacturers and material and equipment manufacturers must, among other things, endeavour to reduce the use of hazardous substances when designing vehicles and make sure that components of vehicles placed on the market after July 2003 do not contain mercury, hexavalent chromium, cadmium or lead (European Com-

---

search project "Transnational Governance and International Law" at the collaborative research center "Transformations of the State" (University of Bremen). The interviews were arranged with representatives of corporations belonging to the automotive and the chemical industry. All in all, ten interviews took place. Five interviews were conducted in the automotive industry (car producers and parts suppliers) and five interviews were conducted in the chemical industry (producers and distributors of chemicals, one chemical consulting firm). The interviews were interpreted according to qualitative-interpretive methods (Froschauer/Lueger 2003; Wernet 2000). Furthermore, environmental reports of corporations, corporation guidelines, management standards and similar documents were analysed. The sources are available from the author.

mission 2000). Further, the directive on the restriction of the use of certain hazardous substances in electrical and electronic equipment stipulates that from July 2006, new electrical and electronic equipment that are placed the market do not contain lead, mercury, cadmium, hexavalent chromium, polybrominated biphenyls (PBB) or polybrominated diphenyl ethers (PBDE) (European Commission 2002).

In the following section, I will demonstrate the efforts of corporations belonging to the chemical industry and the automotive industry relating to the management of hazardous chemical substances. Naturally, inter-organisational relations are most important for the survival of corporations that are involved in the production of manufactured goods because they are in need of the other firms' resources. This article pays attention not only to economic exchange relationships, but also to non-economic relations like communicative activities (cf. Jang 1997: 328p), e.g. the transfer of knowledge, which may move up and down the value chain. The corporations in the production chain that are analysed in this article are formally autonomous organisations that are connected to one another by material and immaterial exchange processes. The relationships between the corporations are formal, e.g. contracts between a supplier and a customer concerning the design of a product, as well as informal, e.g. rather loose arrangements between a customer and a supplier to improve a suppliers' performance if a ranking conducted by an automobile producer reveals undesired results.

International Material Data System/ Global Automotive Declarable Substance List

The development of the automotive industry's international material data system (IMDS), as well as the development of the global automotive declarable substance list are examples of a transnational management of chemical substances. The IMDS was developed by European and American car producers and came into operation in June 2000. Meanwhile, Asian automotive producers have attached themselves to this system. The IMDS, a voluntary industry-led initiative, files and administers all materials used in the automotive manufacturing chain and collects chemical information (Fisher 2005). It is the goal of this initiative to collect data on chemical substances that are a part of the automobiles produced. This system is intended to make it possible for car manufacturers and their suppliers to comply with the different national laws and private standards concerning hazardous substances and, last but not least, to make the recycling of automobiles easier. Suppliers have to produce these data, because they are constrained by law and/or by their customers' delivery conditions. On the one hand, this system is helpful to car producers: If a substance of concern is prohibited by law, a producer knows which of its suppliers uses this substance and can call on to him to remove the substance from his products (Johnson Controls 2001). On the other hand, the suppliers, using the database, are able to monitor the substances used in their products. If a customer has any questions regarding the composition of the products' parts, the supplier is able to answer them. Nonetheless, suppliers initially protested against this system, because they were of the opinion that a data management system must allow them to protect their business know-how. In the initial approach to dealing with declarable substances, each car manufacturer developed individual lists of substances and as a result, suppliers had to consider multiple lists (Interview 2005).

After controversial discussions between the suppliers and the car producers, the international "Global Automotive Stakeholders Group" (GASG) was formed. It consists of automotive manufacturers and the suppliers of the automotive and chemical industry. It is the intention of this stakeholder group to simplify the communication and exchange of information in relation to the use of substances in parts of automobiles all along the production chain. The GASG developed the "Global Automotive Declarable Substance List" (GADSL). The GADSL, implemented in 2005, is a globally uniform list of declarable substances.[3] The decision to list a substance on the GADSL in based on clear criteria. A substance is listed if it is regulated, is projected to be regulated by a governmental agency, or if it is demonstrated – by testing under OECD guidelines – "that the substance may be associated with a significant hazard to human health and/or the environment, and its presence in a material or part in a vehicle may create a significant risk to human health and/or the environment" (GADSL). Accordingly, three so-called "reason codes" have been developed to explain to the participating firms why a substance was included in the GADSL. The first code means that a substance is "legally regulated". The second code "for assessment" indicates that a substance is expected to be regulated by government agencies, and "for information" denotes a substance:

"tracked for information purposes only, upon the decision of the GASG Steering Committee. After discussion at the GASG Steering Committee and on *an exceptional basis*, [a car producer] may include an individual substance or family of substances on the list under this reason code" (ibid., italics in original).

It is anticipated that the GADSL will be a part of the standards of car producers, so the suppliers will have to consider only this list. According to official statements, the purpose of this standard is to "help the automotive industry to monitor the usage of these substances and to facilitate compliance with current

---

3 In April 2005, the GADSL replaced the "International List of Reportable Substances" (ILRS). Like the GADSL, it was the goal of the ILRS to summarise the different requirements of the car producers concerning the declaration of substances. In contrast to the GADSL, the ILRS was planned without the support of the automotive suppliers and the chemical industry.

and future regulations"[4] and to "help take into account customer requirements to ensure sustainable products"[5]. Furthermore, it is the intent of the GADSL

"to become the company specific list for the declaration of parts composition within the automotive industry. It provides a definitive list of substances requiring declaration with the target of minimising individual requirements and ensuring cost-effective management of declaration practice along the complex supply chain" (ibid.).

Empirical evidence shows a different picture. A global automotive manufacturer who is represented in the GASG steering committee has its own restricted substance management standard (RSMS). This standard is, according to the firms' portrayal, global and addresses all legislation on the restriction of substances as well as its own strategy that "may go beyond substance restrictions and bans in local markets." Compliance with this standard is part of the terms of doing business with this car producer. It is the responsibility of the tier-one suppliers to pass on this standard and all its requirements to the sub-tier suppliers. The RSMS exceeds the GADSL. Even after the implementation of the GADSL the RSMS standard is valid and will be updated. The automaker in question regards it as necessary to exceed the existing standards of chemical regulation regarding e.g. the passenger compartment. The suppliers anticipated this reaction of automotive manufacturers. A common standard was in their best interest, because it would have simplified the reporting processes. Complying with this global list would have meant that all laws and the automotive standards were observed. However, the suppliers are aware that they cannot guarantee that the car producers adhere to the common standard and do not demand additional ones. They appreciate that the global list was set up by the industry, because they believe that those actors have a better overview than law-making institutions. The automotive suppliers are of the opinion that the standards of the car producers that exceed the global list, the GADSL, are unwarranted (Interviews 2005).

Material Safety Data Sheets

In short, material safety data sheets contain safety information on the handling of hazardous substances. They provide essential information on chemicals in order to minimise health or environmental dangers (cf. Ronit 2000: 91).

In the 1970s, companies in different industries began to provide their own safety data sheets. For example, car producers and chemical distributors developed their own data sheets as they wanted to be informed by their suppliers on the chemical composition of products as well as on the adequate handling of haz-

---

4 http://www.model.mds.eds.de/html/data/imds_standard101_ilrs.pdf, October 17, 2005.
5 http://gadsl.org/files/2005_Ver_1.0.pdf, October 17, 2005.

ardous chemicals. In the 1980s, the German chemical industry association (VCI) and the German Association of the Automotive Industry (VDA) developed association-specific data sheets. According to a voluntary initiative of the industry, the safety data sheets were harmonised in Germany. At first, these harmonised safety data sheets were not coordinated with foreign data sheets. The situation changed with the European directive on safety data sheets. In the forefront of the directive, the Federation of German Industries (BDI) arranged for a committee of representatives of the VDA and the VCI to participate in the development of a harmonised European safety data sheet. The VDA-data sheet can be said to be the precursor of the forthcoming European data sheet. This can be explained by the fact that as the European Commission, preparing the directive on safety data sheets, was asking for adequate instruments, the VDA-safety-data sheet was widely-used (Interview 2005). The directive determines that any person established within the Community who is responsible for placing a dangerous substance or preparation on the market, whether manufacturer, importer or distributor, shall supply the recipient who is an industrial user of the substance or preparation with a safety data sheet (European Commission 1991).

The major difficulty with the data sheets is that information is often deficient or even lacking or that the wrong data sheet has been used. This can be explained by the fact that the design of safety data sheets is not similar in different regions. So, for example, an Asian corporation that wants to export a dangerous substance has to deal with different data sheets in the USA and in the European Union (EU). If information on chemical substances is lacking, a European corporation uses its personal contacts to its supplier outside of the EU to get the missing information in an informal way. In spite of these problems, safety data sheets are currently more accepted than at the beginning; the corporations' staff pay more attention to them. If they do not want to compile safety data sheets on their own, corporations may contact chemical consulting firms – which emerged in the 1980s – that compile data sheets e.g. under the provisions of the aforementioned directive (Interviews 2005).

Since the implementation of the directive on safety data sheets, the chemical and automotive industries have not been inactive. E.g. some representatives of automotive manufacturers and parts suppliers as well as a representative of a global chemical producer participated in a committee dealing with the development of an efficient electronic system to exchange European data sheets. Finally, a harmonised data format was designed to reduce the corporations' burdens. Before, the data sheet was transmitted in paper form. This was an administrative burden as the data is used for purposes such as compiling registers of hazardous chemicals or operating instructions.

In the 1990s, a globally harmonised system (GHS) for hazard communication was developed that includes a common approach on substance data sheets. Key participants in developing the system include various governments and some international organisations. Work on the GHS has been ongoing since the United

Nations' Conference on the Environment and Development in Rio de Janeiro (Silk 2003: 447).[6] In the case of safety data sheets, the harmonisation process was able to build on the previous efforts of the industry to standardise the approaches of the data sheets requirements. Thus, there was agreement on a sixteen section data sheet (Silk 2003: 451).[7]

Substitution Processes

A last example of an emerging industry-spanning management of chemical substances is the substitution of hazardous chemicals. In recent years, the automotive industry began to substitute other chemicals for methylene chloride, a harmful and presumably cancer-causing solvent. The European Union classifies this substance as ‚category 3', the category containing substances "that need attention due to their possible carcinogenic properties for humans" (Tukker/Simons 1999: 38). A global automotive producer started the replacement of this prevalent substance together with a leading global producer of chemicals. Since replacing of methylene chloride in repairing lacquers proved to be difficult, the car producer first tried to play down the hazardousness of the substance, but the cancer-causing effect of methylene chloride was discussed in public and so the car producer quickly searched for an adequate solution. The corporation contacted a global chemical producer who developed a less harmful repairing lacquer. As this solution proved to be effective, the chemical producer promoted it and offered the new lacquer to other producers of automobiles. Meanwhile, the substitution for methylene chloride in repairing lacquers proceeded in the automotive industry. In another case, a producer of lacquer developed a solvent-free lacquer and ceased the production of lacquers with solvents, so its customer, a global automotive manufacturer, had to purchase it (Interviews 2004, 2005).

Nonetheless, the car producers are critical on the substitution of substances. They are of the opinion that it might be more reasonable to deal with a hazardous, but well-known substance in a careful way than to use a substitute without knowing how to handle it properly. Of course, the substitution processes may fail. This was the case when a US car manufacturer demanded a product free of nitrosamines, a cancer-producing substance, from a supplier outside of the USA. The reason was that the US law prohibits this chemical substance. The supplier regarded this demand as unfair and announced a price increase for the demanded product. This caused the car producer to withdraw its demand.

---

6 According to an international agreement, "it is desirable to have as many countries as possible adopt the GHS by 2008" (Silk 2003: 451).
7 These sections include, among other things, information on ingredients; toxicological, ecological and transport information (Silk 2003: 451).

Transnational Practices and Cognitive Structures

The examples discussed above demonstrate that some common transnational practices have been established and changed in the automotive and chemical industry – corporations have developed new ways of acting or have changed the ways they act – and that a few changes in cognitive structures are observable. Views,[8] norms, values, interpretations or goals of corporations have changed.

First, the international material data system as well as the global automotive declarable substance list – which were invented by different industries and across nation-state boundaries – exemplify how new practices have emerged in relation to the management of chemicals. Also, some cognitive changes have become apparent in this context. For example, the automotive industry thought that a common initiative to collect data on chemical substances was necessary and realised this goal. There are some additional shared views and interpretations such as the recognition of the automotive and the chemical industry that it is necessary to cooperate and to produce a common standard, the GADSL. Thus, they shared and realised a common goal. Yet, the views concerning the benefits of the GADSL seem to differ among automotive producers and their suppliers. While the parts suppliers appreciated the list due to its capacity to make it less difficult to comply with laws and private standards, some car producers believed that their own standards were superior and should not be replaced by a common standard. Hence, it is questionable if the GADSL would guide the behaviour of all involved business partners. Second, the example of the material safety data sheets, illustrates that common practices concerning the handling of safety information on chemical substances emerged. The example shows that some common views and interpretations were established, such as the intention to be informed on the composition of products and their safe handling as well as the enhanced acceptance of safety data sheets in the industry. Requests of different industries for a harmonised European safety data sheet as well as the desire for an electronic exchange system are examples of common goals. Third, the example of the replacement of harmful chemicals demonstrates that practices and cognitive structures have changed. This is true insofar as corporations worked together across the boundaries of firms and industries to reduce environmental and health hazards. Referring to the substitution of methylene chloride with another substance, it is important that the substitute developed by chemical corporations and the automotive industry was diffused throughout the industry by a chemical producer so the whole industry was able to change its practices and benefited from it. Behind this, some cognitive changes are observable. The chemical and primarily the automotive industry turned out to be responsive to public concerns relating to environmental and health dangers. The substitution of chemicals described can be referred to as a re-

---

8 Views may relate to "beliefs about desired product attributes, market structures, appropriate ways of doing business, and the relative quality of member firms" (Porac et al. 2002: 593).

alised goal of corporations in the automotive and the chemical industry. Yet, the interpretations of the automotive manufacturers on the one hand and the interpretations of their suppliers on the other hand seem to be different as the example of the failed substitution process demonstrates. The automotive supplier was of the opinion that the demand of the car producer to phase out nitrosamines in the production of parts was just a strategic decision. Hence, he showed no understanding that this phase-out would be reasonable for environmental and health reasons. Finally, both the American car producer and its supplier were not willing to bear additional costs for a phase-out of nitrosamines voluntarily. It is an indication of changing patterns of thought that some corporations of the chemical as well as of the automotive industry argued that it might be reasonable to use a new, but unknown substance instead of a hazardous but well-known substance.

In the field of chemical regulation, "pure" self-regulation, i.e. strictly autonomous self-regulation, is rare because states or supranational organisations like the EU attempt to influence the firms' behaviour by setting environmental policy targets and/or by creating a framework designed to promote a particular behaviour of private actors (cf. Rehbinder 1997: 2). Even though there are some legal foundations, there are a number of possibilities for self-regulation in a broader sense[9] as the examples illustrated above show and which will be summarised in the following points. The cases of the IMDS and the GADSL show that corporations established data systems that facilitate compliance with different national laws and private standards; corporations are informed on new (foreign) laws and private standards as well as on new scientific evidence concerning the consequences for health and environment by means of the said system. Thus, they were in the position to react quickly to those changes. The case of the automotive producer representing the strategy of exceeding existing public standards of chemical regulation as well as the substitution of methylene chloride shows that corporations go beyond existing legal requirements if they think they are insufficient. Further, the car manufacturer monitored if its suppliers complied with his requirements and ensured that they actively participated in communicating these requirements throughout the value-chain. The example of the VDA-data sheet illustrates that corporations developed a material safety data sheet on their own initiative which was afterwards absorbed by law. Further, corporations man-

---

9   See the concept of Haufler who explains that self-regulation occurs "when those regulated – in this case, corporations – design and enforce the rules themselves. The rules that govern their behaviour are adopted voluntarily, either going beyond current regulatory requirements or establishing new standards in areas in which government rules or standards are lacking" (Haufler 2001: 8). Knill and Lehmkuhl differentiate between "regulated self-regulation" where both public and private actors own a "high level of governance capacity" and "private self-regulation", here the states' capacity to intervene is restricted and private self-regulation is dominant (Knill/Lehmkuhl 2002: 93p.). (For the possibilities of governments to induce corporate self-regulation see Ruhnka/Boerstler 1998; for the relevance of monitoring and sanctioning systems to sustain self-regulation see Ronit/Schneider 2000: 23p.)

aged to develop an electronic system for the exchange of European data sheets without being obliged to do so. In addition, the international approach to harmonising data sheets was based on previous industry efforts.

One reason for the emergence of a private management of hazardous chemical substances in the chemical industry and in the automotive industry is their intention to enhance and not to endanger their reputation. For several decades, chemical corporations have had a "very bad public image", because "[t]hey are seen as causing environmental hazards" (Ronit 2000: 84p.).[10] Especially after some momentous chemical accidents in the past, the public image of the chemical industry has deteriorated. Globally, the most well-known accident was the one in Bhopal (1984) – regarded as the worst accident in industrial history – where thousands of people died and thousands of others were injured when toxic chemicals were released into the atmosphere (Greenpeace 2004; Nathan/Kovoor-Misra 2002: 253).[11] The disaster caused widespread consumer protest against the chemical manufacturer responsible (Kollman/Prakash 2001: 401), and the chemical industry reacted by establishing a global program to ensure the responsible treatment of chemicals (cf. Nathan/Kovoor-Misra 2002: 250). This world-wide, voluntary initiative of the chemical industry ("Responsible Care"), challenges chemical companies "to improve all aspects of performance which relate to protection of health, safety and environment"(Druckrey 1998: 981).[12] The self-portrayals of corporations belonging to the automotive industry, concerning their attitudes towards the protection of the environment are similar to those of the chemical industry. On their web sites, the automotive producers and their suppliers point to their intention to protect human health and the global environment and to their commitment to the concept of sustainable development. A reason for the commitment to sustainable development, as pointed out by one of the global car producers, is that the corporation wants to maintain and expand its societal acceptance. Even though there have been no environmental or health scandals in the automotive industry (cf. Bolli 2000: 55), the discussion of the risks of substances like polyvinyl chloride (PVC), brominated flame retardants (BFRs) and phthalates also concerns the automotive industry as these substances are in their products.[13]

---

10 For the struggle of the chemical industry with its bad reputation since the 1960s see also Ronit/Schneider 2000: 19.
11 The gas explosion in the Indian city of Bhopal is regarded as the worst accident in industrial history. According to Greenpeace, in the first days after the incident 8.000 people died. Since then, more than 20.000 people have died from the direct or indirect consequences of the catastrophe (Greenpeace 2004).
12 One aspect of "Responsible Care" is product stewardship. E.g. chemical distributors pledge themselves to offer only products that can be transported, used and disposed safely according to current knowledge.
13 A recent study of an Austrian environmental protection organisation analysed the contaminant loads in new cars. According to the study, 98 chemicals pollute the air of passenger compartments, among others, the phthalate DEHP, a potentially carcinogenic plasticiser, was detected (Global 2000, 2005).

Another reason for the establishment of a transnational management of chemicals is so-called lead firms.[14] Consequently, the IMDS was initiated by global car manufacturers that built up communication channels among some of the members of the value chain in question. As the example of the substitution of methylene chloride by safer substances reveals, an automotive producer appeared to act as a "pioneer" and thus contributed to changing practices and ideas in the automotive and chemical industry. Last but not least, the car manufacturers produced changes in the value chain through their demands to be informed by their suppliers on the composition of parts and their lists of restricted substances – they were able to dictate to their suppliers the kind of chemical substances they do not want to have in the delivered products. This is because the suppliers depend on their orders. On the other hand the producers depend to a certain degree on their suppliers' willingness to cooperate. This is the case if a car producer depends on a special supplier and can not afford to switch to another one. Suppliers of parts hesitate to exchange information with their customers because they are afraid of revealing sensitive information on the composition of substances and hence to endanger their competitive position.

Conclusion

Above, two reasons were given as an explanation for the emergence of a transnational management of hazardous chemical substances: the interest of the chemical and the automotive industry in having a good reputation and the existence of lead firms that initiated changes concerning the management of chemicals. Of course, there are some other reasons that might explain why corporations engage in the responsible transnational management of chemicals: a careful handling of chemicals reduces risks and contributes to a smooth production; the increased skepticism of the firms' employees who have to handle chemical substances and thus the risk of a lawsuit; the awareness that consumption patters have changed and that the demand for ecologically suitable products has risen. On the other hand, it might be the case that corporations are responsive to societal signals on what is an acceptable behaviour and what is not and that they recognised the environmental consequences of their practices and accordingly have changed their patterns of behaviour to contribute to the protection of the environment (cf. Rehbinder 1997: 2; Ronit/Schneider 2000: 22). To evaluate if economic interests or values and norms explain the emergence of the transnational management of

---

14 According to Gereffi, lead firms "can be located upstream or downstream from manufacturing [...], or they can be involved in the supply of critical components [...]. What distinguishes lead firms from their followers or subordinates is that they control access to major resources (such as product design, new technologies, brand names, or consumer demand) that generate the most profitable return in the industry" (Gereffi 2001: 1622).

chemicals – or if the truth lies somewhere inbetween – is beyond the scope of this article.

Nonetheless, the changing and emerging practices concerning the management of hazardous substances show that the self-regulation of private actors may have some positive effects for the environment and/or for human health. If hazardous substances are known or even avoided, not only the employees of corporations involved in the manufacturing of cars but also consumers will be protected against health risks. Finally, the disposal or recycling of automobiles will be less complicated and more environmental-friendly. In some other cases, empirical examples reveal that self-regulation is useful for the efficient coordination of production processes, but the environmental benefits are questionable. Hence, it may be beneficial for suppliers that it is difficult for car manufacturers to exceed the GADSL; however it may prove to be unfavourable for environmental reasons. This raises the question of whether or not thinking has changed in favour of an enhanced awareness of environmental aspects. One should not take it for granted that the American car manufacturer asked its supplier for a nitrosamine-free part merely because the American law requires a phase-out of nitrosamines. It is by all means possible that the demand was based on environmental considerations as well. But the fact that the car producer was not willing to accept higher prices seems to challenge this.

However, against the background of vanishing borders and the fact that the resources of nation-states are limited, multinational corporations may choose to solve environmental problems by designing and establishing adequate rules and procedures among themselves. Here, their specialised knowledge, financial and management potential as well as their transnational organisational structures (cf. Messner/Nuscheler 2003: 16p; Cutler et al. 1999: 4p) may hopefully be conducive. The empirical cases have shown that corporations identified realms where self-regulation in relation to the transnational management of chemical substances was feasible and necessary and hence created corresponding arrangements. At the same time, it also became apparent that – as e.g. the cases of the IMDS and GADSL showed – it is difficult for practices and ideas to diffuse across the boundaries of industries. Further research will be necessary to determine which factors complicate the diffusion of practices and ideas in transnational value chains.

References

Bolli, Agathe (2000) "Environmental Communication and Competitiveness. A Case Study of the Car Industry." International Institute for Industrial Environmental Economics (IIIEE), Lund: Lund University, February 20, 2006 (http://www.iiiee.lu.se/Publication.nsf/$webAll/7DB36EB102603D37C1256 C37002CC457).

Cutler, Claire/Haufler, Virginia/Porter, Tony (1999) "Private Authority and International Affairs." In: Claire Cutler/Virginia Haufler/Tony Porter (eds.) *Private Authority and International Affairs*, New York: State University of New York Press, pp. 3-23.

Druckrey, Frauke (1998) "How to Make Business Ethics Operational: Responsible Care – An Example of Successful Self-Regulation?" Journal of Business Ethics 17, pp. 979-985.

European Commission (1991) *Defining and laying down the detailed arrangements for the system of specific information relating to dangerous preparations in implementation of Article 10 of Directive 88/379/EEC*, 91/155/EEC.

European Commission (2000) *Management of End-of-Life Vehicles*, 2000/53/EC.

European Commission (2002) *Restriction of the use of certain hazardous substances in electrical and electronic equipment*, 2002/95/EC.

Fisher, Michael (2005) "Standards Development for Reporting of Declarable Substances." American Society for Testing and Materials, October 17, 2005 (http://www.astm.org/SNEWS/JUNE_2005/ fisher_jun05.html).

Froschauer, Ulrike/Lueger, Manfred (2003) *Das qualitative Interview. Zur Praxis interpretativer Analyse sozialer Systeme*, Wien: WUV-Universitätsverlag.

Gereffi, Gary (2001) "Shifting Governance Structures in Global Commodity Chains, With Special Reference to the Internet." American Behavioral Scientist 44/10, pp. 1616-1637.

Global 2000 (2005) "Schadstoffbelastung in Neuwagen.", February 22, 2006 (http://help.orf.at/dateien/1903_Autotest_Luft.pdf).

Greenpeace (2004) "Bhopal 1984 – 2004: Zwanzig Jahre Verantwortungslosigkeit." February 20, 2006 (www.greenpeace.de/ fileadmin /gpd/user_upload/ themen/umweltgifte/greenpeace_bhopal.pdf).

Haufler, Virginia (2001) *A Public Role for the Private Sector. Industry Self-Regulation in a Global Economy*, Washington D.C: Carnegie Endowment for International Peace.

Jang, Ha-Yong (1997) "Cultural Differences in an Interorganizational Network: Shared Public Relations Firms among Japanese and American Companies." Public Relations Review 23/4, pp. 327-341.

Johnson Controls (2001) "IMDS User Guideline.", October 17, 2005 (http://ag.johnsoncontrols.com/SupplierHandbook/pdf/imdsuserd.pdf).

Knill, Christoph/Lehmkuhl, Dirk (2002) "Governance and Globalization: Conceptualizing the Role of Public and Private Actors." In: Adrienne Héritier (ed.) *Common Goods: Reinventing European and International Governance*, Oxford: Rowman & Littlefield, pp. 85-104.

Kollman, Kelly/Prakash, Aseem (2001) "Green by Choice? Cross-National Variations in Firms' Responses to EMS-Based Environmental Regimes." World Politics 53, pp. 399-430.

Messner, Dirk/Nuscheler, Franz (2003) *Das Konzept Global Governance. Stand und Perspektiven*, Duisburg: Institut für Entwicklung und Frieden der Universität Duisburg-Essen.

Nathan, Maria/Kovoor-Misra, Sarah (2002) "Vicarious Organizational Learning. From Crises in an Inter-Organizational Field." The Journal of Applied Behavioral Science 38/2, pp. 245-266.

Porac, Joseph/Ventresca, Marc/Mishina, Yuri (2002) "Interorganizational Cognition and Interpretation." In: Joel Baum (ed.) *Companion to Organizations*. Oxford: Blackwell, pp. 597-598.

Rehbinder, Eckard (1997) *Environmental Agreements. A New Instrument of Environmental Policy*, Florence: European University Institute.

Ronit, Karsten (2000) "The Good, the Bad or the Ugly?"In: Karsten Ronit/Volker Schneider (eds.) *Private Organizations and their Contribution to Problem-Solving in the Global Arena*, London: Routledge, pp. 83-101.

Ronit, Karsten/Schneider, Volker (2000) "Private Organizations and their Contribution to Problem-Solving in the Global Arena." In: Karsten Ronit/Volker Schneider (eds.) *Private Organizations in Global Politics*, London: Routledge, pp. 1-33.

Ruhnka, John/Boerstler, Heidi (1998) "Governmental Incentives for Corporate Self-Regulation." Journal of Business Ethics 17, pp. 309-326.

Silk, Jennifer C. (2003) "Development of a globally harmonized system for hazard communication." International Journal of Hygiene and Environmental Health 206, pp. 447-452.

Tukker, A/Simons, L. Ph. (1999) *Methylene Chloride: Advantages and Drawbacks of Possible Market Restrictions in the EU,* Final report for DG III of the European Commission, March 22, 2006 (http://europa.eu.int/comm/enterprise/chemicals/docs/studies/tno-methylene_chloride.pdf).

Wernet, Andreas (2000) *Einführung in die Interpretationstechnik der objektiven Hermeneutik*, Opladen: Leske Budrich.

IT Usage and
Transnational Identity Formations

'Do you really talk about emotions on the phone..?': Content of Distance Communication as a Structuring Moment of the Modern World Society

MAGDALENA NOWICKA

Introduction

Distance communication tools as a mean of spanning and sustaining personal networks, as well as network analysis and the metaphor of a network have long been a focus of transnational studies (Vertovec 2001). There have also been attempts to make these concepts and objects of study fruitful and interesting to the world society approach. Despite the fact that the two approaches emphas different dimensions of the issue, they are not necessarily contradictory. If we define society as "the inclusion of all possible contacts" (Luhmann 1984: 33) the network perspective can be informative for the model of the modern world society (Stichweh 2006; Holzer 2005). Transnational studies investigate the exact forms and contents of social networks, which can tell the world society approach adherent about their local density and heterogeneity, connectivity and clustering and thus about the structure of world society (Stichweh 2003). Illustrative is the assumption that the modern world society is characterised by universal accessibility – in principle, anybody can be an addressee (and a source) of communication (Fuchs 1997). However, there can be many societal barriers to the possible scope of a social relationship – it is who the participants of social exchange are. From this perspective, distance communication tools – their form and availability – determine the exact form of social relationships yet their nonexistence does not question the existence of the modern world society (Holzer 2005: 320p). Distance communication tools make the social networks possible, insofar they allow the disembedding of communication from physical co-presence (Lübbe 1996). Yet, social networks do not emerge in a vacuum but they are predetermined by particular social specifications on which kind of communication and with which addressee is relevant. Therefore, neither the scope of social networks directly, nor the availability of distance communication tools, structure the world society. Rather, other factors, for example 'mental maps' of the social world and in particular, the way potential contacts are localised, determine the world society's structure. Watts (2003) identified geographical location and profession as two such key factors for selecting communication partners.

However, with few exceptions (Knorr-Cetina/Bruegger 2002), no studies look at structures and dynamics of the modern world society from the microperspective of individual behaviour (Herkenrath et al. 2005). The world society approach has so far given little attention to the question of the defining qualities of the world society, focusing rather on its quantities. The qualitative studies have been a domain of transnational approaches, which, however, scarcely think in more global terms. Moreover, there is more confusion than consensus on the role of long-distance communication tools for the formation and structures of globally spanning social networks. The world society approach sees the spreading of new communication technologies as a substitute for the geographical mobility of people (Stichweh 2005), which might be true in terms of getting in contact with people over geographical distance but is controversial with respect to networks already existing. Another interpretation, which can be located within the transnational approach, is that Internet based exchange platforms play a key role in creating new social interconnectedness and the emergence of 'new imagined communities' (Baym 1995; Jenkins 1997; Miller/Slater 2000; Georgiou 2002; Panagakos 2003) or 'global village' (McLuhan/Powers 1992) or 'world polity' (Meyer 2005). In turn, the distinction between mobility and immobility (Bonß/Kesselring 2001; Kesselring 2001), and 'here' and 'there' is said to be irrelevant; borders seem to disappear and the new space opens out in which the old social order has been replaced by relational complexity (Urry 2004). The opponents of these approaches point to a simplified understanding of space in which the local and the global, as well as place and space are dychotomic, and to the neglected role of various non-spatial boundaries (Berking 1998; Berger 1999; Berker 2003; Massey 2005; cf. Nowicka 2006a). Focusing on individual life courses, some authors (Escobar 1996; Dutton 1999; Jordan 1999; Smith/Kollock 1999) critic pessimistic approaches that perceive in the development of computer mediated communication a danger to mutual trust and collective identity (Tarrow 1998). They also contradict the technological optimism and the opinion that ITC can replace face-to-face interactions (Schwartzman 1989; Boden/Molotch 1994).

There is thus a great need for a grounded empirical research on the exact structures of the modern world society and the involvement of the media of distance communication. The following paper wants to make a contribution to this subject by focusing on the group of transnationally mobile professionals and their small-scale social networks. A rich literature on migrants and diasporas has enhanced our understanding of practices that stretch beyond one locality, and captured how migrants negotiate significant aspects of their lives across borders (Dezalay 1990; King 1990; Glick Schiller et al 1992; Basch et al. 1994; Chan

1997; Cohen 1997; Smith/Guarnizo 1998; Vertovec/Cohen 1999; Faist 2000; O'Riain 2000; Colic-Peisker 2002; Hannerz 2003, to name a few). However, this growing literature has focused on enforced migration, large communities, identity formation and integration in host societies, and little interest has been given to the more informal and interpersonal connections established and sustained by mobile professionals. Further, the premature conclusion that, in the era of distance communication tools, mobility and spatial dispersal do not have any negative effects on individuals' social networks needs to be tested against the empirical data.

The research which focused on family networks has addressed the relationship between spatial ruptures and the negotiation of changes in the gender division of labor, gender relations and ideologies and intergenerational relations within the family (Landolt/Da 2005) but not on the relationship between spatial distance and proximity, use of distance communication tools, and forms of social interaction with family and friends. Similarly, the research on mobile professionals has focused on the consequences of their mobility for family life and the forms and geographical spread of their social networks (Pelizäus-Hoffmeister 2001; Schneider et al. 2002) or on general patterns of sociability, especially on inclusion of foreigners and locals into the networks (Kennedy 2004). There is scant debate on the spatiality of family practices (Kivisto 2003), in particular on the relationship between mobility and changing notions of home and away (Nowicka 2007).

In the following, I consider mobility and distance communication as two aspects of social networking and ask how they complement each other. I look at how the mobile individuals handle their relationships under the condition of geographical dispersal. In particular, I investigate two types of relationships my interview partners sustain with their immediate family (spouse, children, parents and siblings) and friends. These two situations were distinguished by my interview partners according to how physical and emotional distance and proximity interplay.

Further, I look at how distance communication tools' contribute to maintenance of informal social networks. I argue that content of transmitted messages is crucial for sustaining such networks. Under the conditions of almost unrestrained access to high quality distance communication media (due to diminishing financial costs), other factors such as time efficiency structure the world society. Also, other 'residual boundaries' (Berker 2003) to social networks can be identified, such as language, territorial bond, or cultural and life style differences. These should be understood not as barriers to connectivity but as the structuralising moments of the modern world society.

I begin with picturing the context of the empirical study and the description of the sample studied. In particular, I discuss the individuals' mobility practices and their inclusion in complex institutional arrangements and the way their lives are internationalised. I briefly describe their access to distance communication tools. Focusing on distance communication, I do not lose sight of motivation for travel. This brings me to the first claim that communication in distance and proximity are not interchangeable. I carry on analysing each of the relationships' type and the roles the geographical distance and proximity and distance communication have in them. In the last section, I summar the identified transnationalisation of social networks and individualisation of life styles and their temporal fragmentation. In conclusion, I combine these results with the findings on distance communication and ask how distance communication can soften or sharpen the effects of physical distance for remote relationships.

Mobile Transnational Professionals and Their Environment

For a growing number of professionals mobility belongs to their daily routine. Highly-skilled workers move to undertake a job abroad when in danger of unemployment at home, to pursue their careers or to perform their work tasks. They are involved in overlapping multiple social worlds and interpersonal networks, both private and professional, which are the outcome of their mobility and which can also be a reason to become or stay mobile. Every relationship of mobile people is potentially temporally remote: they may be present at home for three weeks and then leave for six weeks to come back and stay a month. The relationship to their spouses and children, but also to clients and work colleagues takes place in momentary proximity and it is affected by their regular absences. Their geographical mobility may thus mean to them a change in forms and intensity of contact to their nearest and dearest.

The particular group I studied is highly mobile employees of an international organisation, one of the specialised agencies within the United Nations system (later on referred to as the IO). The study was conducted between December 2002 and September 2004 and relied on two-to-three-hour-long problem-centered interviews, accompanied by a short questionnaire. I did not restrict my research to any particular location but spoke to the interviewees in their places of their residence and at their business travel destinations. If a meeting was not possible, we phoned, which was the case five times. I interviewed six women and seven men between 31 and 64 years of age. At the time of the interviews, nine people were married, two of them for the second time. There was one widow and one single person in the sample. One interviewee indicated having a steady life partner and another having a girlfriend. Ten people have children; five of them have (also) adult children who do not live with them anymore (some of them live in a different country). All interviewees have higher education, and most of them completed university with an M.A. degree. Spouses of eight interviewees were professionally active, two of them worked from home, and one was retired.

All of them are migrants and frequent travelers. One group can be distinguished. This is the group of those who travel between 100-170 days in a year, to five to seven countries in which they conduct projects (usually over five to seven years). Such short trips are one to four weeks long (only one interviewee travels only to one country in Africa but for one to three months). These individuals reside generally longer (5-15 years) in one country, usually in the USA, but also in Eastern Europe. A second group consists of individuals who undertake three to five years long assignments in a third country, from where they also travel, but less extensively (usually once a month to neighboring countries, and three times a year to the USA). However, in the course of their lives, the two options of re-settlement and extensive mobility mix: some individuals had traveled extensively for a couple of years and then undertook a foreign assignment. On average, the interviewees re-settled two to nine times between countries and continents. My interview partners come originally from South America, Turkey, the Middle East, the USA, Western (continental) Europe, non-continental Europe and Central and Eastern European countries. They were residents of all continents, and they travel (or used to travel) to various continents, except to Australia. Importantly, the migrants do not separate from their spouses and children but move with them to another country. The IO provides extensive support to these families through job searches for spouses and care and schooling opportunities for children.

Distinctively, they dwell in a de-nationalised environment. The disembeddedness from nation-states is the result of immersion in the organisational networks of the United Nations system, with its own pension and health programs, as well as exclusion from national taxation schemes. Unlike migrants living in diasporas, my informants go abroad alone or with their immediate family only (when re-settling); and they tend not to sustain links characteristic to 'transnational social spaces'. Typically, 'transmigrants' uphold close relationships to communities of origin while being well-integrated into the host society. For example, they contribute financially to the development of their hometowns, and are engaged in local politics (Glick Schiller et al. 1992; Basch et al.1994; Pries 2001). This is not the case in my sample. While my informants wish to maintain close links with family and friends at home, it is not their main concern to sustain cultural bonds with the home country. Also their dependency on home-bonds and on local ethnic groups is very weak (which seems typical of highly qualified and middle class professionals – cf. Kennedy 2004).

The technical networks of the organisation guarantee to the individuals an almost unlimited access to the modern distance communication tools, which can be used for business and private purposes: videoconferencing, satellite phone connections, or mobile computers with Internet access. The IO owns a satellite network for remote communication. It permits reducing the costs for the whole organisation but also for its employees, who are allowed to use the connections, above all phones, for private reasons. For example, they may call via the main board worldwide, paying only for a basic outgoing connection. The IO has a well developed Intranet. Many of the internal transactions and processes take place electronically. The IO's field offices are equipped with special rooms for visiting employees who can use a docking station, Internet access, printers, etc. All the mobile employees are equipped with laptops. In this context the choice of the form of communication belongs to the individual.

The availability of distance communication tools in the offices may be the reason why most of my interview partners are not too well equipped at home. Many of them take their business laptops home, and usually they own a personal computer but they use Internet from home only occasionally, typically for shopping or as a source of information (for example route planners or telephone books). Many of them do not carry a mobile phone with them, and if they do they try to switch it off as often as possible, and do not take business calls after hours. On the other hand, the limited private use of such equipment is a result of their protection of their private sphere. Usually, the mobile individuals have even less time at their disposal than their immobile colleagues, and they try to spend this time entirely with the family. They dedicate their spare time to their hobbies, which they carry out either at home or outdoors. Many like gardening and taking of their house, or do individual sports. This precious time should be exclusively devoted to those who are closest to them.

Motivation to Travel or: From Whom Are You Remote?

One of the most important questions for my research was why people are mobile. In the context of this paper, this question is relevant as far as the individuals' decision to become or stay mobile means a choice of from whom they are remote. They conduct projects in distant countries. This means their clients are remote. When deciding to travel, they decide for a physical proximity to them. At the same time, they become remote to their families, who stay at home. A closer look at the individuals' motivation to travel demonstrates some of the issues of remote communication, which I discuss in greater detail when focusing on my interviewees' private relationships.

One reason why my interviewees decide to travel are the deficiencies of distance communication tools. It is expected that physical mobility can be replaced by virtual mobility, it means that instead of traveling, the individuals use distance communication tools to manage their tasks in far destinations. The IO makes three options available to it's employees: they can choose to move to a third country where they stay three to five years and perform their work while residing there; they can undertake an assignment which enables them to reside in the USA, where the IO's headquarters is located and from there they travel regularly to the countries where they participate in projects. They can also choose to stay in their place of residence (usually in the IO's headquarters location) and do their work from 'behind the desk'. All three options are equally supported by the IO. It means someone who does not want to travel (due to family circumstances like a birth of a baby or health problems) can find another, qualitatively equal, assignment within the organisation that does not require them to travel.

However, all the interviewees agree that travel is necessary because nothing can replace personal encounters with people and places. They say "no best equipment can replace traveling" (I1: 51; I4: 57)[1]. They see several reasons for this: First, people – their clients and cooperation partners – are used to communicate face-to-face and they do not want to rely on videoconferencing (I4: 57). More importantly, however, one can benefit more from the "personal touch" that face-to-face meetings give. Further, the interviewees believe that:

"You can use videoconferences when there is kind not a very difficult or controversial issue to be discussed which are also on the further agenda, when you have to convince people then it is better to meet people face-to-face it is videoconferencing are great just to update, to get people informed, but if it is a very critical issue, when you have to convince people then I would still say face-to face discussion in order really to have very detailed discussion." (I3: 36)

They admit that videoconferencing is an improvement to telephone conference or e-mail because one can see people, their faces, expressions, behaviour, and their body language (I3: 152). Observing body language is necessary to understand their motivations and decisions (I3: 57). Yet travel and personal encounter involves another aspect: one meets not only people when traveling, one meets places (I6: 26). Lenka[2] says that she meets people who are not her direct clients or counterparts with whom she could not communicate by e-mail, phone or videoconference but who are affected by the projects she supervises. When she sees what she contributed when preparing the project, a bypass constructed or a bridge built, and when she talks to people who use this infrastructure and thank her for this contribution, she feels satisfaction. She feels rewarded for her efforts and it compensates for her hard work. She is then motivated to continue (I6: 40). Reiner confirms this saying that one gets a much better understanding of the situation of a particular person (a client, an addressee of a project) when visiting a project site. Being physically present in the "field", he talks to people, for example taxi drivers, with whom he otherwise would not have a possibility to communicate. He also observes beggars on the street or passing people laughing, and these impressions cannot be replaced by talking, he stresses (I2: 57). Rainer's words point to the very important issue that communication is not only about talking and that the forms of communication are not exchangeable. The issues, problems and situations he and his colleagues deal with, when supervising a

---

1 The numbers in brackets stand for interview and paragraph number respectively.
2 The names of all the interviewees and of geographic destinations have been changed to assure anonymity.

project, are too complex. Not only it is necessary to see people's faces when they talk to get a full picture of their reactions but it is often necessary to talk to other people, and to see their environment. Therefore, videoconferencing is a poor substitute for travel, and can be used only when travel is not possible for some reasons (I2: 65).

His words make clear that distance communication disconnects people from their environments. When communicating by phone or Internet the partners do not get an impression of how the other lives, how the other fits into the surroundings, and how the location may influence this person. Being physically present in a place gives one a much better understanding of the situation of a particular person. When in place, you can talk to many people, recogn their moods, and get an idea of people's living conditions. You can participate in the stories of others. This knowledge increases the satisfaction my informants feel when performing their professional tasks. Otherwise, they experience others as anonymous recipients of their decisions, who are 'caught in the moment', without their own personal histories, immobilised and atemporalised, extracted from spatial and temporal contexts. We can say thus that the spatial distance increases the emotional distance between people by the means of abstracting them from the particularities of place.

The same does not apply to the communication between the co-workers within the IO, either those who sit in a neighboring office or building or who work in another country. Contrary to what has been said so far, the interviewees use mostly e-mail to communicate within teams, and they rarely meet personally. Besides e-mail, phone, and sometimes also audio-conferencing are the tools used to contact colleagues (I1: 23), depending on what needs to be communicated. Usually, teams exchange documents and other information, and coordinate meetings; seldom, they discuss problems on the phone. One of the reasons for this difference may be a clear division of tasks and responsibilities between the work colleagues, which makes their behaviour predictable. The risk of misunderstandings and the anxiety that they could negatively influence a relationship is much lower in this case. There is no necessity to establish trust since the roles assigned to partners govern their relationships. Should a conflict nevertheless occur, there are conciliation mechanisms in place in the organisation.

Private Social Networks

My interview partners live with the constant anxiety that they may lose contact with their friends when they resettle. Many of them moved out from their parents' house as students and never came back, as a result of having moved to another country right after graduation. Since then, they rely on distance communication tools to keep in touch with their family and friends:

"You know, we live in such a world practically without borders. One day I am at this continent, the other day somewhere else...It is natural that we do not end friendships. Of course, we do not see each other so often, but we contact per e-mail, we talk on the phone. It is not like in nineteenth century when you went to America, got on board of such damper and you cried because you thought you go forever." (I12: 52)

Those who travel over one hundred days a year use distance communication tools to stay in regular contact with the immediate family: wife, husband, and children. The availability of distance communication does not make their mobility unnecessary. It makes it possible. Knowing that they can communicate when traveling, bridging the distance to their nearest and dearest, it is easier for them to decide to leave home for a time.

Families under the Condition of Remoteness

Despite this, the interviewees complain that their contact with family is quite irregular due to mobility. The temporal dimension is of key importance to mobile individuals. First, their contacts to their nearest and dearest suffer due to (real or experienced) time shortages and squeeses (Southerton et al. 2001) anyway. When they are not on trips, they work long hours and have little leisure time available for activities with their families. When they are away, this possibility does not exist at all; they just manage to call their spouse at the end of their work day only if time zones allow for it. Secondly, every trip fragments the private time they spend together with the family, in physical proximity, when the family members hug, kiss, play together, go shopping, or get involved in hobbies. This time is divided over the year into short periods. Thirdly, time delays are a problem to individuals. Often, it is easy to maintain contact either by e-mail or telephone, one can be reached almost in every location. However, not just the fact of information exchange, but immediate reaction, is important. Reiner says he carries a mobile phone with him case his wife needs to get in touch with him:

"I do that because I would like to be in touch, I don't want to miss anything important and also I would like to be contactable in cases of emergencies. Before 1990 when I was in Africa it was really difficult to stay in touch. And I was out of touch with my family for a week or more. That was not really very good – when the child was sick or your wife wasn't able to find a certain file or there was something urgent...It gives the impression that she had to manage on her own. That was quite a problem. It is much less so these days. But still it is an issue. This traveling, the amount of traveling I do is a burden on a family." (I2: 53)

The reaction time is important insofar an immediate response carries an emotional message with it. A delayed reaction makes an impression of less involvement and understanding of the problem and its urgency. Someone who replies with a delay misses a great dose of immediate and strong emotions on a particular, controversial or difficult, issue.

Scarcity of time disrupts the seemingly trivial personal contacts because it disturbs the daily routines. Routine interactions play a significant role in the maintenance of close relationships and defining the roles in each relationship (Duck 1988). How important they are becomes visible first when mobile people decide to change their work assignment to travel less. This is often the case for young mothers, but also other interviewees use this option (I5). Many decide to reduce the number and duration of trips when it becomes a clear burden on their families, like Martin (I3) who reduced his amount of travels by forty percent when his wife gave birth to their daughter.

However, the interviewees differ in their judgment on whether irregular contact is more destructive to relationships with their direct or extended family or to friends. Some claim that their families suffer dramatically from their physical absences referring to their spouses and children. Others say that no matter what, the family members maintain their close ties; they usually mean their parents and siblings. Relationships with the extended family are usually not considered too problematic. Sporadic visits to family members and regular phone calls are sufficient to maintain contact and there is little danger of weakening ties. All the interviewees bridge the distance to their parents with the help of the telephone. Ludmila calls them regularly in spite of the costs because this way she feels comfortable – "I try not to set barriers myself", she says (I7: 51). For those whose friends and families live in the USA, regular contact is even easier because it is cheaper – they use the IO's satellite system to make private calls. One can call for free via the IO's satellite in the US; calling the local number is then free of charge, and long-distance connections are much cheaper than through commercial networks (I4: 109).

Men tend to see their relationship to their parents and relatives as less difficult than women do. Women tend to be more sensitive about distance between family members and often regret being far from their parents. Although their relationship remains intimate, they miss daily contact with their parents; they are worried that they may not be present in case of emergency, and they miss parental advice and warmth. "You cannot call Mum non-stop when you cook and you are not sure what to put in a pot", says Lenka (I6: 70).

Due to physical distance, individuals need to be more flexible in their life arrangements, and they also need to be well organised. They also need to flexibly react to any possibility to meet their extended family members face-to-face: many interviewees combine business travels with visits to their parents (I5, I11). Visits to the parental home of both partners are, on the other hand, arranged so that the time is divided equally between both families, thus requiring certain regular schedule. Many of the interviewees say, they always spend summer holidays in the country of a husband, and winter in the country of his wife's family, and then one week a year by themselves in a third 'neutral' country. Not without importance is their wish to let their own children get to know their grandparents, as well as the country and culture of their parents' origin.

Friendships and Mobile Life-Styles

When asked to describe their social networks the interviewees indicated the nationality and place of residence of their friends, which allowed them to draw their 'social maps'. Most of interviewees stay in touch with friends from school or university. The closer the ties used to be, the better the chance that the friendship survives the distance, note the interviewees (I5: 125, 141). Typically, they accept that their friendships evolve with time and see it as a normal development. They relate this change in the nature and form of a friendship and the intensity of contacts to an evolving life situation rather than physical distance. Reiner who has lived abroad (in several countries) for over thirty years says that one develops different interests and different perspectives, so: "after a number of years" he discovered he "might not have much in common" with his old friends and relatives (I2: 81). In particular, the experience of mobility, frequent changes of residence and exposure to many different cultures disembedds the interviewees from their old networks. Some of my interview partners, however, point to the role of physical absence from friends. Rodrigo believes that after some ten years of being outside of the home country one has to accept that certain contacts, especially those based on professional interests and business co-operation end. It is possible to maintain the interest in one person's life over a longer time but this link has to be emotional; in other cases a friendship ends (I13: 86). Steven, on the other hand, considers mobility as a positive factor in shaping his own social networks; because of frequent changes of residence, he gains possibilities to decide with whom to stay in touch with and with whom not (I4: 121).

Generally, the interviewees judge keeping contact with friends as requiring a lot of effort. Some friendships end with time because the contact is not as regular as it used to be or because not many people are able to express emotions when talking on the phone only or writing e-mails (not to mention that not everybody has e-mail access, though these days it is rarely a problem because everybody has a telephone). The interviewees emphas that direct unmediated contact is the most important to them and their friends (I1: 49). Diego says it is perhaps easier to maintain contact with friends in the age of Internet and e-mails – but, in practice, keeping in touch regularly is difficult. Thus, he re-defined true friendship:

„True friends is that you may not see each other for four, five years, you may actually only once or twice a year write a short note, and then you see each other after four years and it is as you never stopped seeing each other. Because things start clicking immediately. And that is very rare, it doesn't happen very often but when it happens, at least in my definition then you know it is a real friend. And then it has to work both ways as well." (I10: 98)

A friendship under condition of spatial dispersal is also affected by temporal ruptures. This has tremendous consequences for the mobile individuals. Mobile people have to re-establish their relationships to friends again and again. They need to make effort to ensure that people do not forget them, that they stay integrated (I4: 65) despite being absent. Both parties in this relationship need to be patient: Ludmila says that her friends are tired of waiting to organ a party on the particular weekend that she happens to be back in town. Her foreign language teacher resigned from their meetings because she was away too often, and the irregular lessons were of little benefit to either of them. The interviewees usually give up hobbies, which they would share with a group, like team sports or playing in a music band (I3: 86). Rather, they find hobbies which they can do alone, without a need to coordinate the activity with friends. For example, they go to a gym, read books, take care of their own garden, or go jogging regularly (I2: 47). Mobile individuals prefer to spend their time at home and to dedicate their attention to their immediate family. "When you travel, your favourite place is home", says Lenka (I6: 98). Their social engagements are reduced to sporadic informal meetings. All of my interview partners have resigned from memberships in associations. Tolga, for example, is no longer a member in the society which supports young people from her home country. Although she thinks it is a very important activity, she is only able to be a passive member. This option is satisfactory neither to her nor to the society. Life styles of mobile individuals become individualised, and their social practices are fragmented for longer periods of time.

However, the role of spatial ruptures can be relativised when we look at other important events in interviewees' lives. Such "growing apart" between old friends is not confined only to relationships in which one or both friends are mobile. Many adult persons experience friendship as significantly structured by the challenges of everyday life: coordinating couples' activities, aligning family compositions, pursuing careers, and matching different schedules (Sigman 1991; Rawlins 1994: 285). These can be reinforced by extensive mobility. However, many interview partners stress that their circle of friends and acquaintances has changed because of the demands of family life, especially children. When children are born the circle of friends evolves. First one has less spare time, is more constrained, or cannot stay late in the evening. Second, one chooses friends who also have children so that when meeting them, the kids can play together (I5: 73). Martin, the young father and a father-to-be for the second time, notes with some sadness that his criteria for meeting people are driven almost exclusively by children (I3: 92). On the other hand, when one has children, it becomes more important to maintain contact with the family in the home country. Although some ties may become weak, other are refreshed and reinforced.

Another aspect relates to certain homogenisation of social networks. Their friends are typically transnational professionals as well; many work in the IO, they are also expatriates. Martin estimates that some one-thirds of his friends are international (I3: 56). Lenka's friends are mostly international, too: they are either colleagues she met in the IO or in embassies or in the neighborhood (I6: 84). She notices that "somehow foreigners stick together" (I6: 86). Atanas estimates that only 10 percent of his neighbors are "local" people, the rest are migrants like him (I12: 46). Tolga mostly meets parents from the international school her children attend (I5 110). But these "people come and go", says Lenka (I6: 80). She lost many friends because they moved on, and she stayed, at least for a time, or the opposite. It is characteristic of this group that their friends are often as mobile as they are.

Physical and Emotional Distance: What Can and What Cannot be Said

The problem of keeping in touch over longer time and distance is about the content of a transmitted message: about what can be said on the phone, what can be written in an e-mail, and what has to be said when looking into somebody's eyes. The interviewees emphas that e-mails are good for exchanging and informing. They transfer photos or interesting articles (I2: 85), they update friends about the most important events, and they coordinate meetings with them. Martin, for example used to send e-mails like postcards, but "those days are over". He is flooded with e-mails and has no time to answer them. He says "the whole communication traffic is getting too much and it doesn't reflect the substance. It is really hell" (I3: 152). Only when he plans to go to a country where some of his friends live, does he send them a short e-mail and agrees on the time and exact place of a face-to-face meeting. Everybody accepts this and he thinks it does not affect the relationship too much (I3: 156). He regularly forwards them some pictures to keep them updated on the recent developments in his life. "This is nice and helpful", says Reiner, who prefers to call people. He says he is not too good in writing, and neither is his mother nor his siblings. Tolga agrees: she talks regularly to her friends back in Turkey. They chat about children and work. This is much more interesting and allows for more possibilities for spontaneous response than e-mail (I5: 73). However:

"A real serious communication by phone is very limited. Do you really talk about your emotions or really things that are important for you over the phone? You talk about the weather, how are the kids, Hmm....pretty much superficial things or let's say logistical things also. But not really the real stuff." (I2: 83)

Each tool is suitable for different purposes, and it enables a different kind of communication. The best is the face-to-face meeting (I8: 195), because most elements of communication are non-verbal. One can read the emotions of the other and show emotions and make sure they are understood correctly. The second is voice: on the phone one can hear the person and recogn the tone of his or her voice and also their reactions – joy, sadness, and anger. E-mail is like a letter: one can deduct only some moods from the choice of words (I6: 76). The last is therefore the least personal (I9: 64) and therefore the interviewees use e-mails for simple messages, coordination of meetings, and short updates. Despite the fact that e-mails give the recipient the freedom of replying when it is the most suitable to her or him, there is also a danger that e-mails will disappear in the traffic. Especially when business e-mails are a priority, personal messages to friends often go unanswered for a longer time (I8: 191). The interviewees point to an important feature of e-mail communication which is the possibility of control. The receiver can always decide when to answer and can think over an answer (I8: 193). One can plan when to write to whom and what. E-mail remains thus a tool of communication in business and has only a supplementary role in the private life of the interviewees. They tend to communicate primarily on the phone with their families and friends. The possibility of immediate response seems to be an important factor in the choice of this media of communication.

The interviewees tend to 'return' to traditional forms of distance communication. In spite of having access to modern systems, they would rather phone (Vertovec 2004). They often decide to hand write Christmas greetings to give the message a personal touch (I9: 66) instead of sending an e-mail. They mostly use the IO's networks, though they rarely carry their laptops home or have a business mobile phone. They separate business and private life, try to avoid bringing work home and would rather spend their spare time outdoors, gardening, jogging or meeting friends instead of using a computer or Internet. They do not have private e-mail accounts (I2: 87), they trust that the IO will not control their e-mails flow. Very few interviewees use Internet at home. So, then for shopping (I6: 149, I3: 78), especially for rare things like special cameras or gifts for relatives in another country. Sometimes they use search engines to plan their travel.

The choice of media of communication relates to the type of attachment connecting people (Döring/Dietmar 2003). The more intimate the private relationship, the richer, synchronic and more personalised is the medium chosen, for example telephone for family talks, especially when emotions are to be shared. E-mails are chosen when delay in time is an advantage or when practical issues should be discussed. In business, written media are chosen to minim the risk of misunderstandings and secure transmission, but only when a relationship has already been established. When making contact for the first time, and when complicated issues which require proving the partner's understanding of the situation, and to assure the partner of own trustworthiness, richer media like videoconferencing are used. When one's roles are clearly defined and for coordination in teams, e-mails seem to satisfy all participants.

Conclusions

The empirical findings prove that mobility influences individuals' life courses and patterns of socialisation. However, this influence is quite ambivalent. Several other factors, for example birth of a child, may have a comparably large impact on individuals' social networks and daily practices. Mobility is relevant as far as it leads to a geographical spread of families and friendship networks, and a shift in temporal dimension of social practices. Several processes could be identified as a consequence of mobility. First, the analysis of the empirical material shows that practices and also social contacts of the interviewees become individualised. The interviewees tend not to participate in group activities, but rather meet irregularly with individuals whenever they have time. Secondly, their social networks are transnational, in terms of the nationalities represented and the locations involved. Though often enjoyed, the transnationalisation of social networks is not an aim of the interviewees. It is enforced by institutional settings like the IO, international schools, or expatriate communities, and mobility, which makes them spread around the globe.

One aspect of transnationalisation is that the interviewees social with people like themselves, people who have a similar background and life style and who can better understand them easier than their sedentary neighbors or colleagues. The specific experience of mobility, the frequent absences from home and lack of time lead to the situation when the individuals feel emotional distance from their local communities and also to those whom they left behind. Their relationships are in constant danger of misunderstandings and conflicts, resulting also from language barriers. In the place, where the individuals settle for certain periods of time, their attachment to people and their surroundings is temporary, and they tend to develop new acquaintances mostly among their international colleagues and neighbors. Often, they avoid socialising with work colleagues, who often take more of the role of a guide in a foreign country than of a good friend. Despite the fact that the foreigners stick together, individuals of the same nationality are more likely to get together (I6: 88). New friendships usually follow their own rules. Much of how they develop is accidental; also, "the chemistry between people" (I4: 97) is more important than other factors.

The spatial distance from old friends and to families enforces a certain flexibility in the mobile individuals. They use every occasion to visit their nearest and dearest. On the other hand, they may also establish a greater regularity in their long-distance contacts, for example to fairly distribute their attention to families in more than one country. The pressure of mobility often causes social networks of mobile people to be very fragile, despite the fact that they are constantly concerned with keeping in touch with people. Many friendships end with time; they break down as a result of a lack of common daily activities, and the imperfection of distance communication.

Distance communication tools are believed to mitigate the negative effects of mobility and spatial ruptures. However, the literature has focused on the geographical dispersal and technical connectivity. The interviews with the mobile transnational professionals confirm that they use distance communication tools daily for bridging the spatial distance. Yet they are often less successful in bridging emotional distance. Distance communication has several limitations. Not the accessibility of media but the comfort of its usage, its quality or language are among the barriers to communication. Temporal aspects, however, seem to be even more important. Pressure for coordination, temporal fragmentation of social practice, and shortages of time spent in physical proximity matter much to individuals. Especially in emergency and conflict situations temporal delays in response to problems are a serious issue to mobile people.

Mobility does change the form, scope and content of social networks. Paradoxically, however, the social networks of the mobile individuals may not be dramatically different from the social networks of less mobile professionals who work in any company operating transnationally, and who travel for private reasons only. Mobility seems to rather restrict their networks than to enlarge them. The internationalisation of social network may be related to profession to a greater extent than mobility. One thinks here of transnational social networks of scientists (Berker 2003; Scheibelhofer 2003) or journalists (Pelizäus-Hoffmeister 2001) but also of other, more sedentary groups (Mau 2007).

When establishing new acquaintances my informants rely on face-to-face meetings, which may accidentally give rise to a friendship. They are quite traditional technology users; they do not enlarge their networks with help of distance communication tools. Possibly, their mobile life style hinders them in this aspect – they are steadily confronted with new places and people (despite that they may not communicate with them), which is quite stressful. Their non-travel time is a quality and relaxing time which they dedicate to dwell in familiarity and coziness of own house and family.

The relationship between physical movement and the use of distance communication tools is quite complex. One thing determines the other – mobile people who are absent try to be present from a distance and rely on phone or e-mails to achieve it. The deficiencies of distance communication tools may however increase their motivation to travel to project sites. Possibly, their physical mobility hinders their 'virtual' mobility, when they choose to visit their parents despite a large geographical distance rather than increase the frequency of phone conversations.

When focusing on interviewees' practice of communicating from a distance, I could observe a split into the two separate worlds, in which my interview partners live: a 'virtual' one, where business and private coordination is managed (however often with some difficulty), and a 'real' one, where intimate or difficult business matters are shared. The 'virtual' world is characterised by an increasing simplicity; on contrary, the 'real' world is very complex. This division is not the same as the one of private and public or private and business spheres. The division between them is marked by change in content and quality of transferred messages. In the first, messages tend to 'disappear' in huge information traffic, many of them remain unanswered, and despite the flow of information taking place, communication often does not. In this world, certain functions are exercised: coordination, documents and information sharing, updating, scheduling, etc. The tool chosen depends on type of the task which needs to be performed: e-mails for co-ordination of meetings, audio-conferencing for agreeing with a group of people, videoconferencing for solving minor problems and updating, the telephone for exchanging reactions, etc. Location matters here little. 'Real' life is handicapped by extensive mobility. When a person relocates over a long distance, there is an anxiety that the intimacy of relationships with those left behind will deteriorate. The distance communication tools are a poor replacement for physical proximity, as they do not offer the same 'richness' of communication (Jaffe/Aidmann 1998: 180). In this world, physical and temporal proximity gain in importance as a factor influencing intimacy in the relationship.

The distance communication tools are an important component of each remote relationship. However, their power to mitigate the physical distance is imperfect, and this, as I claim, because they insufficiently alleviate the temporal aspects of social practices of mobile individuals. They may have power to 'reduce' the geographical distance between family members and friends in the sense that geographical distance does not necessarily mean loss of intimacy and emotional detachment. Yet the temporal aspects of each relationship remain affected by physical distance in such a way that intimacy and emotional proximity are in danger. Remote relationships are affected more by time shortages and temporal ruptures, which enforce more effort in assuring synchronisation and coordination than by physical distance. The temporal aspects determine an individual's membership in social groups, both in small scale networks as well as larger communities, which has to do with participating in the spatio-temporal trajectories more than being physically present in a place.

We may also look at mobility not as a reason for spatial dispersal of social networks, and distance communication not as a mean of mitigating the negative effects of spatial ruptures but look at both as means of sustaining social networks. If the fact that certain networks are more durable than others is the result of the constant effort put in their maintenance, this is the result of a conviction of all parties involved that this effort is worth it. Kinship networks are quite durable because mobile individuals take the effort to sustain them, also in situations of physical distance, by means of travel (if possible and/or necessary) or by means of distance communication (if possible and/or necessary). Professional networks based on varying interests and commonalities may not be worth such an effort because both, mobility and communicating at a distance are not easy. They are both time and energy consuming.

When we then finally try to think of mobile professionals' social networks in terms of their structure, we need to go beyond geographical patterns of distribution of network members. Transnational social networks are quite complex in terms of their geographical distribution as well as their temporal structure. We can identify their internal transnationalisation at the level of the nuclear family (binational marriages are quite common), as well as within a single locality (expatriate communities and international neighborhoods, international work environment); we can also recogn their pluri-local spread at various levels – family networks dispersed across continents; friendships between people of different nationalities residing in various countries; professional networks stretching beyond borders of one organisation and one country. We also need to consider durability and intensity of such connections, and how they vary in time. The interplay of geographical mobility and use of distance communication tools determine the exact form of these connections insofar as they influence the temporal patterns of social life.

References

Basch, Linda/Glick Schiller, Nina/Szanton Blanc, Cristina (1994) *Nations Unbound: Transnational Projects, Postcolonial Predicaments and Deterritorialized Nation States*, New York: Gordon&Breach.

Baym, Nancy (1995) "The Emergence of Community in Computer Mediated Communication." In: Steven G. Jones (ed.) *CyberSociety – Computer- Mediated Communication and Community*, London: Sage, pp. 138-163.

Berger, Peter (1999) "Anwesenheit und Abwesenheit. Raumbezüge sozialen Handelns." Berliner Journal für Soziologie 5/1, pp. 145-168.

Berker, Thomas (2003) *Boundaries in a Space of Flows: The Case of Migrant Researchers' Use of ICTs*, a report within the European Media and Technology in Everyday Life Network II 2000-2003, Trondheim: NTNU, Department of Interdisciplinary Studies of Culture.

Berking, Helmut (1998) "Global Flows and Local Cultures: Über die Rekonfiguration sozialer Räume im Globalisierungsprozeß." Berliner Zeitschrift für Soziologie 3, pp. 381-392.

Boden, Deidre/Molotch, Harvey L. (1994) "The Compulsion to Proximity." In: Roger Friedland/Deidre Boden (eds.) *NowHere: Space, Time and Modernity*, Berkeley: University of California Press, pp. 257-286.

Bonß, Wolfgang/Kesserling, Sven (2001) "Mobilität am Übergang von der Ersten zur Zweiten Moderne." In: Ulrich Beck/Wolfgnag Bonß (eds.) *Die Modernisierung der Moderne*, Frankfurt a. M.: Suhrkamp, pp. 177-191.

Chan, Bun Kwok (1997) "A Family Affair: Migration, Dispersal and the Emergent Identity of the Chinese Cosmopolitan." Diaspora 6, pp. 195-213.

Cohen, Robin (1997) *Global Diasporas: an Introduction*, London: University Collage London Press.

Colic-Peisker, Val (2002) "Migrant Communities and Class: Croatians in Western Australia." In: Paul Kennedy/Victor Roudometof (eds.) *Communities Across Borders: New Immigrants and Transnational Cultures*, London: Routledge, pp. 29-40.

Dezalay, Yves (1990) "The Big Bang and The Law: The Internationalization And Restructuring Of The Legal Field." In: Mike Featherstone (ed.) *Global Culture: Nationalism, Globalization and Modernity*, London: Sage, pp. 279-294.

Duck, Steve (1998) *Relating to Others*, Chicago: Dorsey.

Dutton, William H. (1999) *Society on the Line: Information Politics in the Digital Age*, Oxford: Oxford University Press.

Döring, Nicola/Dietmar, Christine (2004) "Mediated Communication in Couple Relationships: Approaches for Theoretical Modelling and Initial Qualitative Findings." Forum: Qualitative Social Research 4/3, March 17, 2006 (http://www.qualitative-research.net/fqs-texte/3-03/3-03doeringdietmar-e.htm).

Escobar, Arturro (1996) "Welcome to Cyberia: Notes on the Anthropology of Cyberculture." In: Ziaduddin Sardar/Jerome Revetz (eds.) *Cyberfutures*, London: Pluto, pp. 111-137.

Faist, Thomas (2000) "Transnationalism in International Migration: Implications for the Study of Citizenship and Culture." Racial and Ethnic Studies 23, pp. 189-222.

Fuchs, Peter (1997) "Adressabilität als Grundbegriff der soziologischen Systemtheorie." Soziale Systeme 3/1, pp. 56-79.

Georgiou, Myria (2002) *Diasporic Communities On-Line: A Bottom Up Experience of Transnationalism*, February 10, 2005 (http://www.lse.ac.uk/collections/EMTEL/Minorities/minorities_docs.html).

Glick Schiller, Nina/Basch, Linda/Blanc-Szanton, Cristina (eds.) (1992) *Towards a Transnational Perspective on Migration. Race, Class, Ethnicity, and Nationalism Reconsidered*, New York: New York Academy of Science.

Hannerz, Ulf (2003) "Being There...and There...and There! Reflections on Multi-Sited Ethnography." Ethnography 4/2, pp. 201-216.

Herkenrath, Mark et al. (2005) "Globalizations from 'Above' and 'Below': The Future of World Society." Special Issue, Journal of World-Systems Research 11/3.

Holzer, Boris (2005) "Vom globalen Dorf zu kleinen Welt: Netzwerke Konnektivität in der Weltgesellschaft." Zeitschrift für Soziologie, Sonderheft "Weltgesellschaft", pp. 314-329.

Jaffe, J. Michael/Aidman-Kitron, Amy (1998) "Families, Geographical Separation, and the Internet: A Theoretical Prospectus." In: Ann S. Robertson (ed.)

Proceedings of the Families, Technology, and Education, Conference in Chicago, October 1997, Champaign, IL: ERIC Clearinghouse, pp. 177-187.

Jenkins, Richard (1997) *Rethinking Ethnicity – Arguments and Explorations*, London: Sage.

Jordan, Tim (1999) *Cyberpower: The Culture and Politics of Cyberspace and the Internet*, London: Routledge.

Kennedy, Paul (2004). "Making Global Society: Friendship Networks Among Transnational Professionals in the Building Design Industry." Global Networks 4/2, pp. 157-179.

Kesselring, Sven (2001) "Beweglichkeit ohne Bewegung." Die Mitbestimmung 9, pp. 10-14.

King, Anthony (1990) "Architecture, Capital and the Globalization of Culture." In: Mike Featherstone (ed.) *Global Culture: Nationalism, Globalization and Modernity*, London: Sage, pp. 397-411.

Kieserling, Andre (1999) *Kommunikation unter Anwesenden*, Frankfurt a. M.: Suhrkamp.

Kivisto, Peter (2003) "Social Spaces, Transnational Immigrant Communities, and the Politics of Incorporation." Ethnicities 3/1, pp. 5-28.

Knorr-Cetina, Karin/Bruegger, Urs (2002) "Global Microstructures: The Virtual Societies of Financial Markets." American Journal of Sociology 107/4, pp. 905-950.

Landolt, Patricia/Da, Wei Wei (2005) "The Spatially Ruptured Practices of Migrant Families: A Comparison of Immigrants from El Salvador and the People's Republic of China." Current Sociology 53/4, pp. 625-653.

Lübbe, Hermann (1996) "Netzverdichtung. Zur Philosophie industriegesellschaftlicher Entwicklungen." Zeitschrift für philosophische Forschung 50, pp. 133-150.

Luhmann, Niklas (1984) *Soziale Systeme. Grundriss 2 einer allgemeinen Theorie*, Frankfurt a. M.: Suhrkamp.

Mau, Steffen (2007) *Transnationale Vergesellschaftung. Die Entgrenzung sozialer Lebenswelten*, Frankfurt a. M.: Campus.

Massey, Doreen (2005) *For Space*, London: Sage.

McLuhan, Marshall/Powers, Bruce P. (1992) *The Global Village: Transformations in World Life and Media in the 21st Century*, New York: Communication and Society.

Meyer, John (2005) *Weltkultur. Wie die westlichen Prinzipien die Welt durchdringen*, Frankfurt a. M.: Suhrkamp.

Miller, Dan/Slater, Don (2000) *The Internet: An Ethnographic Approach*, Oxford/New York: Berg.

Nowicka, Magdalena (2006a) *Transnational Professionals and Their Cosmopolitan Universes*, Frankfurt a. M./New York: Campus.

Nowicka, Magdalena (2006b) "Mobility, Space and Social Structuration in the Second Modernity and Beyond." Mobilities 3, pp. 411-436.

Nowicka, Magdalena (2007) "Mobile Locations: Construction of home in the group of chronically mobile transnational professionals." Global Networks 7/1, pp. 69-86.

O'Riain, Sean (2000) "Net-working for a Living: Irish Software Developers in the Global Workplace." In: Michael Burawoy et al. (ed.) *Global ethnography*, Berkeley/Los Angeles: University of California Press, pp. 175-201.

Panagakos, Anastasia N. (2003) "Downloading New Identities: Ethnicity, Technology, and Media in the Global Greek Village." Identities: Global Studies in Culture and Power 10, pp. 201-219.

Pelizäus-Hoffmeister, Helga (2001) *Mobilität: Chance oder Risiko? Der Einfluss beruflicher Mobilität auf soziale Netzwerke – das Beispiel freie JournalistInnen*, Opladen: Leske + Budrich.

Pries, Ludger (2001) *Internationale Migration*, Bielefeld: transcript Verlag.

Rawlins, William (1994) "Being There and Growing Apart. Sustaining Friendships during Adulthood". In: Daniel Canary/Laura Stafford (eds.) *Communication and Relational Maintenance*, San Diego: Academic Press, pp. 275-294.

Scheibelhofer, Elisabeth (2003) *Mobilitätsperspektiven junger WissenschaftlerInnen. Eine qualitative Studie zur Situation österreichischer ForscherInnen in den USA,* Projektbericht, Wien: Institut für Höhere Studien.

Schneider, Norbert/Limmer, Ruth/Ruckdeschel, Kerstin (2002) *Mobil, flexibel, gebunden. Beruf und Familie in der mobilen Gesellschaft*, Frankfurt a. M.: Campus.

Schwartzman, Helen (1989) *The Meeting*, New York/London: Plenum.

Sigman, Stuat (1991) "Handling the Discontinious Aspects of Continuing Social Relationships: Toward Research on the Persistance of Social Forms." Communication Theory 1, pp. 106-127.

Smith, Marc A./Kollock, Peter (eds.) (1999) *Communities in Cyberspace*, London: Routledge.

Smith, Michael P./Guarnizo, Luis Eduardo (eds.) (1998) *The Locations of Transnationalism*, New Brunswick: Transaction Publishers.

Southerton, Dale/Shove, Elisabeth/Warde, Alan (2001) *"Harried and Hurried": Time Shortage and the Co-ordination of Everyday Life*, CRIC Discussion Paper 47, University of Manchester

Stichweh, Rudolf (2003) *Structure Formation in World Society: The Eigenstructures of World Society and the Regional Cultures of the World*, Working Paper 3, Bielefeld: Institut für Weltgesellschaft.

Stichweh, Rudolf (2005) *Migration und Weltgesellschaft,* July 21, 2007 (http://www.unilu.ch/files/16stwmigrationundweltgesellschaft.pdf).

Stichweh, Rudolf (2006) *Structure Formation in World Society. The Structures of World Society and the Regional Cultures of the World,* July 20, 2007 (http://www.unilu.ch/files/5stwworldsociety.eigenstructures.1.pdf).

Tarrow, Sidney (1998) *Power in Movement: Social Movements and Contentious Politics*, Cambridge: Cambridge University Press.
Urry, John (2004) "The Complex Spaces of Scandal." In: Jørgen O. Bærenholdt/ Kirstein Simonsen (eds.) *Space Odysseys. Spatiality and Social Relations in the 21st Century*, Aldershot: Ashgate, pp. 15-26.
Vertovec, Steven (2001) *Transnational Social Formations: Towards Conceptual Cross-Fertilization*, COMPAS Oxford Working Paper WPTC-01-16.
Vertovec, Steven (2004), "Cheap Calls: the Social Glue of Migrant Transnationalism." Global Networks 4/2, pp. 219-34.
Vertovec, Steven/Cohen, Robert (eds.) (1999) *Migration, Diasporas and Transnationalism*, Cheltenham: Edward Elgar Publishing.
Watts, Duncan J. (2003) *Small Worlds: The Dynamics of Networks Between Order and Randomness*, Princeton: Princeton University Press.

Does It Matter Where You Are? – Transnational Migration, Internet Usage and the Emergence of Global Togetherness

HEIKE MÓNIKA GRESCHKE

> The new media influence the course of communication – and possibly its content – in ways that are unknown to date. This is precisely why they can create new modes and types of sociality over time. Both for methodological and factual reasons, it is thus the task of social sciences to investigate these new media in terms of their own logic and dynamics, to describe the forms of interaction and communication that they create and to show how they influence, shape, create or hinder processes of society-building (Bergmann/Meier 2003: 430, *my own translation*).

Introduction

This paper contributes to the development of concepts useful for studying global complexities, i.e. the realisation of the 'World Society', by exploring emerging Internet based forms of *global togetherness*. By focusing on the complex interrelations between migration movements on the one hand and the progressive 'shrinking of distances' through communication technologies on the other, I seek to uncover some of the "global micro-structures" (Knorr-Cetina/Bruegger 2002) that constitute the evolving World Society. This paper draws on data from ethnographic research. The case study consists of www.cibervalle.com,[1] an online discussion forum that connects Paraguayans from all over the world. During the first phase of generating data from the virtual scene, the practice of interrelating local and virtual settings has emerged as a striking phenomenon within this field. In order to comprehend this multilayer techno-social formation properly, a multi-sited-ethnographic approach has been developed, which relates the data gathered on

---

1 The online-discussion forum's name and the nicknames of the users were changed as a means of preserving the participant's identities.

the online discussion forum to data, which was collected face-to-face in some of the places of residence of some of the participants, i.e. in Paraguay, Buenos Aires, California and Germany. The methodological implications of generating and analysing data in a pluri-local and computer-mediated field of research are discussed elsewhere (Greschke 2007b). In this paper I will focus rather on some theoretical and conceptual problems arising from the observations I made during my fieldwork in different parts of the global life-world Cibervalle.

Most of the members of the Cibervalle-community did not know each other when they accessed the online-forum for the first time. Over the years, however some communicative practices have developed within Cibervalle, that allude to the emergence of global forms of living together. By means of sharing everyday-life practices with their distant counterparts, the communication in Cibervalle – despite the geographical dispersion of its members – has reached a high degree of proximity and intimacy. While the degree of engagement differs from one user to the next, the formerly anonymous socio-electronic network has become a community based on solidarity and trust for many of the participants. But how can we imagine people living together although they are not sharing the same geographical space?

In the following I attempt to illuminate the meaning of "living together", while being physically apart by exploring some of the communicative forms that have been developed by the members of Cibervalle. Particularly, I will focus on the interactions between advancing technologies and the social practices of their usage on the one hand, and the relation between co-present and mediated forms of communication, on the other hand. By doing so, I hope not only to uncover the techno-social requirements for global communication but to exemplify further some of the emerging techno-social hybrid forms that enhance global togetherness. Assuming that most of the readers are unfamiliar with techno-social formations like Cibervalle I begin with a short story about an ordinary day[2] within the Cibervalle-community. As its members reside physically in different parts of the world, some travelling will be necessary to catch a glimpse of how the Cibervaller@s[3] are *doing living* (Sacks 1984) globally together.
Have a good trip!

---

[2] The story must not be misunderstood as an account of a factually happened day in Cibervalle. As a matter of course it is impossible to be physically at different places at the same time, as the story may suggest. This mode of story telling may be best described as 'faction'. Faction is a genre that combines facts with fiction. It was introduced by Truman Capote (1965) in the novel "In cold blood". Describing everyday-life in Cibervalle demands fictive elements as it consists of the interrelation of different physically grounded as well as virtual spaces. Nevertheless, the story is based on 'facts' as it relies on data gathered through participant observation in different places. It is in some measure a 'thick description' (Geertz 1973) of some of the main practices and patterns of globally shared everyday-life I could observe in the field.

[3] The suffix @s can be used in written Spanish to include both the masculine and the female gender in only one noun.

Everyday life in Cibervalle:

Monday morning, 8 o' clock: In a small California town Angela is getting up. On her way to the bathroom she casually boots up her computer. After brushing her teeth she goes back to the bed room and logs herself into the instant messenger program she is using. Having a quick look at her buddy list tells her which of her friends are online at present. When she starts the browser she directly enters "Cibervalle", the Paraguayan virtual community she belongs to. A brief glance over the current topics is sufficient to catch up on what has happened within her community while she was asleep. Then she starts her daily work routine with getting the children up. She is sitting in the kitchen having breakfast with the kids when she suddenly hears the familiar sound that notifies her of someone who is trying to communicate with her through the messenger. As she approaches the computer she finds a private conversation window popped up on the screen. Her brother sends his greetings to her. He recently left Paraguay and went to Spain and he wants to tell her that he was able to get a job as a construction worker. They have a brief chat until she has to interrupt the conversation to look after her bickering children.

At the same time, in Paraguay's main city, Eduardo is making himself comfortable in front of the computer screen at his work place. He enters Cibervalle and looks briefly through the current topics. After a busy morning at work he takes advantage of his lunch break to get ahead with this year's fundraising campaign. The online community usually organises one at Christmas time. Suddenly a private conversation window pops up on the screen, it is Angela saying hallo. The kids are absorbed in their game, so she uses the opportunity to get current information about the Christmas fundraising. This year, Eduardo tells her, the fundraising campaign will be in support of a children's home in Asunción. Some of the local Cibervalle – members went there yesterday to meet the person in charge and some of the children. Through their messenger-conversation he sends her the link of the topic he just created, so she can have a look at the images Eduardo took during the visit. Underneath the photos she finds the list of food and basic utilities, which are most urgently required at the children's home. After checking some details, she asks for his bank data and agrees to support the campaign financially. They say goodbye and Angela closes her conversation window feeling slightly sad because this year she won't be able to attend the event personally.

In Buenos Aires, Iwashita bangs the door to the apartment she shares with her Argentinean boyfriend. Impatiently she waits for her computer to boot up just to directly enter Cibervalle. Disregarding the new topics, which were being discussed while she was taking the last exam of this term, she immediately writes a new topic. She almost cries while expressing what happened to her just one hour ago. She does not even care about typing errors but just opens the thread. Then she walks into the kitchen and prepares some Tereré.[4] She approaches her computer again and pushes the refresh button. She already finds answers from some of her friends in Paraguay, USA and Argentina. They all feel sorry for her and try to comfort her because she failed the exam. Especially Belen, one of her compatriots in Argentina supports her impression that she failed the exam because of being a Paraguayan migrant and she advises her to make a complaint

---

4 Beverage on the basis of Paraguayan herbs. Drinking Tereré is usually considered as one of the Paraguayan's main cultural practices.

about her examiner. After reading the comments Iwashita feels somewhat relieved. She turns to a private IM conversation with Belen in order to talk over the possibilities of disputing the result of the examination.

At 1.00 p.m. Irén enters a Cyber café in Asunción and logs herself onto the messenger-program. She is going to meet her boyfriend Tomás in New York. They usually spend their lunch break together. Asunción and New York share the same time zone, so time- coordination is no problem at all. While waiting for him to show up, she examines the current topics in Cibervalle. In Eduardo's topic, she writes her name into the list of participants for the Christmas campaign. Suddenly she realises that the current contributions of her boyfriend are signed with the IP of his home access. Maybe he has not gone to work today? Immediately, she sends a message to his mobile phone, which he uses to keep himself logged onto the messenger permanently. Her mobile phone rings promptly. Tomás tells her that he went to the doctor this morning, because he had suffered from stomach pain the whole night. They have a brief chat, Irén suggests (that he) take some of the yuyos[5] she had sent him recently for preparing Tereré and they arrange to meet at the same time as every night to chat before they end the conversation. There is still some time left to create a get-well-topic for Tomás. Promptly there are some responses from other members expressing get-well wishes and concerns about their friend. Right at the moment when she is about to log herself out of the messenger a window pops up on the screen: Rafael from Switzerland is worried about Tomas after reading her topic and asks her for more information. She tells him everything she knows as quickly as she can type, logs out of the messenger and hurries back to her work place. In the evening, when she arrives home from work, she enters her room straight away to boot up her computer and to log onto the messenger. Tomas is already waiting for her. He rests on his bed with the computer in reach. Irén is able to see him, because he is using a web cam. So she activates hers as well. They chat about this and that. There is trouble again, with a new member on the electronic bulletin board. They assume that it is not really a new person but a regular member, enrolled with an unknown nickname, making waves and messing around with the community. Then they start to play chess through the messenger-program. At the end it is Irén who wins the game. Triumphantly she glances at the webcam, Tomás returns her look laughing with a twinkle in his eye. Tomorrow she won't stand a chance, he presages. They wish one another a good night, before Irén logs herself out of the messenger, shuts down her computer and switches off the light.

The Making of the World Society Real on the Level of Interaction – the Role of Transnational Migration and Means of Global Communication

In 1998, Appadurai already spoke of "a growing number of diasporic public spheres" (22), produced by electronic media, which link together individuals across national boundaries. Three years later Karim still had to claim that "the application of new communication technologies by diasporic groups has largely

---

5   Paraguayan medicinal herbs, used for preparing tea and Tereré.

escaped scholarly scrutiny" (2001: 645). More recently, the new media has been addressed in some studies in the field of transnational research which seek to illuminate various diasporic public spheres. Accordingly, the potential of the Internet for political empowerment and as ways of negotiating ethnic or national identity has taken centre stage in these studies (Graham/Khosravi 2002; Panagakos 2003; Adams 2004).

Despite this, not every person involved in migration, or having transnational ties and practices, necessarily engages in politics. And concerns about belonging to a specific ethnic or national group are just one possible aspect of the transnational population's everyday-life. Besides being a technological tool for creating public discursive spheres, the Internet consists of an advancing set of means of communication that is used increasingly for creating and maintaining social relations at a distance. Referring to the increasing use of e-mail for maintaining relationships in dispersed social networks, Georgiou (2002) stresses the significance of sharing everyday-life experiences for maintaining a sense of community. Miller and Slater assume the Internet constitutes "an inexpensive way not only for families to be in touch, but to be in touch on an intimate, regular, day-to-day basis that conforms to commonly held expectations of what being a parent, child or family entails" (2000: 56).

In other words, it may be helpful to widen the perspective in this field in order to account for the implications of the increasing internet usage of transnational populations. This is helpful not only in terms of political practices but rather to show the consequences for everyday-life. How, for instance does the specific use of the Internet alter senses of love and attachment, family life and other kinds of intimate social relationships? Drawing on the Trinidadian case Miller and Slater (2000) demonstrate how the Internet facilitates the reintegration of the Trinidadians basic social institution 'family' which at first had been challenged by mass emigration. As these studies demonstrate, the Internet turns out to be a convenient tool for the translocal maintenance of formerly locally embedded intimate relationships, which were formed on the basis of co-present interaction.

In the case of Cibervalle however, any kinship between the participants is unlikely. On the contrary, users from all over the world incorporate themselves into the socio-electronic network even when they do not have any personal relations within the group. Furthermore, in contrast to the above mentioned studies which tend to assume the existence of a community with common interests regarding political issues and future perspectives of the 'homeland' as a starting point of the virtual performances, the Paraguayan online discussion forum started neither with a thematic focus nor to reach a common (political) goal. The beginning of this community was an electronic bulletin board, linked to a Paraguayan web portal, provided by an entrepreneur who did no more than provide the platform. One of the principal users explains:

"The first time I entered the forum there were only five users. I have the number 6 *haha*. There was nobody, not even a hair moved. I began to invite friends, that's how the forum began to grow."[6] (Manuela, Asunción, *e-mail interview, my own translation*).

More astonishing appears to be the fact that over the years the members have made themselves comfortable within Cibervalle. They have not only turned the former anonymous socio-electronic network into a community, basing on solidarity and trust, they also have intimately connected the electronic bulletin board with their physically embedded life-worlds thereby transforming the virtual space into a globally shared part of their everyday-life-worlds.

So far it has become obvious, that the development of 'World Society' is neither imaginable without the actual movement of people nor without the use of communication technologies. Particularly in the context of migration, the availability of distance-shrinking communication technologies becomes crucial in terms of creating and maintaining links between sites of being and sites of belonging. The complex interactions between the various means of communication in use and the specific communicative practices developed in transnational migration contexts in turn, seem to engender various forms of social life and bring about new global types of social relations and sociality. Therefore, these kinds of social relations at a distance are considered as a fundamental source for comprehending the growing global linkages between individuals – that is to say, the realisation of World Society on the level of interaction. From a system theoretical point of view however, interaction is supposed to occur only between physically co-present counterparts. The presence of the body is considered a particular condition that needs to be differentiated from other forms of communication. Physical co-presence according to system theory implicates not only perceiving the other but the reflexive awareness about mutual perception as a condition that almost necessarily leads to communication between co-present actors. This is because the bodily presence delivers extra information that is perceived by the counterparts. In order to avoid that this information is being interpreted in an unfavourable manner the actor has to correct his self-presentation according to the assumed perceptions and expectations of the co-present observers (Kieserling 1999: 122).

Global connections and relations on the other hand, are impossible to imagine without mediated forms of communication. With regard to World Society studies this narrow concept of interaction poses a problem. If interaction is always based on physical presence, how are we supposed to analyse global patterns on the level of interaction? The daily practices by which the Cibervaller@s organise their community-life across any distance suggest reconsidering not only the meaning of interaction and co-presence but also the relationship between presence and ab-

---

6 "Cuando entré la primera vez al foro había solo 5 usuarios yo tengo el numero 6 jaja no había nadie ni las moscas volaban empezé a invitar amigos y así empezó a haber más gente".

sence, interaction and communication and different modes of mobility. As will be demonstrated in the following, the communicative forms that I have observed in Cibervalle do indeed conflict with the system theoretical concept as they contain crucial elements of interaction, even without fulfilling the condition of co-presence of the bodies. Social life in Cibervalle relies on a complex relationship between different means of communication in use, including different technologies on the one hand and occasional physical encounters of co-presence on the other hand. In this regard I refer to Urry, who claims that central to sociology should be both the analysis of those processes by which such co-presence is only on occasions and contingently brought about, and the forms of socialities involved when one is *not* involved in ongoing daily interaction, but with which a sense of connection or belonging with various 'others' is sensed and sustained. One should investigate not only physical and immediate presence, but also the socialities involved in occasional co-presence, imagined co-presence and virtual co-presence (2003: 256).

Let us take a closer look at the communicative practices in use in order to identify the patterns that constitute this kind of "strange and uncanny life on the screen" (Urry 2002: 267) and hence to qualify how senses of co-presence are altered by virtual communication.

The Techno-Social Architecture of Global Togetherness

Online-forum. It may be helpful to begin with examining the system infrastructure of the online discussion forum as a source that influences computer-mediated communication and the social organisation of the users (Baym 1995). At the time of writing, Cibervalle has existed for more than six years. The forum is open to the public, that is to say everyone can read the discussions anonymously, but only registered members are allowed to contribute comments. In other words, besides the active participants in this social setting, there is another social role involved, the *anonymous observer*. This refers to the participants' reflexive awareness about a potential global public, which somehow influences their social actions. Furthermore, the moderator's role and status differ from the other participants as he or she is authorised to make sure that every member obeys the rules. In order to accomplish this task, the moderator is enabled to delete topics or particular contributions, as well as to ban a nickname, that is to say, to prevent his or her active participation in the forum. To register, a nickname and an e-mail address are required. There are two ways of contributing. One can propose a new topic for discussion by starting a new thread or participate in ongoing discussions. On the forum's main page there is a list of currently debated topics. This provides the users with some information about the topics, like title, the author's nickname and the country of access,[7] as well as the number of contributions to the topic and the number of visits. The topics or discussion threads provide more information about the participants. Below the particular comments the author's nickname and again the image of the national flag reflecting the IP-address is displayed, as well as the date of issue, and the total number of the nickname's contributions in the forum.

Unlike other internet-based communicative genres like chat or e-mail, the discussion forum provides temporal freedom and the choice between synchronous and asynchronous communication. Users, who are online at the same time, are able to communicate with others in real time. However, users – if they do not spend so much time on the Internet or they are not able to be online at the same time as their counterparts – are still able to reconstruct ongoing discussions and to make contributions. This is because the discussion threads remain displayed and the postings can be read in their chronological order as long as the discussion goes on. In brief, the condition of asyncronicity allows for global communication between actors who live in different time zones (Stegbauer 2000: 25). Synchronicity, on the other hand, leads to time and space compression, and enables real time communication regardless of the distance between counterparts. In the case of the Paraguayan online-forum, it seems as if these features have provided the technological conditions for the development of a global community. The forum bridges temporal and geographical distances. It is able to unify people despite different degrees of involvement and may hence create a sense of togetherness, even under the condition of geographical dispersion.

A participant who lives in Spain posted the following quotation. She addressed the forum's community to share a difficult moment in her life. She found out that a person she loved had died and on the same day she lost her job. Her topic received many responses, all of them expressing compassion and support. This is the response that she posted as she entered the forum two days later:

"Without you, what would I do?!!! THANK YOU A THOUSAND TIMES! ... today I start work in an Italian restaurant and after reading this page again and again I am now going there full with energy and power.. Now I feel like I have many brothers and sisters all over the world. Kisses for all of you!! I love you a lot and whatever I may be able to do for you, do not hesitate to ask for it!" (Betty, Barcelona, Cibervalle-forum, *my own translation*).[8]

---

7   In fact, the image of the national flag reflects the IP-address of the provider in use which does not always coincide with the participant's place of access. In any case many users do not know this and assume that the national flag indicates the place of residence of the participants.

8   "¡Sin ustedes.. que haria?!!! MIL GRACIAS!... hoy empiezo a probar en un restaurant italiano.. y despues de leer y leer y leer otra vez esta pagina me voy llena de energia y fuerzas.. ahora me siento como si tuviera muchos hermanos por todo el mundo un beso a todos!! les quiero mucho y lo que yo pueda por ustedes no duden en pedirme!"

This statement exemplifies a second important aspect of the online forum, namely its basic orientation in the members' every-day lives. Unlike other online discussion forums, the Paraguayan virtual community does not limit the postings to any thematic focus. In fact, most of the activities in this forum reflect shared everyday-life concerns: talking about the film one saw last night, discussing where to get the most authentic ingredients for preparing *sopa paraguaya*,[9] telling jokes and laughing together, inventing forum-games and playing together, teasing each other, debating forthcoming elections, exchanging opinions about homosexuality, abortion, or religious beliefs, sharing happy or difficult moments in life, discussing concerns about the future perspectives of Paraguay, and so forth. In short, the forum reflects a wide range of topics and socialising activities that usually take place in families at lunch time or, among friends who meet each other on the *plaza central*, on the town square. Many of the users consider Cibervalle a central part of their life-worlds, where a significant part of their socialising activities take place.

"It's true that, unconsciously, Cibervalle turns into your everyday-life. At least once a day you have to stop by, in order to know what's going on. You enter because you need to know if everybody feels fine or if someone's having heartache, or because you want to see Eduardo' s current hairstyle …etc. etc. ..." (Carmen, France, Cibervalle-forum, *my own translation*).[10]

However, the participants do not spend all their time in front of the screen, observing the scene or posting comments. Once Cibervalle is entered and the current activities are reviewed, the actors usually leave the website open and get involved in their daily tasks in their physical environments. Every now and then they approach the computer and push the refresh button in order to update the news. In other words, the users engage at least in two different social contexts at the same time and they have to coordinate their activities in the virtual and the local setting.

Instant Messenger. The members of Cibervalle do not only communicate via the online forum. For more private chat, as well as for specific requests that need to be discussed instantly, they also do *instant messaging*. Instant messenger (IM) defines a program that enables instant communication between two or more people over a network such as the Internet. Most programs can be downloaded from the WWW as freeware. The IM program used by most of the Cibervalle members enables one to add and remove the e-mail addresses of contacts who one likes to network with. When logging into the IM, a window pops up (the so called buddy

---

9   A typical dish in Paraguay.
10 "La verdad que sin darte cuenta cibervalle se convierte en tu dia a dia, por lo menos una vez al dia tenes que pasar a ver que hay , si estan todos bien , si no le duele el corazon a nadie , si como se peino hoy Eduardo para ir al trabajo ... etc etc .."

list) in which the collection of names shows which of the contacts are currently online. When clicking on one of the names, a second window pops up (the private conversation window) which is used to send instant messages to one's counterpart. On the screen of the addressed counterpart another window pops up displaying the message that has been sent. Besides the visual information, the program emits a sound every time a message is received or one of the contacts logs in. IM is also used for discussing current topics 'in private' and events both of the counterparts can follow simultaneously on the discussion forum. For example, one sends the link for a topic through the IM to other members, because he or she wants the others to read and post a comment or to exchange opinions about the respective topic before commenting on it. The communication displayed in the public forum thus tends not only to be influenced by private conversations. By combining different technologies, common interests are produced, which in turn constitute a shared social space.

Global Interaction? – The Relation of Global Means of Communication and Global Physical Movements in the Evolving World Society

Angela's practice of using the messenger, as described in the short story above, exemplifies another pattern of use I observed during my fieldwork in the places of residence of some of the users: the users do not only log into the messenger when they actually want to chat with someone. Rather they log in to know which of their contacts are currently online and also to be communicatively reachable for the others. Then they turn to their daily routine and come back to the screen from time to time to have a brief chat, or to see who has logged in, when they hear the sound. For these cases, the IM program provides some tools for communicating the actual status of the user. On the buddy list one can choose between "coming back soon", "out to lunch", "away", "on the phone", etc. Before leaving the screen the user communicates his or her temporary absence. This is in order to avoid confusion in the case that someone would address her while she is not able to answer.

Logging oneself into the instant messenger means seeing who is online as well as being aware that one is being "seen" by the others. Whether one is sitting in front of the screen exchanging messages the whole time or not, the very fact of being within reach, accompanied by the reflexive awareness of mutual perception enhances a sense of proximity and the impression of sharing the same space. This reflexive awareness, in turn, entails the need for correct self-presentation according to the assumed perceptions and expectations of the co-present observers. More precisely, when a user feels the need for communicating her temporary absence from the screen she anticipates that the counterparts will perceive her as present and that she could be addressed by someone who in turn may misinterpret her missing answer.

Entering Cibervalle is like opening up an additional techno-social space with globally shared common interests that overlay the users' local environments and which has to be coordinated with the social relevant details at face. The practice of keeping the page open and refreshing the screen from time to time, may enhance the imagination of approaching and distancing one's self (but not leaving!) a social space created and maintained by the communicative activities of its users. This virtual space and the social activities within it, however, go on independently of the actual participation of the individual user. Chatting with other members via IM about what is going on in Cibervalle as much as joint travel through the online forum may even strengthen the perception of sharing the same space. In fact, this spatial formation is structured through timely coordination rather than in geographical terms. Both, instant messenger and the online forum enhance the sense of being together even if the counterparts are actually separated by thousands of miles.

At the first glance, it seems as if computer-mediated communication has been superseding co-present encounters. The Internet technologies in use enable the users to be in touch on an intimate, regular and day-to-day-basis not only with distant friends and family but also with the social life going on in their place of origin. Apparently, there is no need to travel; the communication within the shared virtual space seems to be a functional equivalent of being physically together in the same place. From a system theoretical perspective on the current state of globalisation, there is nothing astonishing about this assumption. Stichweh argues that

"communication is becoming world communication to the extent that communication substitutes migration for the communicative accessibility of the world. In this respect, world communication is considered as a functional equivalent for the incessant movements of persons across the globe" (Stichweh 2005: 5, *my own translation*).

The central meaning of communication in system theory leads Stichweh to the assumption that, even if the historical realisation of World Society at first was based upon migration, distance-shrinking communication technologies are now considered to be the fundamental carriers of the global social system. Although Stichweh exemplifies his argument by drawing on working practices in transnational enterprises and scientific contexts, he presupposes that "it could be demonstrated that in many other social systems communicative networking has been replacing travel and migration" (ibid: 12, *my own translation*).

However, people still travel. Current statistics allude to an increasing travel and migration movement across the globe. The International Organisation for Migration states that "without the disintegration of the Soviet Union, the number of international migrants worldwide would have risen by 18 million in

1970-1980, 27 million in 1980-1990, and 21 million in 1990-2000" (IOM 2005: 380). Drawing on the worldwide increasing scale of traveling in the last 50 years – e.g. 25m in 1950 to 700m in 2000 international passenger arrivals each year – Urry points to the apparently contradictory simultaneity of increasing global movements and the spread of global communication (2003: 157).

Local Meetings. Even in Cibervalle the virtual activities are just one side of the coin. This is because the members regularly meet each other face-to-face. Locating each other in order to meet personally in fact is one of the fundamental practices I was able to observe in this field. The forum provides the chance for networking with compatriots who may currently live at the same geographical location or nearby, not only for emigrated Paraguayans. For both those at home and abroad, the virtually formed relationships seem to stimulate the need for face-to-face encounters. By organising, regular meetings in their respective localities of residence, so called *encuentros*, the virtual relations are translated to local contexts whenever possible.

By exploring the particulars of mediated vs. co-present communication, Urry demonstrates the significance of co-present encounters for creating and maintaining social networks. As face-to-face encounters afford access to the eyes of the other, they are considered the most direct and reciprocal form of interaction. "Eye contact enables and stabilises intimacy and trust, as well as the perception of insincerity and fear" (2003: 164). The informational thickness of physical co-presence is reached because

"conversations are made up of not only words, but indexical expressions, facial gestures, body language, status, voice intonation, pregnant silences, past histories, anticipated conversations and actions, turn-taking practices and so on" (Urry 2003: 164f).

Besides the embodied particulars, Urry highlights place and time aspects of co-presence. Sharing the same location in a specific moment and experiencing a place with one's own senses, "physically walking or seeing or touching or hearing or smelling a place" (2002: 261) is considered to be a crucial base of co-presence and explains the increasing need for physical travel enhanced by the spread of global means of communication.

Nevertheless, in Cibervalle the face-to-face-relationships, initially enabled by the electronic network, by no means substitute for the virtual ties. Rather the local sub-groups which have been evolving along the way in different parts of the world share the events they organise at the local levels afterwards with the global community. That is to say, soon after a local meeting occurs, the group reports about it on the electronic bulletin board on the basis of some images of the participants and their activities. The distant members of the global community respond, expressing gratitude for sharing the event with them and they usually add some charming or funny comments to the images. In so doing, the events that are first enacted by local sub-groups are reconstructed on a global level as a collective experience of the whole community.

In this regard, I want to highlight one of the main findings of my research, namely the fact that the sense of the local events seems to be strongly shaped by the delayed reconnection with the virtual level. Particularly, the meetings in Paraguay may be taken as performances of everyday-life in Paraguay which are addressed to the people abroad. Accordingly, many of the users living abroad describe Cibervalle as "a window to Paraguay", through which they not only keep themselves up to date regarding current political and social issues but rather keep themselves involved in their socio-cultural context of origin on a regular, intimate and day-to-day basis. With Cibervalle, Paraguayans in Spain, Japan, USA, France, etc … find an easy and inexpensive way to take daily trips to Paraguay, irrespective of their actual geographical distance to their place of origin.[11]

Again, although "virtual travel" (Urry 2002) may "ease nostalgia" and "make one feel closer to home", as some participants explain, it seems also to enhance the need for occasional meetings. For not only the members located geographically near-by have the habit of meeting each other personally. Whenever one of the distant members spends his or her holidays in Paraguay, the local groups organise welcome meetings for the visitor. These meetings, again, are collectively reconstructed and shared with the whole community.

In brief, "meetingness" is assumed to be a fundamental feature of the Cibervalle-community, since

"moments of physical co-presence are crucial to patterns of social life that occur 'at-a-distance' […] 'Meetingness' and thus different forms and modes of travel, are central to much social life, a life involving strange combinations of increasing distance and intermittent co-presence" (Urry 2003:156).

Conclusion

I have demonstrated that social life within Cibervalle is based on a complex relationship between different forms of communication, enhanced by specific combinations of physical, imaginative and virtual travel. The practice of interrelating local events (the meetings) with virtual events on a global level (the meeting's collective narrations) transports the members of the group imaginatively to the localities of residence of their counterparts. The possibility for daily travel to the places of one's origin is assumed to be particularly important for Paraguayans abroad, as it is hard to obtain any images or information about this country through the mass media. The specific use of IM and online forum at the same time, enables joint travel through a shared virtual space in real time, as well as creating experiences of virtual co-presence encounters. This kind of computer-

---

11 These findings are elaborated in detail in my doctoral thesis (Greschke 2007b).

mediated co-presence seems to dissolve the boundary between physical presence and total absence.

The specific use of internet technologies in the context of Cibervalle, in brief, entails new technologically mediated forms of sociality, which are challenging classical concepts of interaction and co-presence as well as altering senses of space and living together. Instead of drawing on apparently clearly bounded concepts, my research calls for a closer examination of the complex interactions between global means of communication, social practices of usage, co-present encounters and various means of mobility, in order to explore the ongoing process of global structuring.

References

Adams Parham, Angel (2004) "Diaspora, Community and Communication: Internet Use in Transnational Haiti." Global Networks 4/2, pp. 199-217.

Appadurai, Arjun (1998) *Modernity at Large: Cultural Dimensions of Globalization*, Minneapolis: University of Minnesota Press.

Baym, Nancy (1995) "The Emergence of Community in Computer Mediated Communication." In: Steven G. Jones (ed.) *CyberSociety – Computer-Mediated Communication and Community*, London: Sage Publications, pp. 138-163.

Bergmann, Jörg/Meier, Christoph (2003) "Elektronische Prozessdaten und ihre Analyse." In: Uwe Flick/Ernst von Kardoff/Ines Steinke (eds.) *Qualitative Forschung. Ein Handbuch*, Reinbeck: Rowohlt, pp. 429-437.

Capote, Truman (1965) *In Cold Blood: A True Account of a Multiple Murder and Its Consequences*, New York: The American Library.

Geertz, Clifford (1973) "Thick Description: Toward an Interpretive Theory of Culture." In: Clifford Geertz (ed.) *The Interpretation of Cultures: Selected Essays*, New York: Basic Books, pp. 3-30.

Georgiou, Myria (2002) "Diasporic Communities On-Line: A Bottom Up Experience of Transnationalism", November 16, 2005 (www.lse.ac.uk/collections/EMTEL/Minorities/papers/hommesmigrations.doc).

Graham, Mark/Khosravi, Shahram (2002) "Reordering Public and Private in Iranian Cyberspace: Identity, Politics, and Mobilization." Identities: Global Studies in Culture and Power 9, pp. 219-246.

Greschke, Heike Mónika (2007a) "Bin ich drin? – Methodologische Reflektionen zur ethnografischen Forschung in einem plurilokalen, computervermittelten Feld." Forum: Qualitative Social Research, 8/3, Art. 32, http://www.qualitative-research.net/fqs-texte/3-07/07-3-32-d.htm.

Greschke, Heike M. (2007b) *Daheim in www.cibervalle.com – Ethnographie einer globalen Lebenswelt*, MS doctoral thesis (submitted), Faculty of Sociology, Bielefeld University.

International Organization for Migration (IOM) (2005) "World Migration 2005: Costs and Benefits of International Migration" Section 3, September 15, 2005 (http://www.iom.int//DOCUMENTS/PUBLICATION/wmr_sec03.pdf).

Karim, Karim H. (2001) "From Ethnic Media to Global Media – Transnational Communication Networks among Diasporic Communities." Nord-Süd aktuell 4, pp. 645-654.

Kieserling, André (1999) *Kommunikation unter Anwesenden*, Frankfurt a.M.: Suhrkamp.

Knorr-Cetina, Karin/Bruegger, Urs (2002) "Global Microstructures, The Virtual Societies of Financial Markets." American Journal of Sociology 107/4, pp. 905-950.

Miller, Daniel/Slater, Don (2000) *The Internet – An Ethnographic Approach*, Oxford: Berg.

Panagakos, Anastasia N. (2003) "Downloading New Identities: Ethnicity, Technology, and Media in the Global Greek Village." Identities: Global Studies in Culture and Power 10, pp. 201-219.

Sacks, Harvey (1984) "On Doing 'being ordinary'." In: John M. Atkinson/John Heritage (eds.) *Structures of Social Action. Studies in Conversation Analysis*, Cambridge [et al.]: Cambridge University Press, pp. 413-429.

Stegbauer, Christian (2000) "Begrenzungen und Strukturen internetbasierter Kommunikationsgruppen." In: Caja Thimm (ed.) *Soziales im Netz. Sprache, Beziehungen und Kommunikationskulturen im Internet*, Opladen: Westdeutscher Verlag, pp. 18-38.

Stichweh, Rudolf (2005) "Migration in der Weltgesellschaft" June 10, 2005 (http://www.uni-bielefeld.de/soz/iw/pdf/stw.migration.PDF).

Urry, John (2002) "Mobility and Proximity." Sociology 36/2, London: Sage, pp. 255-274.

Urry, John (2003) "Social Networks, Travel and Talk." British Journal of Sociology 54 /2, pp. 155-175.

The Indernet – A German Network in a Transnational Space

URMILA GOEL

Communicating Across the World

> It is an Indian portal also for foreign Indians, who can get an insight into the German scene. [...] Like I express myself in the world, thus the Indian community expresses itself in the world: We are there as well! Not only Canada, Great Britain and India, we are also there! We Indians in Germany also do something! We have a cultural scene and we also have our value, our pride, our commitment and our activity. That is the Indernet for me. That is what the Indernet incorporates for me.[1]

In these words Jay, a rap musician whose parents migrated from India to Germany, enthusiastically explains to me the importance of the internet portal http://www.theinder.net, called the *Indernet*. Later in the interview he comes back to this idea and concludes with "The Indernet unites! The world becomes smaller!"

Jay's enthusiasm fits well with the observation that transnational media technologies, and in particular the internet, (cf. Karim 2003; Hannerz 1996; Glick Schiller et al. 1997: 126) are able to connect migrants scattered around the world (Döring 1999: 267; Mitra 1997; Mannur 2003) and give the marginalised a voice (Döring 1999: 148; Miller/Slater 2000: 3; 18; Mandaville 2003: 135). The internet contributes to making the world smaller as it enables everyday togetherness across national borders (Miller/Slater 2000: 55-84; Greschke in this volume) and

---

1 This is a quote from an interview I conducted in the course of the research project "The virtual second generation" (see http://www.urmila.de/UDG/Forschung/forschungindex.html). I conducted all interviews in German and have translated as well as anonymised the quotes for this article.

lets discourses and images travel quickly between different regions of the world (King 2003: 179). According to Jay the virtual space *Indernet* is connecting *"Indian communities"*[2] around the word. This is also the impression of the 'white'[3] journalist Manuel: "Already the fact that there is an English version and a Hindi version makes it possible for Indians around the world to communicate. I think also the choice of topics, i.e. Indian films and music and so on, are encouraging this."

However, both my observation of the *Indernet* and most of my interview partners do not support Jay's and Manuel's impressions. The virtual space the *Indernet* does not indicate any significant interaction with those marked as Indians beyond the German-speaking countries. It neither provides evidence for a worldwide representation of the German cultural scene nor do debates and discourses from other parts of the world seem to be received through it in Germany on a significant scale. In contrast the *Indernet* seems to be very much focused on the German context. In this it differs considerably from virtual spaces like the one analysed by Greschke in this volume, where interactions across borders are everyday practices. In this article I will discuss, in which ways the *Indernet* is nonetheless part of a transnational space and how Jay's and Manuel's impressions can be interpreted. I will do so from the perspective of racism theory[4] and as an outsider to the debates around transnationalism, hoping that this outsider perspective might add productive insights to this volume and the discussions about world society.

In the following I will first provide basic information about the *Indernet* and my research methods, then I will describe the internet portal's localisation through the German language, before I finally return first to Manuel's and then Jay's impression of worldwide communication facilitated through the *Indernet*.

---

2 For a critical discussion of the imagination of an 'Indian community' in Germany see Goel (2007a).
3 I use the term ‚white' to mark the normally unmarked social position of symbolic and practical privilege in the racist reality of contemporary Germany (Mecheril 2004: 199). It indicates that a person or a group of persons participates in the privileges of the racist system. While the privileged are hardly aware of their 'white' privileges, those who are racialised perceive and have to deal with them everyday. The power system and mechanisms of exclusion based on the construction of the 'white' and the racialised are analysed in the Critical Whiteness Studies (in Germany in particular Eggers et al. 2005; Tißberger et al. 2006), on which I base my analysis. I am aware that the term 'white' is prone to evoke essentialised notions about biological differences between persons. Nonetheless, I consider the term 'white' as the analytically most productive term in the German context at the moment to make the privileged position visible.
4 My approach is based on theorists like Mecheril (2003), Rommelspacher (1995) and Terkessidis (2004) as well as on the Critical Whiteness Studies and postcolonial theory (for example Steyerl/Gutiérrez Rodríguez 2003 or Broden/Mecheril 2007).

The Indernet

The internet portal the *Indernet* was founded in the summer of the year 2000 by three young men, who were socialised in Germany and are marked as Indians there.[5] They had already created private websites and wanted to develop their skills through a meaningful project. The campaign *'Kinder statt Inder'*[6] provided them with a starting point for the latter. First they just collected some of the cartoons[7] online, but soon they decided to establish their own network of Indians, hoping to thus get into contact with others socialised like them in Germany and marked as Indians there. The English project description[8] introduced the internet portal as follows:

"We are a young Indian internet community and portal, founded in July 2000, named "the InderNet" ("Inder" is the German word for an Indian, so it becomes an "Indian Network"). [...] Our goal is to bring people via internet together, encourage communication among each other, promote and support projects and to provide you with information on India. [...] Our target group is primarily 2nd generation Indians living in Germany."

---

5 Most of the editors and users of the Indernet are categorised most commonly as Indians (of the second generation). Many identify themselves as such, some identify as Germans, Indo-Germans, German Indians, Asians, Desis, foreigners, Kanaken, etc. Many have relatives in India, some in Pakistan, Bangladesh, Sri Lanka or some other country of the former British empire. Others do not know of any relatives outside of Germany. What is common to them is on the one hand that they were socialised primarily in Germany, live in Germany and plan to live in Germany. On the other hand they share the experience of being considered Indians by others in Germany. As my analysis takes the approach of racism theory (cf. Mecheril 2004: 176-200) I will not use a term referring to an ascribed origin outside Germany to categorise these editors and users of the Indernet but will rather refer to the process of racialisation they experience in Germany. Thus, I will talk of people socialised in Germany and marked (by numerous physiognomic and social attributes) as Indians in Germany. For a discussion of how social and physiognomic attributes play a central role in whether people are considered to belong to a particular natio-ethno-cultural context or not see Mecheril (2003: 211-212). For a discussion of claims and contestations of 'Indianness' in Germany see Goel (2008).
6 In the summer of 2000 the German IT industry was experiencing a lack of skilled professionals. The German government thus announced the introduction of a 'Green Card' scheme to attract foreign IT experts and in particular referred to Indians. The conservative opposition started a campaign against it, which was soon known as 'Kinder statt Inder' (which translates to children instead of Indians). This was the first time that people marked as Indians were at the centre of a racist campaign in Germany.
7 The public debate about the 'GreenCard' scheme was accompanied by a plethora of cartoons, many of them using the image of a 'Computer Indian' or working with the German play of words Indernet, which joins the term internet with Inder (which is German for Indian).
8 http://www.theinder.net/presentation/presentation-eng.htm, September 30, 2001

Through skilful networking and luck the founders were able to make the project known among others active in organising events and spaces for those socialised in Germany and marked as Indians there. The *Indernet* thus gained not only a wider audience, but also more content and new editors. The internet portal grew fast in users, editors and content and by the time I conducted my interviews in the year 2004 it was established as a space of the second generation (Heft/Goel 2006), known not only to young people marked as Indians and socialised in Germany but also to migrants from South Asia and 'white' Germans interested in India. In the summer of the year 2007, at which point I am (re)writing this article,[9] the *Indernet* seems to have passed its zenith.

I got to know the founders of the *Indernet* and thus the internet portal at a networking seminar, which I organised together with others for the German-Indian Society, in November 2000. Since at this point I was already collecting material and writing about people marked (like me and my father) as Indians in Germany, I started to observe the virtual space shortly afterwards. I applied for research funds some time later and began a full-time research project on the *Indernet* in spring 2004. Since then I have been surfing the virtual spaces with few exceptions at least once every day, have occasionally participated in forum discussions, contributed articles to the editorial section, been on few occasions in the *Indernet* chat, have exchanged personal messages and emails with other users and attended offline events. My participation was, however, mainly one of a distanced lurker,[10] staying most of the time an observer and hardly considering myself part of the *Indernet*. Starting in 2004 I conducted more than 80 open interviews about the *Indernet* with the founders, editors and users as well as with observers and people, who know of the internet portal but do not use it. Most of the interviews were conducted face to face with me travelling to meet my interview partners. When this was not possible, either because the interview partner wanted to stay anonymous or I did not have the resources to meet her or him, I also conducted online interviews. For contacting interview partners I used my own networks among people socialised in Germany and marked as Indians there, contacted *Indernet* editors and users and followed other interesting traces found on the internet portal. In doing so I was guided by the principles of grounded theory, adapting my approach, methods and analysis in accordance with the empirical material and my theoretical deliberations.

---

9   This is a total reformulation of a paper presented at the conference "The Making of 'World Society'" at Bielefeld in November 2005. I thank Eva Gerharz for her critical comments, which induced me to rethink my arguments fundamentally.
10 A lurker uses a virtual space, but does not post herself and thus is hardly visible to the other users.

A Space in German

The project description of the Indernet refers to Indians and India, the domain name includes the German term for Indians, the logo is a stylised Indian flag. The main reference point of the Indernet quite clearly is India. The English project description refers to "a global information and communication platform"[11] and the internet portal starts in three languages (German, English and Hindi), thus supporting Jay's and Manuel's impression of the Indernet being a part of a worldwide Indian network. But a closer look questions this impression. In the interactive parts German is the clearly dominant language, there are almost no posts in English and very seldom any in another Indian language. The English version of the Indernet has little and the Hindi version hardly any content.[12] Deepak, one of the three founders, comments this as follows:

"At the beginning the portal was really trilingual. All news were translated into all three languages. But then we stopped because it was too much work and in fact only two people or so per day were interested in the Hindi version, so we left the navigation in Hindi and [...] took the English home page for the Hindi version as well. [...]In the meantime I think there are always about eight people per day, who enter the Hindi version. And one does not know, whether they want to read Hindi or whether they are just interested to see, what Hindi looks like. I do not think that it is a serious content transferring medium [...]"

It is also a lot of work to translate all the articles into English, thus the update of the English version is always a bit behind. Thus everything is only available 100% on the German version.

At the time of the interviews the impression of trilinguality was preserved by the entrance page giving one the choice of the three languages. For users, who entered only the German version like Manuel,[13] it appeared that there were alternative offers in the other languages. Today this impression should be weaker since, some time in the year 2006, the entrance page disappeared and the user now enters directly the German version.[14]

My interviews show that the choice of German as the dominant language is decisive for the success of the Indernet. The most common answer I got, when I

---

11 http://www.theinder.net/presentation/presentation-eng.htm, September 30, 2001
12 The Indernet is not the only ethnically defined internet portal in Germany, which uses German as the main language. Androutsopolous (2006: 9-12) mentions also http://iran-now.de, http://www.greex.net, http://www.asia-zone.de and http://www.dimadima.de.
13 Manuel admitted his ignorance about the Hindi and English version in the interview: "I know in particular, I have to admit, the German version. There is also the English and the Hindi version. But I do not know these, I have at least failed to check."
14 From which the user, however, can still change to the English and Hindi version.

asked what was special about this particular internet portal, was that it is a German-language virtual space. German is the language that those socialised in Germany, are most comfortable with. It is the language, which they read with the least effort and in which they can express themselves best as Deepak among others explained to me:

"There is the medium German language. The people, we want to reach, they know German. [...] Naturally one does not know a foreign language as well as one's own mother tongue. And I want to express myself in my mother tongue, when I am writing an article, it should be rhetorically interesting and not only providing facts, and thus I prefer German."

No other language could be used to the same effect. English is for most of the editors and users of the Indernet a foreign language, which they have learned in school and use seldom in their everyday lives, and there is no Indian language they could use alternatively as Martin, one of the early editors, explains:

"The special thing is that it is an online community, which because it is in German, reaches all Indians. Because India is a country, in which there are so many languages. If the Indernet was only in Hindi, then I think not so many people would come. Because the people, the generation, which grows up here, they grow up with German and many do know a little bit of Malayalam or a bit of Hindi or some other language, but the language, which they learn here, in the school, is German. And the Indernet uses German in order that everybody understands it. Also, an Indian from the North does not understand the languages from the South or from the West or East."

What Martin does not say explicitly here is that many of the editors and users (like himself) do not know any Indian language at all. He was adopted from India as a small child and has been brought up with German, Vietnamese and French. I myself grew up with German and English. Only at university did I start to study the basics of Hindi, which is the mother tongue of my father. Thus, German is really the only language which is understood by all those socialised in Germany and marked as Indians there.

The choice of this language shapes the nature of this virtual space and makes it different from other virtual spaces marked as Indian across the world (eg. Mitra 1997 or Gajjala 2004) and others in Germany. The latter include the mailing group GINDS: Indians in Germany,[15] which is used mainly by IT professionals, the internet portal http://www.indianfootball.com, which was founded by a young man socialised in Germany and marked as an Indian there, or the matrimonial service http://www.shaadi.com, on which many young people socialised in Germany and marked as Indians there are registered. All of the latter use English as their main language, a language which is spoken in India and connects people

---

15 http://groups.yahoo.com/group/GINDS/, September 11, 2007

marked as Indians across the world.[16] These virtual spaces thus enable worldwide interaction and can reach people, the Indernet fails to cater for as Deepak is aware:

"In the editorial team it was always a discussion in how far we will include the Computer Indians and especially how we will do that. We would, for example, have needed to promote the English version. For which we did not have the resources. [...] and due to the language barrier the Computer Indians are already excluded somewhat."

Whoever is uncomfortable with German can read only few articles in English on the Indernet and can access information about India much better on other websites. In the forum and the chatroom one can interact in English (or another Indian language), but there will only be few other users, who will interact readily in these languages, and the majority of the discussions will not be accessible. One can contribute articles in English[17], but this will be a unidirectional involvement in the virtual space. In my observation there are few users, who do not know German and try to interact on the Indernet. I have observed none, who became a regular user actively interacting with others. In my interviews I was, however, told that some of my interview partners contacted Indian migrants on the Indernet chat. Others met migrants, at events marked as Indian in Germany, who found out about these events on the Indernet.

Connecting (with) Germany

The English project description[18] (despite the language barrier) claims to have a global audience: "We do also have [...] members from India, UK, USA or Switzerland." This is supported by the membership list of the Indernet in early 2004.[19] While most of the 442 members were based in Germany, eight had indicated a residence in India and even fewer in other non-German speaking countries. Manish, who went for his postgraduate studies from Germany to the US is one of them:

"When I registered as a member, I was one of the very few abroad. The others were naturally Germans. I used to look at the list occasionally. There were some from the

---

16 Like Spanish connects people marked as Paraguayans across the world in the virtual space, as analysed by Greschke in this volume.
17 There was a regular column in English called Usha's corner (for example http://culture.indian-network.de/ushascorner/usha_indianidentity.htm, September 12, 2007). As there is no further information available about the author Usha, I do not know where she is based and how she made contact with the Indernet. At the time of writing this article the Indernet is looking for a new columnist.
18 http://www.theinder.net/presentation/presentation-eng.htm, September 30, 2001
19 On http://www.indien-netzwerk.de/logo/mitglieder/mitglieder.htm, March 27, 2004 there used to be a list of people who had filled in a membership form.

neighbouring countries like Switzerland, but one could count them with one hand. And at some stage, I still remember it, there were also Indians there, Indians from India. And a few from North America, I think [...] I did not want to lose my connections with the Indian community in Germany. And through the Indernet I was always up to date about what was happening among the Indians in Germany."

Nikhil, another user from Germany told me that he particularly enjoyed using the Indernet, while he was doing a practical training in India:

"It was in the time, when I was in India, when I started to appreciate the internet as such. Because of the distance. Because I had an email address and could email people. And I could chat with them on msn and so on. The value of the internet was more apparent, because I was so far away and could keep the contacts nonetheless. Thus, while I was in India, I also went on the Indernet often in order to know what was happening in the Indian community. [...] And also to write in the guestbook. It was funny to leave messages there and to enter as a location Bangalore. Or to write how I like it there and what I have done today or whatever could be of interest to Indians."

This was echoed by Ishvar, a very active user, who was brought up in Germany and pursued his studies in Great Britain. Like the other two he used the Indernet to keep up to date about what happened among those socialised in Germany and marked as Indians there. As he wrote me in the email interview: "I consider Germany my home.[20] There I grew up and maybe I will settle there for work (let's wait and see)."

The editors of the Indernet observe who is using the internet portal and take pride in the international participation, as the interview with the editor Ranjan illustrates:

"The community spirit is that everyone can be together, that everyone can communicate with one another. That there are no boundaries anymore. That it crosses borders. [...] There are people, who come from England, there are people who come from ... I don't know. Do you know Ishvar? He comes from Britain and I asked him how he came to know the Indernet. He is Indian, born in Germany and went to England to work there."

But it is not only the crossing of international borders which is important for Ranjan. In the quote above I have omitted the following passage:

"One, for example, knows that there are many Indians in Cologne or in Frankfurt or in urban areas and one knows, if one goes on the Indernet, for example in the forum, one meets people from all over Germany."

---

20 He uses the German term Heimat, which has a much stronger sense of belongingness than the English term home.

Only after stressing the fact that the Indernet connects those socialised in Germany and marked as Indians there within the country does Ranjan look across the national border. In this emphasis on networking in Germany he is joined by most of my interview partners. The user Maya, for example, told me:

"The Indernet is unique in being a link between Indians of the second generation, which is at the same time modern and German inspired, as it also does not deny the Indian roots. [...] It provides a German perspective on India."

Important for Maya, and for most others, is that the Indernet links Germany and India, in a way she likes to identify with. The interesting point is that Maya has never lived in Germany, that she has been socialised and lives in Switzerland. Puzzled by her reference to a German perspective I asked her whether she considered herself part of this. She answered:

"There is no Swiss perspective on Indian things. .. In Switzerland everything differs from district to district. The Indians in the district Aargau are so different from those in Basel or Zürich. They are worlds apart. And the French and the Italian Switzerland cannot be compared anyway. There is no Swiss perspective. I think the German Swiss perspective is very similar to the German. [...] The German Swiss can be compared more with the Germans than to the rest of Switzerland. [...] Everything cool comes from Germany. Germany is the big brother and everything that happens, happens first in Germany. [...] Switzerland is always a subchapter of Germany."

In fact, there are several very active users as well as registered members of the Indernet, who were socialised in either Switzerland or Austria and are marked as Indians there. In discussions they sometimes point out to other users that the latter's assumptions that everyone is based in Germany is wrong and that, for example, if a question like "Do you prefer to live in Germany or India?" is posted, then Austria and/or Switzerland should be included as well. Sometimes they also stress their regional identity by writing their posts in Swiss or Austrian German. In general, however, the German language – as well as the absence of a comparable internet portal in Switzerland or Austria – seems sufficient to make them part of the Indernet.

The Topics of the *Indernet*

The Indernet offers two kinds of information: first, information about India and secondly, information about things marked as Indian in Germany.[21] The latter is what Manish, Nikhil and Ishvar mentioned as being particularly important to

---

21 There is hardly ever any information provided about issues directly connected to Austria or Switzerland.

them while they were away from Germany. It is also what many of those based in the German-speaking countries consider as the most important aspect of the Indernet.[22] The internet portal allows its users to learn more about which things marked as Indian happen in Germany through an events calendar, reports about events and the discussions in the forum. Thus they get to know both what is being discussed and where they can participate offline themselves. This information is sought not only to actively interact, but also to just get to know more about what can be considered Indian in Germany. The Swiss user Maya, for example, told me:

"The great thing was in the beginning: Until that time I only knew the British Indian community. It was very interesting for me to see, how the German community differs from the British. Because the British community is very much closed towards the British. I saw that among my relatives, who are much more traditional [...] While the German Indians out of necessity, because there are not so many Indians, are more open towards the German culture. I found that interesting. That there is such a blend."

Maya, like some of the other users, has relatives in the UK and other countries around the world. When she visits them, she observes how they define and cultivate their Indianness, which differs considerably from her positioning in Switzerland. She thus seeks a further comparison and uses the Indernet to get to know more about others, who are marked as Indians in German-speaking countries. She, like others, emphasises the differences she sees among those marked as Indians in Germany and in countries with a larger presence of people thus categorised. It seems that her feeling of belongingness to those marked as Indians in Britain is considerably less than to those in Germany. Ishvar, who is using the Indernet to keep in contact with those marked as Indian in Germany and who lives in a British university town tells me: "There are masses of Indians here. One is no exception anymore. There are certainly also communities here, but I do not have contact with them." It does not seem important for him, to get into contact with the local networks. His point of reference remains Germany.

The focus on Germany can be noticed also in the information provided on the Indernet about India. Hardly ever is there an article, which was written by somebody based (at least temporarily) in India[23] and only seldom are sources based in India quoted. There is hardly any news about Indian domestic issues and in contrast, for example, to the mailing list GINDS hardly ever issues, which are currently debated in India, are taken up on the Indernet. Much of the information provided is very general, giving basic facts about India[24] or Hinduism[25] or provid-

---

22 This is true also for several of the ‚white' observers (like the journalist Manuel) I interviewed. They told me that they were using the Indernet mainly to get to know more about people marked as Indians in Germany.
23 The Indernet claims to have an India office since 2006, but so far I have noticed only one article written there.

ing a list with Indian names and their meanings.[26] Many reports are taken from German media and thus mirror the latter's interests. In general the selection of topics seems rather haphazard depending on the interests and skills of the editors.[27] Thus, while many of my interview partners told me that they appreciate the information provided by the Indernet, all those with a more detailed interest in India said that they rather prefer to refer to other sources such as Indian newspapers online.

Some are also users of the German-language internet portal http://www.suedasien.info, which is an official cooperation partner of the Indernet[28] and was founded shortly before the Indernet by students whose studies have in some way to do with South Asia. The aim of this internet portal is to provide well researched and critically edited information in German about the South Asian countries. Most of the editors are 'white', several travel regularly to South Asia and some have lived there. One of the 'white' editor, I interviewed, had originally volunteered as an editor for the Indernet and then changed to suedasien.info. She not only preferred the academic approach of suedasien.info but also feared that as a 'white' person, she did not fit into the Indernet team. This contrasts with the perspective of Jule, a 'white' user of the Indernet I interviewed, who feels very much accepted in that virtual space:

"Yes, I know suedasien.info. I have printed lots of their articles. [...] I think it is great, a lot of knowledge is communicated, but on the interpersonal level [...] it is better on the Indernet. [...] There I have the impression, these are people who participate, who listen to me. [...] suedasien.info [...] is somehow dead [...] more like a book and the Indernet is more open. There one can communicate with people."

While thus the Indernet is able to bind some 'white' users,[29] it has failed despite several attempts[30] to attract young Indian migrants, who are IT professionals, on a significant scale. Observing the mailing list GINDS shows that this is not only an issue of language but also of topics. On GINDS the contributions are predominantly about the practicalities of migration to and life in Germany. The topics in-

---

24 For example http://www.indien-netzwerk.de/navigation/landleute/bharat-ki-khoj/bharat-ki-khoj.htm, September 12, 2007.
25 For example http://culture.indian-network.de/religion/artikel/hinduismus2.htm, September 12, 2007.
26 For example http://culture.indian-network.de/gesellschaft/artikel/maennl-namen-deu.htm, September 12, 2007.
27 The Indernet is organised fully on a voluntary basis. All the editors work full-time or are students with limited time available for their editorial work. Most of them have neither a training in journalism nor any formal education on Indian issues.
28 The cooperation so far seems restricted mainly to linking each other and very seldomly exchanging articles.
29 In fact, among the most active users in the forum there are several 'white' users.
30 For example, by providing an own section "New in Germany" (http://forum.indian-network.de/viewforum.php?f=18, September 12, 2007).

clude where there are job opportunities, how to apply for a residence permit, what to do about insurance, how to find accommodation and also offers to sell furniture or other household equipment, all of which are absent on the Indernet. From time to time debates from India, for example about a controversial Muslim painter, are also discussed in GINDS. Although there are common users it only rarely happens that issues travel from GINDS to the Indernet or the other way round.

A Space for Those Socialised in Germany

Among the different virtual spaces marked as Indian in Germany, the special thing about the Indernet is that it is a space of those socialised in Germany and marked as Indians there for those socialised in Germany and marked as Indians there as I was told in many of the interviews. As I have argued elsewhere (Goel 2005, 2007b, 2007c; Heft/Goel 2006) the Indernet is an own space in a society perceived as being racist, which is helpful in dealing with experiences of racist exclusion.[31] The user Fatima illustrates this as follows:

"I also went through phases, when I was almost depressive, because I thought: 'Oh no, where do I belong?' A conflict of identity, when one does not know, where ... what am I? You look into the mirror and you see somebody with black hair. You go outside, talk to people and when you listen to yourself, you think: 'Yes, naturally. For myself, I am German.' When I listen to myself thus, but as soon as, I don't know ... there are small things said by others, by friends, small remarks like 'How is it done at your place?' Then it is again: 'Oh no, I am different after all.' And then I found other people with this conflict of identity on [...] the Indernet. There one can talk with each other, exchange experiences. A bit of survival training: how does one deal with this?"[32]

Fatima thus highlights the importance of meeting others with the same experiences of exclusion on the Indernet and being able to discuss with them. The Indernet facilitates this as racist othering is virtually absent there and a sense of natio-ethno-cultural familiarity[33] exists. Mary, an early editor, describes the latter as follows: "There are small examples, in which one can see the familiarity that ex-

---

31 For an analysis of experiences of racism by people socialised in Germany and marked as Indians there see for example Mecheril (2003), Goel (2006) or Paske (2006). The experiences are mostly those of banal racism (Terkessidis 2004). They are encountered in everyday interactions (Battaglia 1995; Ferreira 2003) as well as in legislation, institutions and public discourses (Mecheril 2003).
32 A detailed analysis of the interview with Fatima can be found in Goel (2005).
33 Mecheril (2003) coins the term natio-ethno-cultural to refer to notions of nation, ethnicity and culture, which are used to categorise people in and define their belongingness to Germany. The Indernet users share similar experiences concerning this categorisation, while with respect to others such as gender, sexuality or class they might lack commonality.

ists among Indians without having to explain what it is to be Indian". She later returns to this, when she explains what she considers special about the internet portal: "It is a platform for young people to get to know each other, for young people from Germany to get to know Indians, who are born and brought up like them, and to get to know each other without a need to explain."[34]

The Indernet is a space, where the (multiple) natio-ethno-cultural belongingness (Mecheril 2003) of those socialised in Germany and marked as Indians there is the norm. It allows the (imaginary) movement between different contexts of belongingness and thus constitutes – as Mecheril (2004: 73) in an adaptation of Ludger Pries' work argues – a transnational space. Here the logic of univocal belongingness, which constitutes the basis both of nation states and of racism (Mecheril 2003), is circumvented. Here the users can feel, express and negotiate a simultaneous belongingness to India and Germany (and more natio-ethno-cultural contexts[35]) at the same time, and can expect to be understood and accepted in this without many questions. Here they experience being valued as and can develop pride in being socialised in Germany and marked as Indians there (as Jay wants the world to notice). Here the national borders can be crossed discursively, while staying localised in Germany and without necessarily having to interact with people based in other regions of the world. Those, who are longing for the latter, use other (virtual) spaces like shaadi.com, indianfootball.com or international networks of relatives and friends as well (or exclusively).

The Difficulty to Think Multiple Belongingness

But this (multiple) natio-ethno-cultural belongingness is difficult to think for those, who are socialised with the belief in univocal belongingness to only one natio-ethno-cultural context. The 'white' journalist Manuel is obviously puzzled by what he observes on the Indernet when he talks about an online discussion about the Indian elections:

"One can see that the political development in India is observed [...] it shows that the second and third generation voluntarily occupies itself with political discussions in their original home country[36] [...] This shows clearly that there is a bond. [...] It is important to recognise this need to discuss, which is actually also surprising. If one considers that many Indians were probably born and brought up in Germany, and thus political

---

34 Battaglia (1995) and Ferreira (2003) show how racialised people have to explain themselves in every-day interactions and how this constitutes experiences of racism.
35 This is the case, for example, for the users based in Austria and Switzerland, and also for users like Fatima, who feels a belongingness also to Pakistan and Great Britain (Goel 2005).
36 Manuel uses throughout the interview the German terms Heimatland and Heimat, which express a much stronger natio-ethno-cultural belongingness than the English terms home country or home.

discussions in Germany should be more important to them, because their education and development takes place in Germany. And also political decisions in Germany are more fundamental and important, influencing the people more. But one sees in the discussions, as if they still affect them as much. This shows how strong the roots and the identification with the original home are."

This quote shows that Manuel is aware that, for those who were born and socialised in Germany, this geographical space and the political decisions there are important. He emphasises the point that the latter will influence the lives of those living in Germany fundamentally. He also sees that those marked as Indians in Germany (and called Indians by him throughout the interview) also have a bond to India. But this double bind surprises him ("which is actually also surprising"), he does not seem to consider it a natural outcome of the (multiple) natio-ethno-cultural belongingness. From one discussion about an Indian election he infers a strong identification with what he calls their original home. Doing so Manuel ignores, that discussions about Indian politics form only a small part of the forum debates on the Indernet as well as that there are also numerous discussions about German politics (and probably many more in other spaces). It seems as if he considers it possible to identify with only one natio-ethno-cultural context fully, when he continues this line of thought later in the interview: "The high degree of identification with the original home shows in the reverse that obviously the integration in the new home is not 100%." If one is considered as Indian by Manuel, then being interested in India seems to show that one does not fully belong to Germany.[37] Throughout the interview he keeps referring to the users of the Indernet as Indians, who have their roots and original home in India, who form a community across the world, who prefer partners from these communities,[38] who have identity problems in Germany[39] and about whose skill in German he is surprised.[40] He is thus continuously reproducing the racist dichotomy of 'us' (the Germans) and the 'other' (the Indians) as mutually exclusive and in doing so refers to those, whom he considers to be Indians despite their birth, socialisation and residence in Germany, to India.

Against this discursive backdrop it is not surprising that he takes the seeming trilinguality of the Indernet and the discussions about Indian films and music[41] as

---

37 While Manuel probably does not see his own belongingness to and integration in Germany diminished by his interest in Indian politics.
38 For example: "I can imagine well, one always hears this, that families, Indian families like it and support it, when their own children choose a partner who suits them, who has the same background."
39 For example: "The distancing [to Germany, ug] indicates a problem, which obviously occurs for many people of this population group, i.e. that they have difficulties with their identity."
40 For example: "The way they formulate it is very good. It is perfect German, if one knows that this page is made by migrants."
41 In fact, discussions about Bollywood films and music constitute a large part of the Indernet and can be interpreted as an important point of reference and identification

an indication of worldwide communication in an Indian community. This seems to arise much more from his imagination of those marked as Indians than from what can be observed on the Indernet, and fits the general political atmosphere at the moment, which Karim (2003: 15) describes as:

"[...] the loyalty of minority ethnic groups living in Western countries is becoming suspect and their transnational connections and relationships are coming under scrutiny. The multiple and hybrid identities of diasporic members are under renewed pressure to conform to the mythic notion of a monolithic populace of the traditional nation state."

The *Indernet* and the World

But it is not only the 'white' observer Manuel, who considers the Indernet to enable worldwide communication. The same notion is also found in the English project description and is prominent in Jay's enthusiastic praise of the Indernet. Why do the editors claim this although they know that the actual interaction is rather insignificant? And why does the musician Jay consider this one of the major achievements of the internet portal?

On the one hand, it is part of the joint imagination of the internet portal. The internet gives those socialised in Germany and marked as Indians there a new possibility to position themselves in the global context.[42] The Indernet does so by linking Germany and India. Located in Germany it assumes a shared natio-ethno-cultural belongingness to a place called India.[43] This not only links its users to the people in India but also to others across the world, who are marked as Indians, and are thus seen both by nationalist and racist ideology[44] to share this belongingness. In its English version the editors position the Indernet in this transnational network centring on India with the slogan "Germany's Premier NRI Portal"[45], thus defining their users as Non-Resident Indians (NRI). The seeming trilinguali-

---

for those socialised in Germany and marked as Indians there, in particular since in recent years Bollywood films and music have become increasingly popular in Germany and are now valued more than they used to be. However, by now it, seems that the discussions on the Indernet about film and music are dominated by 'white' fans, who want to share their passion with others.

42 Miller/Slater (2000: 18-21) analyse this as part of the dynamics of positioning.
43 Clifford (1994: 311-312) argues that diaspora consciousness is developed negatively through experiences of exclusion and positively through an identification with an imagined community.
44 See van der Veer (1995) for a discussion of the forms of belongingness of people marked as Indians abroad to India and Glick Schiller et al. (1997: 126-127) for the Greek policy of binding all people marked abroad as Greek to Greece.
45 On http://www.theinder.net/eng/ September 14, 2007. The German slogan is different and translates as "India portal for Germany" (http://www.theinder.net/deu/ September 14, 2007).

ty of the internet portal opens this space symbolically to all NRIs and illustrates that the editors consider it part of a transnational space.

On the other hand the Indernet is more than a virtual space. For those actively involved in it, it opens up new possibilities. The editors of the Indernet can, as journalists, approach people they would not otherwise contact. Those, who had been looking to the British Asian music scene for identification[46] can through the Indernet, come closer to their idols. Already in 2001 Bobby, who was at this time an Indernet editor, interviewed the British musician Apache Indian. Other interviews with international artists marked as Indians followed from time to time. While the frequency of such articles was too low to make the Indernet a prime source for this information, it still showed that the internet portal was able to approach international stars and that these considered the German audience important enough to give an interview. They, at least for the time of the interview, took notice of those marked as Indians in Germany and this makes Jay say: "They gave interviews. They know there is a scene in Germany. They think this is great. We are heard and that is amazing." Even more importantly it provided the Indernet editors with contacts to artists marked as Indians abroad. Bobby used these when he left the Indernet and founded his own event agency, which to all appearances successfully promotes international artists marked as Indians in Germany and organises dance parties marked as Indian. Jay considers Bobby's activities important beyond Germany (and traces them back to the Indernet):

"The British slowly respect the German scene. After all the English scene has grown through Germany. [..]. We are proud that we have boosted the Desi[47] scene. It was us! Punjabi MC grew through Germany. He played in Hamburg [...] and then Bobby invited him to Germany. [...] Bobby did all the translations for Punjabi MC, all the promotion in Germany. That is interesting. We Indians here, we boost everything there. [...] They [the British artists] have all their own radio shows. And everything through Germany and all report about Germany, but more about Bobby's parties, but they report about German. [...] all through the Indernet. Bobby was interviewing as an editor of the Indernet."

Jay is thus able not only to assert a worldwide audience for the German music scene, of which he is a part, he is also able to claim that those socialised in Germany and marked as Indians there gave a boost to the British scene[48], thus locat-

---

46 In the interview Jay, for example, told me about the British musician Apache Indian: "He was the first, who spoke about Indians, who live in the West and the East ... He was the first Indian, whom I heard, who did that. I have always been an Indian rap musician, but I did not know Indian rap musicians and then I got to know Apache Indian and his music. He has given me a lot."
47 Desi is a term used to describe those, who are marked as Indians and live abroad.
48 Jay is my only source claiming that the British Asian scene was boosted through the Indernet and Bobby. Bobby himself did not make such a rather doubtful claim in his interview with me.

ing himself actively in the transnational music scene, discursively proving his value and legitimising his pride.

To what extend there is interaction among the artists across national borders, to what degree artists marked as Indian and placed outside Germany are really observing the German scene and which role the Indernet plays in this, I cannot tell from my observation of the internet portal. For the users the interaction remains rather marginal, but for those actively involved like Bobby or one of the editors of the Indernet, who in the summer of 2007 acted as official press representative for the German tour of a famous Indian singer, it might well be of major importance. For some the Indernet actually seems to have facilitated communication in the transnational space referring to India.

References

Androutsopolous, Jannis (2006) "Mehrsprachigkeit im deutschen Internet: Sprachwahl und Sprachwechsel in Ethno-Portalen." In: Peter Schlobinski (ed.) *Sprache und neue Medien,* Mannheim: Dudenverlag, pp. 172-196.
Battaglia, Santina (1995) "Interaktive Konstruktion von Fremdheit. Alltagskommunikation von Menschen binationaler Abstammung." Journal für Psychologie 3/3, pp. 16-23.
Broden, Anne/Mecheril, Paul (eds.) (2007) *Re-Präsentationen: Dynamiken der Migrationsgesellschaft,* Düsseldorf: ida.
Clifford, James (1994) "Diasporas." Cultural Anthropology 9/3, pp. 302-338.
Döring, Nicola (1999) *Sozialpsychologie des Internet. Die Bedeutung des Internet für Kommunikationsprozesse, Identitäten, soziale Beziehungen und Gruppen,* Göttingen: Hogrefe.
Eggers, Maureen Maisha/ Kilomba, Grada/Piesche, Peggy/Arndt, Susan (eds.) (2005) *Mythen, Masken und Subjekte – Kritische Weißseinsforschung in Deutschland,* Münster: Unrast Verlag.
Ferreira, Grada (2003) "Die Kolonisierung des Selbst – der Platz des Schwarzen." In: Hito Steyerl/Encarnación Gutiérrez Rodríguez (eds.) *Spricht die Subalterne deutsch? Migration und postkoloniale Kritik,* Münster: Unrast, pp. 146-165.
Gajjala, Radhika (2004) *Cyber Selves – Feminist Ethnographies of South Asian Women,* Walnut Creek: Altamira Press.
Glick Schiller, Nina/Basch, Linda/Szanton Blanc, Cristina (1997) "From Immigrant to Transmigrant: Theorizing Transnational Migration." In: Ludger Pries (ed.) *Transnationale Migration,* Baden Baden: Nomos, pp. 121-140.
Goel, Urmila (2005) "Fatima and the inder.net – A Refuge in Virtual Space." In: Angelika Fitz et al. (ed.) *Import Export – Cultural Transfer – India, Germany, Austria,* Berlin: Parhas, pp. 201-207.

Goel, Urmila (2006) "Ausgrenzung und Zugehörigkeit – Zur Rolle von Staatsbürgerschaft und Einbürgerung." In: Christiane Brosius/Urmila Goel (eds.) *masala.de – Menschen aus Südasien in Deutschland*, Heidelberg: Draupadi, pp. 123-160.

Goel, Urmila (2007a) *Indians in Germany' – The Imagination of a Community*, The University of New England, Asia Centre (UNEAC): Asia Papers 20, September 15, 2007 (http://www.une.edu.au/asiacenter/UNEAC_Asia_Papers_20.html).

Goel, Urmila (2007b) "'Kinder statt Inder' – Normen, Grenzen und das Indernet." In: Christine Riegel/Thomas Geisen (eds.) *Jugend, Zugehörigkeit und Migration*, Wiesbaden: VS Verlag, pp.163-181.

Goel, Urmila (2007c) "(Frei)Räume der zweiten Generation – Wege und Formen von Repräsentation." In: Anne Broden/Paul Mecheril (eds.) *Re-Präsentationen: Dynamiken der Migrationsgesellschaft*, Düsseldorf: ida, pp. 203-227.

Goel, Urmila (2008), "'Half Indians', Adopted 'Germans' and 'Afghan Indians' – On Claims of 'Indianness' and Their Contestations in Germany." Transforming Cultures eJournal 3/1 (http://epress.lib.uts-edu.au/journals/TfC).

Hannerz, Ulf (1996) *Transnational Connections*, London: Routledge.

Heft, Kathleen/Goel, Urmila /2006) *Räume der zweiten Generation – Dokumentation eines Workshops*, Frankfurt/Oder: Viadrina, September 15, 2007 (http://www.urmila.de/UDG/Biblio/Raeume_der_zweiten_Generation.pdf).

Karim, Karim (ed.) (2003) *The Media of Diaspora*, London: Routledge.

King, Tony (2003) "Rhodesians in Hyperspace: The Maintenance of a National and Cultural Identity." In: Karim Karim (ed.) *The Media of Diaspora*, London: Routledge, pp. 177-188.

Mandaville, Peter (2003) "Communication and Diaspora Islam: a Virtual Ummah?" In: Karim Karim (ed.) *The Media of Diaspora*, London: Routledge, pp. 135-147.

Mannur, Anita (2003) "PostScript: Cyberspaces and the Interfacing of Diasporas." In: Jana Evans Braziel/Anita Mannur (eds.) *Theorizing Diaspora*, Malden: Blackwell, pp. 283-291.

Mecheril, Paul (2003) *Prekäre Verhältnisse. Über natio-ethno-kulturelle (Mehrfach-) Zugehörigkeiten*, Münster: Waxmann.

Mecheril, Paul (2004) *Einführung in die Migrationspädagogik*, Weinheim: Beltz Studium.

Miller, Dan/Slater, Don (2000) *The Internet: An Ethnographic Approach*, Oxford: Berg.

Mitra, Ananda (1997) "Virtual Commonality: Looking for India on the Internet." In: Steven Jones (ed.) *Virtual Culture. Identity and Communication in Cybersociety*, London: Sage, pp. 55-79.

Paske, Mareile (2006) *'Andere Deutsche' – Strategien des Umgangs mit Rassismuserfahrungen,* Frankfurt/Oder: Viadrina, September 14, 2007 (http://www.urmila.de/UDG/Forschung/publikationen/Paske2006.pdf).

Rommelspacher, Birgit (1995) *Dominanzkultur*, Berlin: Orlanda.
Steyerl, Hito/Gutiérrez Rodríguez, Encarnación (2003) *Spricht die Subalterne deutsch? Migration und postkoloniale Kritik*, Münster: Unrast.
Terkessidis, Mark (2004) *Die Banalität des Rassismus. Migranten zweiter Generation entwickeln eine neue Perspektive*, Bielefeld: transcript.
Tißberger, Martina/Dietze, Gabriele/Hrzan, Daniela/Humann-Kastein, Jana (2006) *Weiß-Weißsein-Whiteness. Kritische Studien zu Gender und Rassismus*, Frankfurt: Peter Lang.
Veer, Peter van der (1995) "Introduction: The Diasporic Imagination." In: Peter van der Veer (ed.) *Nation and migration – The Politics of Space in the South Asian Diaspora*, Philadelphia: University of Pennsylvania Press, pp. 1-16.

Are We All Transnationalists Now?

JOANNA PFAFF-CZARNECKA

Currently, we can look back at fifteen years of transnational research. The transnational paradigm for studying migration and the social (trans)formations instigated by connectivity is certainly a success story – as the rapidly expanding number of studies reveals. The spanning of social relationships beyond borders into new sites and places, continuous spatial movement as an important facet of social life and multiplication of formal memberships and belonging increasingly characterise the social realm all around the world. These trends are well captured in this volume which aptly demonstrates that our conceptual tools geared at grasping the new complexities and subtleties have been considerably refined since the early 1990s. This volume is a valuable collection of contributions combining theoretical and methodological approaches as well as precise empirical analyses conducted in manifold social fields. I see it as a timely contribution to transnational research, demonstrating its strengths and innovative potential. At the same time, this volume uncovers an important problem entailed in transnational research which I would like to discuss in this short essay. Given the novelty of the transnational paradigm, it is oriented by one strong bias that requires closer attention. In the pages that follow, I shall argue that the transnational paradigm privileges an overtly optimistic picture of emerging global connectivity, celebrating in its analyses visions of world-spanning ties of mutuality and collective attachments. It highlights the emergence of bridging ties as well as of communicative channels, while neglecting ruptures, distances as well as boundary dynamics that are part and parcel of transnational processes.

To put it simply: In order to establish the transnational condition, today, it was necessary to stress the relatedness between people and social realms in a world-spanning perspective. However, if we agree that the transnational paradigm is a powerful tool for describing the simultaneity of globally expanding social relations, as well as decentred processes of localisation, then the obstacles to connectivity demand closer attention. These deserve our attention not as an anomaly, but rather as an intrinsic element of transnational processes. Thomas

Faist's reflections (this volume) on the overtly enthusiastic prognoses formulated by system theory scholars conceptualising the world society as of one communicative space, without producing empirical evidence to substantiate this claim, point in the direction of my argument. Urmila Goel's careful analysis of the Indernet (this volume) brings the discrepancy between a celebratory discourse deployed by users of new communicative media, on one hand, and the restricted impact of the new technologies, on the other, to light. By drawing upon the analyses presented in this volume, I intend to highlight the obvious strengths of this approach and then proceed to some apparent weaknesses and blank spots in transnationalist research that the authors of this volume have addressed. A tension is expressed in the title of this essay: The transnational research carried out from industrial centres is biased, suggesting that human life around the globe is characterised and perceived as being forged in and reinforced through transnational ties. But what is the state of the "transnational condition", today?

The Importance of the Transnational Paradigm

Transnational studies provide scholars with refined analytical tools for studying social dynamics in a world increasingly characterised by globality. I follow Nina Glick Schiller's distinction between the terms "transnational" and "global". In her view (2007: 449), speaking about transnationalism or transnational process means to "emphasise" the ongoing interconnection or flow of people, ideas, objects and capital across the borders of nation-states. These flows take place in contexts in which the state shapes but does not contain such linkages and movements. In contrast, the term "global is best deployed for those world system phenomena that affect the planet, regardless of borders and local differences" (ibid.). Following this distinction, studies in the transnational field focus on micro and mezo-constellations that come about under the conditions of globality (see Lachenmann, this volume). They privilege processes that are usually ignored by globalisation or world society studies, i.e. actor-centred perspectives, localisation as well as boundary dynamics. As Faist argues (this volume), transnational studies serve as an important corrective to the overtly systemic and top-down-approaches deployed by world society as well as systemic analyses in the field of globalisation research.

Neither global expansion, nor peoples' movements, nor cultural transfers are recent phenomena. The "transnational condition" is an ongoing, intensifying processes of social exchanges in the field of politics, economy, environmental concerns (see Lindenthal in this volume), social security and artistic production. Scholars working in the fields of globalisation, world society as well as transnational studies, increasingly concur on this point. The novelty of the transnationalist approach is its insistence (demonstrated throughout the work of Ludger Pries

2008) upon the simultaneous embeddedness in distant localities as well as its providing conceptual space to encompass migrants living in more than one society. The proponents of this paradigm are silent, though, regarding whether transnationality is seen by them as the norm in migration, or as one important formation among those who migrate. The former is usually implied, as revealed by Glick Schiller's critique of multiculturalist as well as (neo)assimilationist approaches that focus upon national constellations and suggest that peoples' movements mean the permanent abandoning of one place for another. Transnationality as a general feature of migration is seen by her as an intrinsic element of past societies that has been intensified and become more visible in recent times.

One of the biggest problems of transnational studies is simultaneously also one of their major strengths. Transnationality is observed as occurring and shaped in a wide range of societal spheres. International and national orders, legal systems, capitalist expansion, global cultural flows, modernity, social movements, wars and resistance, to name just some of the most frequently mentioned topics, all provide important contexts for studying transnationality. Social sciences encounter in these circumstances the problem of extending their research to diverse and distant fields of inquiry, putting their conceptual tools to severe tests. At the same time, corrections to established methodologies have become necessary – which is a welcome occasion to re-think some of the basic disciplinary assumptions. In particular, social anthropology embraced for a long time a holistic paradigm that postulated the cultural boundedness of societies, their homogeneity as well as their static character. It invented the notorious "anthropological concept of culture" that many scholars working in this field abandoned a long time ago, but that is nowadays used largely outside the discipline in essentialising discourses of culture. Sociology, as other neighbour disciplines, is prone to methodological nationalism (Wimmer/Glick Schiller 2002), conceiving of societies in their boundedness within borders of the nation-state while neglecting the substantial scope of transnationality shaping the social live. The advantage the transnationalist perspective offers is then given by its quest to develop conceptual tools for analysing cultures in their processual capacities (Wimmer 2005) and societies in their complexities – as interactive spaces constituted through trans-regional exchanges.

Given the problem of how to study societies in their multi-sited locations – by which I do not only mean multi-locality in spatial terms, but also the simultaneous shaping of social relations by different types of formations and organisational levels – transnational approaches deployed in social anthropology as well as in micro-sociology (see Lachemann in this volume) are well advised to start off from actor-centred, interactionist approaches that focus upon individuals, small collectivities as well as personalised networks, and only then cautiously proceeding to their embeddedness in societal formations on a larger scale (while systemic and quantitative approaches in political sciences and sociology provide complementary perspectives). This technique was successfully developed by the team of the Manchester School, centred around Max Gluckman, Clyde Mitchell and others. Mitchell's analysis of the Kalela dance (1956) is one of the finest examples of how a micro-analysis of a leisure activity in a Southern African town can be used to demonstrate broad processes of (late) colonial influence on African societies. These processes include industrialisation, urbanisation as well as emerging urban-rural inter-linkages resulting from labour migration. This procedure resembles peeling an onion in reverse. The analysis of social interactions, on the occasion of group singing and dancing, gradually reveals the larger and larger implications of the meanings of songs as well as of the perfomative acts that mimicry the colonial society's hierarchy and shed light on ethnic categorisations that are shaped through the urban co-existence of migrant workers.

It was the Manchester School that alerted social anthropologists to interactionist perspectives, used in particular for studies of conflicts, by means of the extended case study method. This approach allowed scholars working in this field to observe the transformative properties of conflict for social orders. Furthermore, partly building upon studies of the Chicago School, this team produced rich ethnography challenging simplifying assumptions on migration and integration. This school provides us with analytical tools useful for studying transnational relations which were taken up in other disciplinary fields and in other national contexts. Among them is situational analysis based in observing social interactions in a diachronic perspective, i.e. in the extended case-study method (on parallel research in France, see Salzbrunn, this volume).

The Manchester School contributed furthermore to the elaboration of the concept of network for micro-sociological research, applying mostly qualitative research methods. The concept of social network was brought into social anthropology from other disciplines, while the concept of "social field" developed by the Manchester School spread to other "scientific communities" and is currently informing transnational studies well beyond the disciplinary boundaries of social anthropology (see, Lachenmann, this volume). Today, Alejandro Portes (2001: 812) focuses upon "dense networks across political borders created by immigrants in their quest for economic advancement and social recognition". Glick Schiller (2007: 455) defines "social field" as an "unbounded terrain of multiple interlocking egocentric networks". According to her, the term "network" is best applied to chains of social relationships that are egocentric and are mapped as stretching out from a single individual. "Social field" is a more encompassing term than "network", "taking us to a societal level of analysis" (ibid.).

In the sphere of transnational studies, the notion of "transnational social spaces" is frequently evoked in a metaphoric manner, denoting relationships, aspirations as well as imaginations between those who travel as well as those left behind at home. In this sense, it denotes dense interactive horizons, but does not pay sufficient justice to the social constitution of interactive processes. In this vein, despite the fact that life on the move is a phenomenon restricted to less than 10 % of the global population, almost everybody is becoming a transnationalist.

Almost everybody forms part of social constellations that are shaped in diverse ways by migration practices: through remittances that can play a decisive role in a family's or community's well-being as well as in all those places where the "locals" are confronted with "newcomers" in manifold sites of social interaction.

When we go one step further in the transnationalist conceptualisation, in terms of imagining the world, in relating to other spaces, in the – arguably often very restricted, but nevertheless – enlarged radius of movement and communication (almost) everybody becomes a transnationalist. The old and new means of communication, paired with the available transportation technologies provide people around the globe with a significantly heightened awareness of globality as the very basis of local concerns as well as of converging cognitive frames (see Lindenthal's contribution). With communications occurring increasingly beyond the scope of face-to-face exchanges as Greschke (this volume) argues, the sense of immediacy is significantly hightened. One could even speak of a "celebratory mode" of connectivity – in particular embraced by those involved in transnational communicative networks. With the reinforced reflexivity on globality, actors increasingly conceive of global processes in relation to their own concerns. Their own radius of action is significantly shaped by distant events. Wars, conflicts and calamities are often evaluated with regards to one's own well-being.

Simultaneously, problems and cases of injustice, but also new social projects evolving in distant places may instigate a sense of solidarity and involvement. Therefore, transnational solidarity networks, religious dynamics as well as new social movements can create new transnational social fields. These dynamics are buttressed by the easy availability of information and a heightened sense of immediacy. Thus connectivity appears as one of the major properties of social dynamics in the current world society. It does not come as a surprise that transnational studies have greatly contributed to revealing the importance of transnational flows, the ensuing reflexivity as well as local positionings vis-à-vis global spectators (as analysed by Hering in this volume). However, looking back at the scope of research in this field, it is worth while asking whether the major thrust of research does not cover up dimensions in social relations that are significantly less smooth, less self-evident and more problematic than the term suggests.

Transnational Research Designs and Their Problems

Transnational studies have thus far neglected the necessity to make a close examination of the ruptures, inequalities, power differentials and conflicts entailed in transborder social relations. The thrust of research has so far been geared towards observing how social relations expand in space and time, with scholars mostly trying to demonstrate the durable character and salience of kin and community ties. In order to examine these interconnections methodological choices were necessary that, to some extent, have narrowed the scope of interest. In the following, I shall concentrate on some weaknesses in this field that have not yet received sufficient attention. Above all, it is my contention that while rejecting methodological nationalism, transnational research still tends to endorse methodological ethnicisation. This comes about through some problematic choices in research designs.

Above all, (too) many studies select communities as their social units of observation and take their internal solidarity for granted. In a similar vein, while observing transnational relations, as in the realm of transnational activism, solidarity tends to be taken simultaneously as *explanans* as well as as *explanandum* (see Radcliffe et al. 2002).

Secondly, distances and boundaries are not sufficiently taken into account. The transnational research postulates for very good reasons that spatial distances are to be seen as social constructions. Space-time-compression (Giddens 1991, following Karl Marx) is indeed a feature of contemporary societies that has greatly accelerated in recent decades. Nevertheless, as Vattimo (1992) argued already long time ago, societies continue to be differentiated by unequal distribution of resources which makes for substantial differences in the speed with which people move. While the ability to communicate has been significantly enhanced, transportation is still a scarce commodity for those persons with low income. For many migrant workers as well as for political refugees (though usually for different reasons) as well as their kin and co-fellows, spatial distances and/or political boundaries continue to be a crucial feature affecting their existence – whereas the oversimplifying terminology of transnationality covers up the internal problems in kinship and friendship relations (this issue was already taken up in the introduction to this volume).

Thirdly, most studies concentrate on the transnational social spaces while neglecting processes of localisation, i.e. confrontations with persons, groups and organisations in localised contexts that are characterised by diversity, persistence of social boundaries, limited access to valued resources as well as being prone to conflict and contestation. This issue has been thoroughly criticised by Glick Schiller and Çağlar (forthcoming): Their concept of rescaling constitutes an important corrective to the mainstream transnationalist approaches. Salzbrunn's contribution in this volume recapitulates the thrust of their critique, so that I shall not repeat their arguments here. Instead, I shall concentrate on the related concept of belonging, discerning three major problems.

First. On ethnicisation and (putative) solidarity in transnational social spaces. While there are important exceptions of course, many research designs are prone to methodological ethnicisation by selecting distinct categories of people as their object of observation – i.e. members of religious congregations, ethnic or national groups – and following them around the globe. Such a choice may well reflect persisting boundaries in social interactions. These may be true in the case of irregular migration, when migrants find little opportunity to enter into communication with members of the "societies of arrival", with their employers (beyond taking their commands and receiving salaries), or with migrants coming from other places of origin. Still, rather then taking this state of affairs for granted, researchers should be careful in selecting their units of analysis. As difficult as it may be, other units of analysis would be more likely to reveal whether the concentration of communications within one's own group of origin is really the norm in observed situations; if so, whether it was deliberate or enforced, and if not, who were other interaction partners and which resources and strategies made for particular choices. Is social life really as ethnicised as researchers as well as ethnic activists are trying to convince us? If so, when is the concentration upon interactions among one's own peers regarded by actors as their own choice and when is it seen as forced?

Social relations in transnational spaces tend to be perceived as harmonious and solidary. The transmigrants as well as those who remain at home appear in many studies as characterised by commonality of interest, mutually accepted division of labour as well common aspirations and expectations. When inequality and power differentials come into the picture, these are usually described as instigated by the "systemic colonisation of the life-worlds" (Habermas 1981), i.e. of capital and state as impinging upon individuals and collectivities. That market transactions are realised in social relations is all too often ignored. The very fact that migrants may compete among themselves for jobs, that new sources of income may destabilise relations within families and households; that those who remain at home, on one hand, and the transmigrants, on the other hand, are likely to enter into conflicts over the use of remittances as well as the modalities of sharing diverse types of assets finds little space in the available analyses. Rescher's analysis of gender conflicts ensuing in transnational social spaces (in this volume) provides telling examples of substantial re-arrangements in kin and household constellations. His and other analyses continue to highlight the fascinating fact that the capitalist world's economy necessitates the maintenance of family ties and allegiances among persons spread across the globe. Scholars like Kearney (2004) have described how capitalism has contributed to stabilising traditional kinship and local structures while taking advantage of these formations. In a similar vein, Germana D'Ottawio's contribution in this volume provides a very timely analysis of the mutual reinforcement of interpersonal reciprocity ties and capitalist expansion in the field of human reproduction. Her study reveals the possibility that the problems entailed in these constellations, facing relatives, friends and neighbours, have not received sufficient attention so far.

Transmigrants and those remaining at home tend to be depicted as sharing the same goals, interests and political attitudes. While following discrete groups of people engaged in their daily activities, scholars are prone to concentrate on networks sharing political convictions and endeavours. But transnational space is forged by networks of diverse political allegiance. "Local societies" do not necessarily share political ideologies. On the contrary, factionalism, i.e. political group formation cutting across socio-economic lines and often stabilised through patron-client-relationships, is a wide-spread phenomenon in local societies around the globe. Transnational activism tends to reinforce local conflict lines while local factions are likely to impinge upon their supporters in transnational social spaces. Such phenomena can be observed for instance in the case of the Indian anti-dam movement (Pfaff-Czarnecka 2007) where party politics, economic interests, environmental or human rights concerns instigate local divisions in diverse camps. Gandhi draws our attention to the deeply entangled nature of negotiations in the course of the Narmada project in Gujarat: "Resistance is a process of negotiation between actors who operate from particular positions along a spectrum of power relations. Complex, horizontal engagements of convergence and disengagement rather than static relations of dominance "from above" and resistance "from below" characterise the relationship between the state, *adivasis* and activists" (Gandhi 2003: 486).

Radcliffe et al. (2002) draw our attention to such movements' unruly, complex, and partly contradictory character. On the basis of a study of indigenous and political transnationalism in the Andean region, they argue against a simple "meeting of above and below" model, as reflected in many over-enthusiastic transnationalist models. They suggest that the "issue networks" they have observed operate simultaneously on diverse levels, and are full of entanglements and contradictions: "political transnationalism represents the entanglements of diverse ethnic, class and geographically dispersed institutionalised and politicised social actors around the notion of indigenous needs, and the policy and political frameworks through which to address these needs. ... We find entanglements around gender hierarchies, political affiliations, notions of professionalism, and cultural authenticity" (Radcliffe et al. 2002: 3). "In practice, the work on Andean indigenous transnational issue networks demonstrates that the interests, agendas and practices constitutive of transnational indigenous development are radically heterogeneous" (Radcliffe et al. 2002: 14).

Secondly, while acknowledging the persisting salience of state institutions reinforcing the territorial boundedness, the actual process of transgressing borders has not yet received sufficient attention in transnational research. The thrust of studies concentrates rather on those for whom borders either did not constitute an obstacle, or on those who managed to cross them. Those unable to pursue transnational life, hindered by the insurmountable thresholds of national boundaries are hardly ever objects of inquiries – despite the fact that the wish to move across borders is an important element of their life. While political science and social geography are already dealing with this theme, the importance of boundaries needs to become an object of transnational studies in other disciplines.

Some people experience closed doors when they seek access to a new country, and for others national boundaries can be problematic when temporary permits and national social security systems do not match. Yet other groups of people thrive on the existence of (physical) state boundaries, for instance by engaging in smuggling. This transnational way of life would come more fully to light if social science research would pay more attention to the question of how it is affected by the crossing of national boundaries. The notion of "trans-border", that is frequently evoked, highlights rather the lowering of thresholds when people shift between countries and their institutions rather than the human creativity exercised in dealing with borders as part of a transnational way of life.

Spatial dynamics have always posed difficulties for social science research. Transnational analysis has taken them under consideration more than other fields of social science research. This was made possible in particular by drawing upon the constructivist approaches elaborated in cultural geography as well as by insisting upon the constitution of space through social interactions. The constructivist understanding of space attaches priority to mental maps that may significantly reduce distances or even render them unimportant. But the annihilation of space through time in our current imagery often lacks confirmation in actual social practices. The availability of new communication technologies is changing our sense of the immediacy and the form of human exchanges. Still, the means of communication as well as of transportation are not equally available to all and we are still in the process of establishing when face-to-face communication matters and when other forms of exchange are sufficient. The differences in the ease with which people can travel from place to place are significant. "Being there" has not ceased to be important – as is shown by numerous examples of transnational politics (see Faist's insistence on the importance of face-to-face communication).

The importance of spatial distances and the problem of immediacy through spatial dislocation have been particularly well demonstrated in transmigrants' political action. Transnationalist research has highlighted so far the multiplication of political attachments as well as long-distance political involvement. But the problematic sides of these dynamics need also to come to light. While some migrants lose interest in the politics going on in places of their origin, others tend to acquire more nationalist or particularist positions regarding politics in their places "of origin". This can be seen in the example of the Hindutva movement, i.e. in the Hindu-extremist violence actions against members of other faiths in India – best exemplified in the case of struggles over the spiritual sites in Ayodhya, North India that were hugely supported, financially as well as ideologically, through transnational networks. The forms of involvement and the consequences of political action are very different if you are on the spot, or far away from it. It is one thing to send money and express moral support to co-fellows engaging in local political struggles, and another thing to actually fight, risk bodily harm or death, and bear the consequences. The concept of simultaneity developed by scholars who document that migrants increasingly engage in transnational political networks, in their homelands as well as in new locales, requires therefore some additional consideration. The literature is largely silent on the problem of simultaneous political involvements in contexts of differing immediacy. Eva Gerharz' study makes therefore an import contribution to this field when she observes the increased intensity in exchanges between Jaffna and the Tamil diaspora while simultaneously highlighting processes of closure and of re-affirmation of boundaries, localities and identities.

Thirdly, transmigrants have a problem of belonging. Transnational studies obscure this fact. Indeed, their basic assumption is that transmigrants simultaneously belong to different social configurations by forming part of a transnational social space. I should like to problematise the concept of transnational social space, not by questioning the existence of what it denotes, but rather by drawing attention to the delicacies of belonging in a world on the move. I should like to suggest that problems of belonging are relevant at the places of origin as well as at the places of arrival. And certainly, the relations in the spaces in-between, i.e. during journeys, in exchanges between people living in diverse local contexts as well as in transnational networks are prone to rupture, conflict and to problematic contestations.

The problem of formal membership in transnational spaces has already attracted a lot of attention in the debates on dual as well of multiple memberships. Institutions have not yet been attuned to the continuous flux of people and the resulting necessity to readjust. But some important innovations have taken place. The regional integration of Europe has significantly reduced the importance of national borders between the member countries, but important boundaries still remain, for example in the field of social security systems. Some countries such as Germany have reduced obstacles to dual citizenship. Nevertheless, citizenship remains an important problem for many people seeking access and residency permits in countries of arrival, with legislation discriminating more and more between "haves" and "have-nots". On the other hand, collective duties attached to formal membership may cause problems at the places of origin – as powerfully argued by Ramble in the case of Northern Nepalese communities. Local communities dwelling in marginal locations often dread losing members. Consequently, those who out-migrate are frequently challenged to either come back on a regular basis, or to provide financial support – under the threat of losing membership and the benefits of local solidarity entailed in formalised collective attachments.

Belonging through material attachments is another field worthy of further consideration. The current research tends to concentrate on transnational and translocal networking in the field of finance. Investments in transnational space, loans as well as donations, are certainly important features of the world society. However, from the point of view of migrants, having material possessions at different locales can be cumbersome. Belongings can keep people attached to places that they wish to abandon – as was repeatedly experienced in Nazi Germany, for example, when houses, industries and libraries prevented Jews from leaving early enough to establish a safe existence elsewhere. Also, the social relations of ownership and division of labour can prove to be very problematic: Those who remain at home can exert pressure upon labour migrants to provide goods for conspicuous consumption, rather than opt for long-term investments. Glick Schiller

(2007) rightly argues that kin networks maintained between people who send remittances and those who live on them can be fraught with tension. Often, migrant families living away from their place of origin need to make choices in money allocation between the material well-being of their nuclear families and the demands put upon them by broader kinship and friendship networks in their communities of origin. Time and time again migrants have discovered upon coming home that money they earned under severe conditions was entirely spent by relatives during their absence. Those who remain at home are likely to develop metropolitan imageries of capitalist consumption which can bolster the unproductive use of remittances. Enhanced status considerations are yet another feature of transnational social spaces. These are often mentioned in the relevant studies, but we still know little about their impact upon social relations in kin and communal relations.

Cultural identity, the third dimension of belonging, can become a pawn used in social relations in the transnational space. Transnational attitudes oscillate between two extremes. On one hand, there are cosmopolitan attitudes (that however tends to be elitist as Janoschka highlights in this volume), transcultural rapprochements as well as to reflexive hybridity or creolisation. On the other hand, identity politics can reinforce particularist positioning (on their dynamics in shifting contexts, see Zirh's analysis in this volume); hence, social closure can be the direct result of transnational encounters. These can be caused by the migrants' experiences of exclusion and marginalisation at places of arrival. This experience may buttress nostalgia, but also occur through emotional blackmail exerted upon the transmigrants who may possibly wish to establish durable ties in new contexts far away from their original homes by those living there and seeking their support. We may ask therefore: When is culture "what goes without saying" (an important form of belonging as tacit understanding), when is it located at the very root of people's identity, and when is it a representational devise (i.e. belonging made explicit)? Whether belonging is made to serve as a tool of collective representation depends upon the social relations structuring the transnational space. In this field also, transnational studies open up a broad and fascinating scope for future research.

If we wish to abandon the metaphoric facets of the transnational space concept and establish it as being composed of multi-scalar social relations and transactions, then a closer examination of the social ties making up its fabric is necessary. For instance the term "transnational communities" that informed a lot of research in the early phase of the transnational studies has diverted scholars' attention from some major features of transnational social life. At first glance, "community" denotes equality, sameness and social harmony. But when we look beneath collective representations of commonality, then inequality, conflict as well as mechanisms of negative reciprocity may come into the picture. In this vein, transnational social spaces can be cosy, instigating a warm sense of mutuality, but also can confront members with restrictions and a lot of pressure – within and beyond communal boundaries. A historical perspective is required here in order to grasp the processes of stratification within migratory streams.

The localisation theory developed by Glick Schiller and Çağlar (forthcoming) provides an important corrective to transnationalist approaches when we reflect on the social relations of belonging in transmigrant situations. The problem of migrants' belonging has been discussed time and again in integrationist approaches, but for a long time it was neglected in transnational research which privileged the observation of migratory dynamics, ignoring local attachments at places of "arrival". In dealings with authorities, in interactions at schools and in kindergardens, relations reaching across cultural boundaries, i.e. those forged between the "locals" and the "newcomers", become very important. Salzbrunn illustrates this point in her contribution to this volume. Joint activism can significantly buttress the mutual sense of belonging, but in other instances, the "locals" may wish not to relate with the newcomers. Therefore, "translocal" relations can result in new constellations of reciprocity, but they often tend to be confrontational and put pressures upon newcomers who more often than not may feel that they do not entirely belong – and never will. However, alliances can be created around the notion of belonging to a neighbourhood without regards to national background, especially in multicultural neighbourhoods like Belleville/Paris. But more often than not, the condition of not-belonging comes about through extremely diverse assessments by all the social actors involved in a given "transnationalist situation". While many transnationalists (in particular, scholars examining the transnational dynamics) oscillate towards cosmopolitan positions (even very tacit ones), a significant number of locals acquires xenophobic attitudes. The "right to cultural difference", based upon the "anthropological notion of culture" challenges overtly optimistic depictions of multiple belonging in transnational space.

This short *tour d'horizon* was intended at underlining my contention that transnational studies have contributed greatly to our knowledge of how people relate in the world society and the ensuing transformations. It is obvious that the transnational condition is by no means confined to those who frequently cross borders. The transnational research has powerfully suggested that a myriad of direct as well as indirect connections exist between disparate individuals and collectivities that do not even know about each other, but are shaped by action and events taking place in other parts of the globe. But we need to accept that the constellations of connectivity as well as the configurations of multiple belonging in transnational social spaces, today, confront everybody with challenging options and choices and, with new conflict potentials and uncertainties, that scholars are just starting to explore.

References

Gandhi, Ashok (2003) "Developing Compliance and Resistance: The State, Transnational Social Movements and Tribal Peoples contesting India's Narmada Project." Global Networks 3/4, pp. 481-95.

Giddens, Anthony (1991) *The Consequences of Modernity*, Chicago: Stanford University Press.

Glick Schiller, Nina (2007) "Transnationality." In: David Nugent/Joan Vincent (eds.) *Companion to the Anthropology of Politics*, Oxford: Blackwell, pp. 448-467.

Glick Schiller, Nina/Çağlar, Ayse (forthcoming) "Towards a Theory of Locality in Migration Studies: Migrant Incorporation and City Scale." In: (id.) (eds.) *Rescaling Cities* (working title), Ithaca: Cornell University Press.

Habermas, Jürgen (1981) *Theorie des kommunikativen Handelns,* Frankfurt a. M.: Suhrkamp.

Kearney, Michael (2004) *Changing Fields of Anthropology: From Local to Global*, Lanham: Rowman & Littlefield Publishers.

Mitchell, Clyde (1956) *The Kalela Dance. Aspects of social relationships among urban African in Northern Rhodesia*, Manchester: Manchester University Press.

Pfaff-Czarnecka, Joanna (2007) "Challenging Goliath: People, Dams, and the Paradoxes of Transnational Critical Movements." Political and Social Transformations in North India and Nepal (Social Dynamics in Northern South Asia 2; Japanese Studies on South Asia 6), pp. 399-433.

Portes, Alejandro (2001) "Transnational Entrepreneurs: the Emergence and Determinants of an Alternative form of Immigrant Economic Adaptation." WPTC-01-05.

Pries, Ludger (2008) *Die Transnationalisierung der sozialen Welt*, Frankfurt a. M.: Suhrkamp.

Radcliffe, Sarah/Laurie, Nina/Andolina, Robert (2002) "Indigenous people and political transnationalism: globalization from below meets globalization from above?" WPTC-02-05.

Vattimo, Gianni (1992) *The Transparent Society*, London: Polity Press.

Wimmer, Andreas/Glick Schiller, Nina (2002) "Methodological nationalism and beyond. Nation state formation, migration and the social sciences." Global Networks. A Journal of Transnational Affairs 2/4, pp.301-334.

Wimmer, Andreas (2005) *Kultur als Prozess. Zur Dynamik des Aushandelns von Bedeutungen*, Wiesbaden: Verlag für Sozialwissenschaften.

Contributors

Anghel, Remus Gabriel (MA), is a PhD student in Sociology at the University of Bielefeld, a member in the DFG Research Training Group "World Society - Making and Representing the Global", and a participant in the International Graduate School in Sociology. His PhD thesis is a comparative study of Romanians' transnational practices in Western Europe, in Nuremberg (Germany) and Milan (Italy). He is currently employed at the Romanian Institute for Research on National Minorities, Cluj Napoca, Romania. His research interests are migration, transnationalism, globalisation and post-socialism.

D'Ottavio, Germana (PhD), received the PhD degree in 2006 in Social Policy and Local Development at the University of Teramo (Italy) with a dissertation titled: *Women On The Bus: Domestic and Care Workers Transnational Mobility Strategies in the Enlarged Europe. Case Studies in Poland and Southern Italy*. She graduated with a M.A. in Political Science from the University of Urbino (Italy) and her thesis in cultural anthropology dealt with the impact of fair trade on the living condition of artisans in Kenya.

Faist, Thomas (Prof. PhD), is Professor of Transnational Relations and Development Studies at the Department of Sociology, Bielefeld University (www.comcad-bielefeld.de). He received his PhD from The Graduate Faculty, The New School for Social Research. Thomas Faist was Willy-Brandt-Guest Professor at the University of Malmö and DAAD Visiting Professor at the University of Toronto. Formerly, he developed and directed the Program in International Studies in Political Management (ISPM) in Bremen. He is the deputy editor of *The Sociological Quarterly* and a member of the editorial board of the journals *Ethnic and Racial Studies*, *Migration Letters* and the *International Journal of Indian Diaspora*. His research focuses on international migration, citizenship, and social and development policies. Currently, he is involved in research projects on environmental degradation and forced migration and on transnationalisation and social transformation. His recent book publications include *Dual Citizenship in Europe: From Nationhood to Societal Integration* (Ashgate 2007; reprint 2008), *Citizenship: Discourse, Theory and Transnational Prospects* (with Peter Kivisto, Blackwell, 2007), and *Dual Citizenship in a Globalizing World: From Unitary to Multiple Citizenship* (Palgrave Macmillan 2007; reprint 2008).

Gerharz, Eva (Dr.), is a lecturer in the Department of Sociology, University of Bielefeld since 2007, where she also received her doctoral degree. She studied sociology, political science, law and education in Bielefeld, Würzburg and Leiden (NL). She has been a member of the DFG Research Training Group "World Society - Making and Representing the Global". Her main fields of research are development and reconstruction, globalisation, transnationalisation and migration. She is doing fieldwork in Sri Lanka and Bangladesh and worked at the Centre for Integrated Mountain Development (ICIMOD) in Kathmandu, Nepal as a research associate.

Goel, Urmila (Dr.), is a post-doctoral researcher in social and cultural anthropology based in Berlin (Germany). She conducted her research at the European University Viadrina in Frankfurt/Oder (Germany), at the University of New England in Armidale (Australia) as well as at the University of Bergen (Norway). Currently she is Fellow in the Jacobs Summer Research Group 'Youth - Migration -Religion' at the University of Zürich (Switzerland). Her research interests cover in particular the consequences of racism and heteronormativity as well as the strategies to deal with these power inequalities both by the marginalised and the privileged. She bases her work on critical racism theory, critical whiteness studies as well as gender and queer theory and conducts her ethnographic work in particular among those marked as South Asians in Germany. Currently she analyses ethnographically the interdependency of racism and heteronormativity. More information can be found on her website www.urmila.de.

Greschke, Heike Mónika (Dr.), has studied Social Work, Sociology, and Social Anthropology in Koblenz and Bielefeld (Germany), and in Seville (Spain). As a member of the Research Training Group "World Society - Making and Representing the Global", financed by the German Research Community (DFG) she worked on her doctoral dissertation *Daheim in www.cibervalle.com - Ethnographie einer globalen Lebenswelt*, submitted in July 2007 at the Department of Sociology, Bielefeld University. At the moment she is engaged in the scientific supervision of a pilot program for "effect-oriented improvement of youth welfare services", financed by the German Federal Government. Her main research interests are ethnography, ethnomethodology, transnational migration and youth welfare services.

Hering, Stephanie (Dipl. Soz.), is a sociologist (Dipl. Soz., University of Bielefeld 2002) and presently working on her dissertation on the architectural self-presentation of global finance at the University of Basel. From 2003-2007 she did research on a project on the sociology of finance: *Die visuelle Semantik der globalen Finanzökonomie*, directed by Prof. Dr. Urs Stäheli, funded by the Swiss Nation Science Foundation (SNF). Since 2007 she has been a lecturer for sociology at the Institute of Architecture and Planning, University of Liechtenstein. Research interests are Sociology of Finance, Sociology of Architecture, Postcolonial and Global Studies and Sociological Theory. Stephanie Hering lives in Zürich, Switzerland.

Janoschka, Michael (Dr.), currently works as a Lecturer at the Institute of Human Geography of the Goethe-University of Frankfurt/Main (Germany). His research interests mainly focus on migration processes in a globalised world and the role of identity politics and citizenship practice in geographical and political conflicts. Furthermore, his research concentrates on urban transformation processes and governance, identity politics in shrinking cities and strategies of private urban governance. Michael Janoschka is a graduate geographer from the Humboldt-University of Berlin and received his Dr. phil. at the University of Frankfurt.

Lachenmann, Gudrun (Prof. Dr.), studied sociology, political science and economics (after finishing her education and working as a translator). Former research fellow at German Development Institute, Berlin, Africa Division, doing policy research, advice and training; since 1992 Professor at the Department of Sociology, Sociology of Development Research Centre (professor emeritus since 3/2006). Her current research interests are global and local networking for engendering development policy, civil society, transformation processes, women's and peasant movements in Africa, engendering the embeddedness of economy, methodology of multi-level field research and empirically grounding globalisation and localisation theories. Her empirical research is carried out mainly in francophone West Africa.

Lindenthal, Alexandra (PhD), is a research associate in the project "Transnational Governance and Interlegality" at the collaborative research centre 597 "Transformations of the State" (University of Bremen). As a political scientist she is doing empirical research on public-private partnerships in the context of sustainable development. For example, she analyses to what extent the Marine Stewardship Council, a private standard-setting organisation, contributes to solving the problem of overfishing. Furthermore, she asks the question of how far do nation states react to private solutions to global problems like overfishing and deforestation. Before her current position, Alexandra was a research associate at the Universities of Bielefeld, Oldenburg and Bremen. Her research topics are organisational learning, environmental policy and international relations. Recently, Alexandra completed her PhD project at the International Graduate School in Sociology (IGSS) at the University of Bielefeld. The English title of the dissertation is *Leadership in International Relations. The European Union in the International Regime for Climate Change*. The thesis will be published at the beginning of 2009.

Nowicka, Magdalena (Dr.), is a research assistant at the Institute of Sociology at the Ludwig Maximilian University in Munich, Germany, where she obtained her doctoral title in 2005. She is a graduate of the Philosophical Department of the Jagiellonian University in Krakow and the Center for Europe of the Warsaw University, Poland. Her recent publications include *Transnational Professionals and Their Cosmopolitan Universes* (Campus, Frankfurt a. M. and New York 2006) and *Von Polen nach Deutschland und zurück. Die Arbeitsmigration und ihre Herausforderungen für Europa* (Transcript, Bielefeld 2007). Her research interests encompass sociology of migration, space, cosmopolitanism and European society.

Pfaff-Czarnecka, Joanna (Prof. Dr.), is Professor of Social Anthropology in the Department of Sociology at Bielefeld University. She held academic positions at Zurich University as well as Bonn University and was a Visiting Professor at the University of Tokyo as well as Research Fellow at the Oxford University. She wrote her PhD thesis on "Power and Ritual Purity. The Hindu Caste System and Ethnic Relations in the Process of State-formation in Nepal." and her Habilitation thesis on "From Subjects to Citizens. Ethnopolitology of Development in Nepal-Himalaya." at Zürich University. Her main research areas are political anthropology, ethnicity, integration- and minority research, democratisation processes in sub-national contexts, legal anthropology (in particular: human and minority rights), cultural change and inter-cultural communication and social anthropological perspectives on processes of globalisation. Her publications include (written together with Nandy, A./Rajasingham, D./Gomez, T.) (1999) *Ethnic Futures. State and Identity in Four Asian Countries*. New Delhi : Sage; (ed. with C. Caduff); (1999) *Rituale heute: Theorien, Kontroversen, Entwürfe,* Berlin: Reimer; (2005) "No end to Nepal's Maoist rebellion." Focaal, European Journal of Anthropology 46, pp. 158-168; (2005) "Das Lokale als Ressource im entgrenzten Wettbewerb: Das Verhandeln kollektiver Repräsentationen in Nepal-Himalaya." In: Zeitschrift für Soziologie, Sonderheft "Weltgesellschaft" Stuttgart: Lucius & Lucius, pp. 479-499.

Rescher, Gilberto (Dipl. Soz.), is a doctoral candidate at the International Graduate School in Sociology at the University of Bielefeld. He studied sociology in Bielefeld with a special focus on sociology of development. There he graduated with a diploma thesis on local negotiation of processes of decentralisation in Nicaragua. His research and practical experiences include extended fieldwork on the Philippines, in Nicaragua and Mexico and work experience in governmental and non-governmental institutions in Mexico. As part of his doctoral project he is currently working on the processes of political transformation in the Valle del Mezquital, a rural area in Mexico. His research interests include local political processes, development, transnationality, gender and ethnicity, mainly with a focus on Latin America.

Salzbrunn, Monika (Dr.), teaches sociology and anthropology at EHESS and the universities of Paris XII, Tours and Bielefeld. She wrote her binational PhD dissertation on *Transnational Politics of West African Muslim Migrants in France and Germany*. This work was awarded two doctorates: a French doctorate in Anthropology from the EHESS in Paris and a German doctorate in Sociology from the University of Bielefeld. She is currently doing research on festive events and rituals in the context of migration, and is leading the French Team in the European GEMMA project on policy-making, gender and migration (FP 7), at EHESS Paris. She was an Emmy Nother fellow of the German Research Foundation at the Institute of World Society Studies of the University of Bielefeld and is a member of the French research centres CRIA (UMR 8131 Centre National de Recherche Scientifique/EHESS, Paris), MIGRINTER (International Migration), Poitiers, and "Cultures et Sociétés en Europe", Strasburg. She has published more than 20 articles on Muslims in Europe and the USA, transnational networks, gender issues and festive events in French, English, German and Italian.

Zirh, Besim Can (MSc), graduated from METU Sociology (B.A) and Political Science (MSc). He is currently doing PhD at UCL in the Department of Anthropology and is also affiliated with METU Department of Sociology as a research assistant. His research interests include transnational migration and diaspora politics. He is specifically studying Turkish migration to Europe. His PhD project aims at comparing Alevi associations in three European cities (London, Berlin and Oslo) in the framework of transnational practices, border-crossing activities and identity (re-)formation in different migratory contexts.

Global Studies

Remus Gabriel Anghel,
Eva Gerharz, Gilberto Rescher,
Monika Salzbrunn (eds.)
The Making of World Society
Perspectives from
Transnational Research
November 2008, 332 Seiten,
kart., 27,80 €,
ISBN: 978-3-89942-835-3

Bülent Küçük
**Die Türkei und
das andere Europa**
Phantasmen der Identität
im Beitrittsdiskurs
September 2008, 236 Seiten,
kart., zahlr. Abb., 25,80 €,
ISBN: 978-3-8376-1012-3

Ines Braune
Aneignungen des Globalen
Internet-Alltag in
der arabischen Welt.
Eine Fallstudie
in Marokko
September 2008, 262 Seiten,
kart., 26,80 €,
ISBN: 978-3-89942-971-8

Wiebke Keim
Vermessene Disziplin
Zum konterhegemonialen
Potential afrikanischer
und lateinamerikanischer
Soziologien
September 2008, 564 Seiten,
kart., 35,80 €,
ISBN: 978-3-89942-838-4

Peter Lindner
**Der Kolchoz-Archipel im
Privatisierungsprozess**
Wege und Umwege der
russischen Landwirtschaft in
die globale Marktgesellschaft
März 2008, 282 Seiten,
kart., 27,80 €,
ISBN: 978-3-89942-784-4

Friedrich Arndt, Carmen Dege,
Christian Ellermann,
Maximilian Mayer,
David Teller,
Lisbeth Zimmermann (Hg.)
Ordnungen im Wandel
Globale und lokale
Wirklichkeiten im Spiegel
transdisziplinärer Analysen
Januar 2008, 386 Seiten,
kart., 30,80 €,
ISBN: 978-3-89942-783-7

Moritz Csáky,
Johannes Feichtinger (Hg.)
Europa – geeint durch Werte?
Die europäische Wertedebatte
auf dem Prüfstand
der Geschichte
2007, 218 Seiten,
kart., 24,80 €,
ISBN: 978-3-89942-785-1

Florian Feuser
Der hybride Raum
Chinesisch-deutsche
Zusammenarbeit in
der VR China
2006, 344 Seiten,
kart., 29,80 €,
ISBN: 978-3-89942-581-9

Leseproben und weitere Informationen finden Sie unter:
www.transcript-verlag.de

Global Studies

Helen Schwenken
Rechtlos, aber nicht ohne Stimme
Politische Mobilisierungen um irreguläre Migration in die Europäische Union
2006, 374 Seiten,
kart., 29,80 €,
ISBN: 978-3-89942-516-1

Lutz Leisering, Petra Buhr, Ute Traiser-Diop
Soziale Grundsicherung in der Weltgesellschaft
Monetäre Mindestsicherungssysteme in den Ländern des Südens und des Nordens. Weltweiter Survey und theoretische Verortung
2006, 342 Seiten,
kart., 29,80 €,
ISBN: 978-3-89942-460-7

Christoph Wulf
Anthropologie kultureller Vielfalt
Interkulturelle Bildung in Zeiten der Globalisierung
2006, 164 Seiten,
kart., 17,80 €,
ISBN: 978-3-89942-574-1

Heiner Depner
Transnationale Direktinvestitionen und kulturelle Unterschiede
Lieferanten und Joint Ventures deutscher Automobilzulieferer in China
2006, 240 Seiten,
kart., 25,80 €,
ISBN: 978-3-89942-567-3

Christian Berndt, Johannes Glückler (Hg.)
Denkanstöße zu einer anderen Geographie der Ökonomie
2006, 172 Seiten,
kart., 17,80 €,
ISBN: 978-3-89942-454-6

Ivo Mossig
Netzwerke der Kulturökonomie
Lokale Knoten und globale Verflechtungen der Film- und Fernsehindustrie in Deutschland und den USA
2006, 228 Seiten,
kart., 26,80 €,
ISBN: 978-3-89942-523-9

Ulrich Heinze
Hautkontakt der Schriftsysteme
Japan im Zeichen der Globalisierung: Geldflüsse und Werbetexte
2006, 208 Seiten,
kart., 25,80 €,
ISBN: 978-3-89942-513-0

Christian Kellermann
Die Organisation des Washington Consensus
Der Internationale Währungsfonds und seine Rolle in der internationalen Finanzarchitektur
2006, 326 Seiten,
kart., 28,80 €,
ISBN: 978-3-89942-553-6

Leseproben und weitere Informationen finden Sie unter:
www.transcript-verlag.de